ISBN 978-1-5280-9589-1
PIBN 10969595

English
Français
Deutsche
Italiano
Español
Português

www.forgottenbooks.com

Mythology Photography **Fiction**
Fishing Christianity **Art** Cooking
Essays Buddhism Freemasonry
Medicine **Biology** Music **Ancient
Egypt** Evolution Carpentry Physics
Dance Geology **Mathematics** Fitness
Shakespeare **Folklore** Yoga Marketing
Confidence Immortality Biographies
Poetry **Psychology** Witchcraft
Electronics Chemistry History **Law**
Accounting **Philosophy** Anthropology
Alchemy Drama Quantum Mechanics
Atheism Sexual Health **Ancient History**
Entrepreneurship Languages Sport
Paleontology Needlework Islam
Metaphysics Investment Archaeology
Parenting Statistics Criminology
Motivational

NORTH CAROLINA EASTERN BAPTIST ASSOCIATION

HUNDRED FIFTY-FOURTH ANNUAL SESSION
1827-1981

FIRST DAY—October 26, 1981
CLINTON FIRST BAPTIST CHURCH
SECOND DAY—October 27, 1981
MAGNOLIA BAPTIST CHURCH
(Johnson & Concord, Assisting)

THEME
"CHRIST, THE ONLY HOPE"

OR

L. Mack Thompson
Lucille Yancey

NEXT ANNUAL MEETING
First Day

Mount Olive First Baptist Church
Monday, October 25, 1982

Second Day
Tuesday, October 26, 1982
Mount Gilead Baptist Church
(Union Grove, Assisting)

TABLE OF CONTENTS

RULES OF ORDER

1. At the meeting of the Association the Moderator elected at
the preceding session shall preside. In the case of his absence,
the Vice Moderator shall preside.

2. Each session of the Association shall be opened with reli-
ious exercises.

3. At each daily session and previous to proceeding to business
the Associate Clerk shall be requested to announce the number of
churches represented and the total number of messengers representing
these churches. When it is determined that a majority of the chur-
hes are represented the Moderator shall declare the Association
uly constituted. It shall be necessary for a majority of the
churches to be represented for the Association to transact business
ther than adjournment. The proceedings of the first of the Annual
ession shall be read the morning of the second day and the pro-
eedings of the second day shall be read at the first Council of
he Association to meet following the Annual Meeting.

4. The members shall observe toward the officers and each other
hat courtesy which belongs to Christians.

5. Any member wishing to speak shall arise and address the
residing officer and shall confine himself strictly to the question
nder consideration and avoid personalities.

6. No member shall speak more than twice on the same question
ithout permission.

7. All motions seconded shall be definitely stated by the pre-
iding officer before discussion.

8. No motion shall be withdrawn after discussion.

9. When a question is under discussion, no motion or proposi-
ion shall be received except to adjourn, to lay on the table, to
mend, to commit, or to postpone to a definite time, which several
otions shall have preference in the order in which they are stated.

10. After a motion has been decided, any member having voted
n the majority may move a re-consideration.

11. All questions except such as relate to the Constitution
hall be decided by a majority vote.

12. The Association shall have the right to decide what subjects
hall be admitted to consideration.

13. The rules of order may be altered or amended at any session
f the Association by a Majority vote.

CONSTITUTION

PREAMBLE

We, the Missionary Baptist Churches of Jesus Christ, composing
he EASTERN BAPTIST ASSOCIATION, convinced of the necessity of an
ssociation of churches in order to promote fellowship, missions,
ducation, Christian service, the preaching of the Gospel, and to
ooperate with the Baptist State Convention of North Carolina and
he Southern Baptist Convention in their work, do hereby agree and
ubscribe to the following articles.

Article I. NAME

This Association shall be known and denominated as the North
arolina EASTERN BAPTIST ASSOCIATION.

Article II. PURPOSE

The purpose of this association shall be the promotion of Christ' Kingdom among men, and the means of accomplishing this shall be in strict conformity to the New Testament.

Article III. AUTHORITY

This association claims to be independent and sovereign in its own sphere, but shall never attempt to exercise any authority over the internal affairs of the churches.

Article IV. COMPOSITION

This association shall be composed of all ordained ministers who are members or pastors of member churches, the general officers of the association, the director of missions, and three messengers from each church with one additional messenger for every one hundred members over the first one hundred, no church being allowed more than ten messengers.

Article V. MEETINGS

The annual session of the association shall commence on Monday after the fourth Lord's Day in October. The church year for the churches of the association shall commence on October 1, and end on September 30.

Article VI. OFFICERS

The officers of the association shall be a Moderator, a Vice Moderator, a Clerk, and Associate Clerk, the Chairman of the Historical Committee, a Treasurer and an Associate Treasurer. All officers shall be elected annually except the chairman of the Historical Committee who is the senior member of the Historical Committee. The Moderator shall not be elected to serve more than two full years at one period and shall assume office at the close of the Annual Session at which he is elected.

Article VII. TRUSTEES

The association shall have three (3) trustees who shall serve three-year terms in rotation, the replacement to be elected by the association annually.

Article VIII. ASSOCIATIONAL COUNCIL Executive Board or team

The association shall have an Associational Council consisting of the Moderator, Vice Moderator, Clerk, Associate Clerk, Treasurer, Associate Treasurer, Director of Missions, Associational Church Music Director, Associational Sunday School Director, Associational Church Training Director, Associational Brotherhood, Associational W. M. U. Director, Associational representatives to denominational agencies, each active and retired pastor in the association, and one lay member from each church to be elected by the church whose name shall be included in the church letter to the association.

Article IX. CHURCH PROGRAMS

The association shall organize groups of officers for the five

4

5) church programs: Sunday School, Church Training, Woman's Missionary Union, Brotherhood, and Music.

Article X. VISITORS

The association may invite visiting and corresponding brethren to seats and extend to them the privilege of the body, except that of voting.

Article XI. MISCELLANEOUS

The association shall not maintain fellowship with any church which neglects to observe gospel order.

Article XII. CONSTITUTIONAL CHANGES

This constitution may be amended on the second day of any annual session by a vote of two-thirds of the members present provided the proposed changes have been presented on the first day of the annual session.

BY-LAWS

Article I. DUTIES OF OFFICERS

A. Moderator--The moderator on the first day of each annual session of the Association shall appoint the following committees to function during the session: Place and Preacher; Resolutions; and Memorials. At the last regular meeting of the Association Council before the annual meeting of the Association, the moderator shall appoint a Constitutional Committee to serve during the annual meeting and a Committee on Committees.

It shall be the duty of the moderator to enforce an observance of the constitution, preserve order, decide all questions of order, vote in case of a tie, and act as chairman of the Associational Council.

B. Vice Moderator--It shall be the duty of the vice moderator to preside in the absence or at the request of the moderator, to give other appropriate assistance to the moderator, and to succeed to the office of moderator, if and when during his tenure of office the office of moderator becomes vacant.

C. Clerk--It shall be the duty of the clerk to record the proceedings of each annual session, superintend their printing and distribution, and serve as secretary of the Associational Council and Executive Committee. It shall be his duty to report the actions of the Council to the annual meeting of the Association. He shall report the actions of the Executive Committee to the next meeting of the Council or to the Association, whichever comes first.

D. Associate Clerk--It shall be the duty of the associate clerk to register the messengers, to report upon request the number of churches represented and the total number of messengers representing these churches, and to perform such other duties as are usually performed by an associate clerk.

E. Treasurer--It shall be the duty of the treasurer to receive all funds contributed by the churches or collected during the session of this body, to distribute all funds received as ordered by the association, and to make to the Association an annual report of the condition of the treasury.

F. Associate Treasurer--It shall be the duties of the associate treasurer to assist the treasurer in the performance of his duties as directed by the treasurer.

Article II. DUTIES OF TRUSTEES

The trustees shall be the representatives of the Association in legal matters, and shall perform such duties as the Association or the Associational Council may prescribe.

Article III. ASSOCIATIONAL COUNCIL

A. Officers--The officers of the Associational Council shall be: Moderator, Vice Moderator, Clerk, Associate Clerk, Treasurer, and Associate Treasurer. The corresponding officers of the Association elected during the last annual meeting of the Association shall serve in these positions on the Associational Council.

B. Duties--The Associational Council shall cooperate with the Baptist State Convention of North Carolina in its program for the furtherance of the work fostered by the body within the bounds of our association; it shall act for the Association on any matters requiring attention between the annual session of the Association; and it shall have power to fill any vacancies on the Council during the year. The clerk shall make a report of the work of the Associational Council at the annual session of the Association. The director of missions or other workers employed by the Association shall make a quarterly report to the Associational Council in order that the said Council shall be prepared to make a full report to this body.

C. Meetings--The Associational Council shall meet at least once each quarter at a time and place designated by the Council after the first meeting which will be called by the moderator who shall serve as chairman of the Council. With proper notice being given to all members of the meeting and when it is determined that a majority of the churches are represented the chairman shall declare the Council duly constituted.

D. Election of Committees--The Associational Council shall hold an organizational meeting not later than six weeks following the annual session, and, in cooperation with the Committee on Committees, shall set up the following committees: The Executive, Missions, Program, Stewardship, Audit, Evangelism, Associational Nominating, Ordination, Historical, Pastoral Support, Library, and any other deemed necessary for the proper handling of associational business between the annual sessions.

Article IV. DUTIES OF COMMITTEES

A. ASSOCIATIONAL COUNCIL COMMITTEES--A majority shall constitute a quorum for each committee.

1. EXECUTIVE COMMITTEE: The Executive Committee shall be composed of five (5) members elected from the Association Council together with the officers of said council, the directors of the Associational Church Program Organizations, and the chairmen of the Associational Council Committees. This committee shall handle all matters committed to it by the Associational Council and shall have authority to act for the council only in matters pertaining to the work of the Association that may arise between the regular quarterly meetings of the Council. The action taken by the Executive Committee shall be reported by the clerk to the next meeting of the council or to the Association, whichever comes first, and shall be subject to the approval of the larger body to whom the report is made. In the event the

position of director of missions becomes vacant, the Executive Committee shall recommend to the Associational Council for approval a Search Committee whose duties shall be to seek prayerfully a person to fill the position. The Search Committee shall report to the Executive Committee and shall recommend to the Associational Council a prospective director of missions for approval.. The Executive Committee shall exercise general supervision over the work of the director of missions. The Executive Committee shall meet regularly at least eight times each year.

2. MISSIONS COMMITTEE: The Missions Committee shall be composed of seven (7) members whose duties shall be to work with the director of missions in discovering, analyzing, and presenting mission opportunities to the Association for mission action. The Brotherhood director and the Woman's Missionary Union director shall be members of the Missions Committee. The chairman of the committee shall make periodic reports to the Associational Council and the Association at its annual session.

3. STEWARDSHIP COMMITTEE: The Stewardship Committee shall be composed of nine (9) members. This committee shall be responsible for recommending a budget to the Association in its annual session, for the distribution of all associational funds, and for devising plans for raising such funds as are necessary for carrying on the associational program. The Stewardship Committee shall lead a program of Biblical stewardship education and promotion among the churches and on the associational level. The associational treasurer shall be a member of this committee.

4. EVANGELISM COMMITTEE: The Evangelism Committee shall be composed of five (5) members. It shall be the duty of this committee to promote evangelism both in the local church and on an associational level. It shall serve to link the association with state and south-wide departments of evangelism and shall use every available means for fostering the cause of winning the lost to Christ.

5. LIBRARIES COMMITTEE: This committee shall be composed of three (3) members duly elected by the Association and resources personnel as appointed by the moderator whose duty it shall be to encourage the establishing and promotion of libraries in churches.

6. PASTORAL SUPPORT COMMITTEE: The committee shall be composed of five (5) members whose duties shall be to provide an ongoing, continuing program of help to pastors and church staff members in areas of need. The program shall include guidance for those who are just beginning to prepare for church related vocations; career assessment, spiritual, emotional, and physical needs of pastors and church staff.

B. APPOINTED COMMITTEES:

1. CONSTITUTION AND BY-LAWS COMMITTEE: This committee shall be composed of three(3) members, whose duty it shall be to study and recommend changes in the Constitution and By-Laws and bring reports as necessary to the Association.

2. PLACE AND PREACHER COMMITTEE: This committee shall be composed of three (3) members, whose duty it shall be to make the Association aware of the rotating system of meeting places, and to recommend to the Association in annual session a place or places for meeting, along with a preacher and alternate for the sermon the following year.

3. RESOLUTIONS COMMITTEE: This committee shall be composed of three (3) members whose duty it shall be to study all resolutions referred to it by the Association or the Associational Council, and report suitable resolutions at the annual meeting.

4. MEMORIALS COMMITTEE: This committee shall be composed of three (3) members whose duty it shall be to prepare and present at the annual meeting an appropriate program of memorial for those of our number who have died during the preceeding year. These names may be secured from the letters to the Association from the member churches.

5. COMMITTEE ON COMMITTEES: This committee shall be composed of five (5) members whose duty it shall be to select and nominate persons for the Associational Committees and Associational Council Committees at the first Associational Council meeting, and shall appoint successors when vacancies occur during the year.

C. ASSOCIATIONAL COMMITTEES:

1. PROGRAM COMMITTEE: The Program Committee shall be composed of five (5) members. It shall be their duty to arrange the program of the annual session of the Association and for all other sessions which may be called.

2. AUDITING COMMITTEE: The Auditing Committee shall be composed of three (3) members whose duty it shall be to execute the proper auditing of the financial records of the Association and to bring a report to the Association in its annual session.

3. ORDINATIONS COMMITTEE: The Ordinations Committee shall be composed of three (3) pastors and two (2) deacons. This committee shall offer to any church, upon request, advice and assistance in the examination and ordinations of deacons and ministers.

4. HISTORICAL COMMITTEE: The Historical Committee shall consist of three (3) members. The Committee shall obtain and edit the histories of two churches each year and be included in the minutes, and shall obtain an up-to-date history of the Association. The senior member of the committee shall be the chairman.

5. ASSOCIATIONAL NOMINATING COMMITTEE: The Associational Nominating Committee shall be composed of five (5) members. It shall be the duty of this committee to submit nominations to the Association in session for the associational general officers (with the floor open for nominations) as well as for representatives to denominational agencies and interest for the following year, and to fill any vacancies which may occur during the year.

This committee shall also be responsible for forwarding to the Associational Council at their third meeting for approval and to the Association, for election, the directors of Brotherhood, Sunday School, Woman's Missionary Union, Church Training, and Church Music. The Church Program Organizations directors shall then become members of the Nominating Committee. The Nominating Committee shall present to the Associational Council at their fourth meeting a complete slate of officers for the five Church Program Organizations.

Article V. DUTIES OF CHURCH PROGRAM DIRECTORS

A. THE ASSOCIATION SUNDAY SCHOOL DIRECTOR shall promote and supervise the Sunday School Program of the Association and shall be responsible for the direction of the Vacation Bible School work of the Association in cooperation with the director of missions.

B. THE ASSOCIATIONAL CHURCH TRAINING DIRECTOR shall promote and supervise the Church Training Program of the Association in cooperation with the director of missions.

C. THE ASSOCIATIONAL WOMAN'S MISSIONARY DIRECTOR shall promote and supervise the Woman's Missionary Union Program of the Association in cooperation with the director of missions and in keeping with the Constitution and By-Laws of the Woman's Missionary Union

the EASTERN BAPTIST ASSOCIATION.
D. THE ASSOCIATIONAL BROTHERHOOD DIRECTOR shall promote and
ervise the Brotherhood Program of the Association in coopera-
ŋ with the director of missions.
E. THE ASSOCIATIONAL MUSIC DIRECTOR shall promote and super-
e the Church Music Program of the Association in cooperation
h the director of missions.

PASTORS

CHURCH	PASTOR	ADDRESS	TELEPHONE
Albertson	Caleb Goodwin, Jr.	P. O. Box 276, La Grange 28551	566-9472
Alum Springs	Shelton Justice	Rt. 1, Box 38A-2, Warsaw 28398	293-7524
Bear Marsh	Mitchell D. Rivenbark	Rt. 2, Box 52, Mount Olive 28365	658-5872
Beulah	Willie O. Carr	Rt. 5, Box 50, Clinton 28328	533-3789
Browns	Joseph Walter Moss	Rt. 1, Clinton 28328	592-5642
Calvary	F. J. McCarson	103 Wade Street, Warsaw 28398	293-3467
Calypso	Greg Thornton	Calypso 28325	C-658-6693 H-658-5223
Center	Robert E. Hill	P. O. Box 153, Clinton 28328	592-4910
Clinton, First	William M. Jones	P. O. Box 837, Clinton 28328	C-592-3641 H-592-2472 592-2898
Concord	Eddie Wetherington	Rt. 5, Box 29A, Clinton 28328	296-1473
Corinth	John A. Johnson (Interim)		
Dobson Chapel	Randy Wellman	Rt. 1, Magnolia 28453	
Evergreen	Charles Kirkland	P. O. Box 426, Faison 28341	267-2591
Faison	Wayne Wheeler	Garland 28441	C-529-5431 H-529-5201
Garland			
Garner's Chapel	Michael Lee	Rt. 1, Mount Olive 28365	658-6886
Grove Park	Davis Benton	605 N.E. Blvd., Clinton 28328	592-3513
Immanuel	Vernon Braswell	200 Fox Lake Drive, Clinton 28328	C-592-3854 H-592-4489
Ingold	Robert Miller	P. O. Box 5252, Ingold 28446	529-4181
Island Creek	James Hartsell	Rt. 2, Box 349, Rose Hill 28458	289-2606
Johnson	Kenneth Durham	Rt. 2, Box 71, Warsaw 28398	C-293-4757 H-293-4980
Kenansville	Lauren R. Sharpe	Box 86, Kenansville 28349	296-0659
Magnolia	William B. Shipp	P. O. Box 147, Magnolia 28453	289-2418
Mount Gilead	Oliver Skerrett	Rt. 2, Box 106, Clinton 28328	592-6533
Mount Olive	Anthony Z. Gurganus	301 Chestnut Street, Mount Olive 28365	C-658-2062 H-658-2351
Mount Vernon	Willie O. Carr	Rt. 5, Box 50, Clinton 28328	533-3789
New Hope	Paul Rose	Rt. 1, Box 255, Mount Olive 28365	658-4600

Church	Representative	Address	Telephone
Piney Grove	Ferrell Miller	Rt. 2, Box 122-A, Faison 28341	533-32
Poplar Grove	Andy Wood	Rt. 1, Box 77½, Faison 28341	267-2981
Poston	Donald Coley	Rt. 3, Wallace 28466	285-2476
Rose Hill	Jerry D. Kinlaw	P. O. Box 459, Rose Hill 28458	289-3882
Rowan	Michael Shook	202 Reedsford Road, Clinton 28328	C-592-7508 H-592-7268
Sharon	Phillip R. Denton	P. O. Box 126, Chinquapin 28521	285-3062
Shiloh			
Siloam	Carlton Miller	Rt. 1, Box 67-B, Harrells 28444	638-1394
Teachey	Larry Blount	P. O. Box 38, Teachey 28464	285-2788
Turkey	Larry Padgett	P. O. Box 216, Turkey, 28393	592-2416
Union Grove	L. L. Barnes	Rt. 2, Elizabethtown 28337	588-4422
Warsaw	L. Mack Thompson	205 E. Chelly Street, Warsaw 28398	293-7479
Wells Chapel	Freddie M. Harris	Rt. 1, Wallace 28466	532-4528

COUNCIL LAY REPRESENTATIVES

CHURCH	REPRESENTATIVE	ADDRESS	TELEPHONE
Albertson	Nathan Kelly	Rt. 1, Albertson 28508	***
Alum Springs	Larry Harper	Rt. 2, Mount Olive 28365	658-3614
Bear Marsh	Glanton Holland	Rt. 2, Box 428, Mount Olive 28365	***
Beulah	Willie Carr	Rt. 5, Box 50, Clinton 28328	533-3189
Brown	Jimmy A. Carr	Rt. 3, Box 97, Clinton 28328	564-6584
Calvary	Billy Dail	Rt. 2, Box 220, Warsaw 28398	293-4869
Calypso	Charles Rivenbark	P. O. Box 5, Calypso 28325	658-2019
Center	Jamey West	Rt. 1, Box 184, Garland 28441	532-4995
Clinton	Carles Lee Pope	P. O. Box 514, Clinton 28328	592-2469
Concord	G. E. Drew	Rt. 1, Box 386, Magnolia 28453	289-2782
Corinth	R. Clifton Knowles	206 N. Oak Street, Wallace 28466	285-2285
Dobson Chapel	James P. Brown	Rt. 2, Rose Hill 28458	289-3463
Evergreen	Billy Todd	Rt. 1, Box 321, Magnolia 28453	532-4769
Faison	Clement R. Shine	Faison 28341	***
Garland	Gene Hart	P. O. Box 187, Garland 28441	529-4311
Garners Chapel	Morris Rose	Rt. 1, Mount Olive 28365	658-5425
Grove Park	Gordon Powell	1002 Raleigh Road, Clinton 28328	592-3982
Immanuel			

CHURCH	REPRESENTATIVE	ADDRESS	TELEPHONE
Ingold	Norwood Carter	P. O. Box 3, Harrells 28444	529-4112
Island Creek	Edward Teachey	331 N. Norwood, Wallace 28466	***
Johnson	Robert Southerland	Rt. 2, Warsaw 28398	293-4690
Kenansville	O. R. Blizzard	Rt. 1, Kenansville 28349	296-0749
Magnolia	Jack Joyner	P. O. Box 184, Magnolia 28453	289-2568
Mount Gilead	Lonnie J. Bass	Rt. 2, Box 110A, Clinton 28328	592-4074
Mount Olive	W. K. Lewis	W. Steele Street, Mount Olive 28365	658-4191
Mount Vernon	Edgar Gainey	Rt. 5, Clinton 28328	***
New Hope	R. W. Blanchard, Jr.	Rt. 1, Turkey 28393	533-3586
Piney Grove	J. O. Brewer	Rt. 5, Clinton 28328	***
Poston	John Braswell	Rt. 1, Box 53-A, Watha 28471	285-7133
Rose Hill	Albert Cottle	Hwy. 117 North, Rose Hill 28458	***
Rowan	John E. Yancey	Rt. 4, Clinton 28328	592-5376
Sharon	T. G. Huffman	Rt. 1, Chinquapin 28521	285-3585
Shiloh	P. A. Maready	Rt. 2, Wallace 28466	***
Siloam	R. C. Garris	Rt. 2, Box 125, Harrells 28444	***
Teachey			
Turkey	J. C. Ezzell	Rt. 1, Turkey 28393	533-3368
Union Grove	Glendale Fryar	Rt. 4, Box 27, Clinton 28328	592-4830
Warsaw	John A. Johnson	108 E. Plank St., Warsaw 28398	293-4830
Wells Chapel			

MINISTERS NOT PASTORS

RST: Homer Baumgardner, Rt. 2, Warsaw 28328 (OM)
T. N. Cooper, P. O. Box 55, Clinton 28328 (OM)
J. A. Crowe, Sr., 308 Warsaw Road, Clinton 28328
(OM)
Waldo Early, 207 Dixie Circle, Clinton 28328 (OM)
M. M. Johnson, P. O. Box 1093, Clinton 28328 (OM)
Jasper Hinson, Rt. 6, Box 161, Clinton 28328 (OM)
L. E. Williamson, P. O. Box 837, Clinton 28328 (OM)
E. C. Matthocks, 132 Heath Street, Clinton 28328
(OM)
W. Price Knowles, Rose Hill 28458 (LM)
Billy Todd, Rt. 1, Box 321, Magnolia 28453 (LM)
Timothy Register, Garland 28441 (LM)

K: Albert Hanchey, Rt. 1, Willard 28478
Norman Kennedy, RFD 1, Chinquapin 28521 (OM)
Warren Thomas, Chinquapin 28521 (OM)
Jimmy Johnson, 515 Boney Street, Wallace 28466 (LM)

: Paul Barefoot, Rt. 4, Box 210, Clinton 28328 (OM)
DeWitt W. Branch, 515 E. College Street, Warsaw
28398 (OM)
John A. Johnson, 108 E. Plank Street, Warsaw 28398
(LM)

ASSOCIATIONAL OFFICERS

Missions	Clyde L. Davis, Sr.
	L. Mack Thompson
tor	John Flake
	Lucille Yancey
lerk	Willie O. Carr
	Donald Pope
reasurer	Jo Robinson

TRUSTEES

ay, Jr.	Term Expiring 1982
eel	Term Expiring 1983
n	Term Expiring 1984

CHURCH PROGRAM OFFICERS
SUNDAY SCHOOL

	Don Coley
tor	Charlotte Hartsell
tor	James Hartsell
ren Director	Andy Wood
dren Director	Martha Harris
ldren Director	Sue Padgett
hool Director	Tempie Wood

CHURCH TRAINING

	----
ltant	H. J. Register
Consultant	Larry Padgett
ltant	Michael Lee
nsultant	Jean Hatch

13

BROTHERHOOD

Brotherhood Director	Charles Kirkland
Baptist Men Director	Charles Kirkland
Pioneer RA Director	Michael Shook
Crusader RA Director	Kenny Register

CHURCH MUSIC

Director	Jean Hatch
Council	Janet Register
	Maribell Slemend₂
	Virginia Williams

WOMAN'S MISSIONARY UNION

Director	Mrs. Norwood Cart
Assistant Director	Mrs. Coleman Cart
Secretary-Treasurer	Mrs. Donald Pope
Baptist Women Director	Mrs. Jackie Strou
BYW Director	Miss Glenda Stric
Acteen Director	Mrs. Johnny Carlt
GA Director	Mrs. Steve Matthi
Mission Friend Director	Mrs. Andy Wood
Mission Action Director	Mrs. H. J. Regist
Enlistment & Enlargement Director	Mrs. George McLe]

DENOMINATIONAL REPRESENTATIVES

American Bible Society	H. J. Register
Annuity Board, SBC	Waldo Early
Baptist Children Homes	John A. Johnson
Baptist Foundation	Hubert Phillips
Baptist Homes for Aging	Millard Johnson
Baptist Hospital	Gerald Quinn
Christian Education	Elwynn Murray, J]
Christian Literature	T. N. Cooper
Cooperative Program	Albert Pope

MESSENGERS TO ASSOCIATION

ALBERTSON: Edwin Holt, Douglas Stroud
ALUM SPRINGS: Mr. & Mrs. Euge Outlaw, Mrs. Carolyn
    Larry W. Harper
BEAR MARSH: Leslie Southerland, Elbert Davis, Mitcl
    Gordan Holland, Jr.,E. G. Hatch, Jr.
BEULAH: T. M. Creech, Milton Massey, L. A. Pope, M]
    Mrs. Lee Baxley, Lonnie Carter
BROWN_ Marie Pope, Mrs. Cooper Gore, Mrs. Bessie J₂
    Ruby Hall.
CALVARY: Mr. & Mrs. Bland Raynor, Peggy McCarson.
CALYPSO: Mrs. Jeanne Thornton, Mrs. Louis Turner,]
    Tadlock, Mrs. Frances Powell, James Baker.
CENTER: Doris Hill, Margie Horrell, Leona Blackburr
    David Blackburn
CLINTON: L. E. Williamson, Jasper Hinson, Waldo Ea]
    Kaleel, Everette Peterson, Mrs. Jean Hatch, Jc
    T. N. Cooper, Charles L. Pope

CORINTH: Price Knowles, Mrs. Annie Ruth Hall, Mrs. Ruth Knowles, George Jones, Mrs. Betty P. Butts, Mrs. Thelma Dempsey
DOBSON CHAPEL: Mrs. Betty Brown, Mrs. Julia Brock, Mrs. Sylvia Wellman, Mrs. Florence Register, Mrs. Naomi Brock, Wilbur Brock
EVERGREEN: Jerry Todd, Norman Bennett, James Ezzell
FAISON: Henry Brown, Annie Brown, Vivian Kirkland, Donald Matthews, Ann Matthews, Stella Sutton
GARLAND: Mrs. Wilbert Davis, Mrs. G. A. McLelland, Hugh Hobbs, Mrs. Wayne Wheeler, Mrs. Sudie Rich
GARNER'S CHAPEL: Mr. & Mrs. Varner Garner, Mrs. Nancy Lee
GROVE PARK: ---
IMMANUEL: Mrs. Jeff Honeycutt, Mrs. Frances Tew, Mrs. Mercedes Floyd, Mrs. Bevie Melson, Dick Pope, Mrs. Lynn Adams, Mrs. Martha Tart, Mrs. Rossie Mattocks, Mrs. Nealie Boyette
INGOLD: Henry L. Blackburn, Mrs. Edith Blackburn, Horace Sutton
ISLAND CREEK: Mr. & Mrs. D. E. Rouse, Phillip Pierce, Mrs. Charlotte Hartsell, Mrs. Vivian Brock
JOHNSON: Robert Southerland, Ms. Kathy Mae Kirby, Percy Gavin
KENANSVILLE: O. R. Blizzard, Amos Brinson, Margaret Oakley, Virginia Holland, Sally Tyndall, Macy Brinson
MAGNOLIA: Carlton Smith, Charles Bowman, Mrs. Lee Bowman, Clifton Chestnutt, Mrs. Nellie Burns
MOUNT GILEAD: Mrs. Kate Spearman, Mrs. Elma Warren, Mrs. Christine Puryear, Lonnie J. Bass, Mrs. Eunice Bass, Mrs. Willa Crea Warren, Mrs. Gertrude Powell
MOUNT OLIVE: Mack Herring, Mrs. Mack Herring, Mr. & Mrs. Kenneth Goodson, Mrs. Helen Bell, Mrs. D. W. Cherry, Mrs. Anna Hunter, Mrs. Virginia Lindsay
MOUNT VERNON: Mrs. Ruby Pope, Mrs. Thelma Gainey, Franklin Barber, Milton Gainey
NEW HOPE: Shelby Blanchard, Buck Blanchard, Raymond Blanchard, Sr., Mrs. Ellen Smith, Mrs. Celestial Colwell, Ed Colwell, Mrs. Paul Rose.
PINEY GROVE: Dot Boyette, Mrs. Irene Darden, Francis Clifton
POSTON: Mrs. Bessie Best, Mrs. Annette Henderson, Mrs. Lula Dixon, Mrs. Laura Ramsey, Mrs. Aileen Moore, Mrs. Thelma Murray, Mrs. Effie Kennedy, Mrs. Madge Boney
ROSE HILL: H. G. Blanchard, Mrs. Myrtle Blanchard, Albert Pope, Mrs. Ruth Pope
ROWAN: Jo Neal Robinson, Ruby Peterson, Mozelle Jones, Mr. & Mrs. Frank Wallace, Mrs. R. H. Hairr
SHARON: Mrs. Louise Padgett, Mrs. Hazel Thomas, Jim Southerland
SHILOH: Johnnie Likens, Mrs. Johnnie Likens, Ray Likens, Mrs. Flonnie Hunter, Rifton Raynor, Mary Lee Raynor, Vernon Jenkins, Mrs. Mildred Jenkins
SILOAM: Elizabeth McGill, Louise Maynard, R. C. Garris, Edna King, Pauline Hall, Ezlee Maynard
TEACHEY: Linwood Brinkley, Helen Brinkley, Frank Cottle
TURKEY: Lester D. Massey, H. J. REgister, Creson Ezzell, Mrs. Creson Ezzell, Ruth Ellis, Mrs. Ida Cottle
UNION GROVE: Mrs. R. P. Batts, Eva Fryar, Doris Saunders, Mr. & Mrs. Glendale Fryar, Janie Fryar
WARSAW: John A. Johnson, Blanche Braughan, Bill Knowles, Dote Knowles, Harriet Page, James Page, Dot Rollins, Helen Ann Straughan, Gerald Quinn, Rita Quinn
WELLS CHAPEL: Alma Highsmith, Florence Hoover, Laura G. Moore, Luola P. Rivenbark

1. Moderator Mack Thompson called to order the 154
   sion of Eastern Association at 3:15 P.M. on Oct
   in the Clinton First Baptist Church.
2. Jean Hatch led the singing of "All Hail the Pow
   Name".
3. Church Miller read Matthew 16:21-28 and led in
4. Willie Carr, Associated Clerk, reported registr
   ting 38 churches and moved that the messengers
   tute a quorum. Passed.
5. Program Committee Chairman Tony Gurganus presen
   of service and moved its adoption as the Progra
   address need for minor changes.
6. Lucille Yancey was elected as clerk; Willie Car
7. No response was heard to the call for petitiona
8. The moderator appointed the following committee

      (1) RESOLUTIONS
           Charles Kirkland, Chairman - |
           Freddie Harris
           Oliver Skerrett
      (2) TIME, PLACE & PREACHER
           Davis Benton, Chairman
           Millard Johnson
           Albert Pope
      (3) MEMORIALS
           Tom Cooper, Chairman
           Charles Lee Pope
           Paul Rose

9. Treasurer Donald Pope gave his report, which was
   presented the proposed budget for study and for
   second day of the Session.
10. The clerk reported action taken by the Associat:
    during the year.
11. Miscellaneous Business:
    (1) The moderator read a Mailgram challenge fror
        School Department in Nashville.
    (2) The Clerk recognized Mrs. Jimmy Carr of Brov
        as Church Clerk of the Year.
    (3) Christian Social Ministries, a new proposal,
        by the moderator, who then presented Paula (
        approval as the designated staff person to :
        created position.
    (4) Clyde Davis explained the plight of 20-montl
        Hernan Arteaga -- very ill in Bolivia and be
        the U. S. For treatment at Duke Hospital. :
        given to establish a vehicle for receiving :
        funds for financial assistance by allowing :
        be handled through the associational office.
        pause for special prayer, led by host pastol
    (5) Tony Gurganus requested interpretation and :
        of a motion passed at the September meeting
        tional Council. The moderator explained tha
        Center Building Fund account is open for cor
        that the Council may determine when "suffic:
        available to proceed" should that situation
        the end of the three years commanded by the

. Jean Hatch led the singing of "Standing on the Promises".
. Agency reports were given as follows:
   (1) Annuity Board   - Waldo Earley
   (2) Baptist Foundation   - Kenneth Durham
   (3) American Bible Society - H. J. Register
   (4) Christian Literature   - Tom Cooper
   Dr. Garland Hendrix delivered a message from the Annuity Board.
. L. E. Williamson brought greetings from the host church.
. The congregation sang "Love Lifted Me".
. Reports of Educational Programs were given as follows:
   (1) Brotherhood   - Michael Shook
   (2) Music   - Jean Hatch
   (3) Church Training   - H. J. Register
   (4) Sunday School   - Don Coley
   (5) Vacation Bible School   - Michael Shool
   (6) Woman's Missionary Union - Betsy Carter
. Video presentation: BSC Report to Associations.
. Roger Micks, Pastor of Temple Baptist Church, Raleigh, brought
  a message from the Church Training Department of the Baptist
  State Convention.
. New Pastors and church staff members recognized were:
   (1) Caleb Godwin, Pastor, Albertson
   (2) Mitchell Rivenbark, Pastor, Bear Marsh
   (3) Greg Thornton, Pastor, Calypso
   (4) Randy Wellman, Pastor, Dodsons Chapel
   (5) Kenneth Durham, Pastor, Johnsons
   (6) Wayne Wheeler, Pastor, Garland
   (7) Farrell Miller, Pastor, Piney Grove
   (8) L. E. Williamson, Minister of Education, Clinton
   (9) Don Arnold, Minister of Music, Immanuel
. Davis Benton, Chairman of Pastoral Support Committee, led in
  prayer.
. The Congregation sand "I Am Thine, O Lord".
. Dan Arnold sang a solo, accompanied by Stan Benton at the organ.
. Phillip Denton delivered the Doctrinal Message.
. Lauren Sharpe led in prayer and asked blessings for the evening
  meal.

                  First Day -- Evening Session

. Moderator recalled the association to order at 7:10 P.M.
. The Congregation sang "He Keeps Me Singing".
. Randy Wellman read Acts 1:6-11 and led in prayer.
. Clyde Davis led in a period of recognition of those who serve
  on associational committees and offices.
. Hernan Arteaga, pastor of the Second Baptist Church in Santa
  Cruz, Bolivia, also president of the Bolivian Baptist Conven-
  tion, gave a slide presentation of the work in his country.
  Wayne Wheeler, pastor of Garland Church and Missionary on
  furlough from Honduras, interpreted.
. Video presentation: "Southern Baptist Missions"
. Wayne Wheeler brought the missionary message.
. The moderator adjourned the session with prayer.

                         Second Day

. Moderator Mack Thompson called the meeting to order at 9:30 at
  Magnolia Baptist Church.
. Tony Gurganus led the singing of "Come, Thou Almighty King".
. Freddie Harris read Psalms 126:5-6 and led in prayer.

                             17

4. The clerk reported registration representing 34
   quorum was declared for transaction of business
5. Miscellaneous business:
   (1) Larry Blount asked for ruling in reference
       for definite time" of motion regarding Bapt
       The Moderator ruled the action in order.
   (2) Host pastor William Shipp welcomed the sess

6. Reports from Associational Council committees w
   follows:
   (1) Missions   - Michael Shook
   (2) Library   - Thelma Davis
   (3) Evangelism   - Phil Denton
   (4) Pastoral Support - Davis Benton
   (5) Stewardship---Budget presented during First
                        Session was adopted.
7. Elwynn Murray, Jr., presented his report on Chr
   Education.
8. Officers were elected as recommended by the nom
   tee, allowing the committee to later fill the p
   Training Director.
9. The resolutions committee proposed the followin
   duly adopted:
            WHEREAS, The North Carolina Eastern Bap
   Association held its one hundred and fifty-
   session in the spirit of renewed unity and
   executing its theme "Christ the Only Hope;"
   BE IT RESOLVED:
   1. That the Eastern Association express its
      to our moderator, Mack Thompson, and the
      the Association for the fine manner in w
      ness of the Association has been conduct
   2. That we pledge our love, support and pra
      Director of Missions and his wife, along
      appreciation of their leadership;
   3. That we resolve to encourage the churche
      for unity for the purpose of fulfilling
      God in the proclamation of His Word;
   4. That we express our thanks to the host c
      (First Baptist, Clinton, and Magnolia Ba
      assisted by the Concord and Johnson Chur
      the excellent manner in which they provi
      comfort, the warm fellowship, and the fe
      our messengers;
   5. Finally, we resolve to encourage prayer
      Missions Thrust with the realization tha
      our only hope, and that WE can do ALL th
      Christ who strengtheneth US.
10. The time, place and preacher committee gained a
    recommendation that the 1982 Annual Session be
    Olive on the first day and at Mount Gilead on t
    with Union Grove serving Mount Gilead as joint-
    session be held October 25 and 26, 1982; and th
    Sermon be preached by Lauren Sharpe.
11. Reports of Social Service Institutions were giv
    (1) Baptists Homes for the Aging - Millard John
    (2) Baptist Children's Homes   - John A. John
    (3) Baptist Hospital   - Gerald Ouinn
    Representatives were present to speak for the a
    children's homes and hospital.

2. The annual sermon was brought by Don Coley.
3. The Meeting adjourned.

RESOLUTION COMMITTEE REPORT

1ereas, the North Carolina Eastern Baptist Association held its
1e hundred and fifty-fourth annual session in the spirit of
:newed unity and cooperation executing its theme "Christ the Only
)pe",

: it Resolved:
   1. That the Eastern Association express its appreciation to our
)derator, Mack Thompson, and the officers of the Association for
1e fine manner in which the business of this Association has been
)nducted;
   2. That we pledge our love, support, and prayers to our Direc-
)r of Missions and his wife along with our appreciation for their
:adership;
   3. That we resolve to encourage the churches to strive for unity
)r the purpose of fulfilling the will of God in the proclamation
: His Word;
   4. That we express our thanks to the host churches; First Bap-
ist, Clinton, and Magnolia Baptist - assisted by the Concord and
)hnson Churches, for the excellent manner in which they provided
)r the comfort, the warm fellowship, and the feeding of our mes-
:ngers;
   5. Finally, we resolve to encourage prayer for the Bold Mission
1rust with the realization that Christ is our only hope, and that
: can do ALL things through Christ who strengthenth US.

                          Freddie Harris, Chairman
                          Oliver Skerrett
                          Charles Kirkland

SEVENTY-SECOND ANNUAL SESSION
EASTERN BAPTIST ASSOCIATION
WMU ANNUAL SESSION MINUTES - 1981

   The 72nd WMU Annual Session of Eastern Association WMU met
)ril 16, 1981 with First Baptist Church, Clinton. Mrs. Norwood
irter, Director, presided. The meeting was opened with the singing
: "Take My Life and Let It Be". Prayer Calendar and prayer was
:d by Mrs. Coleman Carter. Mrs. Albert Kaleel, WMU Director of
.rst Church, Clinton, welcomed the 72 Annual Session. Minutes
ire read and approved. It was reported that 27 churches shared
1 sending $130.00 to the Womans' Prison Center in Raleigh.
   The schedule for the annual session for the next five years is
: follows: 1982-Ingold Baptist Church, 1983-Rowan Baptist Church,
)84-Wells Chapel Baptist Church, 1985-Grove Park Baptist Church,
)86-Sharon and Shiloh Baptist Churches.
   The Leadership Conference will be held September 24 at Warsaw.
   Reports and challenges were given from the age level organiza-
-ons. Baptist Young Women Director was absent. Mission Action -
1 the absence of Helen Register, Mary Carter emphasized the impor-
ince of personal evangelism. She said each person should take it
iriously and be available whereever they are, to others who want
) know about Jesus Christ. Helen sent word that she would be
itting in touch with the churches regarding the health kits.
iteen - Connie Carlton, Director, stated that Acteen is a hard

age for girls, but churches can help. They can lov
them. GA - Paula Matthis, Director, said girls thi
about WMU work in the church, mission action, and m
This year there has been one new GA group started a
organized. It is important to plan work a year in
a good organization. Mission Friends - Francis Tew
said the church is most important part in a preschc
Our children are easily influenced at an early age;
not let the church have the most important task.   T
sions is planted here.

Mrs. Robert Miller invited the 73 Annual Session
Ingold Baptist Church.

Special music was given by Norma Jean Jackson.

Rev. Bill Davis, missionary to Bolivia, showed s
information about mission work in Bolivia. He aske
giving support for missions.

Grace was given and the meeting adjourned for su

The evening session began with the singing of "C
is Risen". Baptist Young Women Director, Glenda St
brought an update on BYW. Three BYW's were started

Mrs. Inez Peterson presented the 1981-82 WMU off
Mrs. Norwood Carter; Associate Director, Mrs. Colem
Secretary, Mrs. Donald Pope; BW Director, Mrs. Jack
Director, Glenda Strickland; Acteens Director, Mrs.
GA Director, Mrs. Paula Matthis; Mission Friends Di
Andy Wood; Mission Action Director, Mrs. Helen Regi
Enlargement Director, Mrs. Silas Howell. Motion wa
these officers. Motion carried. The officers were
prayer.

Special music was given by Mr. & Mrs. Van Arnold
Church.

Mrs. Wayne Wheeler, Missionary to Honduras, brou
message, "My Mission to be a Pilgrim". This was a
mission for Christ by faith. God calls each of us
either in a foreign country or at home. We have a
from the day we are saved. That mission is for us
the Lord. In a foreign country we learn the langua
and then we witness. As people become Christians,
pilgrims for Christ. As Southern Baptists, what ca
can take part in BOLD growing, BOLD giving and BOLD
cannot go, we can pray and pray without ceasing. P
missions in Honduras.

86 Registered.   Respectfully submi
                                        Mrs. Norwood Carte
                                        Mrs. Donald Pope,

REPORT OF THE AMERICAN BIBLE SOCIETY

On behalf of the millions of people who learned
Jesus Christ through the pages of Scripture in 1980
like to express its sincere thanks to the churches
the Southern Baptist Convention for their share in
ful programs of Scripture evangelism. The denomina
for each of the past four years has averaged about
member, or a total of $293,000.

During 1980, the Bible Society of Brazil produce
time the Illustrated New Testament in Today's Portu
translation is receiving a tremendous response from

20

and individuals. In addition, work is continuing on the complete Bible in this version. This translation is expected to attain the same popularity in Brazil as the Spanish Version Popular Bible received throughout Latin America. And in Nigeria, new translations have been completed to meet the growing need of Nigerian Christians who are becoming increasingly eager to have the Scriptures in their own languages. Translation of the complete New Testament was reported for the first time ever in the languages of Angas and Yala.

Another example of what your gifts in 1980 have helped to accomplish is seen in the Philippines. Following is a true story about how God is workin in the Phillippines through the Bible Society. A colleague writes: "As I inched my way to the bunkhouse to give out these Scripture selections, a 13-year old boy named Huy from Vietnam followed me. In broken English he said, 'You telling about God? Me know Him little bit.' I told Huy about God and His love.

"Then Huy's father, Le, told how, when the communists overthrew South Vietnam, he and his family escaped in a motorboat--had to endure sharks, violent storms, a pirate attach....they lost everything.

"I explained that God had a reason for bringing them out of their own country -- even though it might be hard to see it just then. I asked if they had ever read the Bible. When they said they hadn't, I gave them some Scripture Selections.

"After awhile, Le's wife said, 'This is good. I feel something in my heart.' Le then volunteered to distribute more scriptures. And he said, 'I want to help you give my people this precious treasure. We will share the Word of God with others.'

"As Le and his family left, I heard him say, 'All along the journey, amidst all kinds of dangers and impending death, I have always felt a loving hand upholding me and my family. Now I know it -- God!'"

To help aid the ABS in its world-wide effort to serve the church and its global ministries, and to strengthen the indispensable partnership between the churches and the ABS, an Advisory Council was held last year. Representatives of many major denominations were present at this Council, to discuss with officials of the ABS ways in which increased support for the worldwide Bible cause and goals for the years to come could be achieved. Representing the Southern Baptist Convention were Dr. Harold C. Bennett, Executive Secretary-Treasurer, Executive Committee of the Southern Baptist Convention and Dr. Porter Routh, his predecessor, both members of the ABS Board of Managers.

At the Advisory Council Meeting, several important resolutions were adopted. Of special significance is the resolution encouraging "...greater financial support from churches and the total Christian community, expecially when viewed in the light of U.S. and world inflation..." and urging "...the churches to set a goal of at least 10% annual growth in financial support to the work of ABS." We sincerely hope that the Southern Baptist Convention will find it possible to assist in the successful fulfillment of this resolution.

Respectfully submitted,
H. J. Register

REPORT OF THE BIBLICAL RECORDER

Again this past year, the "Biblical Recorder" has reminded us all of the value of good church-pastor relations. This is just one of

the many subjects the "Recorder" seeks to cover fo
Baptists.

The editor believes strongly in the local churc
ministry and work of the pastor. As all of us kno
take the place of a good church and a good pastor.

And yet, we also know that there are those in o
not believe in this as much as they should. The "
constant reminder to us that bedrock of Baptist li
local church served by a dedicated pastor.

The "Recorder" also challenges us in many other
ple, it reported that there was a net gain of only
in our convention in the past 10 years. This shoc
especially in view of the number of new churches o
last 50 years and in the population growth of our
last decade.

The "Recorder" was happy to report that the Sou
Convention in Los Angeles was a good one. Those u
were given an accurate and complete picture of wha
--a front seat, as it were, for only 7¢ (cost of o

When people know the truth--and truth must be s
we have a better convention, better churches, bett
and better individual Christians. The "Recorder"
ment of communication that keeps us closer togethe

If you are not receiving the "Recorder", you ar
thing vital to your Christian life. The cost is s
than one-half the price of a first class stamp. S
church and every individual can afford that much.

Respectfully subm
T. N. Cooper

ANNUITY BOARD REPORT

"Nineteen hundred eighty has been a year of unp₁
and startling change," according to Dr. Darold H. ₁
of the Southern Baptist Convention's Annuity Board.
Key statistical highlights in 1980 included:

1. A 13th check amounting to 10 per cent of a y₁
   was mailed to annuitants who retired before ₁
2. A total of $21,059,479 in retirement benefit₁
3. Insurance benefits through the Board's churcl
   seminary programs amounted to $15,955,965.
4. Total assets held in trust at the close of tl
   $806,518,757. This figure represented a gro₁
   $139,043,770 over 1979's total.
5. Premium income totaled $87,938,590, includin₁
   and relief receipts. A total of $42,121,138
   for the Fixed Fund, $3,620,501 was earmarked
   Fund and $11,063,513 went into Plan A. Insu₁
   totaled $24,863,894.
6. At the close of 1980, the Board counted 20,5₁
   agency member accounts in Plan A, 47,701 in ₁
   6,033 in the Balanced Fund and 3,376 in the ₁

STATISTICAL HIGHLIGHTS 1981

Retirement Plans Protection Section of	Member Accounts and Benefits	Insu₁
Southern Baptist Retire- ment Program	8,536	*Health ₁ Group L₁

22

etirement Plans	Member Accounts and Benefits	Insurance	Members
lan A (church agency)	20,527	Group Life (agency)	17,802
ixed Fund (church-agency)	47,701	**Life Benefit Plan	2,328
alanced Fund (church-agency)	6,033	Seminarian Life	1,584
ariable Fund (Church-agency)	3,376	Seminarian Medical	4,245
enefits Paid (retirement and Variable)	$21,059,479	* Includes churches and agencies	
elief Benefits	413,980	** Closed to new members	
elief Recipients	407		

In North Carolina as of March 31, 1981, 3,114 staff members of
,353 churches and associations are participating in the Southern
aptist Retirement Program. Through March 31, 1981, we had proces-
ed the following:
    70 - Southern Baptist Retirement Program applications
    11 - applications for age retirement benefits
    442 - upgrades
    One of the most exciting and far-reaching aspects of our work
or 1980 has been the printing and response to the study guide,
Planning the Rest of Your Life". This is available from our office
or those who wish to have help in planning their retirement years.
    The church's response to upgrading staff member's retirement is
ost encouraging. Ten percent of his/her annual compensation
salary, housing, auto allowance, etc.) should be minimum.
    In Eastern Association 32 churches and 37 staff members are par-
icipating in the retirement program. Of these, 9 are still parti-
ipating on the minimum of $33.34 per month. There is great need
o upgrade this to 10% of total salary for staff members.

Respectfully submitted,
Waldo Early

NORTH CAROLINA BAPTIST FOUNDATION REPORT

During the past year, twenty-three new trust funds valued at
385,016 were established with the N.C. Baptist Foundation. Cou-
led with the additions to existing trusts, total new assets held
or the various missions and institutions increased the value of
rust assets by $453,877.
    -Foreign missions trust fund increased by approximately $26,000.
    -Home missions trusts increased by $8,000.
    -Baptist Childrens Homes of North Carolina trust increased by
        approximately $19,000.
    -Southeastern Seminary by $12,250.
    -Fruitland Bible Institute by $33,000.
    -N.C. Baptist Homes by $1,500.
    -Local church trust funds, including cemetery, scholarship and
        mission funds by $5,000.
    -Cooperative Program by $7,000.
    -Statewide Student loan fund by $115,000.
The Directors of the Foundation made an investment decision in
)78 to increase the yield to the charitable beneficiaries of trust
ncome. Over a two year period investments moved toward high qua-
ity selective bonds to accomplish this goal. The income of yield
ncreased steadily with the rate on December 30, 1980 averaging
).3%. Market value of all assets on December 30, 1980 were
l,586,215.12. The bond portion of the investment portfolio re-
lected the high interest market at the end of the year with market
alues being depressed below inventory value.

Thirty-eight percent of the market value of all a
the Foundation were made as gifts by persons desirin
income for the remainder of their lifetime and at de
trust funds to pay income to missions or Baptist ins
Foundation personnel are available to assist any mem
tist Church in North Carolina to utilize this or oth
giving to provide a perpetual personal support for s
sage of Christ - even beyond one's lifetime.

More families are utilizing the memorial gifts as
viding mission support on a continuing basis. Indiv
accounts are established with only the income being
the name of the deceased family member. Generally t
cause named to receive the income was loved and supp
the lifetime of the family member.

Private and confidential conferences are schedule
staff members with individuals desiring to seek direc
planning and giving.

Respectfully submitt
Hubert Phillips

NORTH CAROLINA BAPTIST HOMES FOR THE AGIN

As we look back over the past thirty years of mini
Baptist Homes, it is a real inspiration to see where
and to meditate on the many blessings that God has so
stowed upon us. He has brought us from one Home in 1
of six Homes, an apartment complex, and a skilled nur
from one resident to a total capacity for 300 persons
These have been good years, and God has used N. C. Ba
bring this special ministry to older people a long way
go from here is certainly, as always, in the hands of
depends largely on where North Carolina Baptists want

Quite frankly, we are at a standstill. Crippling i
caught up with us and is eating into the very vitals (
tence. We are still giving the same high quality of (
to each of the residents in the six Homes, Nursing Car
the apartment complex. It is a struggle and a juggle
come and expenditures. Building plans for a desperate
70-bed addition to our current Nursing Care Unit and i
Home have been held up by regulatory red tape for yea:
the state health laws have been altered to permit the
these beds, it doesn't appear that we could wisely bo:
at the current interest rates.

Though 1980 gifts through our Cooperative Program a
Carolina Missions Offering are a little more than $55(
of all income), these gifts are not commensurate with
population growth and the ministry support needs of tl

Two things are apparent. One - Baptists must be in
needs and do all possible to increase their gifts accc
through the regular channels -- the Cooperative Progra
North Carolina Missions Offering. Two - North Carolin
must help us find ways of raising money for developmen
sion to meet the needs of current residents and the ne
numbers of older adults.

The General Board of the Baptist State Convention I
in our concerns and has appointed a Special Study Comm
a serious and close look at the financial needs of oui
Homes.

continue to trust our Heavenly Father for His blessings
mes' vital ministry to older adults. We will keep faith
d with N. C. Baptists and strive to give the highest
e to each resident of the North Carolina Baptist Homes.
ieve that our future is as bright as the promises of
and as sure as the love and devotion of North Carolina

Respectfully Submitted,
Millard M. Johnson

CHRISTIAN HIGHER EDUCATION REPORT

cil on Christian Higher Education has published a small
ned for study in the churches. The title is "On mission:
College Alliance". By means of a complimentary copy to
iled September 1, 1981, the colleges hope to create
ong the churches for studying the book. Chapter titles

 are the Purposes of a Christian College or University?
are the People Who Make Up the College Community?
Does the College Community Decide on Policies and
rams That Will Genuinely Reflect the Purpose of a
stian Institution?
 are Some of the Distinctive Problems that Baptist
eges Encounter as They Attempt to Fulfill Their
ational Mission in a Christian Context?
do Baptist Colleges Seek to Encourage Students in
Continuing Development of the Religious Dimension of
?
Do Baptist Colleges Decide which Students Should Be
tted? How can Baptist Young People of Limited Means
rd the Cost of Attending a Baptist College?
Sould Baptist People of North Carolina Support Insti-
ons of Higher Learning?
f the book will be sent, free of charge, to those who
 A study guide is also available.
-82 school year is filled with financial uncertainties
nation. North Carolina Baptist colleges, where a total
tudents were enrolled last year, are grateful for the
d growing support through the Cooperative Program and
arolina Missions Offering. In addition to dollars, the
of more Baptist young people from the churches is a
sis of your colleges and universities. Thank you for
ulness in the development of college-related churches.
HOWAN GARDNER-WEBB MARS HILL MEREDITH WAKE FOREST

Respectfully submitted,
Elwynn Murray, Jr.

NORTH CAROLINA BAPTIST HOSPITAL REPORT

he past decade, life expectancy in this country has
y three years, to 73.2 years. Important factors in
se have been the development of new medical technology
lication of new medical knowledge gained through re-

Hospital has had a significant part in this developing

knowledge and technology. During the past year, th
expended more than $3 million on technological equi
the installation of an 18-MEV linear accelerator fo
treatment of patients with certain types of cancer.
catheterization laboratory increases the capability
and locating heart problems. A cell saver, the fir
lina, contributes to the recovery of many surgical
technology salvages the patient's own blood, cleans
it for transfusion back into the patient in a matte
making transfusion faster and less expensive. The
treatment of epilepsy has been greatly enhanced by
of a video telemetry system which uses cameras to r
physical symptoms during a seizure. This makes it
identify a seizure, thus enabling the physician to
precise drug dosage needed.

The hospital's ministry has been aided by comple
tion of the Focus Building. Other hospital space i
renovation for more effective use.

Several staff members from the Medical Center ha
in shortterm mission assignments during the past ye
these in overseas areas.

The Department of Pastoral Care continues to pro
ministry to hospital patients and their families, i
group counseling in crisis situations, clinical pas
in both crisis ministry and pastoral counseling, at
and numerous events in Christian enrichment and dev
Minister's Care Plan continues in which the Baptist
tion provides financial assistance for ministers an
families who seek pastoral counseling through one o
ment's regional centers.

Again this year, our hospital has won awards in c
ness programs, indicating our continuing efforts to
ting costs and patient charges as low as possible.

During the year, the hospital's charter revision
to successful and satisfactory conclusion.

In 1980, our churches contributed $457,459.56 to
through the Cooperative Program, and $353,397.73 thr
Carolina Missions Offering and designated gifts.

Respectfully submit
Gerald Quinn

STEWARDSHIP COMMITTEE REPORT

A dream is only a dream until someone makes it co
Mission Thrust began as a dream for Southern Baptist
a BOLD dream of greater mission support and church q
people are committeed to making this dream a reality
BOLD mission thrust to succeed, many people must ado
ment.

Two important questions must be asked and answere
        1. Do we have the will and commitment to pers
            what we have voted as BOLD mission thrust
        2. Can we learn to live with our commitments?
Officially, Southern Baptists claimed their BOLD
dream in 1977. Looking at the years ahead we have m
of excitement and anxiety. The introduction is over
must demonstrate our willingness to make our BOLD mi
dream come true through our BOLD giving.

Involved in this demonstration are several realities to be considered:
1. Churches need to be faithful in fulfilling their goals of mission giving and church growth.
2. Some churches may need to discover "special roles" in the BOLD endeavors they have adopted;
3. Church leaders must lead the people to adjust lifestyles and values to achieve BOLD Mission Thrust.

Commitment to BOLD Mission calls for specific action on our part as individuals and churches. Each church is challenged to:
1. Give something through the Cooperative Program for BOLD Mission Thrust support.
2. Increase the percentage of its total budget income given through the Cooperative Program.
3. Increase the percentage of total budget income given for the support of associational missions.

Let every church in the Eastern Baptist Association demonstrate its genuine concern for and commitment to world mission support through BOLD living and BOLD giving. The dream is BOLD. The people are excited. The mission is unmistakably before us.

Respectfully submitted,
Jim Hartsell, Chairman

PASTORAL SUPPORT COMMITTEE REPORT

The Pastoral Support Committee, consisting of Davis Benton, Chairman, Tony Gurganus, Gene Hart, Charles Kirkland, and R. O. Sanderson, took the theme of "Strengthen the Pastors" as theme and goal for 1980-81.

We opened the year with a "Get-to-Know-You" Dinner for all new pastors and their wives on Friday, April 10. A total of 7 new pastors have come into our association since October 1, 1980. On May 8, 1981, each pastor and his wife were invited to a Seminar led by Dr. & Mrs. J. Winston Pearce, "Making Good Marriages Better". This was very well attended.

The Committee has met, and some plans have been made to start small "support groups" throughout the Association. This would involve five or six pastors in a given area getting together once or twice per month to give each other prayer and moral support.

Plans have already been made for another Seminar, November 10, 1981, for all pastors and wives. The theme for this seminar, which will be led by Dr. Bob Dale of Southeastern Seminary, will be "Support From Within". This will deal with pastor and wife supporting each other in the ministry.

We are also looking at the possibility of starting a Seminary Extension Course for pastors and their families during the next year.. During the past year more than 10,000 persons enrolled in one or more Seminary Extension programs throughout the United States. This surpassed the enrollment of all six Southern Baptist Seminaries. In North Carolina, the enrollment was 2,300. These people studied primarily in 75 centers throughout the state. Some of them enrolled in the Independent Study Institute. They enjoyed selecting courses in the Basic Curriculum Series and the College-Level Curriculum. As a part of our state missions program, North Carolina Baptist help underwrite the cost of study with Seminary Extension through the Cooperative Program budget. This subsidy helps keep the cost per course within a range every student can afford. It also helps to explain why our state has enjoyed the

largest Seminary Extension program in the United St
seventh consecutive year.

Respectfully submi
Davis Benton, Chai

HISTORY OF FIRST BAPTIST CHURCH
Clinton, North Carolina

On November 16, 1854, a little group of brethren
of Isham Royal on what is now Wall Street in Clinto?
liminary steps to organize a Baptist Church. Isaac
named chairman and Mr. Royal, secretary of this mee?
January 7, 1855 another meeting was held in the Cou?
that time the organization of the Clinton Missionar?
was completed. Records reveal that there were only
namely - Isaac Boykin, Thomas J. Boykin, James M. M?
Brown, James Peterson, James Marsh, George W. Marsh,
Susan Pickett, Celestial P. Bizzell, Sarah B. Mosel?
Carroll, Harriett Roberts, Winnie Johnson, Martha J.
Eliza Boykin.

In the first months after the organization, the ?
held in the Presbyterian Church and the Courthouse.
Isaac Boykin gave the lot for erection of a buildinc
was completed in 1857. It was about 50 feet wide ar
The building was made of lumber and furnished with ?
bell now being used. It was equipped with a baptist
were two balconies for the Negro members.

The church had what they called a "colored member
colored members were subject to the same rules and ?
the white members were and held their own conference
pastor of the church presided and the clerk recorde?
This church continued to receive colored members unt
after this the First Baptist Church (colored) was o?
letters of dismission were granted all colored membe
new church.

The first 20 years or more, the church did not h?
School of its own. Clinton had a union Sunday Schoc
interested church members of all denominations took
Sunday School was organized about 1889.

About 1906 the first pastor's home was built for
Also during his term as pastor, the first church bui
down and what we speak of now as "the old church" w?
1908 the church had a membership of 245. The WMU h?
vital part in the program and ministry of the church

The music program has played an important part in
this church also. A service of love and sacrifice h
by several in this program.

During these years of growth also, many young pec
their lives to full-time Christian work.

The progress of the church with its continual imp
expansion has to a great degree, walked hand in hand
pastors through the years. Each has made his contri
these -- additions to the staff, growth of membershi
buildings, promoting two mission churches, and 17 ye
building of a new sanctuary and educational building
cost of over six-hundred thousand dollars (the entir
is valued at over one and one-half million dollars t

In 1979 the old building was completely renovated
over $600,000. Our resident membership is now over

Total church budget in 1951 = $49,658.00
Total receipts in 1980   = $315,000.00

HISTORY OF MAGNOLIA BAPTIST CHURCH
1835 - 1981

In November, 1835, the Concord Baptist Church granted letters
to twenty-four members to organize a church to be named Beaverdam
Baptist Church. They met in Beaverdam School, located one-half
mile east of Magnolia.

On June 3, 1837, six members were given letters and they organized Kenansville Baptist Church.

In 1846, the members built a church across the road from the
schoolhouse at Beaverdam. In 1872, the church was moved to the
present location in Magnolia. The name was changed to Magnolia
Baptist Church in 1874.

In the year 1913, eleven members from the church organized Oak
Vale Church. (This church is no longer in service.)

Many members have been trained for the Lord's service in the
different organizations of the church. Sunday School has been in
existence for many, many years. In 1905, the WMU was organized;
the Sunbeams in 1907, and in September, 1909 the WMU of the Eastern
Association was founded in this church. The YWA was organized in
1913; RA's and GA's in 1918, and the BYPU in 1921. Only the WMU
and Sunday School is in service today to train our members. In
1959 our church voted for full time worship service and has continued full time since its beginning.

In 1920 the church built a new brick building (present one).
The pastorium was sold in 1959 and a new brick one erected next
to the church on a lot given and dedicated in 1960. In 1969, the
much needed educational unit was begun and was dedicated in 1970.
In observance of the Bicentennial, July 4, 1976, a Historical Room
was dedicated. It is furnished with our old church furniture,
pictures, and records of our church. This also serves as the
pastor's study. (Our records have been microfilmed and are in the
Baptist Historical Collection stored in the State Archives in
Raleigh, N.C.)

In 1977, a brick storage building for the pastorium and the
church was built.

There have been many men and women, who, through their dedicated
Christian lives, have had an influence on the growth of our church.
We also have pastors who are serving other churches. Our church
has been served by forty pastors since 1835 (146 years).

The past is our heritage, the present is what we have, and the
future is our challenge. May we grow in grace and the knowledge
of our Lord and Saviour Jesus Christ be with us now and forever.

BAPTIST CHILDREN'S HOMES REPORT
Pembroke Family Services Area

The ministry of the Baptist Children's Homes in Southeastern
North Carolina continues to grow and develop. This is made possible by the continuing support of many Christian friends. Vital
to the work of the Homes is financial support through special gifts,
the North Carolina Missions Offering and income through the Cooperative Program.

The Family Services Center Office, serving the ten Southeastern
North Carolina counties, is located on the Odum Home Campus, Pembroke,

North Carolina. Through this office all services o
Institution are made available to those who need as
the Homes.

Construction has been completed on the Jimmy Lat
County Cottage and the new cottage is expected to b
children by early fall. The addition of the new co
crease the Odum Home capacity to thirty-four childr
God for His leading in supplying this need on the C

Programs located in the Southeastern area includ
Odum Home, emergency care at Supply, North Carolina
foster homes, mother's aid, social work and counsel
Children and their families from Southeastern North
usually served through these programs.

Good things are taking place in our Baptist Chil
family across the state. Six Family Service Center
opened with three others in the planning stages. C
being provided temporary care in seven Emergency Ca
Therapeutic camping for boys is being expanded at C
near Vass. The Child Development Center in Thomasv
to offer progressive demonstration preschool care a
North Carolina Baptist Churches. The Family Resour
cated in Thomasville is piloting a concept of conti
for people across the State who are in the best pos
families through a concept of preventive care.

Melvin Brown and members of the staff of the Hom
eastern North Carolina are leading the program in a
In the words of Paul we can say "We are laborers to
(I Corinthians 3:9). Thank Him for this relationsh

Respectfully submi
John A. Johnson

MISSIONS COMMITTEE REPORT

The Missions Committee exists to work with churc
to develop a strong mission program in Eastern Asso
possibilities and opportunities for mission action
The years ahead will afford an opportunity to utili
reservoir of expertise represented by dedicated lay
ready and willing to volunteer their services in re
for Christ.

A request for $6,500.00 of Cooperative Missions
to the Baptist State Convention for the purpose of
half-time Christian Social Ministries program in Ea
tion. Should funds be approved, the Christian Soci
worker will be responsible for determining needs in
propose plans to meet those needs; and work with pa
church leaders for the purpose of enlisting volunte

A word of grateful appreciation is due Rev. Larr
the work he has done to establish this program in o
Larry has given a great deal of time and effort in
the Migrant Program and the Youth/Family Ministry P
our hope and prayer that the churches of Eastern As
continue their cooperative spirit as this ministry
the days to come.

Respectfully submi
Michael Shook, Cha

EVANGELISM REPORT

Our main emphasis in evangelism this year has been to help churches make preparations for our 1982 Simultaneous Revivals. In
February of this year we had an Interpretation Meeting for the purpose of informing the churches in our Association about the plans
for our 1982 Revivals--Then two people from our association were
chosen to go to Ridgecrest to receive training for People Search
and Prayer Chairman. Rev. Chuck Miller is our People Search Chairman for the Eastern Association, and Mrs. Helen Register is our
Prayer Chairman.
Each church in our association was contacted and asked to elect
a People Search Chairman and Prayer Chairman from that church--
these people were to attend the Associational Key Leadership Conference on September 15 at Warsaw to receive training. They, in
turn will go back to their churches and take a census of their
church area and find all the lost and unchurched people...At the
same time the Prayer Chairman will be putting emphasis on the importance of prayer in preparation for our 1982 Revivals.
All pastors in our association were contacted and asked to attend
a training program on lay witnessing--This is being done through
video-tapes. The pastors will go back and teach lay witnessing
to people from their churches who volunteer for this program. These
people will go out and witness to all those lost people in their
church area found by the People Search team.
Next spring there will be a mass media campaign to advertise our
1982 Simultaneous Revivals. This will be done through television
commercials, radio announcements and the newspapers.
In March our revivals will begin in the Eastern part of our
state and go across the state--Eastern section March 14-28, in the
Piedmont March 28-April 24 and the Mountains April 18-May 15.
After revivals the new converts will be followed up on and given
new Church Membership Training.
As your Associational Chairman of Evangelism, I am excited about
these revivals because I know that God wants to bless and revive
us; but we must be willing to make the necessary preparations if
we are going to have real revival.
If your Associational Evangelism Committee can be of any help
to you in preparation for your revival or in any other way, please
contact us.

Respectfully submitted,
Phillip R. Denton

ASSOCIATIONAL COUNCIL ACTIVITIES 1980-81

The Council met in 4 regular and 2 special meetings during the
year.
On November 18, an offer was accepted from the Warsaw Church
of a room of additional office space, and appreciation was expressed to the pastor and the members for their hospitality.
At the January 5 meeting at Center Church, new Pastors Ken
Durham of Johnson, and Mike Lee from Garner's Chapel were welcomed.
April 7, instructions were given for purchase of a plaque
expressing appreciation to the Bolivian Baptist Convention for the
fine work being done there for our Lord. The plaque was to be
carried to Bolivia, South America by the missions team, on their
tour to Bolivia. A special committee was appointed to lead a joint
pilot project with the Baptist State Convention for work with

31

migrants.

Approval was given at the July Meeting for a propo
plan and for a proposed financing plan to construct a
ter Building.

Called meetings in August and September resulted i
action on a Baptist Center Building for three years o
time as sufficient funds are available to go forward.

Respectfully submitt
Lucille Yancey

1982 ASSOCIATIONAL CALENDAR

JANUARY
4-8   Bible Study Week
5   7:30 P.M. EXECUTIVE COMMITTEE - MOUNT VERNON C
         8:00 P.M. ASSOCIATIONAL COUNCIL - MOUNT VERNON
8-9   Home Missions Teacher Training - Caraway
10   SBC - Witness Commitment Day
11   10:45 A.M. PASTORS CONFERENCE
11-12   7:00 P.M. MUSIC WORKSHOP
19   7:30 P.M. MISSIONS COMMITTEE - WARSAW
24   Baptist Men Day
26-27   General Board - BSC
27-28   DOAM and Convention Staff
29-30   Church Training Enabling Conference - Caraway

FEBRUARY
2   10:45 A.M. PASTORS CONFERENCE
         7:30 P.M. EXECUTIVE COMMITTEE - WARSAW
8-9   Statewide Evangelism Conference - Greensboro
14-20   WMU Focus Week
28-March 7   Special prayer emphasis for Simultaneous
28   EASTERN ASSOCIATION PRAYER EMPHASIS FOR REVIVAI

MARCH
7-14   Week of Prayer for Home Missions
8-13   Youth Week (Week before SBC to clear Simultanec
            dates)
9   7:30 P.M. EXECUTIVE COMMITTEE
13   7:30 P.M. YOUTH NIGHT - RALLY AND SPEAKERS' TOU
14-28   SIMULTANEOUS JOINT REVIVALS
15   10:45 A.M. PASTORS' CONFERENCE
19-23   Baptist Doctrine Study
28   State Pioneer RA Congress
29-30   7:30 P.M. MEDIA CENTER/LIBRARY WORKSHOP - CLIN1

APRIL
2-3   State Church Media/Library Conference - Raleigl
3   ROYAL AMBASSADOR TRACK MEET
5   7:00 P.M. STEWARDSHIP DINNER - CARSON'S RESTAUI
6   7:30 P.M. EXECUTIVE COMMITTEE - BEULAH
         8:00 P.M. ASSOCIATIONAL COUNCIL - BEULAH
11   EASTER SUNDAY
12   10:45 A.M. PASTORS' CONFERENCE
15   5:00 P.M. ASSOCIATIONAL WMU ANNUAL MEETING - II
19   7:30 P.M. CHURCH VBS WORKERS CLINIC - ROWAN
19-23   Baptist Doctrine Week
23-24   Youth Convention - Charlotte

MAY
1-9   Christian Home Week
1   10:45 A.M. PASTORS' CONFERENCE
1-4   Statewide Senior Adult Rally - Greensboro
10-12   Key Leadership Conference - Ridgecrest
13-15   State RA Track Meet
16   3:00 P.M. CHILDREN'S BIBLE DRILL - GROVE PARK
17-19 & 19-21 Senior Adult Conference - Caraway
17-23   Associational Emphasis Week
21-22   Area Church Training Convention - Goldsboro
22   State Children's Bible Drill/Youth Bible Drill & Speakers'
             Tournament - Goldsboro

JUNE
         10:45 A.M. PASTORS'CONFERENCE
         7:30 P.M. MISSIONS COMMITTEE - FAISON
13-14   WMU Annual Meeting - New Orleans
15-17   Southern Baptist Convention, New Orleans

JULY
         7:30 P.M. EXECUTIVE COMMITTEE - GROVE PARK
         8:00 P.M. ASSOCIATIONAL COUNCIL - GROVE PARK
2   10:45 A.M. PASTORS' CONFERENCE

AUGUST
         PASTORS' CONFERENCE (FAMILY PICNIC)
7   Youth Evangelism Conference - Fayetteville

SEPTEMBER
1-4   Foreign Missions Teacher Training - Caraway
         Labor Day
3   10:45 A.M. PASTORS' CONFERENCE
         7:30 P.M. EXECUTIVE COMMITTEE
4   BOLD MISSIONS RALLY - KEY LEADERS' CONFERENCE - WARSAW
0   7:30 P.M. MISSIONS COMMITTEE - MOUNT OLIVE, FIRST
3   7:30 P.M. WMU LEADERSHIP CONFERENCE - WARSAW
4   6:30 P.M. ASSOCIATIONAL RA CRUSADER FIELD DAY
6-October 3   Sunday School Preparation Week
27-28   7:30 P.M. SUNDAY SCHOOL LEADERS' TRAINING CONFERENCE - WARSAW
28-29   General Board
29-30   DOAM & Convention Staff

OCTOBER
-10   Week of Prayer for State Missions
         Foreign Mission Study Teacher Training
0   World Hunger Day
1   10:45 A.M. PASTORS' CONFERENCE
15-16   Sunday School Convention - Rocky Mount
4   High Attendance Day
5   2:30 P.M. ANNUAL ASSOCIATIONAL MEETING
6   9:00 A.M. ANNUAL ASSOCIATIONAL MEETING

NOVEMBER
-13   Royal Ambassador Week
         10:45 A.M. PASTORS' CONFERENCE
15-17   7:30 P.M. BROTHERHOOD WORKSHOP (Baptist Men & Royal Ambas-
             sadors) - WARSAW
15-17   Baptist State Convention - Fayetteville
)   Crusader RA Congress (State)
2   7:30 p.m. "M" Night - CHURCH TRAINING - ROWAN

33

NOVEMBER (Continued)
25   THANKSGIVING DAY
30   7:30 P.M. EXECUTIVE COMMITTEE - ROWAN
        8:30 P.M. ASSOCIATIONAL COUNCIL - ROWAN
28-December 5   Week of Prayer for Foreign Missions

DECEMBER
13   PASTORS' CONFERENCE (CHRISTMAS PARTY)
25   CHRISTMAS DAY
26-January 2   Association Office Closed

                EASTERN BAPTIST ASSOCIATION GOALS 1981 -

                            GENERAL

1. Assist BSU work at Mount Olive College
2. Provide service, promotion, leadership training
    nate cooperative activities for 40 churches.

                         SUNDAY SCHOOL

Goal #1. Train or retrain 8 Association Sunday Schoo
Goal #2. Provide training for 320 Church Sunday Scho
Goal #3. Lead churches to increase Sunday School enr
Goal #4. Lead churches to begin 8 new Sunday School
Goal #5. Train 200 church VBS workers.
Goal #6. Train 8 Associational VBS workers.

                         CHURCH TRAINING

Goal #1. Lead 50 church Training Leaders to participa
         ship training.
Goal #2. Involve 15 churches in inspiration and train
Goal #3. Lead 5 churches to participate in Bible Dril
Goal #4. Achieve an attendance of 200 at "M" Night.
Goal #5. Train or retrain 2 Associational Church Trai
Goal #6. Lead 12 churches to teach the doctrinal stud
         April.
Goal #7. Organize new Church Training Program in 4 ch

                          BROTHERHOOD

Goal #1. Train or retrain 3 Associational Brotherhood
Goal #2. Involve 50 Baptist Men officers and RA Leade
         training.
Goal #3. Involve 300 men in inspiration and promotion
Goal #4. Provide individual assistance for 3 church B
         groups.
Goal #5. Involve Crusaders from 10 churches in fellow
         sports.
Goal #6. Involve 150 boys in Royal Ambassador sports
Goal #7. Assist 25 churches to improve existing RA Ch
Goal #8. Assist in training 10 persons to teach Forei
         Mission Study books.

WOMANS MISSIONARY UNION

Goal #1. Train or retrain 8 Associational WMU officers.
Goal #2. Train 125 church WMU officers.
Goal #3. Provide inspiration and information for 150 women.
Goal #4. Involve women from 40 churches in Mission Action.
Goal #5. Assist in training 10 persons to teach Foreign and Home Mission Study books.

CHURCH MUSIC

Goal #1. Assist 40 churches to have best music program available.
Goal #2. Provide personal assistance to 40 church music programs.
Goal #3. Provide training for choirs and music directors from 20 churches.
Goal #4. Lead 40 churches to make annual music report.

EVANGELISM

Goal #1 Involve 20 churches in Joint Evangelism Crusade - 1982.
Goal #2. Involve 20 churches in follow-up simultaneous revivals.

STEWARDSHIP

Goal #1. Provide Stewardship training for 40 church stewardship leaders.
Goal #2. Assist the Association to provide training for 300 church key leaders.
Goal #3. Provide individual assistance in stewardship to 5 churches.

MISSIONS COMMITTEE

Goal #1. Provide ministry to 500 migrant and seasonal workers.
Goal #2. Begin Christian Social Ministries Program - part-time.
Goal #3. Provide training for 10 church leaders who work with senior citizens.

PASTORAL SUPPORT COMMITTEE

Goal #1. Involve 20 pastors and their wives in family life enrichment training.
Goal #2. Organize 4 support groups for pastors.
Goal #3. Involve 20 pastors and/or laymen in continuing education.

LIBRARY COMMITTEE

Goal #1. Begin one new church media center.
Goal #2. Train or retrain 30 media center workers.
Goal #3. Add 4 visual aid items to Associational Media Center.

WOMANS' MISSIONARY UNION REPORT

"Life-Changing Commitments" the second of an emphasis series for WMU was the theme stressed during the year.
There were 39 of the 40 churches that reported through the church letters as having a WMU organization.
Associational leaders received training at First Church, Whiteville, and a leadership conference for WMU officers was held September 24, 1981 at Warsaw Church with 100 ladies present.

EASTERN BAPTIST ASSOCIATION

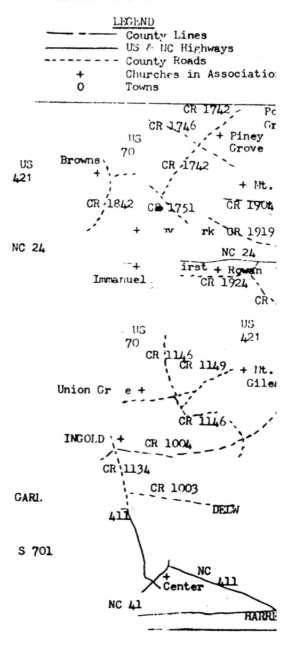

LEGEND
————— — ————— County Lines
————————————— US & NC Highways
- - - - - - - - County Roads
+ Churches in Association
O Towns

CR 1742 Po
CR 1746 Gr
+ Piney Grove
US 70
Browns
+
US 421
CR 1742
+ Mt.
CR 1842 CR 1751 CR 1904
+ rk CR 1919
NC 24
NC 24
+ irst + Rowan
Immanuel CR 1924
CR

US 70 US 421
CR 1146
CR 1149 + Mt.
Union Gr e + Giles
CR 1146
INGOLD + CR 1004
CR 1134
CARL. CR 1003
411 DELW
S 701
NC
411
+ Center
NC 41
HARRI

36

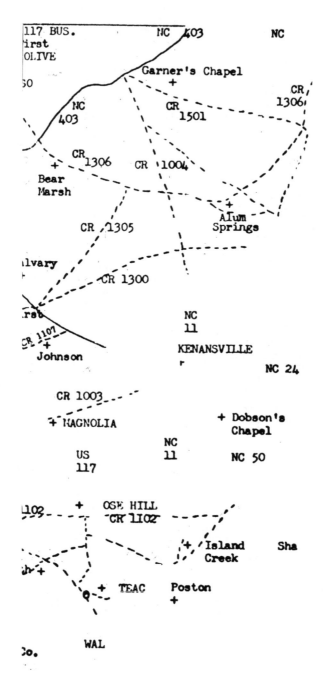

117 BUS.
irst
OLIVE
NC 403
NC

Garner's Chapel
+
50
NC
403
CR
1501
CR
1306

CR 1306
CR 1004

Bear
Marsh

CR 1305
Alum
Springs

lvary
CR 1300

rst
NC
11

CR 1107
+
Johnson
KENANSVILLE
r
NC 24

CR 1003
+ MAGNOLIA
+ Dobson's
Chapel

NC
11
US
117
NC 50

102 +
OSE HILL
CR 1102

+ Island
Creek
Sha

ch +
+ TEAC
Poston
+

Co.
WAL

Gifts of $5.00 per church was collected for North
Correctional Center for Women, in Raleigh. This was
chase matching drapes and bedspreads for the women's
In June, health kits were prepared by the WMU ladi
sented to Migrant children by Helen Register and Larr
Rev. Bill Davis and his wife Judy were given gifts
for their new daughter, Maria, before their departure
South America.
Clinton First Church was host for the Annual Sessi
were Mrs. Wayne Wheeler and Rev. Bill Davis. Dinner
the ladies of the church.
A schedule for 5 years for future meetings was pre:
The 1982 Annual Session will be at Ingold Baptist
Garland Baptist as co-host.

Respectfully submitt
Mrs. Norwood S. Cart

LIBRARY/MEDIA CENTER REPORT

The Spirit of cooperation that exists among our ch
centers in Eastern Association has made this a reward
the Library Committee. This has been demonstrated by
ness to share equipment and personnel.
Some significant improvements in church media cent
the Library Committee is aware are:
Rowan moved from the use of shelves in a class
appointed space in a new educational building
Warsaw added conference table and chairs. The
an increased number of children using the ce
additon of a "show and tell" area.
Clinton First acquired a tape-copying machine
have made available to churches who want to
of their Sunday services for use in tape min
Mount Olive First had a special committee to u
and Regulations" and to discuss new promotio
New Library/Media Centers have been started by Mou
Sharon. This brings the number of church library/Med
reported, to twenty.
Six churches participated in a two-night workshop
First where demonstrations were given on all special
Further assistance was provided through personal c
with church committees and pastors and contacts by te
by letters.

Respectfully submitte
Thelma Davis, Chairm
Library Committee

SUNDAY SCHOOL REPORT

The October, 1980 Sunday School Leadership Confere
at the First Baptist Church, Clinton with 160 teacher
in attendance.
January 16, 1981 the Assost team attended the Sund
Basic Study at Campbell University to prepare for the
leadership conference.
In March, 1981 there were two regional conferences
Sunday School Basic Study with a total attendance of
Twelve churches participated.

Island Creek and Poston Churches reported new Sunday School Classes started.

Five churches were represented by 31 persons, including five pastors at the Regional Sunday School Conference in Goldsboro on September 26-27.

Respectfully submitted,
Don Coley, Chairman

VACATION BIBLE SCHOOL REPORT

One-hundred eight VBS Workers from 19 churches recieved training in the Church VBS Workers Clinic held in Warsaw April 7, 1981.

Associational VBS Workers who received training earlier in the STATE VBS clinic led the conferences.

At the time of this report, 33 churches had reported having a VBS. Those reporting are:

Church	Enroll-ment	Avg. Att.	No Days	Hours Daily	Prof. Faith	Miss. Off.	Achievement
Alum Springs	33	31	5	$2\frac{1}{2}$	0	15.00	*
Bear Marsh	94	78	5	3	0	68.00	Merit
Beulah	49	47	5	2	0	38.00	Merit
Brown	75	62	5	$2\frac{1}{4}$	0	95.00	*
Center	56	39	8	3	0	45.00	Advanced
Clinton	164	152	7	$2\frac{1}{2}$	16	282.00	Merit
Concord	79	67	6	$2\frac{1}{2}$	0	41.00	Advanced
Corinth	59	52	5	$2\frac{1}{2}$	0	0	*
Dobson Chapel	68	54	5	$2\frac{1}{2}$	0	59.00	*
Evergreen	34	32	5	3	0	12.60	Merit
Garland	81	72	5	3	0	58.00	*
Garner's Chapel	31	25	5	2	0	6.98	*
Grove Park	80	77	5	2	0	64.97	*
Immanuel	147	118	5	3	0	43.00	Merit
Ingold	41	31	6	2	0	53.00	*
Island Creek	76	66	5	3	0	69.00	*
Johnson	74	60	5	3	1	80.00	*
Magnolia	36	30	5	$2\frac{1}{2}$	0	17.00	Merit
Mount Olive	106	90	5	3	0	45.00	*
Mount Vernon	36	34	5	2		17.00	Merit
New Hope	42	35	6	2	0	49.00	Merit
Piney Grove	116	85	5	2	0	0	*
Poplar Grove	64	47	6	2	0	0	Advanced
Poston	89	64	5	3	0	45.00	Merit
Rose Hill	90	82	5	3		65.00	
Rowan	131	93	5	3	0	59.00	Distin-guished
Sharon	93	84	5	3	1	57.00	Merit
Shiloh	69	66	5	3	0	47.00	Merit
Siloam	34	32	5	$2\frac{1}{2}$	0	47.00	*
Teachey	47	34	5	$1\frac{1}{2}$	0	28.00	*
Union Grove	40	36	5	2	0	25.00	*
Warsaw	121	108	5	3	0	50.00	*
Wells Chapel	52	48	5	$2\frac{1}{2}$	0	87.00	Merit

39

CHURCH TRAINING REPORT

Church Training is the organization assiqned the
church members, new church members, and church leade
potential church leaders, qrow in their christian di
The Church Training program does not compete with ot
programs but, when properly administered, enhances t
of the church.

The Church Training program has responsibility fo
five major content areas: Christian Doctrine, Christ
Christian History, Church Policy and Organization, a
lopment (in performing the function of a New Testame
During the past year our Associational Church Tra
Sent Jean Hatch, Carroll Buckner, Sue and Larry
to the Area Church Training Enabler Conferenc
Elizabethtown.
Sponsored a leadership conference at Grove Park
with 13 churches represented.
Invited Pete Black to speak at one of our pasto
ferences to stress the importance of doctrina
to the pastors of our association.
Other highlights of the Church Traininq year incl
standing "M" Night at the First Baptist Church of Cl
Glenn Smith of the SBC Church Training Department as
enthusiastic and well attended Youth Rally and Youth
Tournament at the Warsaw church;. and one of the best
Bible drills, at the Rose Hill Church. We also sent
to the State Bible Drill at Goldsboro and one youth
Speakers' Torunament in Winston Salem. Congratulatic
order for the Turkey Church for being one of the firs
Southern Baptist Convention to do Masterlife (discip.
and to the First Church of Clinton for hosting the re
ren's Bible Drill Rally.
Next year we hope to begin some new Church Trainir
increase the number of churches involved in the Bible
Speakers' Tournament. We are looking forward to anot
ing "M" Night at the Poston Church.

Respectfully submitt
Larry D. Padgett
Church Traininq Dire

EASTERN BAPTIST ASSOCIATION BUDGET 1981-{
BASIC

A. MISSION ADVANCE
    1. Mount Olive College BSU $100.00
            Sub-Total

B. ASSOCIATION OFFICE
    1. Equipment and repairs   200.00
    2. Routine printing & minutes   1,900.00
    3. Office Supplies   650.00
    4. Postage   700.00
    5. Telephone   600.00
            Sub-Total

C. SALARIES
    1. Director of Missions   10,400.00

```
ALARIES (Continued)
2. Secretary                        4,138.00
3. Director of CSM (9 months)      ·3,375.00*
              Sub-Total                            17,913.00

THER PERSONNEL EXPENSE
1. Retirement and Insurance         2,400.00
2. Social Security                    225.00
3. Housing                          5,900.00
4. Convention and Conferences         600.00
5. Travel: Director of Missions     3,000.00
           CSM Director (9 mos)       750.00*
              Sub-Total                            12,375.00

DUCATION AND PROMOTION
1. General Promotion & Training     1,000.00
2. Sunday School                      720.00
3. Church Training                    660.00
4. Brotherhood                        975.00
5. Womans' Missionary Union           750.00
6. Church Music                       250.00
7. Audio-Visuals                      100.00
8. Evangelism Committee               250.00
9. Stewardship Committee              600.00
0. Missions Committee               1,100.00*
1. Pastor Support Committee           500.00
2. Library Committee                  300.00
              Sub-Total                             7,295.00

ISCELLANEOUS
Unforeseen                            300.00
              Sub-Total                               300.00

  BASIC BUDGET                                    $42,533.00
```

                        PHASE II
      (To be expended after Basic Budget has been met)

```
ise copier for Association Office   3,000.00

  TOTAL                                           $45,533.00
```

	ANTICIPATED INCOME	(BASIC)	(PHASE II)
IES' CONTRIBUTIONS		$36,358.00	$39,358.00
:S		1,300.00	1,300.00
'T STATE CONVENTION ((Mos))		4,875.00	4,875.00
		$42,533.00	$45,533.00

The Association approved a recommendation that all churches
bute 3% of receipts for Associational Missions. Total tithes
ferings received by all churches in 1979 was $1,722,711.00.
per cent of that amount would have been $51,681.00.

ems where Baptist State Convention funds are placed in budget.

CHURCH MUSIC REPORT

An Associational Music Workshop was held on Janua
at Warsaw Baptist Church. Mr. Charles Storey from t
State Convention Music Department led the workshop i
choir members how to read music and also rehearsal p
the choir directors. Mr. Clyde Patterson, minister
First Baptist Church, Wilson, led the simultaneous c
pianists and organists. Total attendance was over 2
churches. A similar workshop is being planned for 1
activities have included providing special music for
15 churches in the association.

Our association is beginning to grow in church mu
our hope that 1982 will be the best year ever to PRA
THROUGH EXCELLENT MUSIC!

Respectfully submit
Jean Hatch, Directo
Martha Pierce, Co-D

TREASURER'S REPORT

CHURCHES CONTRIBUTIONS TO ASSOCIATIONAL MISSIONS - Y
September 30, 1980, compared to Year ending Septembe

CHURCH	1980	1981	CHURCH	1980
Albertson	154.00	166.00	Johnson	509.7
Alum Springs	250.00	250.00	Kenansville	300.00
Bear Marsh	300.00	300.00	Magnolia	618.08
Beulah	530.33	606.42	Mt. Gilead	1693.00
Browns	253.50	350.00	Mount Olive	1937.50
Calvary	699.93	633.96	Mount Vernon	300.00
Calypso	280.00	280.00	New Hope	400.00
Center	467.06	387.53	Piney Grove	300.00
Clinton First	3300.00	1900.00	Poplar Grove	66.00
Concord	321.98	366.87	Poston	780.00
Corinth	1320.00	1440.00	Rose Hill	1050.00
Dobson Chapel	326.18	390.18	Rowan	985.00
Evergreen	240.00	240.00	Sharon	650.00
Faison	339.70	440.01	Shiloh	560.98
Garland	511.07	939.01	Siloam	380.00
Garner's			Teachey	575.00
Chapel	135.00	150.00	Turkey	655.20
Grove Park	1858.19	1521.63	Union Grove	146.25
Immanuel	2990.00	3329.00	Warsaw	1436.40
Ingold	350.00	400.00	Wells Chapel	662.40
Island Creek	240.00	240.00		
			TOTALS	$28,872.46

FINANCIAL STATEMENT
GENERAL FUND

RECEIPTS

Brought Forward
(Less $68.79 employees withholdings on hand)

Net Balance brought forward

```
Balance brought forward                                      $   7,331.64

Regular Contributions (from churches)           29,825.59

Designated Contributions
    State Convention Assistance        $500.01
          (3 mos)
    Migrant Ministry                    800.00
    Youth & Family Ministry             900.03
    Lucille Lanning - Postage            10.00
    Minutes                             893.50
Total Designated                                 3,103.54

REFUNDS
    General Promotion & Training          2.43
    Sunday School                        93.65
    Pastor Support                      135.00
    North Carolina Sales Tax            194.80
Total Refunds                                      425.88

TOTAL RECEIPTS                                               33,355.01

TOTAL RECEIPTS + BALANCE BROUGHT FORWARD (Available
                                          Funds)             40,686.65

DISBURSEMENTS:
A.  MISSION ADVANCE
    Mount Olive College (BSU)           100.00
    Migrant Missions                    800.00
    Youth & Family Ministry             900.03
                                                  1,800.03
B.  ASSOCIATIONAL OFFICE
    1. Equipment                        301.38
    2. Printing                       1,554.16
    3. Office Supplies                  520.28
    4. Postage                         851.99
    5. Telephone                       646.31
         Sub-Total                                3,874.12

C.  SALARIES
    1. Director of Missions         10,000.00
    2. Secretary                     3,080.00
         Sub-Total                               13,080.01

D.  OTHER PERSONNEL EXPENSES
    1. Retirement & Insurance         2,398.68
    2. Social Security (Employer)       192.52
    3. Housing                        5,900.00
    4. Convention & Conferences         600.00
    5. Travel                         2,400.00
         Sub-Total                               11,491.20

E.  EDUCATION & PROMOTIONS
    1. General Promotion and
            Training                    727.38
    2. Sunday School                    590.51
    3. Church Training                  283.21
    4. Brotherhood                      511.25
    5. WMU                              520.00
    6. Music                            184.58
```

```
     7.  Audiovisuals                     20.50
     8.  Evangelism Committee            120.00
     9.  Stewardship Committee            -0-
    10.  Missions Committee              165.00
    11.  Pastoral Support Committee      372.40
    12.  Library                           2.07
              Sub-Total                                 3,496.9

F.  MISCELLANEOUS
     1.  Unforeseen                      233.61
     2.  N.C. Sales Tax                  117.18
     3.  Land Payment                  2,900.00
     4.  Transfer to new account
         (Baptist Center Fund)          187.71
              Sub-Total                                 3,438.5
```

TOTAL EXPENDITURES

Balance

Plus employees' withholdings on hand

NET BALANCE - SEPTEMBER 30, 1981

RESERVE FUND

RECEIPTS
    Bank Deposits, October 1, 1980
    Interest on Money Market Notes
            Total

DISBURSEMENTS
    Land Payment

Balance, September 30, 1981

BAPTIST CENTER FUND

RECEIPTS
    Brought Forward, October 1, 1980 (Shiloh Church)
    Church Contributions:
```
        Mount Vernon             $1,000.00
        Sharon                      267.00
        Magnolia                     15.00
        Calvary                      74.25
        Alum Springs                250.00
        Poston                      354.20
        Poplar Grove                110.00
        Union Grove                 530.00
        Rowan                       381.00
```
TOTAL

DISBURSEMENTS
```
    Check Book Printing             12.17
    Applied on Land Payment        167.35
    Bank Service Charge               .17
    Total
```
BALANCE, September 30, 1981

44

General Fund Balance (Less Withholdings)	$ 3,596.52
Reserve Fund Balance	25,498.76
Baptist Center Fund Balance	2,989.47
Total Cash Assets	$32,084.75

Funds deposited with Southern Bank and Trust
    as Follows:

Checking Account (General Fund)	3,596.52
Money Market Notes @14.379%	28,000.00
Checking Account (BAPTIST CENTER FUND)	488.23
TOTAL	$28,084.75

Donald Pope, Treasurer
Jo Neal Robinson, Assistant
Treasurer

M E M O R I A L S

ALBERTSON: Lattie Rouse

ALUM SPRINGS: Theodore Herring
Oliver Herring
Mrs. Bertie Kelly

BEAR MARSH: N. O. Holmes
Mary Jane Wilson
Edwin Dixon

BROWNS: Mrs. Annie Catherine Gore, Pianist for 50 years

CENTER: Mrs. Eulas Marshall

CLINTON: Mrs. E. G. Harris
T. E. Blount, Sr.
Sam McCullen, Sr.
Mrs. C. C. Robinson
Rev. R. H. Kelly
Mrs. Jasper Holland
W. J. Stewart
Lynwood Hall
Wayne Warren
Leamon Bradshaw
Mrs. Hilda Starling
David Welsh
Cynthia O'Rear
Charles Butler

CORINTH: David Hall, Sr.
Mrs. Naomi Dixon
Snyder Dempsey
Cleve Savage, Sr., Deacon
Alton Matthews, Deacon

DOBSONS CHAPEL: Mrs. Mary Ellen Brinson
Jenning Brown

FAISON: Jimmy Padgett
Miss Rossie Waters

45

GARLAND:	Pearlie Matthews
	Mrs. Eula Watson
	Mrs. Anna Cain
GARNERS CHAPEL:	Mrs. Donnie Whitfield
GROVE PARK:	Mrs. H. R. Howard
	Mrs. Mabel Kennedy
IMMANUEL:	Earl Coley
	Raymond Justice
	Bobby Miller
	Vernell Miller
INGOLD:	Lois B. Bradsher
	LeRoy Smith
ISLAND CREEK:	Hallie C. Brinson
	Miss Dorothy Watkins
JOHNSON:	Nathan Brown
	Ms. Mary Byrd
	Ms. Essie Kennedy
	Harry Phillips, Sr.
	Johnny Todd
KENANSVILLE:	Mrs. Katherine Wallace
	David J. Kilpatrick, Deacon
	Charles Yelverton, Deacon
	Mrs. Alma Brinson
	Colon Holland
	Mrs. Brilla Dobson
	J. B. Wallace
MAGNOLIA:	Carlos Batts, Deacon
	Mrs. Oscar Drew
	Miss Betty Horne
	Mrs. Anna Riley
MOUNT GILEAD:	Mrs. Ina Marvin Purtle
	Major Burke
	Miss Sallie Merritt
	George Rackley
	James Bell Cashwell
	Mrs. Bessie Carter
	Mrs. Lonie Register
MOUNT OLIVE:	Mrs. Willie Powell
	C. B. Bullock
	Mrs. Pinkney Price
	Mrs. Kate Lancaster
	Eugene Dall
	Denman Martin
	Mark Rivenbark
	John Ivey Amon
MOUNT VERNON:	Mrs. Betsy Hudson
	Marion Gainey, Deacon
	Yancey Delano Frederick

Miss Annie Johnson
Asa Johnson
Lloyd Drew
Sam Williams
Mrs. Emma Drew

Mrs. Thelma Miller

Mack Rivenbark

Thomas Knowles
Miss Annie Ruth Murray
Mrs. Ellen Savage
Mrs. Arlene Fussell

Vaston Byrd
Miss Janie Chesnutt
Paul R. Jones, Jr.
A. G. Smith

Mrs. Myrtle Futreal

Paul Henderson

Robert L. Wadsworth, Deacon
Arthur M. Kenan

H. C. Faulkner, Deacon
Bobby Carter

Raeford H. Carter, Sr.
Colon B. Fryar
Mrs. Dollie Fryar

Miss Ann Padgett
R. J. Lewis
Mrs. Marie King
Ed Strickland, Deacon
General W. M. Buck
Mrs. Sallie Honeycutt

Fred Pigford
William L. Matthews

SCHEDULE OF MEETING PLACES OF EASTERN ASSO(

	1982		1987
1st Day	Mount Olive	1st Day	*Kenan:
			Albert
2nd Day	*Mount Gilead	2nd Day	*Corin1
	Union Grove		Teache
	1983		**1988**
1st Day	*Siloam	1st Day	Rose I
	Evergreen		
2nd Day	*Turkey	2nd Day	Immanι
	Beulah - New Hope		
	1984		**1989**
1st Day	*Piney Grove	1st Day	*Calyp:
	Mount Vernon		Faisor
2nd Day	*Sharon	2nd Day	*Garlar
	Shiloh		Ingolι
	1985		**1990**
1st Day	Rowan	1st Day	*Islanι
			Dobsoι
2nd Day	*Poston	2nd Day	*Grove
	Wells Chapel		Brown:

1986

1st Day   *Warsaw
          Calvary
2nd Day   *Bear Marsh
          Garners Chapel - Alum Springs

* Meeting Place -- other listed churches assisting ι
              respective days.

HISTORICAL AND STATISTICAL TABLES

HISTORICAL TABLE

YEAR	PLACE	MODERATOR	CLERK	PREACHER
1827	Beulah	James Matthews	J. L. Britt	J. B. Taylor
1828	South West	James Matthews	V. N. Seawell	W. M. Kennedy
1829	Limestone	James Matthews	J. R. Oliver	C. A. Jenkins
1830	Bull Tail	James Matthews	F. H. Ivey	W. B. Pope
1831	Island Creek	James Matthews	L. T. Carroll	J. B. Harrell
1832	Browns	James Matthews	J. T. Bland	Hiram Stallings
1833	Lisbon	James Matthews	Allen Morriss	John Cornto
1834	Bear Marsh	W. J. Findley	Allen Morriss	Allen Morriss
1835	Limestone	W. J. Findley	Allen Morriss	George Fennell
1836	Beaver Dam	George Fennell	Allen Morriss	H. Swinson
1837	Well's Chapel	W. J. Findley	G. W. Hufham	George Fennell
1838	Rowans	W. J. Findley	G. W. Hufham	Hiram Stallings
1839	Johnson's	James Mathis	G. W. Hufham	G. W. Hufham
1840	Concord	James Carroll	G. W. Hufham	George Fennell
1841	Bear Marsh	James Carroll	G. W. Hufham	G. W. Hufham
1842	Red Hill	James Carroll	G. W. Hufham	H. Stallings
1843	Beulah	James Carroll	G. W. Hufham	R. McNab
1844	Kenansville	James Carroll	G. W. Hufham	W. J. Findley
1845	Lebanon	Benjamin Oliver	J. G. Dickson	David Rogers
1846	Wilmington	James McDaniel	J. G. Dickson	W. J. Findley
1847	Harriet's Chapel	James McDaniel	J. G. Dickson	David Thompson
1848	White Oak	James McDaniel	J. G. Dickson	James Rogers
1849	Mt. Gilead	James McDaniel	J. G. Dickson	Isaac W. West
1850	Bear Marsh	James McDaniel	Robert McNab	W. J. Findley
1851	Little Creek	Benjamin Oliver	A. J. Battle	A. J. Battle
1852	New Hope	G. W. Wallace	A. J. Battle	D. Furman
1853	Moore's Creek	G. W. Wallace	A. J. Battle	L. F. Williams
1854	Beulah	G. W. Wallace	D. Cashwell	M. R. Forey
1855	Concord	G. W. Wallace	D. Cashwell	W. P. Riddle

Year	Location			
1865	Moore's Creek	Owen Fennell	J. G. Dickson	J. S. Wathall
1866	Union Chapel	W. M. Kennedy	J. N. Stallings	R. F. Marable
1867	Bear Marsh	W. M. Kennedy	J. N. Stallings	J. L. Pritchard
1868	Beulah	Hugh McAlphin	Isham Royal	Hugh McAlpin
1869	Lisbon	Hugh McAlphin	Isham Royal	W. M. Kennedy
1870	Well's Chapel	J. L. Stewart	Isham Royal	G. S. Best
1871	New Hope	Hugh McAlpin	Isham Royal	J. E. King
1872	Union Lenoir	Hugh McAlpin	Isham Royal	W. M. Kennedy
1873	Shiloh	Hugh McAlpin	Isham Royal	W. M. Young
1874	Island Creek	J. N. Stallings	Isham Royal	J. N. Stallings
1875	Beaufont	J. N. Stallings	Isham Royal	G. S. Best
1876	Mt. Olive	J. L. Stewart	Isham Royal	J. P. Faison
1877	Corinth	J. L. Stewart	Isham Royal	J. C. Hiden
1878	New Bern	J. L. Stewart	Isham Royal	A. D. Cohen
1879	Piney Grove	J. L. Stewart	Isham Royal	J. N. Stallings
1880	Bethel	J. L. Stewart	Isham Royal	S. W. Westcot
1881	Magnolia	J. L. Stewart	J. R. Oliver	J. L. Stewart
1882	Emma's Chapel	J. L. Stewart	J. R. Oliver	A. C. Dixon
1883	Bethlehem	J. L. Stewart	J. L. Britt	F. H. Ivey
1884	Pollocksville	J. L. Stewart	J. L. Britt	J. R. Taylor
1885	Mt. Olive	J. L. Stewart	J. L. Britt	J. W. Eason
1886	Clinton	J. L. Stewart	J. L. Britt	J. L. Stewart
1887	Well's Chapel	J. L. Stewart	J. L. Britt	C. C. Newton
1888	Warsaw	J. L. Stewart	J. L. Britt	T. H. Pritchard
1889	Concord	J. L. Stewart	J. L. Britt	F. R. Underwood
1890	Riley's Creek	J. L. Stewart	J. L. Britt	C. A. Jenkins
1891	Dodson's Chapel	J. L. Stewart	Oliver Blackburr	O. P. Meeks
1892	Emma's Chapel	J. L. Stewart	Oliver Blackburr	J. L. Stewart
1893	Johnson's	J. L. Stewart	Oliver Blackburr	O. P. Meeks
1894	Lisbon	J. L. Stewart	A. R. Herring	John Mitchell
1895	Corinth	S. D. Swaim	A. R. Herring	A. A. Butler
1896	Island Creek	S. D. Swaim	A. R. Herring	C. G. Wells
1897	Kenansville	J. L. Stewart	A. R. Herring	I. F. Bone
1898	Harrell's Store	J. L. Stewart	A. R. Herring	J. L. Stewart
1899	Mount Holly	J. L. Stewart	A. R. Herring	N. B. Cobb
1900	Mount Olive	J. L. Stewart	A. R. Herring	R. H. Gilbert
1901	Mount Gilead	J. L. Stewart	A. R. Herring	N. B. Cobb
1902	Hallsville	J. L. Stewart	A. R. Herring	J. M. Alderman
1903	Rose Hill	J. L. Stewart	A. R. Herring	J. L. Stewart

Year	Place			
1904	New Hope	J. L. Stewart	A. F. Robinson	V. N. Johnson
1905	Mount Olive	C. E. Daniel	A. F. Robinson	J. H. Booth
1906	Lisbon	C. E. Daniel	A. F. Robinson	J. L. Stewart
1907	Clinton	C. E. Daniel	A. F. Robinson	C. M. Rock
1908	Warsaw	C. E. Daniel	H. L. Stewart	J. M. Page
1909	Corinth	C. E. Daniel	A. R. Herring	J. M. Alderman
1910	Bethel	C. E. Daniel	A. R. Herring	P. A. Anthony
1911	Rowan	C. E. Daniel	A. R. Herring	E. J. Harrell
1912	Bear Marsh	C. E. Daniel	A. R. Herring	W. B. Rivenbark
1913	Beulaville	C. E. Daniel	A. R. Herring	J. G. Newton
1914	Oak Vale	C. E. Daniel	A. R. Herring	B. G. Early
1915	Johnson's	C. E. Daniel	A. R. Herring	C. H. Cashwell
1916	Calypso	C. E. Daniel	A. L. Carlton	W. N. Johnson
1917	Piney Grove	C. E. Daniel	A. L. Carlton	R. H. Herring
1918	Concord	H. L. Stewart	A. L. Carlton	B. T. Vann
1919	Hallsville	H. L. Stewart	E. P. Blanchard	D. P. Harris
1920	Clinton	H. L. Stewart	E. P. Blanchard	R. W. Cawthon
1921	Siloam	H. L. Stewart	E. P. Blanchard	L. R. O'Brien
1922	Sharon	H. L. Stewart	E. P. Blanchard	R. T. Vann
1923	Corinth	H. L. Stewart	D. J. Middleton	J. M. Duncan
1924	Dobson's Chapel	H. L. Stewart	D. J. Middleton	G. W. Rollins
1925	Turkey	H. L. Stewart	D. J. Middleton	T. H. King
1926	Island Creek	T. H. King	C. I. Robinson	S. L. Naff
1927	Beulah	T. H. King	C. I. Robinson	J. H. Barnes
1928	Bear Marsh	H. L. Stewart	C. I. Robinson	W. R. Beach
1929	Ingold	H. L. Stewart	C. I. Robinson	C. V. Brooks
1930	Hallsville	H. L. Stewart	C. I. Robinson	E. N. Johnson
1931	New Hope	F. W. McGowen	C. I. Robinson	R. C. Foster
1932	Kenansville	F. W. McGowen	C. I. Robinson	T. H. Williams
1933	Mount Gilead	F. W. McGowen	C. I. Robinson	L. M. Holloway
1934	Concord	F. W. McGowen	C. I. Robinson	R. F. Marshburn
1935	Magnolia	F. W. McGowen	C. I. Robinson	L. L. Johnson

Year	Churches			
...	r. w. rcGowen	C. I. Robinson	G. van stephens	
1945	Ingold	F. W. McGowen	C. I. Robinson	J. V. Case
1946	Nw Hope & Mount Vernon	G. Van Stephens	C. I. Robinson	G. W. Lambert
1947	Island Creek & Corinth	G. Van Stephens	C. I. Robinson	Gil mr Beck
1948	Garland & Cedar Fork	G. Van Stephens	C. I. Robinson	A. L. Benton
1949	Rose Hill & Clinton	Thomas L. Rich, Jr.	Paul L. Cashwell	E. N. ye
1950	Magnolia & Mt. Gilead	Mk Herring	Paul L. Cashwell	J. C. Conoly
1951	Piney Grove & Warsaw	Mk Herring	Paul L. Cashwell	J. P. Royal
1952	Siloam & Dobson's Chapel	Mack Herring	Paul L. Cashwell	Elliot B. Stewart
1953	Mount Olive & Turkey	A. W. Greenlaw	Paul L. Cashwell	E. F. Knight
1954	Rowan & Johnson's	Mk Herring	Paul T. Mull	T. W. Williams
1955	Sharon & Beulaville	Paul L. Cashwell	H. M. Baker	Julian Motley
1956	Warsaw & Bear Marsh	J. C. Mitchell	Eugene B. Hager	Robert A. Melvin
1957	Immanuel & Kenansville	T. W. Williams	Eugene B. Hager	M. M. Turner
1958	Rose Hill	C. F. Shipp	Paul T. Mull	M. M. Johnson
1959	Calypso & Ingold	C. F. Shipp	Paul T. Mull	Lauren Sharpe
1960	Island Creek & Grove Park	D. E. Parkerson	Paul T. Mull	Jerry DeBell
1961	Clinton, First & Magnolia	D. E. Parkerson	Paul T. Mull	L. H. Knott
1962	Mt. Olive & Mt. Gilead	Mack Herring	Paul T. Mull	A. Quakenbush
1963	Siloam & Turkey	Milton Boone	Paul T. Mull	Hugh R. Williams
1964	Piney Grove & Sharon	Milton Boone	Paul T. Mull	D. E. Parkerson
1965	Rowan & Well's Chapel	M. M. Johnson	E. L. Eiland	Wayne Wheeler
1966	Warsaw,First & Bear Marsh	Hugh Ross Williams	M. S. McLain	R. H. Kelley
1967	Kenansville & Corinth	Hugh Ross Williams	M. S. McLain	R. A. Thompson
1968	Rose Hill & Immanuel	John R. Johnson	M. S. McLain	Glen Holt
1969	Calypso & Garland	John R. Johnson	M. S. McLain	Norman Dk
1970	Island Creek & Grove Park	John A. Johnson	M. S. McLain	Waldo Early
1971	Clinton, First & Magnolia	Norman Dk	M. S. McLain	Anthony Gurganus
1972	Piney Grove & Mt. Gilead	Vernon Braswell	R. B. Little	J. Boyce Brooks
1973	Siloam	Vernon Braswell	R. B. Little	W. M. Jones
1974	Mt. Olive & Dobson Chapel	Vernon Braswell	R. B. Little	Huber Dixon
1975	Rowan & Shiloh	John Flake	R. B. Little	R. B. Little
1976	Warsaw & Bear Marsh	John Flake	R. B. Little	W le O. Carr
1977	Kenansville & Corinth	Anthony Gurganus	Richard Whitley	Vernon Braswell
1978	Rose Hill & Immanuel	Anthony Gurganus	Charles Jolly	Michael Shock
1979	Island Creek & Calypso	Gene Hart	Lucille Yancey	Joseph Willis
1980	Garland & Grove Park	Gene Hart	Lucille Yancey	Paul Rose
1981	Clinton,First & Magnolia	L. Mk Thompson	Lucille Yancey	Donald Coley

Total church debt at end of
this associational year

State: NORTH CAROLINA
Director of Associational Missions: CLYDE L. DAVIS, SR.
Address: P.O. Box 712, Warsaw, North Carolina, Zip 28398
EASTERN

CHURCHES	PASTORS & ADDRESSES (INCLUDE ZIP CODE)	County	Year organized as a church	Location	Services held twice on Sunday?	Total Baptisms	Other additions (by letter, statement, etc.)	Members lost (by letter, death, statement, etc.)	Present resident members	Present nonresident members	Grand total present members	No. members received from non‑Baptist Churches	No. members lost to non‑Baptist Churches	Value of pastor's home if owned by the church	Value of church property including pastor's home	Total church debt at end of this associational year
MOUNT VERNON	Willie O. Carr, Rt. 5, Box 50, Clinton, NC 28328	Sampson	1910	1	x	12	2	5	172	30	202	1	1	37,500	100,800	0
NEW HOPE	Paul Rose, Rt. 1, Box 355, Mount Olive, NC 28365	Sampson	1817	1	x	7	0	5	99	29	128	0	0	0	50,000	0
PINEY GROVE	Farrell H. Miller, Rt. 2, Box 122‑A, Faison, NC 28341	Sampson	1844	x		1	3	8	172	55	227	1	0	50,000	225,000	12,194
POPLAR GROVE	Andy Wood, Rt. 1, Box 77½, Faison, NC 28341															
POSTON	Donald R. Coley, Rt. 3, Box 67, Wallace, NC 28466	Duplin	1958	2	x	4	6	6	237	49	286	0	3	53,000	435,000	10,156
ROSE HILL	Jerry David Kinlaw, P.O. Box 459, Rose Hill, NC 28458	Duplin	1930	3	x	2	14	12	318	117	435	1	0	45,000	370,000	0
ROWAN	Michael Shook, 202 Reedsford Road, Clinton, NC 28328	Sampson	1749	4	x	20	13	6	370	119	489	0	0	65,000	500,000	65,000
SHARON	Phillip R. Denton, P.O. Box 126, Chinquapin, NC 28521	Duplin	1850	1	x	11	6	10	232	52	284	1	0	40,000	100,000	0
SHILOH	Jimmy Johnson (Interim)	Duplin	1940	x	x	4	3	3	180	54	234	2	0	40,000	250,000	24,090
SILOAM	Carlton G. Miller, Rt. 1, Harrells, NC 28444	Sampson	1889	2	x	0	2	3	130	54	184	0	0	25,000	150,000	3,000
TEACHEY	Larry Blount, Teachey, NC 28464	Duplin	1885	2		3	0	2	115	45	160	0	0	75,000	225,000	0
TURKEY	Larry D. Padgett, Box 216, Turkey, NC, 28393	Sampson	1908	3	x	1	1	7	201	77	278	0	0	22,500	135,000	0
UNION GROVE	L.L. Barnes. Rt. 2, Elizabethtown, NC, 28337	Sampson	1915	1	x	8	1	3	112	81	193	0	0	0	55,000	0
WARSAW	L. Mack Thompson, 205 E. Chelly St., Warsaw, NC 28398	Duplin	1856	4	x	26	8	10	485	101	686	4	0	49,500	1,048,548	31,500
WELLS CHAPEL	Freddie Harris, Rt. 1, Wallace, NC 28466	Sampson	1756	1	x	2	0	8	206	53	259	0	2	50,000	235,000	14,800
TOTALS						255	198	398	8,655	2,702	11,515	31	49			

Total V B S enrolment

State: NORTH CAROLINA

Associational Sunday School Director: DONALD R. COLEY

Address: Rt. 3,   City: WALLACE,   State: NORTH CAROLINA   Zip: 28466

CHURCHES	SUNDAY SCHOOL DIRECTORS & ADDRESSES (INCLUDE ZIP CODE)	Cradle Roll enrollment (Birth to 2 years)	Preschool enrollment (Birth through 5 years)	Children enrollment (6-11 years or Grades 1-6)	Youth enrollment (12-17 years or Grades 7-12)	Young Adult enrollment—Single (18-29 years or H.S. graduate through 29 years)	Young Adult enrollment—married (18-29 years or H.S. graduate through 29 years)	Adult enrollment (30-59 years)	Senior Adult enrollment (60 and over)	Adults Away enrollment	Homebound enrollment	General officers enrollment	Enrollment of mission(s) of church	Total ongoing Sunday School enrollment	Average weekly Sunday School attendance	Number of Bible Study Groups	Bible Study Groups enrollment	Total enrolled in Bible Study	Church V.B.S. enrollment	Mission V.B.S. enrollment	Total V.B.S. enrollment
MOUNT VERNON	Marshall Falatovich, Clinton 28328	9	6	3	3	4	7	21	32	0	3	0	0	93	85	3	0	93	65	0	65
NEW HOPE	Ed Colwell, Rt. 1, Turkey 28393	1	6	4	10	14	7	17	18	0	5	20	0	10?	49	0	0	0	0	0	0
PINEY GROVE	DeWitt King, Rt. 2, Box 122, Faison 28341	0	5	20	10	11	20	59	39	0	0	4	0	168	72	0	0	168	116	0	116
POPLAR GROVE																					
POSTON	Dulan Murray, 211 N. 1st Street, Wallace, 28466	6	32	33	26	14	26	61	23	0	1	6	0	228	194	0	0	0	89	0	89
ROSE HILL	M.M. Bowling, P.O. Box 5, Rose Hill, 28458	10	5	27	30	24	33	88	19	10	8	4	0	258	127	0	0	0	90	0	90
ROWAN	Jo Neal Robinson, Rt. 2, Box 269, Clinton 28328	0	16	37	38	30	26	72	59	0	0	4	40	332	164	0	0	332	131	0	131
SHARON	Jimmy Mercer, Chinquapin, 28521	3	9	31	34	28	33	45	14	0	0	3	0	200	115	30	0	200	93	0	93
SHILOH	David Maready, Rt. 1, Chinquapin, 28521	7	12	16	17	4	22	25	35	0	0	3	0	141	87	0	0	141	55	0	55
SILOAM	G.W. King, Rt. 2, Harrells, 28444	1	0	8	15	8	12	18	34	0	0	6	0	112	52	0	0	112	30	0	30
TEACHEY	Graham Kilpatrick, Rt. 3, Wallace 28466	0	5	12	16	0	0	38	10	0	0	2	0	83	49	0	0	83	47	0	47
TURKEY	David Hudson, Rt. 1, Turkey, 28393	0	22	25	20	7	10	27	40	0	3	4	0	158	88	0	0	158	79	0	79
UNION GROVE	Paul Barefoot, Rt. 4, Box 210, Clinton 28328	4	23	12	25	2	20	30	10	0	0	0	0	126	105	1	0	30	40	0	40
WARSAW	Charles Taylor, Rt. 1, Box 266B-2, Kenansville 28349	0	13	61	45	12	15	99	67	0	18	4	0	342	150	0	0	342	95	0	95
WELLS CHAPEL	Gene Sandlin, Rt. 1, Wallace, 28466	0	12	15	13	10	16	44	37	0	0	3	0	151	91	0	0	151	52	0	52
TOTALS		81	591	873	338	338	741	1,761	1,291	40	124	147	82	7,017	3,774	38	15	3,598	2,497	47	2,544

BSSB - 1297 (Rev. 11-80)

57

Preschool enrollment
(5 years and under—not in school)

Children enrollment
(6-11 years or grades 1-6)

Youth enrollment
(12-17 years or grades 7-12)

Adult enrollment
(18 and over)

Equipping Centers
enrollment

N C M T children
enrollment

N C M T youth
enrollment

N C M T adult
enrollment

Hold File
enrollment

Enrollment of mission(s)
of church

Total Church
Training enrollment

Average weekly Church
Training attendance

CHURCHES	CHURCH TRAINING DIRECTORS & ADDRESSES (INCLUDE ZIP CODE)	City	State	Zip	Preschool enrollm. (5 years and under school)	Children enrollme (6-11 years or gr.)	Youth enrollment (12-17 years or g)	Adult enrollme (18 and over)	Equipping Cen enrollment	N.C.M.T. child enrollment	N.C.M.T. youth enrollment	N.C.M.T. adult enrollment	Hold File enrollment	General officers e	Enrollment of mis of church	Total Church Training enrollm	Average weekly C Training attendan
MOUNT VERNON	None				0	0	0	0	0	0	0	0	0	0	0	0	0
NEW HOPE	Danny Johnson, Rt. 1, Turkey 28393				2	8	5	20	0	0	0	0	0	0	0	35	18
PINEY GROVE	None				0	0	0	0	0	0	0	0	0	0	0	0	0
POPLAR GROVE																	
POSTON	Eleanor Poston, Rt. 3, Wallace, 28466				15	21	11	53	0	0	0	0	0	4	0	104	46
ROSE HILL	None				0	0	0	0	0	0	0	0	0	0	0	0	0
ROWAN	Lucille Yancey, P.O. Box 711, Clinton 28328				3	13	21	28	0	0	0	0	0	3	0	68	43
SHARON	Carol Hatcher, Rt. 1, Chinquapin 28521				0	6	5	24	0	2	1	9	0	2	0	49	33
SHILOH	None				0	0	0	0	0	0	0	0	0	0	0	0	0
SILOAM	None				0	0	0	0	0	0	0	0	0	0	0	0	0
TEACHEY	None				0	0	0	0	0	0	0	0	0	0	0	0	0
TURKEY	H.J. Register, Rt. 1, Turkey 28393				1	14	11	27	0	0	0	0	0	?	0	55	?7
UNION GROVE	None				0	0	0	0	0	0	0	0	0	0	0	0	0
WARSAW	John Gurganus, 106 W. Chelly Street, Warsaw 28398				11	38	48	26	14	0	0	0	0	2	0	139	45
WELLS CHAPEL	Florence Hoover, Rt. 2, Box 18, Harrells 28444				4	13	11	35	0	2	0	0	0	3	0	66	44
TOTALS					83	210	259	370	68		19	9	39	36	0	1,105	684

59

BSSB - 1297 (Rev. 11-68)

Association

State EASTERN

NORTH CAROLINA

Associational Music Director JEAN HATCH,

Address P.O. Box 837,   City Clinton,   State North Carolina   Zip 28328

E ZIP CODE)

Preschool enrollment (4-5 years)

Children enrollment (6-8 years or grades 1-3)

Children enrollment (9-11 years or grades 4-6)

Youth enrollment (12-14 years or grades 7-9)

Youth enrollment (15-17 years or grades 10-12)

Adult enrollment (18 and over)

Handbell ringers enrollment

Vocal ensembles enrollment

Instrumental ensembles enrollment

General music leaders enrollment

Enrollment of mission(s) of church

Total ongoing Church Music enrollment

Address: **JEAN HATCH**
P.O. Box 837, City **CLINTON**, State **NORTH CAROLINA**, Zip **28328**

CHURCHES	MUSIC DIRECTORS & ADDRESSES (INCLUDE ZIP CODE)	Preschool enrollmen (4 & 5 years)	Children enrollment (6-8 years or grades)	Children enrollment (9-11 years or grad)	Youth enrollment (12-14 years or gra)	Youth enrollment (15-17 years or gra)	Adult enrollment (18 and over)	Handbell ringers en	Vocal ensembles e	Instrumental ensem enrollment	General music leaders enrollment	Enrollment of missio of church	Total ongoing Chu enrollment
MOUNT VERNON	Callie Carr, Rt. 5, Box 50, Clinton 28328	0	0	12	0	15	18	0	0	0	0	0	45
NEW HOPE	None	0	0	0	0	0	18	0	0	0	3	0	21
PINEY GROVE	Ruby Engles, Rt. 2, Faison 28341	2	6	2	0	0	16	0	0	0	2	0	28
POPLAR GROVE													
POSTON	Annette Henderson, Rt. 3, Box 63, Wallace 28466	0	0	0	0	0	51	0	0	0	8	0	59
ROSE HILL	Linda Murphy, Rt. 1, Rose Hill 28458	0	0	2	9	9	19	0	0	0	10	0	49
ROMAN	Lucille Yancey, P.O. Box 711, Clinton 28328	0	0	0	0	0	16	0	0	0	?	0	18
SHARON	Betty Brant, Chinquapin 28521	3	3	5	10	10	22	0	0	0	6	0	59
SHILOH	Rifton Raynor, Rt. 2, Wallace 28466	0	0	0	0	0	15	0	0	0	3	0	18
SILOAM	Angelyn Burgess, Rt. 1, Harrells 28444	0	0	0	0	0	10	0	0	0	2	0	12
TEACHEY	None	0	0	0	-	4	15	0	1	1	5	0	26
TURKEY	Sue Padgett, Box 216, Turkey 28393	0	-	10	3	15	15	0	0	0	5	0	45
UNION GROVE	Roger Wells, Rt. 4, Clinton 28328	5	10	0	10	7	8	0	0	0	5	0	38
WARSAW	Catherine Vestal, Box 455, Warsaw 28398	6	11	25	10	10	20	8	3	0	-	0	94
WELLS CHAPEL	Geraldine Johnson, Harrells 28444	0	0	0	3	5	15	0	0	0	5	0	28
	T O T A L S	126	131	190	110	210	678	20	29	6	149	0	1,594

BSSB - 1287 (Rev. 11-80)

61

Total ongoing
WMU enrolment

Address: P.O. Box 2, City: HARRELLS, State: NORTH CAROLINA, Zip: 28444

CHURCHES	WMU DIRECTORS & ADDRESSES (INCLUDE ZIP CODE)	Mission Friend (under 5 yrs) — No. of Orgs.	Girls in Action (6-11 yrs or Grades 1-6) — No. of Orgs.	Acteens (12-17 yrs or Grades 7-12) — No. of Orgs.	Baptist Young Women (18-25 yrs or...) — No. of Orgs.	Baptist Women (30 and over) — No. of Orgs.	Mission(s) of church — No. of Orgs.	Total number of organizations	Mission Friend (5 yrs and under, not in school)	Girls in Action (6-11 yrs or Grades 1-6)	Acteens (12-17 yrs or Grades 7-12)	Baptist Young Women (18-29 yrs or grad. through)	Baptist Women (30 and over)	WMU officers	Mission(s) of church	Total WMU enrollment
MOUNT VERNON	Ruth Ann Johnson, Rt. 2, Faison 28341	1	1	1	0	1	0	3	0	7	8	0	17	6	0	38
NEW HOPE	Thelma Ware, Rt. 1, Turkey, 28393	0	2	1	1	1	1	6	0	9	3	7	11	1	0	31
PINEY GROVE	Ruth King, Rt. 2, Box 111, Faison 28341	0	0	0	1	1	0	2	0	0	0	5	40	1	0	46
POPLAR GROVE																
POSTON	Martha Teachey, Rt. 3, Wallace 28466	1	1	1	0	1	0	4	8	15	0	0	47	4	0	84
ROSE HILL	Linda Hawes, Rt. 2, Rose Hill 28458	1	1	1	0	1	0	4	9	7	10	0	60	3	0	91
ROWAN	Lillian Pope, P.O. Box 411, Clinton 28328	1	1	1	1	1	0	5	3	7	9	7	40	7	0	73
SHARON	Shirley Denton, Box 126, Chinquapin 28521	1	1	1	1	0	1	5	7	6	8	19	12	5	0	57
SHILOH	Berena Alston, Rt. 2, Wallace 28466	0	0	1	0	1	0	2	0	0	6	0	10	5	0	21
SILOAM	Mrs. S.F. Burgess, Rt. 1, Harrells 28444	0	0	0	0	1	0	1	0	0	0	0	28	0	0	28
TEACHEY	Mrs. Elwood Fussell, P.O. Box 1, Teachey 28464	0	0	0	0	1	0	1	0	0	0	0	14	2	0	16
TURKEY	Mae Pinyatello, Rt. 1, Turkey, 28393	1	1	1	1	1	0	5	4	6	5	6	12	6	0	39
UNION GROVE	Brenda Stancil, Rt. 4, Box 303, Clinton 28328	0	0	0	0	0	1	1	0	4	0	10	4	3	0	17
WARSAW	Carolyn Drew, Rt. 1, Box 185, Warsaw 28398	1	2	1	0	1	0	5	8	22	25	0	97	7	0	159
WELLS CHAPEL	Florence Hoover, Rt. 2, Box 18, Harrells 28444	1	1	1	1	1	0	5	3	3	4	11	33	5	0	59
TOTALS		17	24	24	14	59	10	126	131	224	177	146	1,034	150	5	1,864

BSSB-1297 (Rev. 11-80)

63

123

Crusaders
(6-11 years or Grades 1-6)

Pioneers
(12-17 years or Grades 7-12)

RA director and committee

Baptist Men enrollment-
Basic

Baptist Men enrollment-
Prayer

Baptist Men enrollment-
Mission Action

Baptist Men enrollment-
Witnessing or Lay Renewal

Brotherhood director and
other general Brotherhood
Officers

Enrollment of mission(s)
of church

Total ongoing Brotherhood
enrollment

State: NORTH CAROLINA

Associational Brotherhood Director: REV. CHARLES KIRKLAND

Address: P.O. BOX 426, **City:** FAISON **State:** NORTH CAROLINA **Zip:** 28341

CHURCHES	BROTHERHOOD DIRECTORS & ADDRESSES (INCLUDE ZIP CODE)	Crusaders (9-11 years or grades 1-6)	Pioneers (12-17 years or grades 7-12)	RA director and committee	Baptist Men enrollment— Basic	Baptist Men enrollment— Prayer	Baptist Men enrollment— Mission Action	Baptist Men enrollment— Witnessing or Lay Renewal	Brotherhood director and other general Brotherhood Officers	Enrollment of mission(s) of church	Total ongoing Brotherhood enrollment
MOUNT VERNON	None	0	0	0	0	0	0	0	0	0	0
NEW HOPE	None	4	1	1	0	0	0	0	0	0	6
PINEY GROVE	None	0	0	0	0	0	0	0	0	0	0
POPLAR GROVE		6	6	2	14	0	0	0	1	0	29
POSTON	John Braswell, Rt. 1, Box 53-A, Matha 28471										
ROSE HILL	None	0	0	0	0	0	0	0	0	0	0
ROMAN	Walter Merritt, P.O. Box 112, Clinton 28328	9	7	6	0	0	0	0	3	0	40
SHARON	Larry Mercer, Chinquapin 28521	12	15	1	15	0	0	0	1	0	34
SHILOH	Ray Likens, Rt. 1, Chinquapin 28521	11	5	1	5	0	0	0	1	34	19
SILOAM	None	0	0	0	0	0	0	0	0	0	0
TEACHEY	None	0	0	0	0	0	0	0	0	0	0
TURKEY	George Pinyatello, Rt. 1, Turkey 28393	7	4	2	10	0	0	0	1	0	24
UNION GROVE	None	0	0	0	0	0	0	0	0	0	0
WARSAW	J.B. Herring, 307 Walnut Street, Warsaw 28398	2	0	4	24	0	0	0	3	0	53
WELLS CHAPEL	Rufus C. Wells, Rt. 1, Willard 28478	6	0	2	0	12	0	0	1	0	21
TOTALS		192	79	42	281	33	55	0	33	44	725

65

Total local
expenditures

EASTERN

State	NORTH CAROLINA	
Associational Treasurer	DONALD E. POPE	
Address	P.O. BOX 411, CLINTON,	State NORTH CAROLINA, Zip 28328

CHURCHES	TREASURERS & ADDRESSES (INCLUDE ZIP CODE)	Number of tithers	Cooperative Program pick as percent of total budget	Associational missions goal as percent of total budget	Budget promotion or emphasis used (None / Forward Program or Alternate / Committed to Ministries / Tithers Commitment / Other)	Budget YES	Budget ON	Total tithes, all offerings, and special gifts	All other receipts	Total receipts	Money borrowed during the year	Church staff salaries	Money paid out on new construction during the year	Debt retirement during the year	Church literature	All other local expenditures	Total local expenditures
MOUNT VERNON	Ruby Pope, Rt. 5, Box 60, Clinton, 28328	15	0	0	None x	x		26,886	600	27,486	0	8,785	0	11,650	792	2,578	23,805
NEW HOPE	R.F. Leonard, Rt. 1, Turkey 28393	13	5	3		x	x	19,921	236	20,157	0	13,470	0	0	883	0	14,353
PINEY GROVE	Marion Darden, Rt. 2, Faison 28341	10	2.5	1.5		x	x	39,589	0	39,589	0	10,444	8,027	3,936	981	14,612	38,000
POPLAR GROVE																	
POSTON	Althea Blanton, P.O. Box 92, Wallace 28466	130	10	.01	Forward x	x	:	65,942	263	66,205	0	12,010	0	20,600	3,202	27,585	63,397
ROSE HILL	John Moore, 313 W. Main St., Rose Hill 28458	0	16.7	2	x	x	:	79,166	0	79,166	0	19,080	0	0	2,357	17,574	39,011
ROWAN	Donald Pope, P.O. Box 411, Clinton 28328	—	9	3	x	x	:	91,917	760	92,677	65,000	13,810	188,000	0	4,350	21,000	227,160
SHARON	Homer James, Rt. 2, Wallace 28465	25	14	3	x		:	30,000	0	30,000	0	16,000	0	0	1,890	12,100	29,990
SHILOH	Cornelia Brown, Rt. 1, Chinquapin 28521	23	5	3		x	:	36,113	0	36,113	0	14,957	0	8,760	1,388	10,568	35,673
SILOAM	R.O. Sanderson, Barrells 28444	10	2.4	1.5		xx	:	24,733	0	24,733	0	8,400	0	5,459	1,071	12,956	31,001
TEACHEY	Elwood Fussell, P.O. Box 1, Teachey 28464	12	13.3	3	Forward x	x	:	43,666	361	44,027	0	14,600	0	0	994	12,054	27,648
TURKEY	Helen Register, Rt. 1, Turkey 28393	20	10	3		x	x	35,151	0	35,151	0	17,140	0	0	2,400	475	70,015
UNION GROVE	Louise Carter, Rt. 4, Box 301, Clinton 28328	5		1.3	x	x	x	10,314	233	10,547	0	3,000	0	14,500	66	3,846	7,508
WARSAW	W.G. Britt, 301 N. Front Street, Warsaw 28398	78	6.9			x	x	119,440	0	119,440	0	34,000	0	0	3,818	54,379	106,697
WELLS CHAPEL	Brenda Bowen, Rt. 1, Wallace 28466	—	11	3	Forward x		x	37,030	164	37,194	0	15,454	1,373	5,550	1,220	8,219	31,816
TOTALS		342						1,908,182	29,863	1,941,049	67,500	655,801	215,564	245,048	82,241	600,392	1,801,718

BSSB - 1397 (Rev. 11-80)

67

Grand Total
Mission expenditures

State: NORTH CAROLINA			
Associational Clerk	LUCILLE E. YANCEY		
Address	City CLINTON,	State NORTH CAROLINA	Zip 28328
P.O. BOX 711,			

CHURCHES	CHURCH CLERKS & ADDRESSES (INCLUDE ZIP CODE)	Money paid out on new construction during the year	All other church sponsored mission expenditures	Total church sponsored mission expenditures	Cooperative Program	Associational missions program	Designated: State missions	Designated: SB Home missions (incl. Annie Armstrong Easter offering)	Designated: SB Foreign missions (incl. Lottie Moon Christmas offering)	Designated: SB Christian education (schools, etc.)	Designated: SB Children's homes (cash plus goods)	Designated: SB Hospitals	Designated: SB Homes for the aged	Designated: All other (Bible Society, Temperance League, etc.)	Total other mission cause expenditures	Mission expenditures Grand Total
MOUNT VERNON	Gurley Quinn, 301 Fairfax Street, Clinton 28328	0	0	0	0	1,400	0	52	61	454	492	551	555	0	3,565	3,565
NEW HOPE	Shelby Blanchard, Rt. 1, Box 269, Turkey 28393	0	0	0	1100	500	150	285	150	0	150	150	150	0	1,585	2,685
PINEY GROVE	Melrose Thornton, Rt. 5, Clinton, 28328	0	0	0	500	300	175	305	882	0	0	0	0	0	1,662	2,162
POPLAR GROVE																
POSTON	Louise Hardison, 201 South Teachey Road, Wallace 28466	0	0	0	6441	1,000	211	518	683	0	0	0	0	100	2,512	8,953
ROSE HILL	Norman Z. Teachey, P.O. Box 71, Rose Hill 28458	0	0	0	11677	1,098	705	2,800	6,292	0	0	0	0	354	11,289	22,966
ROWAN	Barbara Briggs, 1311 S.W. Blvd., Clinton 28328	0	0	0	3600	1,496	463	642	1,144	0	40	0	0	723	4,468	8,068
SHARON	Madeline Norris, Rt. 1, Box 2-E, Chinquapin, 28521	0	0	0	3320	650	205	414	658	0	0	0	0	0	1,927	5,247
SHILOH	Cathy Jarosewicz, Rt. 2, Box 250-B, Wallace, 28466	0	0	0	758	624	0	285	369	0	0	0	0	0	1,278	3,036
SILOAM	Louise Maynard, Rt. 2, Box 124, Harrells 28444	0	0	0	600	380	325	498	916	0	28	0	0	116	2,963	2,863
TEACHEY	Judy Hall, 502 W. Westbrook Street, Wallace 28466	0	0	0	3906	450	1,332	1,070	4,487	0	0	0	0	1,270	8,604	12,509
TURKEY	Lettie-Phipps, Box 96, Turkey 28393	0	0	0	2870	861	717	601	1,101	0	0	0	0	109	3,389	6,259
UNION GROVE	Louise Carter, Rt. 4, Box 301, Clinton 28328	0	0	0	175	662	103	103	100	0	123	180	0	0	1,168	1,343
WARSAW	Peggy Grice, 309 E. Pollock Street, Warsaw 28398	0	0	0	5596	1,331	1,874	667	1,888	0	0	0	0	1,387	7,147	12,743
WELLS CHAPEL	Luola P. Rivenbark, Rt. 1, Box 221, Willard 28478	0	0	0	2747	746	391	472	663	0	0	0	0	87	2,359	5,106
TOTALS		9,358	0	9,538	140,186	33,997	15,028	24,282	46,428	2,464	4,408	1,331	1,105	20,738	150,310	298,414

69

0538 - 1287 (Rev. 11-80)

State: **NORTH CAROLINA**
Moderator: **I. MACK THOMPSON**
Address: **205 E. CHELLY STREET, WARSAW,** State **NORTH CAROLINA** Zip **28398**

EASTERN ASSOCIATION

CHURCHES	CHAIRMEN OF DEACONS & ADDRESSES (INCLUDE ZIP CODE)	No. church-type missions started during the year	No. church-type missions currently operating	No. other-type missions started during the year	No. other-type missions currently operating	No. New Sunday School Ministry	Christian day school enrollment	Annie Armstrong Offering ($)	No. of adult Sunday school classes	N=none TV=tv R=radio B=both	Number of revivals	No. of Spanish Sunday School classes	No. of college students baptized	No. of persons who served in a missions/evangelism project	Library	Deacon F.M.P.	S.S. Lead. Prep. Week	Biblical Doctrine Study	Audio. data processing	Bapt., Sem., Col. Day	Minutes microfilmed	Evangelism committee	Annuity Board protection for the pastor	Brotherhood Lead., Week	Seminary study	Christian Life Comm.	State paper in budget
ALBERTSON	Thurman Stroud, Rt. 1, Albertson 28508	0	0	0	0	4	0	287	3	N	2	0	0	0	n	n	n	n	n	n	n	n	n	n	n	n	y
ALUM SPRINGS	Sam Waller, Rt. 2, Mount Olive 28365	0	0	0	0	6	0	0	2	N	0	0	0	0	n	n	n	n	n	n	n	n	n	n	y	n	n
BEAR MARSH	Elbert Davis, Rt. 2, Mount Olive 28365	0	0	0	0	6	0	430	5	N	1	0	0	0	n	n	n	y	n	n	n	n	n	n	y	n	n
BEULAH	L.A. Pope, Rt. 2, Box 409B, Clinton 28328	0	0	0	0	11	0	0	1	N	1	0	0	0	n	n	y	n	n	n	n	n	n	n	n	n	y
BROWNS	Herbie L. Jordan, Rt. 3, Box 97, Clinton 28328	0	0	0	0	22	0	105	3	N	1	0	0	0	y	n	n	n	n	n	y	n	n	n	y	n	n
CALVARY	Billy Dail, Rt. 2, Box 220, Warsaw 28398	0	0	0	0	8	0	125	3	N	2	0	0	0	n	y	n	n	n	n	n	y	n	y	y	n	y
CALYPSO	Roy Davis, Calypso 28325	0	0	1	0	0	0	463	3	N	1	0	0	0	y	y	n	y	n	n	n	n	n	n	n	n	n
CENTER	James A. Taft, Rt. 1, Harrells 28444	0	0	0	0	3	0	20	1	N	2	0	0	0	n	n	n	n	n	n	n	n	n	y	n	y	n
CLINTON	Bill Miller, 504 Allen Street, Clinton 28328	0	0	0	0	26	0	4,001	18	R	2	0	0	0	y	y	n	y	n	n	n	n	y	y	y	y	y
CONCORD	Gary Bell, Rt. 1, Box 238, Rose Hill 28458	0	0	0	0	18	0	46	3	N	2	0	0	0	n	n	n	n	n	n	n	n	n	n	n	n	n
CORINTH	J.C. Savage, Jr., Rt. 1, Teachey 28464	0	0	0	0	0	0	1,114	7	N	2	0	0	0	y	y	n	n	n	n	n	y	n	n	y	y	n
DOBSON CHAPEL	Wilbur W. Brock, Rt. 2, Box 146, Rose Hill 28458	0	0	0	0	0	0	62	4	N	2	0	0	0	n	y	n	n	n	n	n	n	n	n	n	n	n
EVERGREEN	James Ezzell, Rt. 1, Magnolia 28453	0	0	0	0	0	0	159	2	N	1	0	0	0	n	n	y	n	n	n	n	n	y	n	y	n	y
FAISON	?	0	0	0	0	0	0	88	3	N	1	0	0	0	n	n	y	n	n	n	n	n	n	n	n	n	y
GARNERS CHAPEL	Varner Garner, Rt. 1, Mount Olive 28365	0	0	0	0	0	0	277	3	N	1	0	0	0	n	n	n	n	n	n	n	y	n	n	n	n	n
GROVE PARK	Freddy Bogue, Rt. 1, Box 13, Clinton 28328	0	0	0	0	22	0	1,105	9	R	2	0	0	0	y	y	y	y	y	y	n	n	y	y	y	y	n
IMMANUEL	Charles Adams, Rt. 1, Box 23X, Clinton 28328	0	0	0	0	0	0	1,044	11	R	1	0	0	0	y	y	n	n	y	n	n	n	n	y	n	y	n
INGOLD	Bobby H. Lamb, Rt. 1, Box 138, Garland 28441	0	0	0	0	0	0	175	5	N	1	0	0	0	n	n	y	n	n	n	n	n	y	y	n	n	y
ISLAND CREEK	Garland King, Rt. 1, Teachey 28464	0	0	0	0	0	0	—	6	N	2	0	0	0	n	y	n	n	n	n	n	n	n	n	n	n	y
JOHNSON	Norwood Phillips Rt. 1, Warsaw 28398	0	0	0	0	12	0	431	4	N	1	0	0	0	n	n	n	n	n	n	y	n	y	n	n	n	n
KENANSVILLE	James B. Blanchard, Kenansville 28349	0	0	0	0	0	0	450	3	N	0	0	0	0	n	y	n	n	n	n	n	n	n	y	n	y	n
MAGNOLIA	Carlton Smith, Box 182, Magnolia 28453	0	0	0	0	0	0	220	4	N	2	0	0	0	n	y	n	y	n	n	n	n	n	n	n	n	n
MOUNT GILEAD	Nathan Gay, Rt. 4, Box 166-B, Clinton 28328	0	0	0	0	3	0	377	6	N	2	0	0	0	n	y	y	n	n	n	n	n	n	y	n	n	n
MOUNT OLIVE	Kenneth Goodson, Rt. 4, Box 389, Mount Olive 28365	0	0	0	0	25	0	2,138	8	R	1	0	1	0	y	y	n	y	n	y	y	n	y	y	y	y	n
GARLAND	Hugh Hobbs, Box 151, Garland 2844	0	0	0	0	32	0	500	4	N	2	0	0	0	y	y	n	y	y	n	y	n	y	y	y	n	y

8668 - 1297 (Rev. 11-80)

EASTERN ASSOCIATION

State: NORTH CAROLINA
Moderator: L. MACK THOMPSON
Address: 205 E. CHELLY STREET, City: WARSAW, State: NORTH CAROLINA, Zip: 28398

CHURCHES	CHAIRMEN OF DEACONS & ADDRESSES (INCLUDE ZIP CODE)	No. church-type missions started during the year	No. church-type missions currently operating	No. other-type missions started during the year	No. other-type missions currently operating	No. New Sunday School Members	Christian day school enrollment	(3) Annie Armstrong Offering	No. of adult Sunday school classes	N=none R=radio TV=TV B=both	Number of revivals	No. of Spanish Sunday School classes	No. of college students baptized	No. of persons who served on a missions/ evangelism project	Library	Deacon F.M.P.	S.S. Lead. Prep. Week	Baptist Doctrine Study	Auto. data processing	Bapt. Sem. Col. Day	Minutes microfilmed	Evangelism committee	Annuity Board protection for the pastor	Brotherhood Lead. Week	Seminary study	Christian Life Comm.	State paper in budget
MOUNT VERNON		0	0	0	0	12	0	300	4	N	2	0	0	0	n	n	n	y	n	n	n	n	y	n	n	n	y
NEW HOPE	Raymond Blanchard, Sr., Rt. 1, Turkey 28393	0	0	0	0	27	0	150	4	N	2	0	0	0	n	n	n	n	n	y	n	n	n	n	n	n	n
PINEY GROVE	DeWitt King, Rt. 2, Box 111, Faison 28341	0	0	0	0	8	0	305	5	N	1	0	0	0	n	n	n	n	n	n	y	y	n	n	y	n	n
POPLAR GROVE																											
POSTON	John Braswell, Rt. 1, Box 53A, Watha 28471	0	0	0	0	29	0	518	8	N	2	0	0	0	y	n	y	n	y	n	n	n	y	y	y	y	y
ROSE HILL	William E. Wells, Rt. 1, Box 47, Teachey 28464	0	0	0	0	---	0	---	6	N	1	0	0	0	y	n	n	n	n	n	n	n	n	n	y	n	y
ROWAN	Ralph Robinson, Rt. 2, Box 269, Clinton 28328	0	0	0	0	21	0	642	8	R	2	0	0	0	y	y	y	y	n	y	y	n	n	y	y	n	y
SHARON	Carol Hatcher, Rt. 1, Chinquapin 28521	0	0	0	0	20	0	414	5	N	2	0	0	0	y	n	y	n	n	y	y	n	y	n	y	n	y
SHILOH	G.C. Raynor, Rt. 2, Wallace 28466	0	0	0	0	2	0	285	3	N	2	0	0	0	n	n	n	n	n	n	n	n	n	n	n	n	n
SILOAM	Charles Murphy, Tomahawk 28465	0	0	0	0	0	0	498	4	N	1	0	0	0	y	n	n	n	n	n	n	y	n	y	n	y	y
TEACHEY	Joe Ward, RFD, Teachey 28464	0	0	0	0	7	0	1,070	4	N	2	0	0	0	n	n	n	n	n	n	y	n	y	n	y	n	y
TURKEY	H.J. Register, Rt. 1, Turkey 28393	0	0	0	0	13	0	601	7	N	2	0	0	0	n	y	n	y	n	n	n	n	n	n	y	n	y
UNION GROVE	I.K. Carter, Jr, Rt. 4, Box 300, Clinton 28328	0	0	0	0	0	0	103	2	N	3	0	0	0	n	n	n	n	n	y	n	n	n	n	n	n	n
WARSAW	Graham Hood, 106 W. College Street, Warsaw 28398	0	0	0	0	29	0	591	8	R	1	0	0	0	y	n	n	n	n	n	n	y	n	y	n	y	y
WELLS CHAPEL	Bland Carr, Rt. 1, Willard 28478	0	0	0	0	17	0	472	6	N	2	0	0	0	n	n	n	y	n	n	n	n	y	n	n	n	y
	TOTALS			1		383		19,566	195		61		1	1													

72

Minutes * Church Histories * Church Directories * Sermon Books * Genealogies
A Division of Henington Publishing Co., Inc.

SOUTHERN BAPTIST PR
Wolfe City, Texas 754
214 496-2226

EASTERN
Baptist Association
North Carolina   1982

NORTH CAROLINA EASTERN BAPTIST ASSOCIATION

ONE HUNDRED FIFTY-FIFTH ANNUAL SESSION
1827-1982

FIRST DAY
October 25, 1982
Mt. Olive First Baptist Church

SECOND DAY
October 26, 1982
Mt. Gilead Baptist Church
Union Grove, Assisting

THEME

GO YE AND REACH PEOPLE, DEVELOP BELIEVERS, STRENGTHEN
FAMILIES

MODERATOR
. Mack Thompson

CLERK
Phillip Billings

NEXT ANNUAL MEETING
First Day
Siloam Baptist Church
(Evergreen Assisting)
Monday, October 24, 1983
Second Day
Tuesday, October 25, 1983
Turkey Baptist Church
(Beulah - New Hope Assisting)

TABLE OF CONTENTS

IN MEMORIUM

Katie Murray 1897-1982

Rosa Hocutt Powell
(Mrs. Julius C.)
1891-1982 1982

In gratitude to God and to the memory of two saints of the Lord who gave their lives in dedicated and faithful Christian service, we dedicate the 1982 MINUTES OF EASTERN BAPTIST ASSOCIATION to MISS KATIE MURRAY and MRS. ROSA HOCUTT POWELL.

KATIE MURRAY was born February 8, 1897 at Kenansville, North Carolina. Following her graduation from Meredith College in 1919, she taught one year at Dell High School at Delway. She graduated from Carver School of Missions in Louisville, Kentucky in 1922, and that same year she was appointed a career missionary to China by the Foreign Mission Board, SBC. She served in evangelism and as Bible teacher in Chengchow, Honan from 1925 through 1948; in Kweilin 1948-50; and in Kaohsiung, Taiwan 1954-62. Upon retirement in 1962, Miss Katie made her home among friends and family in Rose Hill, North Carolina, until her death on October 22, 1982.

ROSA HOCUTT POWELL was born on September 27, 1891 at Ashton, North Carolina. She graduated from Meredith College in 1917 and received additional training at the University of North Carolina and North Carolina College for Women. She taught school until her appointment by the Foreign Mission Board to be a career missionary to Oyo, Nigeria. She served as a women's worker; advisor to associational WMU; teacher in Oyo day school, Elam Memorial Girls' School in Shaki, Principal of Oyo Baptist Boy's High School, and taught in the language and orientation school. She and her husband, Reverend Julius C. Powell, retired in 1956 and made Warsaw, North Carolina their home. Following the death of her husband, Julius, Rosa continued living with their daughter, Mary Hester Powell, until her death on June 13, 1982.

PASTORS

CHURCH	PASTOR	ADDRESS	TELEPHONE
Albertson	Caleb Goodwin, Jr.	P.O. Box 37, Albertson, NC 28508	568-951
Alum Springs	Shelton Justice	Rt. 1, Box 38A-2, Warsaw 28398	293-7524
Bear Marsh	Mitchell D. Rivenbark	Rt. 2, Box 52, Mount Olive 28365	658-5872
Beulah	Willie O. Carr	Rt. 5, Box 50, Clinton 28328	533-3789
Browns	Joseph Walter Moss	Rt. 6, Box 389, Clinton 28328	592-5642
Calvary	F. J. McCarson	103 Wade Street, Warsaw 28398	293-3467
Calypso	Greg Thornton	P.O. Box 248, Calypso 28325	C-658-6693
Center	Robert E. Hill	P.O. Box 153, Clinton 28328	H-658-5223
Clinton, First	William M. Jones	P.O. Box 837, Clinton 28328	592-4910
Concord	Eddie Wetherington	Rt. 5, Box 29A, Clinton 28328	H-592-2472
Corinth	John A. Johnson (Interim)	108 Plank Street, Warsaw 28398	592-2898
Dobson Chapel	Randy Wellman	Rt. 1, Box 118-A, Magnolia 28453	289-3928
Evergreen	Donald W. Ailsworth	Rt. 1, Rose Hill, 28458	296-1473
Faison	Charles Kirkland	P.O. Box 426, Faison 28341	532-4757
Garland		Garland 28441	267-2591
Garner's Chapel	William B. Shipp	Rt. 1, Mount Olive 28365	C-529-5431
Grove Park	Davis Benton	605 N.E. Blvd., Clinton 28328	658-3503
Immanuel	Vernon Braswell	200 Fox Lake Drive, Clinton 28328	592-3513
Ingold	Robert Miller	P.O. Box 5252, Ingold 28446	C-592-3854
Island Creek	James Hartsell	Rt. 2, Box 349, Rose Hill 28458	H-592-4489
Johnson	Kenneth Durham	Rt. 2, Box 71, Warsaw 28398	529-4181
Kenansville	Lauren R. Sharpe	P.O. Box 517, Kenansville 28349	289-2606
Magnolia			C-293-4757
Mount Gilead	Oliver Skerrett	Rt. 2, Box 106, Clinton 28328	H-293-4980
Mount Olive	Anthony Z. Gurganus	301 Chestnut Street, Mount Olive 28365	296-0659
			592-6533
			C-658-2062
			H-658-2351

CHURCH	PASTOR	ADDRESS	TELEPHONE
Mount Vernon	Willie O. Carr	Rt. 5, Box 50, Clinton 28328	533-3789
New Hope	Paul Rose	Rt. 1, Box 255, Mount Olive 28365	658-4600
Piney Grove	Ferrell Miller	Rt. 2, Box 122-A, Faison 28341	533-3212
Poplar Grove	Andy Wood	Rt. 1, Box 77 1/2, Faison 28341	267-2981
Poston	Donald Coley	Rt. 3, Wallace 28466	285-2476
Rose Hill	Jerry D. Kinlaw	P.O. Box 459, Rose Hill 28458	289-3882
Rowan	Michael Shook	202 Reedsford Road, Clinton 28328	C-592-7508
			H-592-7268
Sharon	Phillip R. Denton (Interim)	P.O. Box I26, Chinquapin 28521	285-3062
Shiloh	James W. Johnson	515 W. Boney, Wallace 28466	285-7403
Siloam	Phillip Billings	Rt. 1, Box 19, Harrells 28444	532-4444
Teachey	Larry Blount	P.O. Box 38, Teachey 28464	285-2788
Turkey	Larry Padgett	P.O. Box 216, Turkey 28393	592-2416
Union Grove	L. L. Barnes	Rt. 2, Box 584, Elizabethtown 28337	588-4422
Warsaw	L. Mack Thompson	205 E. Chelly Street, Warsaw 28398	293-7479
Wells Chapel	Freddie M. Harris	Rt. 1, Wallace 28466	532-4528

MINISTERS NOT PASTORS

CHURCH	MINISTER	ADDRESS	TELEPHONE
Bearmarsh	Homer Bumgardner (OM)	Rt. 2, Warsaw 28398	293-7072
Clinton	Jean Hatch (OM)	309 Fairfax St., Clinton 28328	592-8124
	T. N. Cooper (OM)	P.O. Box 55, Clinton 28328	592-2293
	J. A. Crowe, Sr. (OM)	190 Jasper St., Clinton 28328	592-8758
	Clyde Davis, Sr. (OM)	P.O. Box 263, Clinton 28328	293-7077
	Waldo Early (OM)	207 Dixie Circle, Clinton 28328	592-2704
	Jasper Hinson (OM)	Rt. 6, Box 161, Clinton 28328	592-2088
	M. M. Johnson (OM)	P.O. Box 1093, Clinton 28328	592-2296
	L. E. Williamson (OM)	P.O. Box 837, Clinton 28328	592-8124
	Bob Doan (OM)	Rt. 6, Clinton 28328	564-6145

CHURCH	MINISTER	ADDRESS	TELEPHONE
Corinth	W. Price Knowles (LM)	115 E. Main, Rose Hill 28458	289-3741
Evergreen	Billy Todd (LM)	107 Dee St., Clinton 28328	592-3441
Garland	Timothy Register (LM)	504 Ingold Ave., Garland 28441	529-2411
Island Creek	Albert Rivenbark (OM)	Rt. 1, Willard 28478	285-2639
Mount Gilead	Scott Bass (LM)	Rt. 2, Box 101-A, Clinton 28328	592-4074
	Randy Powell (LM)	Rt. 2, Box 122, Clinton 28328	592-5520
Rose Hill	Albert Pope (LM)	Rt. 1, Box 239, Warsaw 28398	289-2755
Sharon	Warren E. Thomas (OM)	Chinquapin 28521	285-7956
Shiloh	James W. Johnson (OM)	515 W. Boney St., Wallace 28466	285-4206
Turkey	Richard Ellis (LM)	Rt. 1, Turkey 28393	592-5746
Union Grove	Paul Barefoot (LM)	Rt. 4, Clinton 28328	592-5572
Warsaw	D. W. Branch (OM)	515 E. College St., Warsaw 28398	293-4986
	John A. Johnson (LM)	108 E. Plank St., Warsaw 28398	293-4958

EXECUTIVE BOARD REPRESENTATIVES

CHURCH	REPRESENTATIVE	ADDRESS	TELEPHONE
Albertson			
Alum Springs	Larry W. Harper	Rt. 2, Box 281, Mount Olive 28365	658-3614
Bear Marsh	Stanley Byrd	Rt. 2, Mount Olive 28365	
Beulah	George Cox	Rt. 1, Turkey 28393	
Brown	Grover Sinclair	Rt. 3, Box 97, Clinton 28328	
Calvary	Curtis Pope	305 Inverness Road, Clinton 28328	592-5209
	Rev. Jay McCarson	103 Wade St., Warsaw 28398	293-3467
	Russell Killette	Rt. 1, Warsaw 28398	293-7674
Calypso	Mrs. Jeanne Thornton	Box 248, Calypso 28325	658-5223
Center			
Clinton	Charles Lee Pope	P.O. Box 514, Clinton 28328	592-2469
Concord	Gary Bell	Rt. 1, Box 238, Rose Hill 28458	289-3226

CHURCH	REPRESENTATIVE	ADDRESS	TELEPHONE
Corinth	Price Knowles	Rose Hill 28458	289-2733
	George Jones	Rt. 1, Rose Hill 28458	289-3463
Dobson Chapel	James P. Brown	Rt. 2, Rose Hill 28458	
Evergreen	Grover, Ezzell	Rt. 1, Rose Hill 28458	
Faison	Rev. Charles Kirkland	P.O. Box 426, Faison 28341	267-2591
	Clement R. Shine	Faison 28341	
Garland	Gene Hart	P.O. Box 187, Garland 28441	529-4311
Garner's Chapel	Morris Rose	Rt. 1, Mount Olive 28365	658-5425
Grove Park	Gordon Powell	002 Raleigh Road, Clinton 28328	592-3982
Immanuel	Dick Pope	621 NW Blvd., Clinton 28328	592-4221
	Wilbert Massey	1001 Naylor Street, Clinton 28328	592-2642
Ingold	Norwood Carter	P.O. Box 3, Harrells 28444	529-4112
Island Creek	Edward Teachey	215 E. Boney St., Wallace 28466	293-4690
Johnson	Robert Southerland	Rt. 2, Warsaw 28398	
Kenansville	Amos Brinson	Box 8, Kenansville 28349	296-4529
Magnolia			
Mount Gilead	Lonnie J. Bass	Rt. 2, Box 110-A, Clinton 28328	592-4074
	Max Peterson	Rt. 2, Box 152, Clinton 28328	592-6737
Mount Olive	W. K. Lewis	W. Steele Street, Mount Olive 28365	658-4191
Mount Vernon	Reboyd Warwick	Rt. 5, Clinton 28328	592-5852
New Hope			
Piney Grove	Oscar Thornton	Rt. 2, Faison 28341	
	Wayne Thornton	Rt. 2, Faison 28341	
Poplar Grove	Garland Britt	Rt. 2, Box 176, Faison 28341	
Poston	John Braswell	Rt. 1, Box 53-A, Watha 28471	
Rose Hill	W. S. Wells, Jr.	P.O. Box 66, Rose Hill 28458	285-7133
Rowan	Donald Pope	P.O. Box 411, Clinton 28328	
	Barbara Briggs	717 S. West Blvd., Clinton 28328	592-3437
Sharon	Rev. Phillip Denton	P.O. Box 126, Chinquapin 28521	592-7845
Shiloh	P. A. Maready	Rt. 2, Wallace 28466	285-3062
Siloam	R. O. Sanderson	Rt. 1, Harrells 28444	532-4211
Teachey			
Turkey	Creson Ezzell	Rt. 1, Turkey 28393	
Union Grove	Glendale Fryar	Rt. 4, Box 27, Clinton 28328	592-4830
	Morris Ezzell	Rt. 4, Box 315-A, Clinton 28328	592-2280

CHURCH	REPRESENTATIVE	ADDRESS	TELEPHONE
Warsaw	John A. Johnson	108 E. Plank St., Warsaw 28398	293-4830
Wells Chapel	John W. Johnson	Rt. 1, Wallace 28466	
	Jim Moody	Rt. 1, Wallace 28466	

GENERAL ASSOCIATIONAL OFFICERS

Moderator	John Flake, P.O. Box 1106, Clinton 28328	592-3194(Store)
		592-2973(Home)
Vice Moderator	Donald Coley (See under Pastors)	
Clerk	Phillip Billings (See under Pastors)	
Associate Clerk	Willie O. Carr (See Pastors)	
Treasurer	Walter Thomasson, 307 Fox Lake Dr., Clinton 28328	592-5807
Associate Treasurer	Jo Neal Robinson, Rt. 2, Box 269, Clinton 28328	592-3044

CHURCH PROGRAM OFFICERS

BROTHERHOOD:

Director	Charles Kirkland (See Pastors)	
Crusader Director	Ken Register, Rt. 1, Turkey 28393	533-3845
Pioneer Director		

9

CHURCH MUSIC:

Director   Jean Hatch (See Ministers not Pastors)
Council Members   Janet Register, Rt. 2, Rose Hill 28458   289-3367
                 Vivian Kirkland, P.O. Box 426, Faison 28341 267-2591
                 Curtis Pope (See Executive Board Representatives)

CHURCH TRAINING:

Director   Lucille Yancey, P.O. Box 711, Clinton 28328 592-7061(Office)
                                                 592-3080(Home)

Pastor Leader
Adult Director   H. J. Register, Rt. 1, Turkey 28393   533-3845
Youth Director   Rose Pleasant, P.O. Box 203, Mount Olive 28365 658-3036
Children's Director Jean Hatch (See Ministers not Pastors)
Preschool Director
Other Officers:
  Bible Drill Consultant Jo Robinson (See General Associational Officers)
  Deacon Ministry Training Donald Coley (See Pastors)
  New Member Consultant   Larry Padgett (See Pastors)

SUNDAY SCHOOL:
Director   James Hartsell (See Pastors)
Outreach Director Jimmy Mercer, Chinquapin 28521
VBS Director   Greg Thornton (See Pastors)
8.5 x '85 Representative Larry Padgett (See Pastors)
Adult Leader   Charlotte Hartsell, Rt 2, Box 349, Rose Hill 28458 289-2606
Youth Leader   Sue Padgett, P.O. Box 216, Turkey 28393   592-2416
Older Children Leader Andy Wood (See Pastors)
Younger Children Leader Tim Bass, 502 Allen Street, Clinton 28328   592-5813
Preschool Leader   Tempie Wood, Rt. 1, Box 77 1/2, Faison 28341 267-2981

10

GA Director	Mrs. Steven Matthis, Rt. 4, Clinton 28328	592-5802
Mission Friends	Mrs. Andy Wood (See Sunday School)	
Mission Action Director	Mrs. Elliott Tew, Warren Street, Clinton 28328	592-3745
Missions and Enlargement	Mrs. H. J. Register, Rt. 1, Turkey 28393	533-3845

DENOMINATIONAL REPRESENTATIVES

American Bible Society	H. J. Register (See Church Training)	
Childrens' Home	John A. Johnson (See Ministers not Pastors)	
Homes for Aging	Millard Johnson (See Ministers not Pastors)	
Christian Education	Tony Gurganus (See Pastors)	
Cooperative Program	Albert Pope (See Ministers not Pastors)	
Annuity Board	Waldo Early (See Ministers not Pastors)	
Foundation	Ken Durham (See Pastors)	
Hospital	Gerald Quinn, Wards Bridge Road, Warsaw 28398	293-4579
Christian Literature	T. N. Cooper (See Ministers not Pastors)	

TRUSTEES:

Jane E. Kaleel (1983)	401 Pineview Road, Clinton 28328	592-2043
Wayne Wilson (1984)		
Carroll Turner (1985)		

11

COMMITTEE-ON-COMMITTEES:

Chairman

Donald Coley (See Pastors)
James P. Brown, Rt. 2, Rose Hill 28458   289-3463
R. C. Garris, Rt. 2, Box 125, Harrells 28444   532-4365
Anthony Gurganus (See Pastors)
Freddie Harris (See Pastors)

(OTHER COMMITTEES NOT ELECTED AT TIME MINUTES WERE PREPARED)

12

MESSENGERS TO THE ANNUAL SESSION

M SPRINGS:
R MARSH: Hazel Pipkin, Sam Pipkin, E. G. Hatch, Jr., Mitchell Rivenbark, Stanley Byrd, Ethel Pridgen (Alternate).
LAH: T. M. Creech, Adell Creech, Mr. Cox, Mrs. Callie Carr, Lillie Headley, Lonnie Carter
WN: Mrs. Cooper Gore, Effie Bass, Edna Powell, Doris Sinclair, Herbie Jordan
VARY: Ethel Batts, Peggy McCarson
YPSO: Rev. Greg Thornton, Jeanne Thornton, Frances Powell, Nina Faye Harris, Marie Tadlock
TER:' Doris Hill, Gail Hair, David Blackburn, Barbara Thornton, Louis Register
NTON: L. E. Williamson, Jean Hatch, Charles L. Pope, M. M. Johnson, Martha Pierce, Everette Peterson, Claudius Peterson, Waldo Early, Edith Lee, Eleanor Early
CORD: Mrs. Francis Usher, Mrs. Steve Boone, G. R. Brice
INTH: Betty P. Butts, Inez Baker, Annie Ruth Hall, Charles Knowles, J. C. Savage, Jr., Delana Johnson
SON CHAPEL: Betty Brown, Ruby Rouse, Kate Kilpatrick, Eva Bland, Julia Brock, Naomi Brock
RGREEN: Jerry Todd, Mrs. Tom Straughn, Billy Todd
SON: Rev. Charles Kirkland, Vivian Kirkland, Lucy Custer, Telsie Frank, Helen Flowers, Annie Brown
LAND: Hazel Fields, Mary Carter, Mary Ethel Smith, Anna B. McClelland, Hugh Hobbs, Gene Hart, Mrs. Sudie Rich
ER'S CHAPEL: Randolph Garner, Theron Garner
E PARK:
NUEL: Mildred Honeycutt, Mrs. Bill Honeycutt, Janice Braswell, Dick Pope, Carolyn Sessoms, Dan Arnold, Frances Tew, Bevie Melson (Alternate), Mercedes Floyd, Martha Tart (Alternate), Lynn Adams
OLD:
AND CREEK: Charlotte Hartsell, Centelle Hanchey, Edward Teachey, Daphne Teachey
NSON: Robert Southerland, Katie Mae Kirby, Kenneth Durham
ANSVILLE: O. R. Blizzard, Amos Brinson, Margaret Oakley, Virginia Holand, Sally Tyndall, Rose Swain
NOLIA: Clifton Chesnutt, Roberta Chesnutt, Charles Bowman, Mrs. Lee Bowman
NT GILEAD: Lonnie J. Bass, Pearl Merritt, Joe Barefoot, Fay Gay, Alma Bryant, Gertrude Powell, Pauline Wiggins
NT OLIVE: Mack Herring, Mrs. Mack Herring, Rose Pleasant, Mrs. Kenneth Goodson, Virginia Lindsay, Mrs. D. W. Cherry, Mrs. J.T. Williams (Alternate), Mrs. Norman Anderson, Kenneth Goodson (Alternate)
NT VERNON: Edgar Gainey, Milton Gainey, Franklin Barber, Gladys Martin, Callie Carr, Willie O. Carr
HOPE: Thelma Ware, Raymond Blanchard, Jr., Shelby Blanchard, Paul Rose, Betty Sue Rose, Celestial Colwell
EY GROVE: Eloise Clifton, Irene Darden, Dot Boyette, Blanche Casey, Rev. Farrell H. Miller
LAR GROVE:
TON: Rev. Donald R. Coley, John Braswell, Annette Henderson, Thelma Murray, Lula Dixon, Deane Murray

13

ROSE HILL: William E. Wells, Mrs. William E. Wells
ROWAN: James Yancey, Dixie Yancey, Lela Wallace, Mozelle Jones, Mary Bell Daughtry, Cooper Hairr
SHARON: Jimmy Mercer, Eunice Hursey, Jim Southerland, Annie Cavenaugh, T. G. Huffman, Clara Huffman, Louise Southerland, Madeline Norris
SHILOH: Rifton Raynor, Mary Lee Raynor, Margaret Hunter, Rev. Jimmy Johnson
SILOAM: Roger Garris, C. P. Eakins, Mildred Garris, Norma Johnson, Louise Maynard, Julia Peterson
TEACHEY: Joe Ward, Linwood Brinkley, Katie Wells
TURKEY: Lester Massey, Naomi Brinkley, Ruth Ellis, Lettie Phipps
UNION GROVE: Rodella Batts, Evelyn Fryar, Jessie Fryar
WARSAW: Bill Knowles, Helen Ann Straughan, Dot Knowles, Rita Quinn, James Page, Gerald Quinn, Harriett Page, Dot Rollins, Blanche Draughan
WELLS CHAPEL: Luola Rivenbark, Florence Hoover, Alma Highsmith, Laura G. Moore, Catherine Thornton, Freddie Harris

PROCEEDINGS

First Day - Afternoon Session

1. Moderator Mack Thompson called to order the 155th Annual Session of EASTERN ASSOCIATION at 3:15 p.m. on October 25, 1982 in the First Baptist Church, Mount Olive.
2. Jean Hatch led the singing of "We Are Called to be God's People".
3. Phil Billings read Ephesians 3:14-21 and led in prayer.
4. Callie Carr, substituting for the associate clerk who was ill, reported registration representing 32 churches and moved that the messengers present constitute a quorum. Passed.
5. Program Committee Chairman, Vernon Braswell, presented the order of service and moved its adoption as the order of business for the 155th Annual Session. Passed.
6. Tony Gurganus, nominating committee chairman, presented for nomination Phil Billings as clerk and Willie Carr as associate clerk. Both were elected.
7. No response was heard to the call for petitionary letters.
8. The moderator appointed the following committees:
   A. RESOLUTIONS
      Jerry Kinlaw, Chairman
      Mitchell Rivenbark
      Phillip Denton
   B. TIME, PLACE & PREACHER
      Millard Johnson, Chairman
      Robert Miller
      Eddie Weatherington
   C. MEMORIALS
      Michael Shook
      Farrell Miller
      Paul Rose
9. Treasurer, Donald Pope, presented Treasurers Report which was adopted.

Lucille Yancey presented Associational Council Report. Ac-
d.

Miscellaneous Business:
A. Davis Benton, Chairman, Constitution Committee presented
tudy proposed changes to the Constitution and By-Laws and a
e revised Constitution and By-Laws. The moderator promoted
nation by all messengers.
B. Jim Hartsell, Stewardship Chairman presented the pro-
budget for study and for vote on the second day of the Ses-

C. Lucille Yancey gave her appreciation for associations
h clerks for their reporting of Church Letters.
D. Larry Padgett made the motion that the 1982 Minutes be
ated in the memory of Rosa Powell and Katie Murray. Passed
unanimous standing vote.
Jean Hatch led the singing of "We Thank Thee That Thy Man-
.

Agency reports were given as follows:
A. Annuity Board   Clyde Davis
B. Christian Literature/
     Biblical Recorder   Tom Cooper
C. Baptist Foundation   Ken Durahm
Tony Gurganus brought greetings from the host church
Jean Hatch led the singing of "Footprints of Jesus".
Gene Puckett, the new editor of the "Biblical Recorder"
ht a message about the "Biblical Recorder's" past, its pres-
and its future. He used "peace" as its key. As editor he ex-
ed his commitment to Jesus, the Christ.
Jean Hatch led the singing of "O, Lord, Who Came to Earth
ow".
Reports of Social Services Institutions were given as fol-

A. Baptist Homes for Aging   Millard Johnson
B. Baptist Children's Homes   Mack Thompson
     Gerald Garner, Director of Odom Home, spoke
     on opportunities and needs of Odom Home.
C. Baptist Hospital   Gerald Quinn
Calvin Knight, Baptist Hospital Representative, brought a
ge from the Baptist Hospitals.
Video Presentation: "Sharing Christ's Hope", General Board
t.

New Pastors and church staff members recognized were:
A. Phil Billings, pastor, Siloam
B. Donald Ailsworth, pastor, Evergreen
C. Rose Pleasant, Minister of Education, Mount Olive, First
Jean Hatch led in the singing of "Dear Lord and Father of
nd".
Marilyn Phelps sang a solo of inspiration, "Bless This
".

Mack Thompson delivered the Doctrinal Message, "Doctrine
e Family" from Genesis 2:18ff.
Tony Gurganus led in prayer and asked blessings for the
ng meal.

FIRST DAY - EVENING SESSION

October 25, 1982

1. Moderator, Mack Thompson, called the Association to order
at 7:10 P.M.
2. Jean Hatch led in the singing of "Rescue the Perishing".
3. Dan Arnold read Acts 1:8 and Proverbs 14:25a and led in
prayer.
4. Clyde Davis gave the Associational Mission Update by intro-
ducing the current staff and its dynamics, commission, and needs.
5. Video presentation: Foreign Mission Board
6. Paula Clayton presented Associational Christian Social Ministries activities of the past year based on Isaiah 58. After a
film presentation of associational involvement of the past year,
she invited all churches to involve themselves in the new year.
7. Jean Hatch led in the singing of "Send Me, O Lord, Send
Me".
8. Mount Olive Baptist Church Adult Choir brought the special
music: "Break Thou the Bread of Life" and "The Man With Many
Names".
9. J. Edwin Bullock, Consultant in the Department of Volunteer
Services of the Foreign Mission Board, brought the Missionary
Message based on Acts 1:8.
10. The moderator adjourned the session with prayer by Larry
Padgett.

SECOND DAY

October 26, 1982

1. Moderator, Mack Thompson called the association to order at
9:30 A.M. at Mount Gilead Baptist Church.
2. Jean Hatch led the singing of "Footsteps of Jesus".
3. L. E. Williamson read 2 Timothy 4:1-8 and led in prayer.
4. Callie Carr, acting for the associate clerk, reported registration representing 34 churches and moved that the messengers
present constituted a quorum. Passed.
5. Clerk, Phil Billings, reported on the events of the previous day.
6. Miscellaneous Business:
    A. Davis Benton, Chairman of the Constitution Committee,
read the proposed constitutional changes in article VIII and the
addition of Articles IX and X and made the motion that they be
adopted. Farrell Miller seconded the motion. After a brief discussion the question was called for. Following the majority vote
to end discussion, the original motion was approved.
    B. Davis Benton, Chairman of the Constitutional Committee,
read the proposed By-Laws changes which involved editing of the
By-Laws to conform to the Constitution as amended; deletion of
section D of Article III; changes in Article IV as follows,

1) Change "Duties of Committees" to "Committees"
2) Change "Associational Council Committee" to "Standing Committees"
3) Deletion of sub-section 1 of Section A
4) State procedures for election of committees
5) Rewriting of sub-section 2 "Mission Committee"
6) Authorization of Stewardship Committee to have financial records audited
7) Discontinue the Audit Committee
8) Add Articles VI and VII

Davis Benton moved the adoption of the above changes as presented. Farrell Milled seconded the motion.

1) Larry Blount made the following motion to amend; delete "or the director of missions may . . . as determined by the Council" and insert "shall".
The amendment was approved.
2) By Common Consent the word "members" in Article VII was changed to "messengers".

Vernon Braswell, Chairman of the program committee moved the time be extended to allow for further discussion. Motion carried.

Mitchell Rivenbark presented the motion to amend Article IV, Section A, Subsection 1 dealing with the election of standing and special committees; Section A, Sub-section 2 Mission Committee to change working original members to At-large members; to have new committees approved by Executive Board and proved for writing the prescription; delete "be authorized to" from section A, Sub-Section 3; and in Article VII, require two-thirds vote to amend the By-Laws.

Tony Gurganus made the motion to refer the motion to amend to the Constitution Committee and Mitchell Rivenbark assist the committee in clarifying the proposed changes. Motion carried.

C. Greg Thornton made motion the Nominating Committee present its report on the first day and action taken on the second day. Motion carried.

D. Moderator, Mack Thompson, deferred continuation of the Miscellaneous Business to a later time of this session and continued with orders of the program.

7. The following Associational Committees reports were given and adopted.

A. Missions   Michael Shook
B. Library Committee   Thelma Davis
C. Evangelism   Phillip Denton
D. Pastoral Support
     Committee   Davis Benton
E. Stewardship Committee   Clyde Davis

8. Mitchell Rivenbark moved that the 1982-83 budget presented on the previous day be accepted. The budget was adopted.

9. Anthony Gurganus presented the Nominating Committee Report. The moderator opened the floor for further nominations. Michael Shook nominated Larry Padgett as moderator and Jimmy Johnson as vice moderator. The Shook nominations were defeated. The Nominating Committee's report was adopted as submitted.

10. Jimmy Johnson made a motion to table until the July Council meeting. This motion was defeated.

11. Tony Gurganus made the motion to close debate. Motion carried.

12. Vernon Braswell, Time and Place Committee Chairman, moved to extend miscellaneous business session five minutes. Motion passed.

13. Motion on changes by By-Laws as revised and presented by the Constitution Committee was approved.

14. Clyde Davis presented a report of Christian Higher Education. Report was adopted.

15. Charles Allen, Campbell University, brought message on education.

16. Jean Hatch led in the singing of "Teach Me, O Lord, I Pray".

17. Jerry Kinlaw, Chairman, gave the Resolutions Committee Report (located in this Associational Minutes titled RESOLUTION COMMITTEE REPORT) which was duly adopted.

18. Millard Johnson, Chairman, Time, Place and Preacher Committee, presented the following report by motion:

The Time, Place and Preacher Committee recommends that the 156th Annual Session be on October 24, 1983 at Siloam and October 25 at Turkey and the preacher be Larry Padgett with Jerry Kinlaw as alternate preacher.

19. Michael Shook, Chairman Memorial Committee, presented the following report (located elsewhere in these minutes as "Our Beloved Dead"). The report was adopted.

20. The following church programs directors submitted their reports for the 1981-82 year:

A. Brotherhood	Charles Kirkland
B. Church Music	Jean Hatch
C. Church Training	Greg Thornton
D. Sunday School	Donald Coley
E. Vacation Bible School	Michael Shook
F. Woman's Missionary Union	Betsy Carter

21. Tommy Puckett, N.C. Brotherhood Department, brought a message of evangelistic opportunities through the Brotherhood Department.

22. Jean Hatch led in the singing of "Savior, Like A Shepherd Lead Us".

23. Davis Benton, Chairman of the Constitution Committee, was recognized to present changes the Committee had in the original motion on By-Laws changes: (A copy of this motion as amended appears elsewhere in these minutes under "Constitution Committee Report").

24. Mrs. Martha Pierce brought special music.

25. Lauren Sharpe brought the Annual Sermon based on 2Corinthians 8:1ff.

26. Moderator, Mack Thompson, adjourned the 155th Annual Session of the Eastern Baptist Association, with a prayer.

RESOLUTION COMMITTEE REPORT

Whereas: being conscious of the presence of God, and the leadership of the Holy Spirit during this, the one-hundred and fifty-fifth session of Eastern Baptist Association Meeting with Mount Olive First Baptist Church and Mount Gilead Baptist Church,

Be it resolved: that the Eastern Baptist Association express it's appreciation to and for the following:

1. To God for His mercies and leadership during this meeting as well as His blessings of the past year.
2. To God for giving us time with Rosa Hocutt Powell, Missionary to Nigeria and Katie Murray, Missionary to China. To these two warriors of prayer, we dedicate this Annual Session.
3. That the Eastern Association express its appreciation to our moderator, Mack Thompson, and the officers of the Association for the fine manner in which the business of this Association has been conducted.
4. That we pledge our love, support, and prayers to our director of missions and his wife, along with our appreciation for their leadership.
5. That we resolve to encourage the churches to strive for unity for the purpose of fulfilling the will of God in the proclamation of His Word.
6. That we express our thanks to the host churches, Mount Olive, First Baptist Church, Mount Olive and Mount Gilead Baptist Church, Clinton, assisted by Union Grove Baptist Church, for the excellent manner in which they provided for the comfort and the feeding of our messengers.
7. That we dedicate ourselves to the task of witnessing for our Lord and seeking to lead people into a closer walk with our Heavenly Father, which is our Theme "Affirming Christ's Bold Commands".

Jerry D. Kinlaw, Chairman
Mitchell D. Rivenbark
Phillip R. Denton

WMU SEVENTY-THIRD ANNUAL SESSION MINUTES

The 73rd WMU Annual Session of Eastern Association met April 15, 1982 at the Ingold Baptist Church with Garland Baptist Church assisting as host. Mrs. Norwood Carter, Director, presided. Meeting was begun by singing "O Zion Haste".

Mrs. Coleman Carter presented the Prayer Calendar and read the Scripture (John 10:1-10). Minutes were read and after corrections were made, were approved. Report was made of Christmas gifts sent to Woman's Prison in Raleigh ($15.00 and 183 scarves).

A delightful skit was performed by Connie Carlton, emphasizing the need of a friend. It encouraged all women and girls in or outside their church to be aware of people in need of friends.

AGE-LEVEL REPORTS AND CHALLENGES:

BAPTIST WOMEN: No report due to absence of leader. MISSION ACTION: Helen Register praised churches for their support of her during the past five years as director; but most of all, she praised them for their support of missions - mission projects throughout the community and Eastern Association. She gave information regarding our summer youth workers we will have this summer to work among the migrants. ACTEENS: Skit was given by Connie Carlton - "Little Red Ride Hooding"; it showed us that acteens are a difficult age, needing love and support - each church needs to have Acteens to love and support throughout their Christian journey. We will miss Connie as this is her last year as Acteen Director. MISSION FRIENDS: Mrs. Andy Wood reminded us of Proverbs 22:6 "Train up a child -" stating that love and patience are necessary when working with children. A child learns much before he starts to school. We cannot let this opportunity pass. Each church was encouraged to start a Mission Friends group.

Mrs. Donald Pope extended invitation for the 74th Annual Session to be held at Rowan Baptist Church. Afternoon speaker was Mrs. Florence Hoover who showed slides and brought information of Bolivia, following a trip to South America by several volunteers. She gave her testimony as a Christian while in Bolivia and told us of the mission work being done in that country. She requested continuation of our prayers and monetary support for that work.

Rev. Robert Miller pronounced grace. Meeting adjourned for supper.

Evening session was opened with singing of hymn "I Love to Tell the Story". Baptist Young Women report was given by Glenda Strickland, Director. GA Report was brought by Paula Matthis, Director.

Mrs. Florence Hoover presented the following names for 1982-83 WMU Officers:

Director	Mrs. Norwood Carter
Assistant Director	Mrs. Coleman Carter
Secretary-Treasurer	Mrs. Donald Pope
Baptist Women Director	Mrs. Jackie Stroud
BYW Director	Miss Glenda Strickland
Acteens Director	Mrs. Ted Lockerman
GA Director	Mrs. Steven Matthis
Mission Friends Director	Mrs. Andy Wood
Mission Action Director	Mrs. Elliott Tew
Enlistment & Enlargement	Mrs. H.J. Register

Motion was made to accept these officers.

Music was presented by Martha Pierce. Evening Speaker was Rev. Paula Clayton, Director of Christian Social Ministries in Eastern Association. She asked for WMU support through prayers and giving, especially to the Migrant Ministry this summer. An offering of $168.75 was received for this cause.

Rev. Clyde Davis gave the benediction.

> Respectfully submitted,
> Mrs. Norwood Carter, Director
> Mrs. Donald Pope, Secretary

THE BIBLICAL RECORDER
CHRISTIAN LITERATURE REPORT
1982

Workers change but the work goes on. This is the simple message from the Biblical Recorder this year.

Marse Grant, editor for nearly 23 years, retired September 13, his 62nd birthday. Succeeding him will be R.G. (Gene) Puckett who has served as editor of two other Baptist state papers and associate editor of a third one.

He came to the Recorder from the position of executive director
f Americans United for the Separation of Church and State where
e was also publisher of the magazine, Church and State.
Editorials and letters have praised his ability. In addition to
is 20 years of editorial work on Baptist papers, he has been
astor of churches in Kentucky, Ohio and Florida. He was interim
astor of the largest Southern Baptist Church in Maryland, the
iddle River Church near Baltimore. He will carry on the tradition
f our Baptist state paper as it looks forward to its 150th an-
iversary next January 17.
It has not been an easy year for the Biblical Recorder, pri-
arily because mailing costs increased 160 per cent, from $2,500
week to $6,500 a week. Another increase may come this fall. The
ecorder has been through hard times before and will make it this
time, thanks to the continuing support of North Carolina Baptists.
Please remember the new Recorder editor and his family. As his
chedule permits, he will be speaking in churches and in associational meetings. He wants to know more about our state and these
ppearances will help him. Remember him in your prayers as he
ndertakes this difficult and demanding job.
A LOOK AT THE BIBLE - The Old Testament is an account of a
ation.
The New Testament is an account of a Man - Christ.
The Nation was founded and nurtured of God to bring the MAN
into the World.
The appearance of Christ on the Earth is the central event of
ll history. The Old Testament sets the stage for it. The New
estament describes it. The challenge of the hour IS TO READ GOD'S
ORD - to prayerfully interpret the word to a lost and dying world.
A LOOK AT OUR MISSION - TO PRAY - TO THINK - TO DO. The Theme
for 1982 for State Missions is: "HOPE IS SOMETHING YOU GIVE".
Never in our world have we needed HOPE as we do today.
There is so much depression, so much hostility, so much neg-
ativism, so much distrust, our generation is searching for HOPE as
never before.
Mr. Keith Parks of our Foreign Mission Board tells us "In the
United States and too often overseas, we tend to say 'unless you
say what I tell you to say, do what I tell you to do and unless
you measure up to my standard - you CANNOT BE A PART OF MY BAPTIST
CHURCH'. Why not let God's Holy Spirit lead us through the deep
waters of the AGE?"
A LOOK AT THE WORLDS' GREATEST NEED - "ENCOURAGEMENT" - Many
sermons and many words are spoken in these times that express our
longing - oh give me something New the old is outdated. The pastor
and the people need encouragement - Positive words, carefully
chosen and sincere should be offered in many situations. The man
in the pew and the pastor are both ministers -Amen.
A LOOK AT OUR HELPS - The Bible and the quarterlies, periodicals,
reading helps, all of these are good and need our constant attention, but my Friend lets the Sunday School book and the lesson
in the Recorder be the Bible. We say, "Back to Basics".
A LOOK AT OUR STATE PAPER - THE RECORDER - In our mail this
morning (Sept. 28, 1982) we have the latest facts and message from
the Biblical Recorder Staff by Larry E. High. We are informed that
the circulation of the Recorder this week (Sept. 16, 1982) is
107,678 per week. Mr. R.G. Puckett, Editor and Business Manager,
Larry E. High, Managing Editor. We, of our Association - welcome
and feel proud of our new Recorder Staff and Administration for
the future of our Convention. We have a good record in our churches

21

in our Association for the Recorder. We still need more churches
and people to participate.
    REPORTING - 13 Clubs in EASTERN ASSOCIATION
               20 churches include Recorder in church budget
          ‘   1,326 individual persons subscribing
    A LOOK AT CHARITY & CHILDREN - This important new organ needs
more careful attention; it may look old but the news is the latest
from our child care institutions. "God Loves The Little Children -
All the Children of the World".

Respectfully submitted,
T.N. Cooper

BAPTIST CHILDREN'S HOMES REPORT

    The Pembroke Family Services Center serves nine Southeastern
counties: Robeson, Columbus, Bladen, Sampson, Cumberland, Harnett,
Hoke, Scotland and Richmond. Central to this service area is Odum
Home, Pembroke.
    Significant growth has occurred at Odum Home. The Home is
operating at near capacity with applications constantly being
serviced. The Jimmy Latta-Harnett County Cottage is operating as
an Emergency Care Home and fills a vital need in this area of the
State. Darrell Garner has been named as Resident Director of Odum
Home and is available to provide any service offered by the
Children's Homes anywhere in North Carolina. The Baptist Children's
Homes has affected the lives of more than five thousand people
during the past twelve months. With more than a dozen programs of
care and with services being offered from twenty-five locations
across North Carolina. Baptists can be confident that the Baptist
Children's Homes is seeking every means possible to serve needy
people in Christ's name.
    The quality of life for our children has been enhanced this year
by the addition of a therapeutic recreation team. Mr. and Mrs. Jim
Martin have a fine background that will enable them to help our
staff statewide to plan and provide recreation with purpose. They
work out of Thomasville.
    A new 16mm thirty minute film was released in July called "You
Needed ME" and is available for use in our churches. Contact the
Children's Homes to schedule this inspiring, instructive film.
    We are grateful for the continuing support of our fellow Baptist
through the Cooperative Program, the North Carolina Missions Offering and designated gifts. Like everyone else, we are being affected
by short-falls in anticipated income. Programs have to be adjusted
but we are careful to maintain quality care for those whom we
serve.

Respectfully submitted,
John A. Johnson

22

ANNUITY BOARD REPORT 1982

"Solid Growth and Expanding Achievements"

"Despite the economic problems in the nation, 1981 was a year of solid growth and expanding achievements with record number in assets, benefits paid and member accounts" said Darold H. Morgan, president of the Annuity Board of the Southern Baptist Convention. Key statistical highlights in 1981 included:

1. A 10 percent 13th check was sent to annuitants who retired before 1980. Those annuitants who retired in 1980-81 received their 13th check bonus in monthly checks.
2. A total of $24,298,521 was paid in retirement benefits.
3. Total assets administered by the board as of Dec. 31, 1981 were $896,535,999 compared with $806,518,757 in December 31, 1980.
4. Relief funds from the Cooperative Program totalled $357,200.
5. Membership records indicated that 19,299 persons were en-rolled in Plan A, 58,930 in Plan B and 4,193 in Plan C.
6. Premium income reached $72,854,632. Of this amount, $45,443,258 was designated for the Fixed Fund and $10,294,788 for Plan A.

STATISTICAL HIGHLIGHTS 1982

Retirement Plans	Member Accounts and Benefits	Insurance	Members
Plan A (church-agency)	19,299	*Health Insurance	23,327
Fixed Fund (church-agency)	49,103	Group Life (church)	15,666
Balanced Fund (church-agency)	9,826	Group Life (agency)	19,744
Variable Fund (church-agency)	4,193	**Life Benefit Plan	2,136
Benefits Paid (retirement and		Seminarian Life	1,738
Variable)	$24,298,521	Seminarian Medical	4,549
Relief Benefits	$411,093	*Includes churches and	
		agencies	
Relief Recipients	396	** Closed to new members	

NORTH CAROLINA

As of March 31, 1982, 3,288 staff members of 2,316 churches and associations are participating in the Southern Baptist Retirement Program.

As of March 31, 1982, we had process the following:
  70 - Southern Baptist Retirement Program applications
  14 - applications for age retirement benefits
  501 - retirement program upgrades

The church's response to upgrading the staff member's retirement program continues to be encouraging. Ten (10%) percent of his/her annual compensation (salary, housing allowance, auto allowance, etc.) should be the minimum. In 1981 North Carolina reported 1,032 upgrades!

Six (6) VIDEO TAPES are now available for churches and associations to assist in understanding the protection programs of the Annuity Board. Order from the Film Library, Baptist State Convention.

VT16-1 "Planning The Rest of Your Life"
VT16-2 "Retirement - The Way It Is"
VT16-3 "Purpose and Meaning in Retirement"
VT16-4 "Mental and Physical Health in Retirement"
VT16-5 "Continuing Education and Mental Alertness"
VT16-7 "Route 10: The Road to Financial Security"

ASSOCIATION

In EASTERN ASSOCIATION 33 churches and 43 staff members are participating in the retirement program. Of this number 10 are still participating on the minimum of $33.34 per month. There is a great need to upgrade this to 10% of total salary for staff members.

NORTH CAROLINA BAPTIST FOUNDATION REPORT

When it was chartered in 1920, the North Carolina Baptist Foundation was charged with the responsibility of promoting the making of gifts, receiving and managing the gifts, and distributing the income earned from the investment of those gifts to the objects and causes specified by their donors. The charter further provided that those designated causes should be any and all objects and causes of the "Missionary Baptist denomination".

Today, the purpose remains the same. Baptist Foundation is the only agency of the Baptist State Convention which receives gifts for all Baptist causes: the colleges, universities and seminaries, Baptist Homes and Children's Homes, Baptist Hospital and the school of medicine, churches and associations, Foreign and Home Mission Boards, special mission offerings, Cooperative Program, and all other concerns of Baptists.

During 1981, new trusts were created and old trusts had additions which together totaled $855,991.00 bringing the assets in all trusts to almost five million dollars. (Real estate is stated in the assets at the value when given, which is on the books at approximately 2.4 million dollars less than the current market value.)

Through the trusts created prior to 1981, investments earned $418,529.70 during 1981 for distribution to beneficiaries named by the trust donors. During the years of the Foundation's existence, the sum of $2,610,299.00 has been distributed to all beneficiaries of trusts held by the Foundation, all according to the instructions provided by the donors.

The objective and future plans of the Foundation are summarized in a brief phrase - promoting mission support through estate stewardship. Through conferences and seminars, through counseling with individuals and speaking to church groups, the Foundation will continue to support North Carolina Baptists in their efforts to become better managers and stewards of their material possessions. Through its role as trustee agency, the Foundation will serve North Carolina Baptists by enabling them to enjoy Christian stewardship in its fullest sense - even after death.

Respectfully submitted,
Hubert Phillips

24

REPORT OF NORTH CAROLINA BAPTIST HOMES, INC.

The past year in our North Carolina Baptist Homes has been a good one. We have had 45 persons admitted to the ministry of our Homes and apartments. This represents 98,065 days of special care for an average daily population of 269 persons. The Lord's blessings continue to be poured out upon us.

Great things are in store for our Homes as we look to the Lord, to North Carolina Baptists, and to the future! The Trustees made a decision of far-reaching significance at their May meeting in approving a Capital Funds Campaign. The existing needs at the Hayes Home and the Nursing Unit in Winston-Salem present a primary challenge of this campaign. With success, we will be well on our way to adding much-needed nursing care beds, and resident rooms. We will also be able to provide much-needed upgraded services in relation to our present Nursing Unit, and also construct a desperately-needed Administration Building. We covet your prayers for the success of this effort.

Our major concern presently in our Homes' ministry is in regard to our benevolent care, assisting those who need supplementing financially. Gifts through the Cooperative Program and the North Carolina Missions Offering go a long way in undergirding those who cannot pay the full cost of care. These gifts, totalling $516,804.00, provided 57% of benevolent care. The many residents who will be looking to the Baptist Homes' ministry for their care and the 43% short fall in mission gifts will place increasing demands on the already over-taxed benevolent funds. Also, many persons on the Homes' waiting list who cannot pay the full cost of care may have a longer period to wait because of limited benevolent funds.

We believe, therefore, that if you know the need, you will respond to it by the increasing support that you will give through the Cooperative Program and through the North Carolina Missions Offering. We will be looking to the Lord and to you to help us continue to be the benevolent ministry that we have always been.

We love you, and we thank you for your love, your gifts, and your prayers. As Abraham was about to deliver the fatal blow to his son, Isaac, he asked, "Father, where is the sacrifice?" Whereupon Abraham replied, "God will provide!" And so He did! And so, we believe that you will provide!

Respectfully submitted,
Millard M. Johnson

CHRISTIAN HIGHER EDUCATION REPORT

CALLING THE ROLL

North Carolina Baptists have founded and continue to support seven colleges and universities. (This number is second only to Texas, which sponsors eight Baptist schools.) What are the names of the North Carolina Baptist colleges, and where are they located? Perhaps calling the roll will prove helpful. Imagining a map of the state and reading from left to right, the Baptist colleges are: Mars Hill, in the mountains 18 miles north of

Asheville, in the town of Mars Hill: <u>Gardner-Webb</u>, in the town of Boiling Springs, nine miles from Shelby and not far from the South Carolina border; <u>Wingate</u>, 30 miles east of Charlotte, in the town of Wingate, also near the South Carolina line; <u>Wake Forest</u>, in the centrally located city of Winston-Salem; <u>Meredith</u>, in the capitol city of Raleigh; <u>Campbell</u>, 30 miles south of Raleigh, in the town of Buies Creek; and <u>Chowan</u>, in the Northeast town of Murfreesboro, and not far from the Virginia state line.

LOOKING INSIDE
During the 1981-82 school year, there were 15,798 students and 1,768 faculty and staff comprising the human side of the seven schools. Foreign students numbered 224 from 57 countries and territories from Australia to Zimbabwe. North Carolina Baptist college students are preparing for a variety of vocations, for example: church-related vocations 665, teaching 1,314; medicine (including nursing) 1,329; law 961; social work 384. Approximately 9,700 of the students received financial aid. The seven colleges have practiced the ministry of Christian education for a cumulative total of 757 years. These colleges are proud of their Baptist heritage and are wanting to be effective missions partners with the churches.

SERVING THE CHURCHES
The business of Baptist colleges is the education of young people. This is the primary service provided by the colleges to the churches. The college presidents have asked that the churches-pastors and lay people alike - help them by pointing young people from the churches toward Baptist colleges. Often there are Baptist youth who would prefer a Baptist college, but who fail to apply out of the belief that they cannot afford the cost. It is often the case that a person can attend a Baptist school as inexpensively-sometimes more inexpensively, depending upon the aid available - as he or she can attend a state institution.

GRATITUDE
For students, for generous support through the Cooperative Program and for a meaningful place in the great mission to the world, your Baptist Colleges are grateful.

Respectfully submitted,
Elwynn Murray, Jr.

NORTH CAROLINA BAPTIST HOSPITAL

Believing that North Carolina Baptists have a right and a responsibility to know as much as possible about their institutions, we submit the following information on Baptist Hospital:
With 673 beds in use, the hospital admitted 23,350 patients during the past year and provided a total of 210,000 days of patient care. There were 65,381 additional visits to the hospital's out-patient clinics and the emergency room. These patients came from across North Carolina, from other states, and even from other countries to receive the specialized hospital care which our institution offers.

Many of these patients received traditional types of hospital and medical care, but others benefited from new procedures: (1) a new method of delivering anti-cancer drugs by means of an "infusion pump," which is implanted in the patient somewhat like a pacemaker for heart patients. For many patients this has proven to be a more effective and more convenient form of chemotherapy. (2) A new type of x-ray called "digital radiography," used principally for examination of blood vessels, which virtually eliminates expensive and cumbersome x-ray film. This method uses less radiation and requires less dye than standard angiography. It also requires less time and can sometimes be done on an outpatient basis. It is expected that this method can eventually be used in many areas of the body where x-rays are required. (3) A new type of dialysis for patients with kidney disease called "continuous ambulatory peritoneal dialysis," which involves leaving a special fluid within the peritoneal cavity for several hours while impurities (normally removed by the kidney) are taken from the blood. This type of dialysis not only frees the patient from dependence on a machine but it is also less expensive than the more conventional forms of dialysis. The Pastoral Care Department continues to provide a pastoral ministry to both in-patients and out-patients and to their families. During the past year, chaplains made a total of 48,209 visits with patients. They provided 923 "on call ministries" and led 262 worship services in Davis Chapel. The Pastoral Counseling Division provided 8,684 hours of counseling for 855 persons. A total of 63 students were enrolled in various levels of clinical - pastoral education. The Winston-Salem center and also the satellites in Fayetteville, Raleigh, Morganton, and Charlotte all continued to experience growth both in the types of services provided as well as in the number of people served.

During the year, our hospital again received a two-year approval by the Joint Commission on Accreditation of Hospitals.

Despite many economic pressures, our hospital continues to operate in the black. It has recently adopted a budget for the new fiscal year which for the first time exceeds $100,000,000.

Gifts from churches during the past year through the Cooperative Program amounted to $479,997 and through the North Carolina Missions Offering and designated gifts totalled $345,765. We are indeed grateful to the churches and their members for this continuing financial support.

Respectfully submitted,
Gerald Quinn

STEWARDSHIP REPORT

Developing Christian Stewards is imperative in the light of biblical teachings and the Bold mission thrust of giving every person in the world an opportunity to head and respond to the gospel of Jesus Christ by the year 2000. This calls for faithful stewardship and growth in Christian giving. Having a Bold mission thrust stewardship presentation in every church is a major concern for 1983.

The Stewardship Commission of the SBC provides leadership,

practical aids, and biblically-based materials for assisting
churches in developing individual Christian stewards. The current
stewardship theme is "Give Boldly - Defining My Growing Commitment". Magnifying giving through the local church is a primary
emphasis.
  Providing year-round stewardship development activities will
help members grow spiritually. Tracts, activity guides, study
course books, visual aids, budget programs, and money management
materials are available to help churches in planning and conduct-
ing these activities. The materials cover the broad areas of stewardship education, missions, budget development and promotion,
and accounting.

WE RECOMMEND:
  1. That every church encourage its members to grow in the grace
     of giving, and in light of our BOLD mission thrust goals,
     to give a greater percentage of their income through their
     church.
  2. That every church accept the responsibility of teaching its
     members the principles of biblical stewardship and provide
     studies and activities throughout the year to accomplish
     this goal.
  3. That every church seek to increase its budget giving to the
     Cooperative Program and to the Associational Missions causes.
     We encourage each church to seek to increase their budget
     giving to the association to 3% of their budget income.
  4. That every church conduct a budget program that would em-
     phasize the importance of each individual member's giving
     and involvement in the life and work of the church.
  5. That every church elect and train a stewardship committee
     to assist the church in developing Christian stewards.
  6. That the association assist the churches in accomplishing
     their task of developing Christian stewards by providing
     information and/or a conference explaining the stewardship
     resources available to the churches.

                              Respectfully submitted,
                              James L. Hartsell

                PASTORAL SUPPORT COMMITTEE REPORT

  The Pastoral Support Committee, consisting of Davis Benton,
Chairman, Don Coley, W.K. Lewis, Charles Kirkland, and R.O. Sanderson, took the theme of "Support The Pastors" as our theme and
goal for 1981-82.
  We had our annual "Get-to-Know-You" Dinner for all new pastors
and their wives on July 23, 1982 at the Sizzlers Steak House in
Wallace. During the year, October 1, 1981 - September 30, 1982,
only one new pastor has come into our association.
  The committee has met and several promising events have been
planned for 1982-83. Two "Get-to-Know-You" Dinners have been
planned, February 18 and August 15, 1983. Two "Family Counseling
and Guidance" meetings are planned for April 15, and September 16,
1983. An all day Seminary on "Sermon Development" is planned for
February 21, 1983, led by Dr. J. Winston Pierce. A representative

                              28

from the Fayetteville Family Life Center will be invited to share in a Seminar on Counseling and Referrals, to be held on May 16, 1983.

It is the purpose and aim of the Pastoral Support Committee to support and strengthen the pastors and their families of the Eastern Baptist Association. May we always be aware of the needs of others!

Respectfully submitted,
Davis Benton, Chairman

CHURCH TRAINING REPORT

We have seen some very positive things happen this year in Church Training. We began our year in November with a very successful "M" Night. Then, in January, our Church Training team went to Caraway for the Regional Enabler Conference where we studied the book, "Equipping Disciples through Church Training". Those attending were Larry Padgett, New Member Training; Mike Lee, Youth; Jean Hatch, Children; and Greg Thornton.

In March we experienced one of the most successful Youth Nights the Association has held, with 20 churches represented with 171 in attendance. The program was led by the Matthis Puppetts from Ingold Baptist Church and singing group Morning Sky from Campbell University. Much of the success goes to our Youth leader, Michael Lee, who planned and coordinated this event, and who is now pastor of the Cape Carteret Baptist Church in Swansboro. The event was hosted by First Baptist Church in Warsaw.

In May, 1982 we had a very exciting Speakers Tournament and Bible Drill as many of our children, youth and senior-high youth participated. Many of them represented our Association in the regional tournament in Goldsboro.

Respectfully submitted,
Greg Thornton

BROTHERHOOD REPORT

Ninteen hundred eighty-two has been a year of training and planning to prepare our associational brotherhood leaders for a process of exercising Bold Mission Thrust for 1983. During the Key Leadership Conference in May special training was given to provide our Baptist Men (BM) and Royal Ambassador (RA) leaders with adequate information and knowledge to carry forth the purpose of their organizations - to teach Missions and encourage Mission Service.

This year we were fortunate in having leaders from the N.C. Brotherhood Department come to a training session at Warsaw Bapt. Church and encourage B.M. and R.A. organizations to use SBC printed materials and programs as an aid in planning and presenting weekly and monthly programs. Several churches which did not have B.M. groups indicated a desire to begin such work.

This summer our B.M. worked with Christian Social Ministries in a combined effort to provide a playground and shelter for migrant children at the Tri-County Health Clinic at Newton Grove.

During the winter months of 82-83, B.M. hope to construct several pieces of playground equipment for this same playground.

Goals for Brotherhood for 82-83

1. Train or retrain 3 associational Brotherhood officers
2. Involve Baptist Men officers and RA leaders in leadership training
3. Involve associational men in inspiration and promotion
4. Provide individual assistance for 3 church Baptist Men groups
5. Involve Crusaders from 10 churches in fellowship and sports
6. Involve RA's in sports activities.
7. Assist churches that desire to improve existing RA chapters
8. Assist in training 10 persons to teach Foreign Mission and Home Mission Study books

The Associational Brotherhood Department exists for the sole purpose of bringing men and boys to a saving knowledge of Jesus Christ. Our desire is to assist you in any way.

Please call us. TO HIM BE THE GLORY!

Respectfully submitted,
Charles Kirkland

LIBRARY COMMITTEE REPORT

Participating in the mission to be of mutual assistance in their endeavor to grow stronger Christians and reach new persons for Christ, the Associational media/library committee has carried out the following tasks:

Purchased new books for associational office to be made available for individual or group study.
Encouraged observance of Media/Library Week with special emphasis on display and use of mission books.
Assisted 3 churches with individual conferences
Held a two-night workshop at Clinton First Baptist Church
Key leadership conference at Warsaw was a time of sharing experiences encountered at Ridgecrest by media staff from Poston.
Plans were discussed for Media Library Week at Ridgecrest in 1983.
Rowan Media/Library center was the focal point for a conference with staff members from Grove Park.

Respectfully submitted,
Thelma Davis, Chairman

EVANGELISM REPORT

Reports were good from our "Here's Hope" Joint Evangelistic Crusade held in March and April of this year. Interpretation Meetings were held across the state to suggest plans and basic thrusts for the Joint Crusade effort, sponsored jointly by the Baptist State Convention of North Carolina and the General Baptist Convention. Many of our churches conducted "People Search" and "Lay Evangelist Schools", followed by local revivals. February 28 through March 7 was set aside for special prayer in preparation for our Associational Simultaneous Revivals.

Churches were grouped together and came together for a special service and prayer in preparation for our revivals. March 14-28 we had our Simultaneous Revivals throughout the Eastern Association. We have had good reports from most of our churches and we give God the praise and glory for what He has done.

"Here's Hope North Carolina" was the theme for the 36th annual Statewide Evangelism Conference, February 8-9, 1982 in Greensboro, with 2500 people in attendance; the best consistant attendance in recent years.

On February 1, 1982, J.W. Hutchens, Jr. became the Director of the Division of Evangelism for the Baptist State Convention of North Carolina.

The Statewide Evangelism Conference for 1983 will be held in Charlotte's Ovens Auditorium during February 7-8, 1983, with Dr. Wayne Ward leading Bible Study; Dr. Landrum Leavell, Dr. B.O. Baker, Dr. Joe Ford preaching, and Dick Baker leading the music.

For 1983, our emphasis will be on Growing an Evangelistic Church, and CWT will be the new witness training method, some pilot churches have already started the programs.

Respectfully submitted,
Phillip R. Denton

MISSIONS COMMITTEE REPORT

Opportunities for mission action abound in virtually every section of our world. The Missions Committee of the EASTERN BAPTIST ASSOCIATION exists to help explore new areas of involvement, to encourage and aid churches in both individual and cooperative ventures in missions, and to develop ministries to meet local needs and opportunities. Developing long-range and annual planning is essential to effectively achieve this purpose. To this end we strive. Funds were made available this past year to begin a half-time Christian Social Ministries program. Rev. Paula Clayton was enlisted to fill the position of Christian Social Ministries Director. A Pilot Project in Migrant Ministries was carried out under the able direction of Miss Clayton. Work began on a ten-weeks summer program in June. Four summer workers spearheaded this ministry with volunteers from several churches assisting. Two of the workers directed a child development program at the Tri-County Community Health Center and two workers directed the work at the Migrant Ministries Center in the old King Methodist Church. Numerous articles of clothing were given to those in need, as well as health kits.

Worship services were conducted in Spanish and Creole. Two mission tour groups participated in ministries in migrant camps along with church groups from within the association. Many good things happened as a result of hard work, planning, cooperation and prayer.

Hopefully we will see ministries for the blind, deaf, illiterate and many others in the future. Possibilities abound for other ministries. Where will these opportunities for ministry lead us in the future? What new avenues of service will be developed? These are questions to which only time will reveal answers. With continued prayer, hard work, and sacrifice much can be done. Hopefully we can count on you to help.

Respectfully submitted,
Michael Shook, Chairman

ASSOCIATIONAL COUNCIL REPORT

The Associational Council met the Association's constitutional requirements of four quarterly meetings for the purpose of acting for the Association between Annual Meetings. Significant actions taken by the Associational Council are summarized below:

December 1, 1981 - Sharon Church was host to representatives from 27 churches. Routine reports were heard and committees approved.

JANUARY 5, 1982 - Representatives from 22 churches met at Mount Vernon Church. Paula Clayton, the new director of Christian Social Ministries was welcomed and at-large members were added to the Executive Committee.

April 6, 1982 - A quorum was not achieved; therefore, another meeting date was set for April 20 at Grove Park Church. Reports were given for information. Michael Shook displayed a certificate from the Baptist State Convention in recognition of 97.5% of Eastern Association churches having Vacation Bible Schools in 1981.

April 20, 1982 - Twenty-four churches were represented at Grove Park Church. Approval was given for the Missions Committee to appeal to the churches for a special offering to support the work with migrant farm laborers. Paula Clayton reported on plans underway for migrant ministries and called attention to the $168.00 gift having been received from the Associational WMU. She presented a list of anticipated expenditures amounting to $5,950.00.

July 27, 1982 - Grove Park Church was host to representatives from 26 churches. Significant actions taken by the Council were as follows: approved of returning to the Reserve Fund $33000.00 which had been advanced to Migrant Ministries at an earlier date; approved the purchase of a copier for the Association office; approved a motion that interest from investment of funds received from sale of the missionary home be used for housing when needed or be re-deposited in the interest-bearing account when not needed. John Flake, acting in the absence of the moderator, appointed two committees -

CONSTITUTION COMMITTEE: Davis Benton, Chairman
                         John Braswell
                         Farrell Miller
COMMITTEE-ON-COMMITTEES: Don Coley, Chairman
                         Tony Gurganus
                         James P. Brown
                         Freddie Harris
                         R.C. Garris

                              Respectfully submitted,
                              Lucille Yancey, Clerk

                    SUNDAY SCHOOL REPORT

    The Sunday School officers attended special training in Fayette-
ville, North Carolina on January 12, 1982 for the purpose of
becoming better equipped to assist churches in our association.
Plans were made for the 1982 Sunday School leaders training conference to be held in Warsaw, September 27-28; due to a conflict
of meetings, this conference was rescheduled for November 1-2.
The books to be studied this year are the HOW TO GUIDE series.
They are excellent helps for Sunday School teachers and we encourage all of our churches to make it possible for their teachers
to participate.
    It has been a privilege for me to serve as your Sunday School
director for these past two years.
    Now, may I commend to you, Rev. Jim Hartsell who will be serv-
ing as Associational Sunday School director. Jim is a state approved worker and is highly qualified in the area of Sunday School
work. We are looking forward to a great year with Jim and the
Assist Team as we strive to enlarge and improve our Sunday School
work.

                              Respectfully submitted,
                              Don Coley, Director

                VACATION BIBLE SCHOOL REPORT

    One-hundred one VBS Workers from 17 churches received training
in the Church VBS Workers Clinic held in Warsaw April 20, 1982.
    Associational VBS Workers who received training earlier in the
STATE VBS CLINIC led the conferences.
    At the time of this report, 32 churches had reported having a
VBS.
    Those reporting are:

Church	Enroll-ment	Avg. Att.	No. Days	Hours Daily	Prof. Faith	Miss Off.	Achieve-ment
Alum Springs	34	32	2	2½	0	30.00	Merit
Beulah	72	69	5	2	0	50.00	*
Brown	75	60	5	2¼	0	65.00	Merit
Calvary	20	18	5	2	0	37.00	Advanced
Calypso	60	48	5	2½	0	24.00	*
Clinton, First	150	131	7	2½	16	101.00	Advanced
Concord	72	69	6	2½	0	23.00	Advanced
Corinth	59	48	5	2½	0	70.00	Advanced
Evergreen	59	49	5	3	0	55.00	Advanced
Faison	101	68	6	2½	3		*
Garland	87	70	5	3	0	42.00	*
Garner's Chapel	32	30	5	2	0	30.00	Merit
Grove Park	123	86	5	2½	0	120.00	Merit
Immanuel	116	88	5	2½	0	-0-	*
Ingold	39	37	5	2	0	52.00	Merit
Island Creek	85	65	5	2	0	22.00	*
Johnson	75	66	5	2½	0	64.00	Merit
Kenansville	69	65	5	3	0	42.00	Merit
Mount Olive	112	92	5	3	0	35.00	Merit
Mount Vernon	40	37	5	2	2	23.00	Merit
New Hope	49	35	5	2	0	47.00	Merit
Piney Grove	122	88	5	2	0	-0-	Spec. Honor
Poston	95	87	5	3	3	87.00	Merit
Rose Hill	91	82	5	3	0	19.81	*
Rowan	119	110	5	3	0	47.00	Distin-guished
Sharon	87	69	5	3	0	85.00	Merit
Siloam	35	35	6	2½	0	36.00	Advanced
Teachey	42	24	5	2	0	28.00	*
Turkey	96	69	5	2½	0	20.00	*
Union Grove	44	36	5	2½	0	23.00	*
Warsaw	137	110	5	3	3	49.00	*
Wells Chapel	49	44	5	2½	0	44.00	Merit

*Achievement not indicated on report.

CHURCH MUSIC REPORT

On January 18-19, 1982, a music workshop was held in the Warsaw Baptist Church under the leadership of Charles Gatwood from the Baptist State Convention. Seventeen churches were represented with a total attendance of 92. Through this workshop, choir members were taught the basics of music reading and choir directors were given several suggestions on rehearsal procedures and performances.

The associational music director attended the Key Leadership Conference in May, 1982, and as an outgrowth of this training, led the Associational Bold Missions Rally in September. Eighteen choir directors attended this conference. Special music for revivals and associational meetings has been provided throughout the year.

As we look toward another year in our association, may we continue to work together and strive to provide music that first and foremost, brings honor and glory to the name of our Lord.

Respectfully submitted,
Jean Hatch, Director

EASTERN BAPTIST ASSOCIATION
BUDGET - 1982-83

A. MISSION ADVANCE
1. Mount Olive College BSU $ 200.00
  Sub-total $ 200.00

B. ASSOCIATION OFFICE
1. Equipment and Repairs   300.00
2. Routine Printing and Minutes   1,900.00
3. Office Supplies   900.00
4. Postage   1,000.00
5. Telephone   900.00
  Sub-total   5,000.00

C. SALARIES
1. Director of Missions   11,500.00
2. Director of Christian Social Min.   4,750.00
3. Secretary   4,800.00
  Sub-total   21,050.00

D. OTHER PERSONNEL EXPENSE
1. Retirement and Insurance   2,600.00
2. Social Security   312.00
3. Housing: Director of Missions   5,900.00
   Director of Christian Social Min.   1,000.00
4. Travel: Director of Missions   3,600.00
   Director of Christian Social Min.   1,500.00
5. Conventions and Conferences   600.00
  Sub-total   15,512.00

E. EDUCATION AND PROMOTION
1. General Promotion and Training   1,000.00
2. Sunday School   700.00
3. Church Training   660.00
4. Brotherhood   300.00
5. Womans Missionary Union   750.00
6. Church Music   250.00
7. Sudio-Visuals   100.00
8. Evangelism Committee   250.00
9. Stewardship Committee   600.00
10. Missions Committee   7,100.00
11. Pastors Support Committee   545.00
12. Library Committee   150.00
13. Pastors Conference   350.00
  Sub-total   12,755.00

F. MISCELLANEOUS
1. Unforeseen Expenses   300.00
  Sub-total   300.00

TOTAL BUDGET $54,817.00

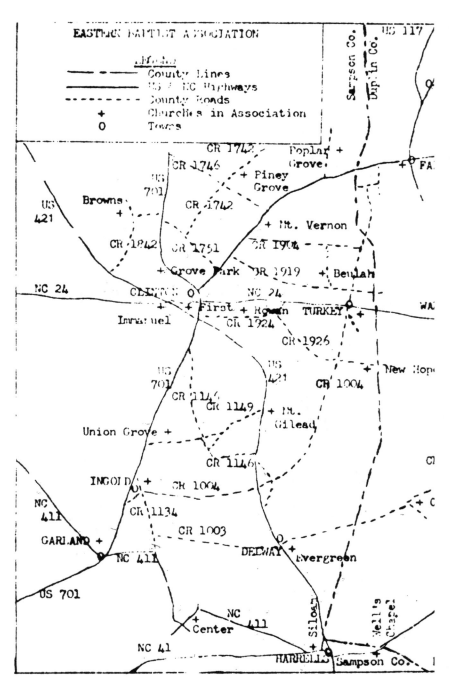

EASTERN BAPTIST ASSOCIATION

Legend
——— • —— County Lines
——————— US & NC Highways
- - - - - - - County Roads
    +   Churches in Association
    O   Towns

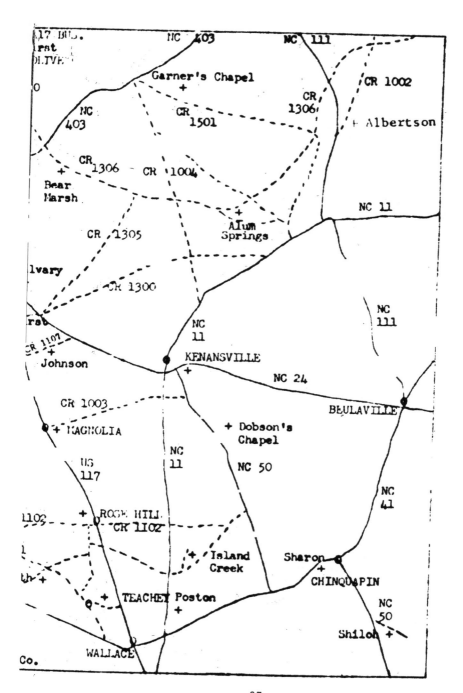

TREASURER'S REPORT

BROUGHT FORWARD October 1, 1981 $ 3,596.52
    (Employees W/h Included $90.63)

RECEIPTS
    Undesignated:
        Church Contributions   34,453.65
        Interest from NOW Account   192.34
        Total Undesignated   34,645.99
    Designated:
        Baptist State Convention:
          Youth and Family Min.   200.01
          Christian Social Min. 5,374.98
          Total   5,574.98
        Churches for Minutes   1,028.17
        Arteaga Fund   2,779.61
        Migrant Ministry Fund   6,337.43
        Baptist Center Fund   204.48
        Total Designated   15,923.67
    Refunds:
        To Convention Expenses   450.00
        North Carolina Sales Tax   102.10
        To General Promotion and Train.   425.00
        Total Refunds   977.10
    Transferred:
        From Bap. Cen. Fund (NOW Acc.)   42.17
        From Reserve Fund for Mi. Min.   3,300.00
        From Int. on Fund from Sa. of
          Home   3,220.76
        Total Transferred   6,562.93
TOTAL RECEIPTS   58,110.69

TOTAL RECEIPTS PLUS AMOUNT BROUGHT FORWARD   61,707.21

DISBURSMENTS
    ASSOCIATIONAL OFFICE
        Equipment and Repairs   329.00
        Printing   1,148.67
        Office Supplies   1,068.65
        Postage   1,105.21
        Telephone   831.99
        Total   4,483.52
    SALARIES
        Director of Missions   10,400.01
        Dir. of Christian Social Min.   2,375.00
        Secretary   4,137.88
        Total   16,912.89
    OTHER PERSONNEL EXPENSE
        Retirement and Insurance   2,607.60
        Soc. Sec. (Em. part)   255.26
        Housing:
         Director of Missions 5,900.00
         Director of CSM   1,000.00
         Total   6,900.00
        Travel:
         Director of Mis.   3,000.00
         Director of CSM   750.00

38

```
        3,750.00
          705.00
               14,217.86

   in.1,222.69
        395.67
        364.99
        205.08
        179.63
         -0-
         98.00
        249.60
        268.10
        280.79
        148.65
         43.67
               3,456.87
                  -0-
                200.59
   S                        39,271.73

             3,000.00
             2,529.61
             7,230.55
   TURES                   12,760.16
                                      52,031.89

             3,300.00
   ND          246.65
                           3,546.65
   NSFERRED FUNDS                    55,578.54
                                      6,128.67
   holdings                            167.01
   1982                               6,295.68

OSIT IN SOUTHERN BANK AND TRUST

   1981
             22,394.00
              2,501.24
              3,104.76
                                     28,000.00

              3,220.76
                453.12
                229.28
                                      3,903.16

Ctr. Fund) 1,467.46
r. Fund)     246.65
Fund)      3,300.00
                                      5,014.11
BROUGHT FORWARD                      36,917.27
```

DISBURSEMENTS:
    Transferred from Reserve to General
                        Fund   3,300.00
    Trans. from Home Sale to
            General Fund-Housing   3,220.76
    TOTAL DISBURSEMENTS   6,520.76
BALANCE Re-deposited September 30, 1982 $30,396.51

SUMMARY
October 1, 1982

CERTIFICATE OF DEPOSIT
    Fund from Sale of Home   22,394.00
    Baptist Center Fund   4,668.47
    Reserve Fund   3,334.04
    TOTAL   30,396.51
GENERAL FUND:
    Total on deposit in Southern Bank and Trust,
        (October 1, 1982) $36,692.19

CHURCHES' CONTRIBUTIONS TO ASSOCIATIONAL MISSIONS

CHURCH	1980	1981	1982
Albertson	154.00	166.00	150.00
Alum Springs	250.00	250.00	300.00
Bear Marsh	300.00	300.00	300.00
Beulah	530.33	606.42	696.31
Brown	253.50	350.00	350.00
Calvary	699.93	633.96	875.49
Calypso	280.00	280.00	280.00
Center	467.06	387.53	527.76
Clinton, First	3,300.00	1,900.00	3,350.00
Concord	321.98	366.87	636.80
Corinth	1,320.00	1,440.00	1,440.00
Dobson Chapel	326.18	390.18	745.70
Evergreen	240.00	240.00	240.00
Faison	339.70	440.01	470.49
Garland	511.07	939.01	1,036.19
Garner's Chapel	135.00	150.00	150.00
Grove Park	1,858.19	1,521.63	1,635.96
Immanuel	2,990.00	3,329.00	3,332.00
Ingold	350.00	400.00	400.00
Island Creek	240.00	240.00	600.00
Johnson	509.72	613.66	748.58
Kenansville	300.00	300.00	300.00
Magnolia	618.08	695.20	642.07
Mount Gilead	1,693.00	1,326.73	825.00
Mount Olive	1,937.50	2,375.00	2,875.00
Mount Vernon	300.00	400.00	400.00
New Hope	400.00	550.00	650.00
Piney Grove	300.00	375.00	225.00
Poplar Grove	66.00	398.24	398.24
Poston	780.00	1,000.00	1,500.00
Rose Hill	1,050.00	1,006.00	1,196.00
Rowan	985.00	1,110.00	1,385.00

aron	650.00	766.40	860.00
iloh	560.98	624.14	766.47
loam	380.00	380.00	380.00
achey	575.00	450.00	500.00
rkey	655.20	860.88	907.20
ion Grove	146.25	132.07	197.69
rsaw	1,436.40	1,452.00	1,452.00
lls Chapel	662.40	679.66	728.70
TALS	$28,872.46	$29,825.59	$34,453.65

Respectfully submitted,
Donald Pope, Treasurer

CONSTITUTION COMMITTEE REPORT
(As Amended)

e Constitution Committee recommends the following Constitutional changes:

I. That Article VIII be changed:

From: ARTICLE VIII. ASSOCIATIONAL COUNCIL

The Association shall have an Associational Council consisting of the Moderator, Vice Moderator, Clerk, Associate Clerk, Treasurer, Associate Treasurer, Director of Missions, Associational Church Music Director, Associational Sunday School Director, Associational Church Training Director, Associational Brotherhood, Associational WMU Director, Associational representative to denominational agencies, each active and retired pastor in the association and one lay member from each church to be elected by the church whose name shall be included in the church letter to the association.

To: ARTICLE VIII, EXECUTIVE BOARD

The Association shall have an Executive Board consisting of the general officers of the association; the director of missions, the director of Christian social ministries, the directors of associational Brotherhood, Church Music, Church Training, Sunday School, and Womans Missionary Union; the chairpersons of associational standing committees, each active and retired pastor in the association; and two lay persons (men or women) from each church to be elected by the church and whose name shall be included in the church letter to the association.

II. That a new article be added as follows:

ARTICLE IX. ASSOCIATIONAL COUNCIL

The Association shall have an Associational Council consisting of the officers of the Executive Board; the directors of Brotherhood, Church Music, Church Training, Sunday School, and Womans Missionary Union; the committee chairpersons of Evangelism, Media/Library, Missions, Pastoral Support, and Stewardship; the director of Christian Social Ministries; and the director of missions.

III. That a new article be added as follows:

ARTICLE X. COMMITTEES

The Association shall have such committees as may be deemed necessary for orderly and efficient achievement of the Association's purpose. Membership on standing committees shall be on the rotating basis with one-third of the

members rotating off each year. Members completing a
three year term shall not be eligible for re-election
until one year has passed. A member elected to fill an
unexpired term shall be eligible for election to a full
term following the completion of the unexpired term.
IV. That all articles following Article X be renumbered as
follows:
ARTICLE XI, ARTICLE XII, ARTICLE XIII, ARTICLE XIV

The Constitution Committee recommends the following by-laws
changes:
I. That wherever the names "Associational Council" and "Executive Committee" appear in the By-Laws appropriate editing
be done to conform to the Constitution as amended, and that
the number of members on the various standing committees
be adjusted to facilitate the rotation system.
II. That section D of Article III be deleted and provisions
for election of committees be included under Article IV.
III. That Article IV be changed as follows:
1. Change Article IV DUTIES OF COMMITTEES to Article IV
COMMITTEES
2. Change section A from ASSOCIATIONAL COUNCIL COMMITTEES
to STANDING COMMITTEES and list Standing Committees in
keeping with the Constitution as amended.
3. Sub-section 1 of section A. be deleted, and that the
content of this sub-section be contained in a new article (see recommendation IV below).
4. That sub-section 1 under Section A be as follows:
1. ELECTION OF COMMITTEES: All committee members shall
be persons who have demonstrated talent for performing the work of the committee, or who have stated a
willingness to receive training to equip them for the
work of the committee.
Standing Committees shall be formed from a slate of
persons selected, notified, secured to serve, and
nominated by the Committee on Committees. The nominees, then, must be elected by the Association in
its annual session. Special committees shall be recommended when deemed appropriate to perform the
business and ministry of the Association, and are
subject to the approval of the Executive Board. These
committee posts shall be filled by the Committee on
Committees from a slate of persons selected, notified,
secured to serve, nominated, and presented to and
elected by the Executive Board. These committees
shall have definitely prescribed duties and a definite term of service before they are established.
5. Change sub-section 2 MISSION COMMITTEE:
From: The Missions Committee shall be composed of seven
(7) members whose duties shall be to work with the
director of missions in discovering, analyzing,
and presenting mission opportunities to the Association for mission action. The Brotherhood director and the Woman's Missionary Union director
shall be members of the Missions Committee. The
chairman of the committee shall make periodic reports to the Associational Council and to the Association at its annual session.

TO: MISSIONS COMMITTEE: The Missions Committee shall
        be composed of three (3) at large members, the
        chairpersons of standing committees whose duties
        relate to Christian Social Ministries, the di-
        rector of Christian Social Ministries, and the
        associational directors of Brotherhood and Womans
        Missionary Union. The rotation system shall apply
        to the three at-large members only. Chair persons
        from other committees shall be rotated from with-
        in their individual committees. The Missions Com-
        mittee shall work with the director of Christian
        Social Ministries in discovering, analyzing, and
        presenting to the Association opportunities for
        mission action; and in coordination of the as-
        sociation's mission activities. Upon determining
        that new committees are needed to direct specific
        social ministries, the Missions Committee shall
        bring to the attention of the Executive Board the
        need for such committees. The Missions Committee
        shall work with the director of Christian Social
        Ministries in writing the prescription as re-
        quired by ARTICLE IV of the By-Laws.
  6. Add the following sentence to Article IV section A sub-
     section 3:
     "The Stewardship Committee shall have the financial re-
     cords of the Association audited annually."
  7. Discontinue the Audit Committee from the list of Stand-
     ing Committees.
IV. That two new articles be added as follows:
          ARTICLE VI. ASSOCIATIONAL COUNCIL
  A. Purpose - The purpose of the Associational Council shall
     be to provide a consultative, advisory, and coordinative
     service to the Association and its various programs and
     committees.
  B. Duties - The duties of the Associational Council shall be:
     provide for communication between the associational of-
     ficers, organizations, and committees; study church needs
     in the association and needs of the people in the area of
     the Association; propose long-range and short-range goals
     for the Association; prepare and recommend plans for in-
     volving organizations and committees appropriately in at-
     taining goals; review and coordinate plans made by the
     organizations and committees and relate these to the at-
     tainment of goals; evaluate the use of resources; and re-
     port through appropriate channels progress made toward at-
     tainment of associational goals. The Council shall exercise
     general supervision of the work of the director of mis-
     sions. In the event the position of director of missions
     becomes vacant, The Council shall recommend to the As-
     sociation or the Executive Board for approval, a search
     committee whose duties shall be to seek prayerfully a
     person to fill the position.
  C. Officers - The officers of the Associational Council shall
     be the chairman and the secretary. The moderator shall
     serve as chairman as determined by the Council. The as-
     sociational clerk shall be the secretary. In the absence
     of the secretary, the chairman shall appoint a temporary
     secretary.

ARTICLE VII BY-LAWS CHANGES

These by-laws may be amended on the second day of any annual session by a vote of the majority of the messengers present and voting provided the proposed changes have been presented on the first day of the annual session.

OUR BELOVED DEAD

ALBERTSON:

ALUM SPRINGS: Mrs. Randolph Taylor

BEAR MARSH: Mr. George Davis
Ms. Ina Swinson
Mr. Randall Hargrove
Ms. Vennie Hargrove
Mrs. Jack Cherry
Mrs. Major Barwick

BEULAH:

BROWNS: Mrs. Fannie Herring
Mrs. Myra Tew Robinson
Mrs. Carol Britt

CALVARY: Deacon Bland Raynor

CALYPSO: Mr. Atwood S. Harris
Mrs. Julia Byrd Waller
Mrs. Inez Nunn Davis

CENTER:

CLINTON FIRST: Mrs. Cober Burge
Mrs. Mary B. Autry
Mrs. E.B. Hales
Mrs. Mary Brantley
Mr. Oliver Barfield
Miss Lucille Peterson
Mrs. Donna McLamb Heath
Mrs. Sallie Pike
Mrs. Paul Shipp
Miss Jane Thompson
Mrs. Viola Bennett
Mrs. Elma Williamson
Mrs. Ada Hargrove
Mrs. Margaret Jordan
Mr. Bennie Weeks

CONCORD: Mr. Lloyd Williams
Mrs. Mazie Herring

CORINTH: Mr. Raymond Knowles
Mr. Wallace Ellis
Mr. John (Buddy) Pike
Mr. Clifton Savage

Mr. Adrian Teachey
Mrs. Mary Rouse Dobson
Mrs. Docia Brock

Mr. Hampton Hobbs
Mrs. Susan Kennedy
Mrs. Minnie Brock
Mr. Bobby Cottle

Mr. Jay Roberson
Mr. Ed Royall
Mr. Hubert Howard
Deacon H.A. Jackson

Mr. Curtis Clewis
Mrs. Emma Bearfield

Mrs. Annie F. Blackburn

Mr. Ben Rivenbark
Mr. Herring Mobley
Mrs. Vada Cavenaugh
Mrs. Katie Teachey

Mrs. Mildred Carlton
Mr. J.D. West

Mrs. Betsy J. Sharpe
Mr. Adrian Bostic
Ms. Carolyn Hall

Mr. Owen Bishop
Mr. John David Brooks
Ms. Laura Merritt
Mr. Glenn Tucker
Ms. Minnie Wood
Ms. Bessie Rackley

Mr. Fred Carter
Mr. Albert Bland
Mrs. Nettie Matthis

ST: Ms. Rachel Jennette
        Ms. Lillie B. Bird
        Mr. D.O. Thompson
        Ms. Thelma Davis
        Mrs. Mattie Williams
        Mr. Ray Scarborough
        Ms. Anna Jones
        Mrs. W.B. Murray, Sr.
        Mrs. J.F. Troutman
        Mrs. Lula King

45

MOUNT VERNON:

NEW HOPE: Mrs. Livvie Corbett
                            Mrs. Edna Johnson

PINEY GROVE: Mr. William D. Casey
                            Mrs. Maie Thornton
                            Mrs. Cannie Belle Brewer

POPLAR GROVE:

POSTON: Mrs. Florence Watkins
                            Mrs. Dorothy Register

ROSE HILL: Deacon W.S. Butler
                            Mr. W.E. Cole
                            Mr. M.E. Edwards
                            Mrs. Selma Teachey

ROWAN: Mrs. Nell Hall
                            Mrs. C.P. Hairr
                            Mr. Alman D. Strickland
                            Mr. King Byrd
                            Mr. William D. Waters
                            Mr. Elliott Chesnutt
                            Deacon Gilbert Chesnutt
                            Mr. R.J. Rackley, Jr.
                            Deacon Frank Wallace
                            Mr. Owen Malpass

SHARON: Mr. Butler Cavenaugh
                            Mrs. Plina Pierce

SHILOH: Mrs. Rubena Jones
                            Mr. James Turner
                            Mr. Luther Brown

SILOAM: Mr. Cecil Sawyer
                            Mrs. Ida Johnson Bostic
                            Mr. A.D. Vernelson

TEACHEY: Mrs. Dorothy K. Peterson
                            Mr. W.E. (Sam) Wells

TURKEY: Mrs. Eva West
                            Mr. H.W. Pope, Jr.
                            Mrs. Rosa Meyer

UNION GROVE: Mrs. Eula Hairr

WARSAW: Ms. Martha Potter
                            Mrs. Carrie Revelle
                            Ms. Arlene Jones
                            Deacon Claud Divine
                            Ms. Marion Creech
                            Mrs. Rosa Powell, Retired Missionary
                                to Nigeria

CHAPEL: Mrs. Thelma Bland
                 Deacon R.S. Highsmith

HISTORY OF FIRST BAPTIST CHURCH OF MOUNT OLIVE

First Baptist Church of Mount Olive was organized in
r, 1863, by a group of Baptists in the Thunder Swamp Baptist
. The original building was erected on Breazeale Avenue and
e Streets. C. Peter Bogart of Goldsboro was the pastor, and
were 19 members.
1875 the church building was moved to the present site at
rner of North Chestnut and West John Streets. John Nicholas
ngs was pastor at the time, and membership stood at 131. In
911, this church building was sold, and moved across the
from the church site to serve as a dwelling. Then began
n a new church structure, to cost "not less than $10,000."
il 7, 1912, was a happy day for members of the church. Sun-
hool and preaching services were held in the new church,
gh the sanctuary was not completed until June 16, 1912. Dr.
m B. Oliver was the pastor.
bers of the church will also remember the excitement and
they felt when the pipe organ, with chimes, was installed
ember, 1927, at a cost of $5,000. Pastor Samuel I. Naff
ly stimulated interest in purchasing the pipe organ, but
aged the church in beginning Vacation Bible School in the
of 1928. The school was successful, with an enrollment

ius Paul Gulley became pastor of the church in March, 1937.
ived interest in all phases of the church program. The
t Training Union for all ages was organized, and six young
's organizations formed. Young Women's Auxiliary; two Girls
aries; two Royal Ambassador groups; and one Sunbeam band.
. membership grew from about 400 to 500 during his pastorate.
nted the seeds of growth which eventually culminated in the
uction of a new educational building.
was during the pastorate of John Wesley Lambert that the
. began a building fund for an educational building. During
storate, which extended from 1944 to 1949, the church pur-
. property from Jack Knowles to be used as the church annex.
uring these years the Rev. L.R. (Billy) Brock, a native of
Olive and member of the church, was ordained as a minister.
now serving as a Southern Baptist missionary in Brazil.
October 31, 1954, during the pastorate of Theodore W. (Ted)
ms, the church declared itself ready to proceed with plans
e educational building. However, it was not until 1959,
the leadership of Milton James Boone, that plans were
ly drawn. The church purchased the Knowles property on the
of Center and John Streets for $22,500. The house, most
ly the dwelling of Mrs. Eva Knowles, widow of Henry Knowles
zed in 1961 and on April 23, 1961, ground-breaking services
eld for the new educational building, expected to cost
91.
20, 1962, was a memorable day for it was then the new
ional building was occupied and dedicated, with Dr. Herman
of the N.C. State Baptist Convention's Sunday School Depart-
preaching the dedicatory sermon. The modern plant was
ted and furnished at a total cost of $215,000.

47

On September 7, 1969, a sanctuary renovation study committee was named by the church. October 1, 1969, Anthony Z. Gurganus became pastor of the church. On January 13, 1970, the church made its final payment on the educational building, and the note was burned in special services at the church, held during the time Mount Olive was noting its centennial celebration.

Mrs. Effie Martin Matthis, lifetime faithful member of the church, had willed the church $16,864.48 and with this starting fund plans began to take shape to renovate the sanctuary. Conrad Wessell, Goldsboro architect, was retained. In May, 1972, workmen moved in to begin the work, and the first act was dismantling of the organ. June 11, 1972, was the last Sunday on which services were held in the old sanctuary.

During the year of renovation work all congregational meetings were held in the fellowship hall of the educational building, and it was in this room that Mr. Gurganus conducted three worship services each Sunday-at 9 and 11 a.m., and 7:30 p.m.

On Sunday, June 24, 1973, in an "Opening the Doors" ceremony, keys to the newly-renovated sanctuary were presented to the chairmen of the renovation committee, and Russell Kelly opened the doors officially to the church congregation.

The dedication ceremony was delayed until new pulpit furniture could be installed. Upon completion of the installation of this furniture a dedication date of Sunday, November 11, 1973, was approved by the membership.

In 1978, under the leadership of the pastor, the church began the Family Ministry Plan for the Diaconate consisting of 16 deacons and 16 co-workers to minister to the church congregation.

During 1979 First Baptist voted to call a full time Minister of Education. Miss Wilda Armstrong came to the church to fill this position. Miss Rose Pleasant is now Minister of Education.

The church lost a long time member, and beloved custodian, Nick Uzzell in the year 1979. As a result of Nick's death, a security system was installed in his memory, in the education plant.

In 1982, Vee Williams resigned as Church Organist and Chancel Director, having served in this position for over 20 years. The church voted to hire a Choir Director and Organist. Mrs. Williams is now full time Church Secretary.

The year 1982 will be remembered long by the church congregation. This year the church paid off the note and is now completely debt-free! On October 3, a day of Homecoming, Thanksgiving and Note Burning was observed!

HISTORY OF MOUNT GILEAD BAPTIST CHURCH

The exact date Mount Gilead was organized is obscured by the lack of information. Early records indicate several denominations shared the Red Hill Union Meeting House. Baptist worshiped in the building as early as 1934. In 1842, Eastern Baptist Association met at Red Hill. Neither Red Hill nor Mount Gilead is listed among churches present at the organizational meeting of Eastern Baptist Association in 1827. Therefore, it is assumed the church began between 1827 and 1834 as Red Hill Baptist Church and later became Mount Gilead Baptist Church.

After the building burned, Jimmy Vann gave land and built a wood frame building on the present site in 1848. Additional buildings have been constructed through the years. Special mention is made in the records of the building erected in 1943 and dedicated in 1950. A steeple was added to the present building in 1971 and complete renovation of the sanctuary was made in 1974.

Music has had a prominent place in the life of Mount Gilead Church. A wind organ was purchased in 1906. The organ was replaced by a piano in 1930. Other musical instruments have been purchased since 1930.

The church has been influential in aiding men in their decision to accept their call to the ministry. Names mentioned in available records are: Billy Powell, L.M. Curtis, C.T. Tew, Leland (L.J.) Powell, K.E. Bryant, Bernice Bass and J.M. Alderman. Among missionaries to China sponsored by the church are such well known persons as T.L. Blalock and D.W. Herring.

Mount Gilead has been and still is, strong in the area of evangelism. Among the outstanding evangelists preaching revivals with good results are: Charles Howard, Forest C. Feezor, and Carl M. Townsend.

Records having been lost for a period of time, the names of all former pastors are not known. However, from available records those known to have served are: Hugh McAlphin, J.N. Stalling, J.L. Stewart, W.E. Crocker, Charles F. Hopper, John J. Douglas, J.M. Alderman, B.F. DeLoach, Fred Collins, L.L. Johnson, H.S. Swain, N.E. Gresham, T.H. King, N.D. Blackburn, W.R. Beach, W.D. Morris, R.F. Marshburn, Thomas Rich, Paul Curry, Claude Asburn, B.C. Lamb, Graham Elmore, Waldo Early (Interim) and Robert Phipps. Oliver Skerrett, the present pastor, came to the church in 1979.

YEAR	PLACE	MODERATOR	CLERK	PREACHER
1827	Beulah	James Matthews	J.L. Britt	J.B. Taylor
1828	South West	James Matthews	V.N. Seawell	W.M. Kennedy
1929	Limestone	James Matthews	J.R. Oliver	C.A. Jenkins
1830	Bull Tail	James Matthews	F.H. Ivey	W.B. Pope
1831	Island Creek	James Matthews	L.T. Carroll	J.B. Harrell
1832	Browns	James Matthews	J.T. Bland	Hiram Stallings
1833	Lisbon	W.J. indley	Allen Morriss	John Cornto
1834	Bear Marsh	W.J. indley	Allen Morriss	Allen Morriss
1835	Limestone	Georg Fennell	Allen Morriss	George Fennell
1836	Beaver Dam	W.J. indley	G.W. Hufham	H. Swinson
1837	Well's Chapel	W.J. indley	G.W. Hufham	George Fennell
1838	Rowans	James Mathis	G.W. Hufham	Hiram Stallings
1839	Johnson's	James Carroll	G.W. Hufham	G.W. Hufham
1840	Concord	James Carroll	G.W. Hufham	George Fennell
1841	Bear Mash	James Carroll	G.W. Hufham	G.W. Hufham
1842	Red Hi 1	James Carroll	G.W. Hufham	H. Stallings
1843	Beulah	James Carroll	G.W. Hufham	R. McNab
1844	Kenansville	Benjamin Oliver	J.G. Dickson	W.J. Findley
1845	Lebanon	James McDaniel	J.G. Dickson	David Rogers
1846	Wilmington	James McDaniel	J.G. Dickson	W.J. Findley
1847	Harriet's Chapel	James McDaniel	J.G. Dickson	David Thompson
1848	White Oak	James McDaniel	J.G. Dickson	Isaac W. West
1849	Mt. Gilead	James McDaniel	Robert McNab	James Rogers
1850	Bear Marsh	Benjamin Oliver	A.J. Battle	W.J. Findley
1851	Little Creek	G.W. Wallace	A.J. Battle	A.J. Battle
1852	New Hope	G.W. Wallace	A.J. Battle	D. Furman
1853	Moore's Creek	G.W. Wallace	D. Cashwell	L.F. Williams
1854	Beulah	G.W. Wallace	D. Cashwell	M.R. Forey
1855	Concord	G.W. Wallace	D. Cashwell	W.P. Riddle
1856	Boykin's Chapel	G.W. Wallace	G.W. Wallace	James McDaniel
1857	Warsaw	G.W. Wallace	G.W. Hufham	C.C. Gordon
1858	Bear Marsh	Benjamin Oliver	G.W. Hufham	G.W. Wallace
1859	Beaver Dam	Benjamin Oliver	Amos Royal	W.M. Kennedy
1860	Lebanon	Benjamin Oliver		G.W. Wallace

Year	Location			
1861	Piney Grove	Benjamin Oliver	J.G. Dickson	Hugh McAlpin
1862	Mt. Gilead	S.J. Faison	J.G. Dickson	J.B. Taylor
1863	Beulah	S.J. Faison	J.G. Dickson	J.L. Pritchard
1864	Boykin's Chapel	Owen Fennell	J.G. Dickson	G.W. Wallace
1865	Moore's Creek	Owen Fennell	J.G. Dickson	J.S. Wathall
1866	Union Chapel	W.M. Kennedy	J.N. Stallings	R.F. Marable
1867	Bear Marsh	W.M. Kennedy	J.N. Stallings	J.L. Pritchard
1868	Beulah	Hugh McAlphin	Isham Royal	Hugh McAlpin
1869	Lisbon	Hugh McAlphin	Isham Royal	W.M. Kennedy
1870	Well's Chapel	J.L. Stewart	Isham Royal	G.S. Best
1871	New Hope	Hugh McAlpin	Isham Royal	J.E. King
1872	Union Lenoir	Hugh McAlpin	Isham Royal	W.M. Kennedy
1873	Shiloh	Hugh McAlpin	Isham Royal	W.M. Young
1874	Island Creek	J.N. Stallings	Isham Royal	J.N. Stallings
1875	Beaufort	J.N. Stallings	Isham Royal	G.S. Best
1876	Mt. Olive	J.L. Stewart	Isham Royal	J.P. Faison
1877	Corinth	J.L. Stewart	Isham Royal	J.C. Hiden
1878	New Bern	J.L. Stewart	sham Royal	A.D. Cohen
1879	Piney Grove	J.L. Stewart	Isham Royal	J.N. Stallings
1880	Bethel	J.L. Stewart	Isham Royal	S.W. Westcot
1881	Magnolia	J.L. Stewart	J.R. Oliver	A.C. Dixon
1882	Emma's Chapel	J.L. Stewart	J.R. Oliver	F.H. Ivey
1883	Bethlehem	J.L. Stewart	J.L. Britt	J.R. Taylor
1884	Pollocksville	J.L. Stewart	J.L. Britt	J.W. Eason
1885	Mt. Olive	J.L. Stewart	J.L. Britt	J.L. Stewart
1886	Clinton	J.L. Stewart	J.L. Britt	C.C. Newton
1887	Well's Chapel	J.L. Stewart	J.L. Britt	T.H. Pritchard
1888	Warsaw	J.L. Stewart	J.L. Britt	F.R. Underwood
1889	Concord	J.L. Stewart	J.L. Britt	C.A. Jenkins
1890	Riley's Creek	J.L. Stewart	J.L. Britt	O.P. Meeks
1891	Dobson's Chapel	J.L. Stewart	Oliver Blackburr	J.L. Stewart
1892	Emma's Chapel	J.L. Stewart	Oliver Blackburr	O.P. Meeks
1893	Johnson's	J.L. Stewart	Oliver Blackburr	John Mitchell
1894	Lisbon	J.L. Stewart	A.R. Herring	A.A. Butler
1895	Corinth	S.D. Swaim	A.R. Herring	C.G. Wells
1896	Island Creek	S.D. Swaim	A.R. Herring	I.F. Bone
1897	Kenansville	J.L. Stewart	A.R. Herring	J.L. Stewart
1898	Harrell's Store	J.L. Stewart	A.R. Herring	

Year	Church			
1899	Mount Holly	J.L. Stewart	A.R. Herring	N.B. Cobb
1900	Mount Olive	J.L. Stewart	A.R. Herring	R.H. Gilbert
1901	Mount Gilead	J.L. Stewart	A.R. Herring	N.B. Cobb
1902	Hallsville	J.L. Stewart	A.R. Herring	J.M. Alderman
1903	Rose Hill	J.L. Stewart	A.R. Herring	J.L. Stewart
1904	New Hope	J.L. Stewart	A.F. Robinson	V.N. Johnson
1905	Mount Olive	C.E. Daniel	A.F. Robinson	J.H. Booth
1906	Lisbon	C.E. Daniel	A.F. Robinson	J.L. Stewart
1907	Clinton	C.E. Daniel	A.F. Robinson	C.M. Rock
1908	Warsaw	C.E. Daniel	H.L. Stewart	J.M. Page
1909	Corinth	C.E. Daniel	A.R. Herring	J.M. Alderman
1910	Bethel	C.E. Daniel	A.R. Herring	P.A. Anthony
1911	Rowan	C.E. Daniel	A.R. Herring	E.J. Harrell
1912	Bear Marsh	C.E. Daniel	A.R. Herring	W.B. Rivenbark
1913	Beulaville	C.E. Daniel	A.R. Herring	J.G. Newton
1914	Oak Vale	C.E. Daniel	A.R. Herring	B.G. Early
1915	Johnson's	C.E. Daniel	A.R. Herring	C.H. Cashwell
1916	Calypso	C.E. Daniel	A.L. Carlton	W.N. Johnson
1917	Piney Grove	C.E. Daniel	A.L. Carlton	R.H. Herring
1918	Concord	C.E. Daniel	A.L. Carlton	B.T. Vann
1919	Hallsville	H.L. Stewart	E.P. Blanchard	D.P. Harris
1920	Clinton	H.L. Stewart	E.P. Blanchard	R.W. Cawthon
1921	Siloam	H.L. Stewart	E.P. Blanchard	L.R. O'Brien
1922	Sharon	H.L. Stewart	E.P. Blanchard	R.T. Vann
1923	Corinth	H.L. Stewart	D.J. Middleton	J.M. Duncan
1924	Dobson's Chapel	H.L. Stewart	D.J. Middleton	G.W. Rollins
1925	Turkey	H.L. Stewart	D.J. Middleton	T.H. King
1926	Island Creek	T.H. King	C.I. Robinson	S.L. Naff
1927	Beulah	T.H. King	C.I. Robinson	J.H. Barnes
1928	Bear Marsh	H.L. Stewart	C.I. Robinson	W.R. Beach
1929	Ingold	H.L. Stewart	C.I. Robinson	C.V. Brooks
1930	Hallsville	H.L. Stewart	C.I. Robinson	E.N. Johnson
1931	New Hope	H.L. Stewart	C.I. Robinson	R.C. Foster
1932	Kenansville	F.W. McGowen	C.I. Robinson	T.H. Williams
1933	Mount Gilead	F.W. McGowen	C.I. Robinson	L.M. Holloway
1934	Concord	F.W. McGowen	C.I. Robinson	R.F. Marshburn
1935	Magnolia	F.W. McGowen	C.I. Robinson	L.L. Johnson
1936	Rowan	F.W. McGowen	C.I. Robinson	W.P. Page

Year	Church			
1937	Warsaw	F.W. McGowen	C.I. Robinson	J.L. Powers
1938	Beulaville	F.W. McGowen	C.I. Robinson	W.R. Stephens
1939	Rose Hill	F.W. McGowen	C.I. Robinson	J.P. Gulley
1940	Clinton	F.W. McGowen	C.I. Robinson	S.L. Morgan, Jr.
1941	Bear Marsh	F.W. McGowen	C.I. Robinson	J.B. Sessoms
1942	Johnson's	F.W. McGowen	C.I. Robinson	J.L. Jones
1943	Turkey	F.W. McGowen	C.I. Robinson	T.N. Cooper
1944	Mount Olive	G. Van Stephens	C.I. Robinson	G. Van Stephens
1945	Ingold	G. Van Stephens	C.I. Robinson	J.V. Case
1946	New Hope & Mount Vernon	G. Van Stephens	C.I. Robinson	G.W. Lambert
1947	Island Creek & Corinth	Thomas L. Rich, Jr.	Paul L. Cashwell	Gilmer Beck
1948	Garland & Cedar Fork	Mack Herring	Paul L. Cashwell	A.L. Benton
1949	Rose Hill & Clinton	Mack Herring	Paul L. Cashwell	E.N. Teague
1950	Magnolia & Mt. Gilead	Mack Herring	Paul L. Cashwell	J.C. Conoly
1951	Piney Grove & Warsaw	A.W. Greenlaw	Paul L. Cashwell	J.P. Royal
1952	Siloam & Dobson's Chpl.	Mack Herring	Paul L. Cashwell	Elliot B. Stewart
1953	Mount Olive & Turkey	Paul L. Cashwell	Paul T. Mull	E.F. Knight
1954	Rowan & Johnson's	J.C. Mitchell	H.M. Baker	T.W. Williams
1955	Sharon & Beulaville	T.W. Williams	Eugene B. Hager	Julian Motley
1956	Warsaw & Bear Marsh	C.F. Shipp	Eugene B. Hager	Robert A. Melvin
1957	Immanuel & Kenansville	C.F. Shipp	Paul T. Mull	M.M. Turner
1958	Rose Hill	D.E. Parkerson	Paul T. Mull	M.M. Johnson
1959	Calypso & Ingold	D.E. Parkerson	Paul T. Mull	Lauren Sharpe
1960	Island Crk. & Grove Pk.	Mack Herring	Paul T. Mull	Jerry DeBell
1961	Clinton, 1st & Magnolia	Milton Boone	Paul T. Mull	L.H. Knott
1962	Mt. Olive & Mt. Gilead	Milton Boone	E.L. Eiland	A. Quakenbush
1963	Siloam & Turkey	M.M. Johnson	M.S. McLain	Hugh R. Williams
1964	Piney Grove & Sharon	Hugh Ross Williams	M.S. McLain	D.E. Parkerson
1965	Rowan & Well's Chapel	Hugh Ross Williams	M.S. McLain	Wayne Wheeler
1966	Warsaw, 1st & Br. Marsh	John R. Johnson	M.S. McLain	R.H. Kelley
1967	Kenansville & Corinth	John R. Johnson	M.S. McLain	R.A. Thompson
1968	Rose Hill & Immanuel	John A. Johnson	M.S. McLain	Glen Holt
1969	Calypso & Garland	Norman Aycock	R.B. Little	Norman Aycock
1970	Island Crk. & Grove Pk.	Vernon Braswell	R.B. Little	Waldo Early
1971	Clinton, 1st & Magnolia	Vernon Braswell		Anthony Gurganus
1972	Piney Gr. & Mt. Gilead			J. Boyce Brooks
1973	Siloam			W.M. Jones

Year	Churches			
1974 –	Mt. Olive & Dob. Chpl.	Vernon Braswell	R.B. Little	Huber Dixon
1975 –	Rowan & Shiloh	John Flake	R.B. Little	R.B. Little
1976 –	Warsaw & Bear Marsh	John Flake	R.B. Little	Willie O. Carr
1977 –	Kenansville & Corinth	Anthony Gurganus	Richard Whitley	Vernon Braswell
1978 –	Rose Hill & Immanuel	Anthony Gurganus	Charles Jolly	Michael Shook
1979 –	Island Crk. & Calypso	Gene Hart	Lucille Yancey	Joseph Willis
1980 –	Garland & Grove Park	Gene Hart	Lucille Yancey	Paul Rose
1981 –	Clinton, 1st & Magnolia	L. Mack Thompson	Lucille Yancey	Donald Coley
1982 –	Mt. Olive & Mt. Gilead	L. Mack Thompson	Phillip Billings	Lauren Sharpe

ETING PLACES OF EASTERN ASSOCIATION

1987

1st Day	*Kenansville
	Albertson
2nd Day	*Corinth
	Teachey

1988

1st Day	Rose Hill
2nd Day	Immanuel

Hope

1989

1st Day	*Calypso
	Faison - Poplar Grove
2nd Day	*Garland
	Ingold - Center

1990

1st Day	*Island Creek
	Dobsons Chapel
2nd Day	*Grove Park
	Browns

el - Alum Springs

1991

1st Day	Clinton, First
2nd Day	*Magnolia
	Concord - Johnson

1992

1st Day	Mount Olive
2nd Day	*Mount Gilead
	Union Grove

assisting with meal on respective days

55

RULES OF ORDER

1. At the meeting of the Association the Moderator elected at the preceding session shall preside. In the case of his absence, the Vice Moderator shall preside.

2. Each session of the Association shall be opened with religious exercises.

3. At each daily session and previous to proceeding to business the Associate Clerk shall be requested to announce the number of churches represented and the total number of messengers representing these churches. When it is determined that a majority of the churches are represented the Moderator shall declare the Association duly constituted. It shall be necessary for a majority of the churches to be represented for the Association to transact business other than adjournment. The proceedings of the first of the Annual Session shall be read the morning of the second day and the proceedings of the second day shall be read at the first Council of the Association to meet following the Annual Meeting.

4. The members shall observe toward the officers and each other that courtesy which belongs to Christians.

5. Any member wishing to speak shall arise and address the presiding officer and shall confine himself strictly to the question under consideration and avoid personalities.

6. No member shall speak more than twice on the same question without permission.

7. All motions seconded shall be definitely stated by the presiding officer before discussion.

8. No motion shall be withdrawn after discussion.

9. When a question is under discussion, no motion or proposition shall be received except to adjourn, to lay on the table, to amend, to commit, or to postpone to a definite time, which several motions shall have preference in the order in which they are stated.

10. After a motion has been decided, any member having voted in the majority may move a re-consideration.

11. All questions except such as relate to the Constitution shall be decided by a majority vote.

12. The Association shall have the right to decide what subjects shall be admitted to consideration.

13. The rules of order may be altered or amended at any session of the Association by a Majority vote.

CONSTITUTION

PREAMBLE

We, the Missionary Baptist Churches of Jesus Christ, composing the EASTERN BAPTIST ASSOCIATION, convinced of the necessity of an association of churches in order to promote fellowship, missions, education, Christian service, the preaching of the gospel, and to cooperate with the Baptist State Convention of North Carolina and the Southern Baptist Convention in their work, do hereby agree and subscribe to the following articles.

ARTICLE I. NAMES

This association shall be known and denominated as the North Carolina EASTERN BAPTIST ASSOCIATION.

ARTICLE II. PURPOSE

The purpose of this association shall be the promotion of Christ's Kingdom among men, and the means of accomplishing this shall be in strict conformity to the New Testament.

ARTICLE III. AUTHORITY

This association claims to be independent and sovereign in its own sphere, but shall never attempt to exercise any authority over the internal affairs of the churches.

ARTICLE IV. COMPOSITION

This association shall be composed of all ordained ministers who are members or pastors of member churches, the general officers of the association, the director of missions, and three messengers from each church with one additional messenger for every one-hundred members over the first one-hundred, no church being allowed more than ten messengers.

ARTICLE V. MEETINGS

The Annual Session of the Association shall commence on Monday after the fourth Lord's Day in October. The church year for the churches of the association shall commence on October 1, and end on September 30.

ARTICLE VI. OFFICERS

The officers of the association shall be a moderator, a vice moderator, a clerk, and associate clerk, the chairman of the Historical Committee, a treasurer and an associate treasurer. All officers shall be elected annually except the chairman of the Historical Committee who is the senior member of the Historical Committee. The moderator shall not be elected to serve more than two full years at one period and shall assume office at the close of the annual session at which he is elected.

ARTICLE VII. TRUSTEES

The association shall have three (3) trustees who shall serve three-year terms in rotation, the replacement to be elected by the association annually.

ARTICLE VIII. EXECUTIVE BOARD

The association shall have an Executive Board consisting of the general officers of the association; the director of missions, the director of Christian Social Ministries; the directors of associational Brotherhood, Church Music, Church Training, Sunday School, and Womans Missionary Union; the chairpersons of associational standing committees; each active and retired pastor in the association; and two lay persons (men or women) from each church to be elected by the church and whose name shall be included in the church letter to the association.

ARTICLE IX. ASSOCIATIONAL COUNCIL

The association shall have an Associational Council consisting of the officers of the Executive Board; the directors of associational Brotherhood, Church Music, Church Training, Sunday School and Womans Missionary Union: the chairpersons of Evangelism, Media Library, Missions, Pastoral Support, and Stewardship; the director of missions, and the director of Christian Social Ministries.

ARTICLE X. COMMITTEES

The association shall have such committees as may be deemed necessary for orderly and efficient achievement of the association's purpose. Members on standing committees shall be on the rotating basis with one-third of the members rotating off each year. Members completing a three year term shall not be eligible for re-election until one year has passed. A member elected to fill an unexpired term shall be eligible for election to a full term following the completion of the unexpired term.

ARTICLE XI. CHURCH PROGRAMS

The association shall organized groups of officers for the five (5) church programs: Sunday School, Church Training, Women's Missionary Union, Brotherhood, and Music.

ARTICLE XIII. MISCELLANEOUS

The association shall not maintain fellowship with any church which neglects to observe gospel order.

ARTICLE XIV. CONSTITUTIONAL CHANGES

This constitution may be amended on the second day of any annual session by a vote of two-thirds of the messengers present provided the proposed changes have been presented on the first day of the annual session.

BY-LAWS

ARTICLE I. DUTIES OF OFFICERS

A. MODERATOR - The moderator on the first day of each Annual Session of the Association shall appoint the following committees to function during the session: Place and Preacher; Resolutions; and Memorials. At the last regular meeting of the Executive Board before the Annual Session of the Association, the moderator shall appoint a Constitutional Committee to serve during the Annual Session, and a Committee on Committees.

It shall be the duty of the moderator to enforce an observance of the constitution, preserve order, decide all questions of order, vote in case of a tie, and act as chairman of the Executive Board.

B. VICE MODERATOR - It shall be the duty of the vice moderator to preside in the absence or at the request of the moderator, to give other appropriate assistance to the moderator, and to succeed to the office of moderator, if and when during his tenure of office the office of moderator becomes vacant.

C. CLERK - It shall be the duty of the clerk to record the proceedings of each Annual Session, superintend their printing and distribution, and serve as secretary of the Executive Board and the Associational Council.

It shall be his duty to report the actions of the Executive Board to the Annual Session of the Association. He shall report the actions of the Associational Council to the next meeting of the Board or to the Annual Session of the Association, which-ever comes first.

D. ASSOCIATE CLERK - It shall be the duty of the associate clerk to register the messengers, to report upon request the number of churches represented and the total number of messengers representing these churches, and to perform such other duties as are usually performed by an associate clerk.

E. TREASURER - It shall be the duty of the treasurer to receive all funds contributed by the churches or collected during the Annual Session of this body, to distribute all funds received as ordered by the association, and to make to the Association an annual report of the condition of the treasury.

F. ASSOCIATE TREASURER - It shall be the duties of the associate treasurer to assist the treasurer in the performance of his duties as directed by the treasurer.

ARTICLE II. DUTIES OF TRUSTEES

The trustees shall be the representatives of the Association in legal matters, and shall perform such duties as the Association or the Executive Board may prescribe.

ARTICLE III. EXECUTIVE BOARD

A. OFFICERS - The officers of the Executive Board shall be: moderator, vice moderator, clerk, associate clerk, treasurer, and associate treasurer. The corresponding officers of the Association elected during the last Annual Session of the Association shall serve in these positions on the Executive Board.

B. DUTIES - The Executive Board shall cooperate with the Baptist State Convention of North Carolina in its program for the furtherance of the work fostered by the body within the bounds of the Association; it shall act for the Association on any matters requiring attention between Annual Sessions of the Association, and it shall have power to fill any vacancies on the Board during the year. The clerk shall make a report of the work of the Executive Board at the Annual Session of the Association. The director of missions or other workers employed by the Association shall make a quarterly report to the Executive Board in order that the said Board shall be prepared to make a full report to this body.

C. MEETINGS - The Executive Board shall meet at least once each quarter at a time and place designated by the Board after the first meeting which will be called by the moderator who shall serve as chairman of the Board. With proper notice being given to all members of the meeting, and when it is determined that a majority of the churches are represented the chairman shall declare the Board duly constituted.

ARTICLE IV. COMMITTEES

A. STANDING COMMITTEES - A majority shall constitute a quorum for each committee.
1. ELECTION OF COMMITTEES: All committee members shall be persons who have demonstrated talent for performing the work of the committee, or who have stated a willingness to receive training to equip them for the work of the committee.
Standing Committees shall be formed from a slate of persons selected, notified, secured to serve, and nominated by the Committee on Committees. The nominees, then, must be elected by the Association in its annual session. Special committees shall be recommended when deemed appropriate to perform the business and ministry of the Association, and are subject to the approval of the Executive Board. These committee posts shall be filled by the Committee on Committees from a slate of persons selected, notified, secured to serve nominated, and presented to and elected by the Executive Board. These committees shall have definitely prescribed duties and a definite term of service before they are established.
2. MISSIONS COMMITTEE: The Missions Committee shall be composed of three (3) at-large members, the chairpersons of standing committees whose duties relate to Christian Social Ministries, the director of Christian Social Ministries, and the associational directors of Brotherhood and Womans Missionary Union. The rotation system shall apply to the three at-large members only. Chair persons from other committees shall be rotated from within their individual committees. The Missions Committee shall work with the director of Christian Social Ministries in discovering, analyzing, and presenting to the Association opportunities for mission action; and in coordination of the association's mission activities. Upon determining that new committees are needed to direct specific social ministries, the Missions Committee shall bring to the attention of the Executive Board the need for such committees. The Missions Committee shall work with the director of Christian Social Ministries in writing the prescription as required by ARTICLE IV of the By-Laws.
3. STEWARDSHIP COMMITTEE: The Stewardship Committee shall be composed of nine (9) members. This committee shall be responsible for recommending a budget to the Association in its Annual Session, for the distribution of all associational funds, and for devising plans for raising such funds as are necessary for carrying on the associational programs. The Stewardship Committee shall lead a program of Biblical stewardship education and promotion among the churches and on the associational level. The associational treasurer shall be a member of this committee. The Stewardship Committee shall have the financial records of the association audited annually.
4. EVANGELISM COMMITTEE: The Evangelism Committee shall be composed of three (3) members. It shall be the duty of this committee to promote evangelism both in the local church and on an associational level. It shall serve to link the Association with state and south-wide departments of evangelism and shall use every available means for fostering the cause of winning the lost to Christ.

5. MEDIA LIBRARY COMMITTEE: The Media Library Committee shall be composed of three (3) members duly elected by the Association and resource personnel as appointed by the moderator whose duty it shall be to encourage the establishing and promotion of libraries in churches.

6. PASTORAL SUPPORT COMMITTEE: The Pastoral Support Committee shall be composed of three (3) members whose duties shall be to provide an ongoing continuing program of help to pastors and church staff members in areas of need. The program shall include guidance for those who are just beginning to prepare for church related vocations; career assessment; spiritual, emotional, and physical needs of pastors and church staff.

7. PROGRAM COMMITTEE: The Program Committee shall be composed of three (3) members. It shall be their duty to arrange the program of the annual session of the Association and for all other sessions which may be called.

8. ORDINATION COMMITTEE: The Ordination Committee shall be composed of six (6) members (Pastors and Deacons). This committee shall offer to any church, upon request, advice and assistance in the examination and ordination of deacons and ministers.

9. HISTORICAL COMMITTEE: The Historical Committee shall consist of three (3) members. The committee shall obtain and edit the histories of two churches each year to be included in the minutes, and shall maintain an up-to-date history of the Association. The senior member of the committee shall be the chairman.

10. NOMINATING COMMITTEE: The Nominating Committee shall be composed of six (6) members. It shall be the duty of this committee to submit nominations to the Association in session for the associational general officers (with the floor open for nominations) as well as for representatives to denominational agencies and interests for the following year and to fill any vacancies which may occur during the year.

This committee shall also be responsible for forwarding to the Executive Board at their third meeting for approval and to the Association for election, the directors of Brotherhood, Sunday School, Woman's Missionary Union, Church Training, and Church Music. The Church Program Organizations directors shall then become members of the Nominating Committee. The Nominating Committee shall present to the Executive Board at their fourth meeting a complete slate of officers for the five Church Program Organizations.

B. APPOINTED COMMITTEES:

1. CONSTITUTION AND BY-LAWS COMMITTEE: This committee shall be composed of three (3) members, whose duty it shall be to study and recommend changes in the Constitution and By-Laws and bring reports as necessary to the Association.

2. PLACE AND PREACHER COMMITTEE: This committee shall be composed of three (3) members, whose duty it shall be to make the Association aware of the rotating system of meeting places, and to recommend to the Association in Annual Session a place or places for meeting, along with a preacher and alternate for the sermon for the following year.

3. RESOLUTIONS COMMITTEE: This committee shall be composed of three (3) members whose duty it shall be to study all resolutions referred to it by the Association or the Executive Board and report suitable resolutions at the Annual Session.

4. MEMORIALS COMMITTEE: This committee shall be composed of (3) members whose duty it shall be to prepare and present at the

Annual Session an appropriate program of memorial for those of
our number who have died during the preceeding year. These names
may be secured from the letters to the Association from the
member churches.

5. COMMITTEE ON COMMITTEES: This committee shall be composed
of six (6) members whose duty it shall be to select and nominate
persons for the standing committees and shall appoint successors
when vacancies occur during the year.

ARTICLE V. DUTIES OF CHURCH PROGRAM DIRECTORS

A. The ASSOCIATION SUNDAY SCHOOL DIRECTOR shall promote and
supervise the Sunday School Program of the Association, and shall
be responsible for the direction of Vacation Bible School work
of the Association in cooperation with the director of missions.

B. THE ASSOCIATIONAL CHURCH TRAINING DIRECTOR shall promote
and supervise the Church Training Program of the Association in
cooperation with the director of missions.

C. THE ASSOCIATIONAL WOMAN'S MISSIONARY DIRECTOR shall promote
and supervise the Woman's Missionary Union Program of the Association cooperating with the director of missions and in keeping
with the Constitution and By-Laws of the Woman's Missionary Union
of the EASTERN BAPTIST ASSOCIATION.

D. The ASSOCIATIONAL BROTHERHOOD DIRECTOR shall promote and
supervise the Brotherhood Program of the Association in cooperation with the director of missions.

E. THE ASSOCIATIONAL MUSIC DIRECTOR shall promote and supervise
the Church Music Program of the Association in cooperation with
the director of missions.

ARTICLE VI. ASSOCIATIONAL COUNCIL

A. Purpose - The Purpose of the Associational Council shall
be to provide a consultative, advisory, and coordinative service
to the Association and its various programs and committees.

B. Duties - The duties of the Associational Council shall be:
provide for communication between associational officers, organizations, and committees; study church needs in the association and
needs of the people in the area of the Association; propose
long-range and short-range goals for the Association; prepare and
recommend plans for involving organizations and committees appropriately in attaining goals; review and coordinate plans made
by the organizations and committees and relate these to the attainment of goals; evaluate the use of resources; and report
through appropriate channels progress made toward attainment of
associational goals. The Council shall exercise general supervision of the work of the director of missions. In the event the
position of director of missions becomes vacant, the Council shall
recommend to the Association or the Executive Board for approval
a search committee whose duties shall be to seek prayerfully a
person to fill the position.

C. Officers - The officers of the Associational Council shall
be the chairman and the secretary. The moderator shall serve as
chairman.

The associational clerk shall be the secretary. In the absence
of the secretary, the chairman shall appoint a temporary secretary.

ARTICLE VII BY-LAWS CHANGES

by-laws may be amended on the second day of any Annual
by a vote of the majority of the messengers present and
rovided the proposed changes have been presented on the
y of the annual session.

64

TABLE A CHURCH MEMBERSHIP AND OTHER INFORMATION 1982

Association: **EASTERN**
State: **NORTH CAROLINA**
Director of Associational Missions: **CLYDE L. DAVIS**
Address: **P.O. Box 712** City: **Warsaw** State: **North Carolina** Zip: **28398**

CHURCHES	PASTORS & ADDRESSES (INCLUDE ZIP CODE)	County	3 Year organized as a church	4 Location	5 Services held twice on Sunday?		13 Total Baptisms	14 Other additions (by letter, statement, etc.)	15 Members lost (by letter, death, statement, etc.)	16 Present resident members	17 Present nonresident members	18 Grand total present members	19 No. members received from non-Baptist churches	20 No. members lost to non-Baptist Churches	24 Value of pastor's home if owned by the church	25 Value of church property including pastor's home	26 Total church debt at end of this associational year
					Y	N											
Albertson	Shelton Justice, Rt. 1/Box 3B, A-2, Warsaw 28398	Duplin	1902	1		X	3	4	1	60	22	82	2	20	0	75000	0
Alum Springs	Mitchell Rivenbark, Rt. 2, Mt. Olive 28365	Duplin	1763	1	X		0	0	9	255	49	304	0	0	25000	150000	0
Bear Marsh	Willie O. Carr, Rt. 5, Box 50, Clinton 28328	Sampson	1814	1		X	3	0	3	74	25	99	0	3	0	100000	6500
Beulah	Joseph W. Moss, Sr., Rt. 6, Clinton 28328	Sampson	1778	1		X	4	1	9	140	16	156	0	2	0	150000	0
Browns	Franklin J. McCarson, 103 Wade St., Warsaw 28398	Duplin	1959	3	X		8	8	4	149	54	203	2	1	55000	160000	0
Calvary	Greg M. Thornton, Box 248, Calypso 28325	Duplin	1908	3	X		2	4	9	202	73	275	1	0	35000	175000	500
Calypso	Robert Hill, Box 153, Clinton 28328	Sampson	1901	1	X		4	4	4	149	19	168	0	0	0	100000	0
Center	Wm. M. Jones, 110 Forest Dr., Clinton 28328	Duplin	1854	5		X	18	24	38	1052	363	1415	4	10	0	2750000	547143
Clinton	Eddie Wetherington, Rt. 5, B-29A, Clinton 28328	Duplin	1825	1		X	2	65		86	34	120	1	1	0	80000	0
Concord	John A. Johnson, (Int.) 108 E. Plank St., Warsaw 28398	Duplin	1853	1	X		2	1	14	351	70	421	1	2	35000	200000	0
Corinth	Albert R. Wellman, Rt. 1, Box 118A, Magnolia 28453	Duplin	1861	4		X	2	3	4	127	58	185	0	1	40000	200000	0
Dobson Chapel	Ailsworth	Sampson	1919	1			1		4	89	61	150	0	0	55000	162500	12363
Evergreen	Charles Kirkland, Faison 28341	Sampson	1885	3		X	9	4	6	126	39	165	1	1	35000	85000	
Faison							9	6	8	166	80	246	1		60000	250000	0
Garland																	
Garner's Chapel	None	Duplin	1927	5	X		0	0	3	57	55	112	0	1	25000	60000	25000
Grove Park	Davis E. Benton, 609 NE Blvd., Clinton 28328	Sampson	1954	5	X		27	9	11	428	103	531	0	2	70000	850000	294262
Immanuel	Vernon Braswell, 200 Fox Lake Dr., Clinton	Sampson	1956	2	X		7	9	20	564	114	678	0	2	50000	800000	0
Ingold	Robert W. Miller, Ingold 28446	Sampson	1925	1		X	1	0	6	102	28	130	0	0	25000	100000	0
Island Creek	James L. Hartsell, Rt. 2, Box 349, Rose Hill 28458	Duplin	1802	1	X		5	5	6	269	60	329	2	3	32000	187000	0
Johnson	Kenneth Durham, Rt. 2, Warsaw 28398	Duplin	1793	3	X		3	6	4	150	111	261	1	1	39000	185000	0
Kenansville	Lauren R. Sharpe, Box 517, Kenansville 28349	Duplin	1837	3	X		0	11	5	135	39	217	1		0	130000	0
Magnolia	Wm. B. Shipp, Magnolia 28453	Duplin	1835	4	X		6	7	8	137	80	217	5		44000	319000	0
Mount Olive	Anthony Z. Gurganus, 301 N. Chestnut St., Mt. Olive 28365	Duplin	1863	4	X		6	7	27	419	169	588	5	1	0	1000000	0
Mount Vernon	W.O. Carr, Rt. 5, Box 50, Clinton 28328	Sampson	1910	1			1	0	3	175	30	205	1	5	37500	100800	0
Mount Gilead	Oliver Skerrett, Rt. 2, Box 106, Clinton 28328	Duplin	1834	4	X	X	6	6	7	299	65	364	2	0	54000	308520	0
New Hope	Paul Rose, Rt. 1, Box 355, Mt. Olive 28365	Sampson	1817	1	X	X	6	0	0	97	28	126	0	6	0	60000	10000
Piney Grove	Farrell H. Miller, Rt. 2, Box 122A, Faison 28341	Sampson	1844	1			2	3	2	171	51	222	0	0	50000	250000	0
Poplar Grove	Andy M. Wood, Rt. 1, Box 77½, Faison 28341	Duplin	1880	2	X		7	1	0	68	70	138	0	1	45000	75000	10400
Poston	Donald R. Coley, Rt. 3, Wallace 28466	Duplin	1958	1	X		10	19	10	257	55	312	6	0	63000	455000	0
Rose Hill	Jerry Kinlaw, Box 459, Rose Hill 28458	Duplin	1900	4	X			8	8	319	116	435	0	0	47000	388000	0
Rowan	C. Michael Shook, 202 Reedsford Rd., Clinton 28328	Sampson	1749	1	X		3	2	21	368	107	475	0	6	65000	500000	25000
Sharon	Phillip Denton, P.O. Box 126, Chinquapin 28521	Duplin	1860	1	X		12	3	11	237	51	288	1	0	40000	90000	0
Shiloh	James W. Johnson, 515 W. Boney, Wallace 28466	Sampson	1940	2	X		7	1	5	189	47	236	0	0	40000	250000	15330
Siloam	Phillip Billings, Rt. 1, Box 19, Harrells 28444	Sampson	1889	2	X		4	1	39	120	59	154	0	0	25000	200000	3000
Teachey	Larry Blount, Box 38, Teachey 28464	Duplin	1885	2	X		2	2	8	109	45	154	0	3	85000	125000	0
Turkey	Larry D. Padgett, Box 216, Turkey 28393	Sampson	1908	1	X		2	1	9	197	77	274	1	1	22500	135000	0
Union Grove	L.L. Barnes, Sr., Rt. 2, Box 584, Elizabethtown 28337	Sampson	1915	4			3	2	6	114	80	194	0		0	70000	0
Warsaw	L. Mack Thompson, 205E Chelly St., Warsaw 28398	Duplin	1856	4	X		3	5	2	487	200	687	1	1	49500	1048548	11500
Wells Chapel	Freddie Harris, Rt. 1, Wallace 28466	Sampson	1756	1	X		4		5	201	53	254	1		65000	250000	13320
TOTALS							162	220	318	8693	2856	11549	31	67			

TABLE B SUNDAY SCHOOL — 1982

Association: EASTERN
State: NORTH CAROLINA
Associational Sunday School Director: JAMES HARTSELL
Address: Route 2, Box 349 **City:** Rose Hill **State:** North Carolina **Zip:** 28458

Church	Sunday School Directors & Addresses (Include Zip Code)	54 Cradle Roll enrollment (Birth to 2 years)	55 Preschool enrollment (Birth through 5 years)	56 Children enrollment (6-11 years or grades 1-6)	57 Youth enrollment (12-17 years or grades 7-12)	58 Young Adult enrollment Single (18-29)	59 Young Adult enrollment Married (18-29)	60 Adult enrollment (30-59 years)	61 Senior Adult enrollment (60 and over)	62 Adults Away enrollment	63 Homebound enrollment	64 General officers enrollment	65 Enrolment of mission(s) of church	66 Total ongoing Sunday School enrollment	67 Average weekly Sunday School attendance	68 Bible Study groups enrollment	69 Total enroled in Bible Study	70 Number ethnic Sunday School members	71 Church V.B.S. enrollment	72 Mission V.B.S. enrollment	73 Backyard Bible Club enrollment
Albertson	Larry Herring, Rt. 1, Mt. Olive 28365	0	8	7	6	8	8	28	15	0	0	0	0	80	45	0	80	0	32	0	0
Alum Springs	Timothy Bell, Rt. 5, Mt. Olive 28365	4	5	31	20	11	14	20	29	0	0	2	0	135	84	15	135	0	64	0	0
Bear Marsh	Lonnie Carter, Rt. 2, Box 193B, Clinton 28328	0	5	16	7	7	7	25	4	0	0	7	0	75	64	0	90	0	72	0	0
Brown	Herbie Jordan, Rt. 3, Box 97, Clinton 28328	0	14	9	15	10	17	24	8	0	0	7	0	106	63	0	0	0	70	0	0
Calvary	Bill Savage, Rt. 2, Box 95R, Warsaw 28398	3	11	13	8	7	4	19	8	0	0	2	5	85	55	0	0	0	18	0	0
Calypso	A.D. Johnson, Box 27, Calypso 28325	0	7	3	5	7	7	18	30	0	0	3	99	48	48	0	99	0	60	0	0
Center	Ray Allen Cannon, Rt. 1, Garland 28441	6	8	9	15	7	9	28	2	0	0	3	0	76	386	0	76	0	152	0	0
Clinton	Keith Jones, 606 Park Ave., Clinton 28328	0	60	90	109	21	51	127	205	30	42	10	0	745		0	0	0	72	0	0
Concord	Gary Bell, Rt. 1, Box 238, Rose Hill 28458	7	17	9	16	2	5	9	9	0	0	4	0	231	104	0	231	0	65	0	0
Corinth	Bill Rogers, Magnolia 28453	0		22	36	17	17	89	34	0	0	2	0	107	60	0	0	0	54	0	0
Dobson Chapel	James P. Brown, Jr., Rt. 2, Rose Hill 28458	3	4	11	16	11	7	17	21	0	0	3	0	84	44	0	0	0	59	0	0
Evergreen	Jerry Todd, P.O. Box 20, Harrells 28444	5	17	8	15	12	8	18	15	0	0	3	0	111	42	20	0	0	101	0	0
Faison	Henry Brown, Faison 28341	0		9	10	7	16	42	22	0	0	3	0	111	68	0	131	0	87	0	0
Garland	Woodrow Jarvis, Box 326, Garland 28441	0	12	23	12	12	9	28	23	0	0	3	0	60	33	0	60	0	32	0	35
Garner's Chapel	Albert Britt, Rt. 1, Mt. Olive 28365	4	30	6	54	25	9	12	20	0	0		0	382	180	0	382	0	123	35	0
Grove Park	Ronnie Warren, 132 Kimberly Dr., Clinton 28328	0	76	41	45	0	11	175	40	0	10	5	0	425	263	0	425	0	120	0	0
Immanuel	Wilbert Massey, 1001 Naylor St., Clinton 28328	0	5	46	15	10	76	124	45	0	0	3	0	105	48	0	105	0	37	0	0
Ingold	Gordon Cashwell, Box 5212, Ingold 28446	0	7	12	22	0	12	30	20	0	0	4	30	174	105	0	174	0	85	0	0
Island Creek	George Brown, Rt. 3, Wallace 28466	2	7	17	10	13	22	24	27	0	0	6	0	101	66	0	101	0	70	0	0
Johnson	Mavis Pigford, 501 Forrest Rd., Warsaw 28398	0	7	12	10			41	9	0	0	3	0	86	63	0	86	0	60	0	0
Kenansville	F.F. Oakley, Box 216, Kenansville 28453	0	0	12	7	6	12	23	12	0	0	4	83	110	68	0	0	0	31	0	0
Magnolia	Kenneth Baker, Magnolia 28453	0	8	67	57	10	19	138	32	0	20	3	56	506	185	0	0	1	86	0	0
Mount Olive	Richard Blackwelder, Box 91, Mt. Olive 28365	8	33	8	40	15	65	33	81	0	0	9	0	140	75	0	140	0	40	0	0
Mount Vernon	Tony Rackley, Rt. 2, Clinton 28328	0	8	13	11	5	21	78	36	0	0		0	75	126	140	0	0	109	0	6
Mount Gilead	Lonnie J. Bass, Rt. 2, Box 110A, Clinton 28328	0	2	36	14	13	17	14	20	0	0	2	0	263	42	0	263	0	49	0	0
New Hope	C. Ed Colwell, Rt. 1, Turkey 28393	0	8	13	11	5	24	57	31	0	0	4	0	64	75	0	64	0	122	0	0
Piney Grove	DeWitt King, Rt. 2, Faison 28341	0	12	16	16	13	32	24	22	1	0	2	0	141	45	0	141	0	68	0	0
Poplar Grove	Jane Brashaw, Rt. 2, Faison 28341	0	0	10	11	14	10	74	21	0	1	5	0	82	135	0	82	0	105	0	7
Poston	Mary Colby, Rt. 3, Wallace 28466	4	43	36	23	0	32	83	62	0	0	5	0	251		0	251	0	91	0	0
Rose Hill	J.T. Kelly, Box 122, Rose Hill 28458	9	37	21	28	0	10	98	96	0	0	3	0	250	120	0	325	0	119	0	0
Rowan	Jo Robinson, Rt. 2, Box 261, Clinton 28328	0	8	28	20	23	25	40	24	0	0	3	0	325	165	0	160	0	87	0	0
Sharon	Jimmy Mercer, Chinquapin 28521	5	7	31	25	0	30	40	40	0	0	2	0	160	101	0	141	0	65	0	0
Shiloh	David Maready, Rt. 1, Chinquapin 28521	0	1	18	15	8	4	14	34	0	0	2	0	141	87	0		0	35	0	0
Siloam	Wayne Cannady, P.O. Box, Harrells 28444	0	6	6	22	0	4	14	18	0	0	5	0	78	49	0	78	0	42	0	0
Teachey	Jerry Dempsey, Rt. 1, Teachey 28464	0	5	13	8	8	6	34	30	0	0	2	0	151	52	0	151	0	95	0	0
Turkey	David Hudson, Rt. 1, Turkey 28393	0	20	26	21	10	17	33	34	0	0	5	0	129	79	0	129	0	44	0	0
Union Grove	Raeford H. Carter, Jr., Rt. 4, Clinton 28328	0	19	25	47	2	19	34	52	19	2	4	0	337	107	0	337	0	138	0	0
Warsaw	Lawton Kitchin, 602 Curtis Rd., Warsaw 28398	0	13	57	13	10	15	110	38	0	1	3	0	337	145	0	153	0	42	0	0
Wells Chapel	Florence Hoover, Rt. 2, Harrells 28444			17	10	13	44							153	93				49		
TOTALS		**56**	**614**	**845**	**872**	**306**	**620**	**1861**	**1309**	**37**	**96**	**129**	**273**	**6778**	**3606**	**35**	**4590**	**1**	**2870**	**35**	**42**

TABLE C CHURCH TRAINING — 1982

Association: EASTERN
State: NORTH CAROLINA
Associational Church Training Director: LUCILLE YANCEY
Address: P.O. Box 711 — **City:** Clinton — **State:** North Carolina — **Zip:** 28328

CHURCHES	CHURCH TRAINING DIRECTORS & ADDRESSES (INCLUDE ZIP CODE)	74 Preschool enrolment (5 yrs & under—not in school)	75 Children enrolment (6-11 yrs or grades 1-6)	76 Youth enrolment (12-17 yrs or grades 7-12)	77 Adult enrolment (18 and over)	78 Equipping Centers enrolment	79 N.C.M.T./Survival Kit enrolment	80 MasterLife enrolment	81 Other enrolment	82 Hold File enrolment	83 General officers enrolment	84 Enrolment of mission(s) of church	85 Total Church Training enrolment	86 Baptist Doctrine Study Y=Yes No=No
Albertson	None	0	0	0	0	0	0	0	0	0	0	0	0	N
Alum Springs	None	0	0	0	0	0	0	0	18	0	1	0	19	Y
Bear Marsh	None	0	0	0	0	0	0	0	0	0	0	0	0	N
Beulah	None	0	0	0	0	0	0	0	0	0	0	0	0	Y
Browns	None	0	0	0	0	0	0	0	25	0	0	0	25	Y
Calvary	None	0	0	0	0	0	0	0	0	0	0	0	0	N
Calypso	None	0	0	0	0	0	0	0	0	0	0	0	0	N
Center	None	0	0	0	0	20	0	0	0	38	4	0	0	N
Clinton	None	5	20	30	48	0	0	0	0	15	1	0	183	Y
Concord	None	0	0	0	14	0	0	0	0	0	2	0	31	Y
Corinth	J.C. Savage, Rt. 1, Teachey 28464	0	0	15	8	0	16	0	0	0	2	0	25	N
Dobson Chapel	Sylvia Wellman, Rt. 1, Box 118A, Magnolia 28453	0	0	0	8	0	0	0	0	0	5	0	74	N
Evergreen	None	0	0	0	0	0	11	0	16	0	4	0	0	Y
Faison	None	6	17	7	28	20	18	0	0	0	3	0	31	N
Garland	Mary Carter, Box 334, Garland 28441	0	0	0	0	0	0	0	45	0	0	0	61	N
Garner's Chapel	None	0	0	0	0	0	0	0	0	0	0	0	0	Y
Grove Park	None	24	14	0	0	0	0	0	0	0	0	0	0	N
Immanuel	Phil Harrison, 214 Moore St., Clinton 28328	0	0	33	69	0	0	0	0	0	3	0	143	Y
Ingold	None	0	0	0	0	0	0	0	0	0	0	0	0	Y
Island Creek	None	0	0	13	22	0	0	0	0	0	4	0	41	N
Johnson	None	0	0	0	0	0	0	0	0	0	0	0	0	N
Kenansville	None	0	0	0	0	0	0	0	0	0	0	0	0	Y
Magnolia	None	20	18	28	0	0	0	0	27	0	6	0	0	N
Mount Olive	Steve Duncan, 412 W. Main St., Mt. Olive 28365	0	0	0	0	30	0	0	25	35	0	40	221	Y
Mount Vernon		0	0	0	17	0	0	0	0	0	6	0	25	Y
Mount Gilead	Myron Bass, Rt. 2, Box 101A, Clinton 28328	1	9	7	7	0	0	0	5	0	5	0	33	Y
New Hope	Danny Johnson, Rt. 1, Turkey 28393	0	6	5	19	0	0	0	0	0	1	0	52	N
Piney Grove	None	0	0	0	0	0	0	0	0	0	0	0	0	N
Poplar Grove	None	14	16	16	0	0	0	0	0	0	5	0	0	N
Poston	Eleanor Thompson, Rt. 3, Wallace 28466	0	0	0	66	0	3	0	0	0	0	0	119	N
Rose Hill	None	4	17	18	30	0	0	0	0	11	3	0	83	N
Rowan	Mozelle R. Jones, Rt. 2, Clinton 28328	0	0	0	25	0	10	0	0	0	3	0	83	Y
Sharon	Louise Padgett, Wallace 28466	0	7	10	0	0	0	0	0	0	3	0	55	Y
Shiloh	None	0	0	0	0	0	0	0	0	0	0	0	0	N
Siloam	Shirley Jones, Harrells 28444	0	0	0	0	25	0	0	0	0	0	0	25	N
Teachey	None	9	14	16	11	0	0	0	0	0	3	0	61	N
Turkey	H.J. Register, Rt. 1, Turkey 28393	0	0	0	0	0	0	0	0	0	0	0	61	Y
Union Grove	None	8	38	42	29	0	0	0	0	0	2	0	0	N
Warsaw	John Gurganus, 106 W Chelley St., Warsaw 28398	5	17	9	36	0	22	0	12	0	3	0	131	N
Wells Chapel	Mary J. Bland, Box 90, Harrells 28444	0	0	0	92	0	0	0	0	0	0	0	92	N
TOTALS		**96**	**194**	**249**	**529**	**83**	**80**	**0**	**173**	**99**	**59**	**40**	**1530**	

66

TABLE D CHURCH MUSIC — 1982

Association: **EASTERN**
State: **NORTH CAROLINA**
Associational Music Director: **JEAN HATCH**
Address: **P.O. Box 837** — City: **Clinton** — State: **North Carolina** — Zip: **28328**

Churches	Music Directors & Addresses (include zip code)	87 Preschool enrolment (4-5 years)	88 Children enrolment (6-8 years or grades 1-3)	89 Children enrolment (9-11 years or grades 4-6)	90 Youth enrolment (12-17 years or grades 7-12)	91 Adult enrolment (18 and over)	92 Handbell ringers enrolment	93 Vocal ensembles enrolment	94 Instrumental ensembles enrolment	95 General music leader enrolment	96 Enrolment of mission(s) of church	97 Total ongoing Church Music enrolment	98 Church Music Average Weekly Ongoing Attendance
Albertson	Connie Jones, Rt. 1, Mt. Olive 28365	0	0	0	0	16	0	0	0	2	0	18	12
Alum Springs	Mrs. Kay Warren, 120 E. John St., Mt. Olive 28365	0	12	0	16	25	0	0	0	6	0	69	50
Bear Marsh	Tex Cline, 205 Dogwood Dr., Warsaw 28398	0	2	5	15	12	0	0	0	2	0	26	26
Beulah	Curtis W. Pope, 305 Inverness Rd., Clinton 28328	0	0	0	11	26	0	0	0	3	0	40	28
Browns	Russell Killette, Rt. 1, Warsaw 28398	0	0	0	0	0	0	0	0	0	0	10	8
Calvary	Mrs. Jeanne Thornton, Box 248, Calypso 28325	0	0	0	0	7	0	0	0	2	0	20	12
Calypso	Joyce Hudson, Rt. 1, Harrells 28444	0	8	6	7	25	0	0	0	0	0	42	35
Clinton	Jean Hatch, 309 Fairfax St., Clinton 28328	18	29	41	31	48	16	12	5	6	0	204	123
Concord	Mrs. Muriel Wetherington, Rt. 5, Box 29A, Clinton 28328	0	0	0	2	10	0	0	0	4	0	16	13
Corinth	Mrs. Lena Benton, Rt. 1, Teachey 28464	0	0	3	7	20	0	0	0	4	0	34	15
Dobson Chapel	Janet Register, Rt. 2, Rose Hill 28458	0	1	5	21	12	0	0	0	2	0	46	18
Evergreen	Mrs. Jerry Todd, Box 20, Harrells 28444	0	6	0	7	12	0	0	0	4	0	29	12
Faison	Henry Brown, Faison 28341	0	0	0	0	15	0	0	0	2	0	19	14
Garland	Sarah Tingle, Garland 28441	0	0	0	0	15	0	0	0	2	0	17	11
Garner's Chapel	None	0	0	0	0	0	0	0	0	0	0	0	0
Grove Park	Stan Benton, 1108 Bass Dr., Clinton 28328	13	4	4	25	32	0	0	0	2	0	67	48
Immanuel	Dan Arnold, 1000 Naylor St., Clinton 28328	0	12	11	20	34	0	10	0	15	0	115	90
Ingold	Bobby H. Lamb, Rt. 1, Box 138, Garland 28441	0	0	0	0	0	0	0	0	0	0	0	0
Island Creek	Johnny Norris, Rt. 2, Rose Hill 28458	0	0	5	9	20	0	5	0	4	0	43	25
Johnson	John W. Boyette, Jr., Rt. 1, Warsaw 28398	3	4	5	5	22	0	0	0	6	0	45	14
Kenansville	Henry M. West, Jr., Rt. 2, Warsaw 28398	0	3	3	0	7	0	0	0	3	0	16	9
Magnolia	Rita Brown, Magnolia 28453	0	0	0	0	11	0	0	0	3	0	14	10
Mount Olive	Barbara Strickland, Rt. 4, Box 514, Mt. Olive 28365	10	23	8	14	25	0	0	0	15	0	87	55
Mount Vernon	Callie Carr, Rt. 5, Box 50, Clinton 28328	0	0	0	10	20	0	4	0	4	0	46	15
Mount Gilead	None	0	3	12	6	8	0	0	0	5	0	34	20
New Hope	Mrs. Nell Corbett, Rt. 1, Turkey 28393	0	2	10	0	12	0	0	0	4	0	16	12
Piney Grove	Ruby Engles, Rt. 2, Faison 28341	0	2	10	1	20	0	0	0	3	0	36	14
Poplar Grove	Elaine S. Jordan, Rt. 1, Faison 28341	14	10	6	10	20	0	0	0	2	0	30	20
Poston	Annette Henderson, Rt. 3, Wallace 28466	0	0	12	0	40	0	0	0	3	0	79	50
Rose Hill	Linda Murphy, Rt. 1, Rose Hill 28458	2	0	0	15	20	0	0	0	6	0	41	22
Rowan	Lucille Yancey, Box 711, Clinton 28328	2	3	3	11	26	0	0	0	3	0	48	21
Sharon	Betty Brant, Chinquapin 28521	0	1	3	15	22	0	0	0	5	0	46	35
Shiloh	Rifton Raynor, Rt. 2, Wallace 28466	0	0	0	3	22	0	0	0	3	0	28	18
Siloam	Angelyn Burgess, Rt. 1, Harrells 28444	0	0	0	0	8	0	0	0	2	0	10	6
Teachey	None	3	8	0	4	12	0	0	0	0	0	27	12
Turkey	Sue Padgett, Box 216, Turkey 28393	5	6	7	6	20	0	0	0	8	0	47	30
Union Grove	Roger Wells, Rt. 4, Clinton 28328	4	5	5	7	18	0	0	0	3	0	44	28
Wallace	Catherine Vestal, Box 453, Warsaw 28398	0	7	24	20	24	0	0	0	2	0	89	75
Wells Chapel	Geraldine Johnson, Harrells 28444	0	0	0	12	15	8	0	3	3	0	33	20
TOTALS		72	151	188	311	706	24	31	8	149	0	1631	1026

67

TABLE E WOMAN'S MISSIONARY UNION — 1982

Association: EASTERN
State: NORTH CAROLINA
Associational WMU Director: BETSY CARTER
Address: P.O. Box 2 — City: Harrells — State: North Carolina — Zip: 28444

CHURCHES	WMU DIRECTORS & ADDRESSES (INCLUDE ZIP CODE)	99 Mission Friends (5 yrs & under—not in school)	100 Girls in Action (6-11 yrs or grades 1-6)	101 Acteens (12-17 yrs or grades 7-12)	102 Baptist Young Women (18-29 yrs or H.S. grad through 29 yrs)	103 Baptist Women (30 and over)	104 Mission(s) of church	105 Total number of organizations	106 Mission Friends (5 yrs & under—not in school)	107 Girls in Action (6-11 yrs or grades 1-6)	108 Acteens (12-17 yrs or grades 7-12)	109 Baptist Young Women (18-29 yrs or H.S. grad through 29 yrs)	110 Baptist Women (30 and over)	111 WMU officers	112 Mission(s) of church	113 Total ongoing WMU enrolment
		Number of Organizations							Enrolment							
Albertson	Marie K. Harper, Rt. 2, Box 281, Mt. Olive 28365	0	0	0	0	0	1	1	0	0	0	0	0	2	10	12
Alum Springs	Hazel Pipkin, Rt. 5, Mt. Olive 28365	0	1	1	0	1	1	3	0	5	5	0	35	7	0	58
Bear Marsh	Betty Jackson, Rt. 2, Clinton 28328	0	1	0	0	1	1	1	0	0	0	3	10	9	13	13
Beulah	Doris Sinclair, Rt. 3, Box 97, Clinton 28328	0	1	0	0	1	1	4	5	6	7	5	14	3	0	40
Browns	Ruth Dail, Rt. 2, Box 220, Warsaw 28398	0	0	0	0	0	0		0	0	0	0	0	1	0	6
Calvary	Virginia Hines, Box 86, Calypso 28325	0	0	1	0	1	3	6	5	5	0	0	13	3	0	16
Center	Ardith Cannon, Rt. V, Garland 28441	0	2	1	0	1	2	3	0	0	0	0	10	2	0	12
Clinton	None	1	1	1	1	1	2	9	12	30	10	12	90	5	12	171
Concord	Mary Lee Usher, Rt. 1, Box 86, Rose Hill 28458	1	1	1	1	1	2	1	0	0	0	0	9	7	0	11
Corinth	Allene Knowles, Rt. 1, Rose Hill 28458	1	1	1	1	1	0	6	10	5	5	10	42	7	0	79
Dobson Chapel	Betty Brown, Rt. 2, Rose Hill 28458	1	1	0	0	1	0	5	7	9	9	5	7	4	0	44
Evergreen	Mrs. Billy Chestnutt, Rt. 1, Magnolia 28453	1	1	1	0	1	2	4	3	3	6	0	22	1	0	34
Faison	Nellie Ferland, Faison 28341	1	1	0	1	1	0	3	6	10	7	4	17	4	17	33
Garland	Mary E. Smith, Box 573, Garland 28441	1	1	1	1	1	0	5	6	17	7	4	27	3	0	64
Garner's Chapel	Debbie Rose, Rt. 1, Mt. Olive 28365	0	0	0	0	1	0	1	0	0	4	8	0	6	0	8
Grove Park	Velva Lindsay, Rt. 1, Box 21B, Clinton 38328	1	1	1	1	1	0	8	15	15	4	0	59	6	0	99
Immanuel	Madelle Ellis, Rt. 1, Box 20G, Clinton 28328	1	1	1	1	1	0	8	16	10	8	12	45	6	0	97
Ingold	Mrs. Winnie Matthis, Rt. 4, Clinton 28328	1	0	0	0	1	0	1	0	0	0	0	12	0	0	12
Island Creek	Charlotte Hartsell, Rt. 2, Box 349, Rose Hill 28458	1	1	1	1	1	0	4	3	6	10	0	15	3	0	37
Johnson	Sammie Southerland, Rt. 2, Box 5, Warsaw 28398	1	1	1	1	1	1	5	4	5	3	14	20	6	0	54
Kenansville	Edna E. Brinson, Box 8, Kenansville 28349	0	0	0	0	2	0	4	4	0	0	0	20	0	2	29
Magnolia	Nellie M. Burns, Magnolia 28453	1	1	1	0	1	1	4	6	5	5	0	47	3	0	52
Mount Olive		0	2	1	0	1	1	3	9	18	8	0	85	6	0	123
Mount Vernon	Gail Gainey, Rt. 5, Clinton 28328	0	1	1	0	1	1	3	0	7	0	0	18	5	2	39
Mount Gilead	Eunice Bass, Rt. 2, Box 110A, Clinton 28328	0	0	0	0	1	0	4	6	12	8	4	12	5	0	43
New Hope	Thelma Ware, Rt. 1, Turkey 28393	0	1	0	1	1	0	3	0	6	0	0	9	1	0	20
Piney Grove	Gail Naylor, 607 Thornton St., Clinton 28328	0	0	0	0	1	0	3	0	12	0	4	36	5	0	57
Poplar Grove	None	0	0	0	0	0	0	0	0	0	0	0	0	0	0	0
Poston	Martha Teachey, Rt. 3, Wallace 28466	0	1	1	1	1	0	4	15	19	13	14	56	6	0	123
Rose Hill	Mrs. W.B. Hawes, Rt. 2, Box 7, Rose Hill 28458	1	1	1	1	1	0	5	10	10	8	0	60	3	0	87
Rowan	Ruby Peterson, Rt. 2, Clinton 28328	0	1	1	1	1	4	5	6	5	8	11	40	7	0	73
Sharon	Clara Huffman, Chinquapin 28521	0	0	1	1	1	4	8	2	12	7	15	16	5	0	55
Shiloh	Mrs. Nellie Mobley, Rt. 1, Chinquapin 28521	0	0	0	0	1	0	2	0	0	1	0	10	5	26	10
Siloam	Linda Billings, Rt. 1, Box 19, Harrells 28444	0	1	1	0	1	1	1	0	0	0	0	24	3	0	27
Teachey	Mrs. Willard Fussell, P.O. Box, Teachey 28464	1	0	0	0	1	1	4	1	8	5	0	0	3	14	17
Turkey	Miss Dot Smith, Turkey 28393	0	1	1	0	1	1	4	0	5	0	0	20	1	0	35
Turkey Grove	Brenda Sancil, Rt. 4, Box 303, Clinton 28328	0	2	1	0	1	0	5	0	22	9	0	12	2	0	51
Warsaw	Cecelyn Drew, Rt. 1, Box 185, Warsaw 28398	1	1	1	1	1	1	5	7	4	4	0	88	7	0	133
Wells Chapel	Catherine Thornton, Rt. 1, Willard 28478	1	1	1	1	1	0	5	9	3	4	10	25	3	0	54
TOTALS		20	28	22	12	41	19	139	145	269	160	131	1033	145	94	1891

68

TABLE F BROTHERHOOD

Association: EASTERN

State: NORTH CAROLINA

Associational Brotherhood Director:

Address: P.O. Box — **City:** Warsaw — **State:** North Carolina — **Zip:** 28398

1982

CHURCHES	BROTHERHOOD DIRECTORS & ADDRESSES (INCLUDE ZIP CODE)	114 Crusaders (6-11 years or grades 1-6)	115 Pioneers (12-17 years or grades 7-12)	116 RA director and committee	117 Baptist Men enrolment—Basic	118 Baptist Men enrolment—Prayer	119 Baptist Men enrolment—Mission Action	120 Baptist Men enrolment—Witnessing or Lay Renewal	121 Brotherhood director and other general Brotherhood officers	122 Enrolment of mission(s) of church	123 Total ongoing Brotherhood enrolment
Albertson	None	0	0	0	0	0	0	0	0	0	0
Alum Springs	None	6	9	3	0	0	8	11	2	0	39
Bear Marsh	None	0	0	0	0	0	0	0	0	0	0
Beulah	None	8	5	3	18	0	0	0	1	0	35
Browns	Curtis Pope, 305 Inverness Rd., Clinton 28328	0	0	0	0	0	0	0	0	0	0
Calvary	Jamie Baker, Greenwood Terrace, Mt. Olive 28365	0	0	0	0	0	0	0	1	0	1
Calypso	Jamey West, Rt. 1, Box 184, Garland 28441	0	0	3	40	0	0	0	1	0	2
Center	Gene Pierce, 103 Denton Ave., Clinton 28328	20	0	0	0	6	2	2	1	0	74
Clinton	None	0	0	0	5	0	0	0	0	0	0
Concord											
Corinth	None	10	0	3	15	0	0	0	1	0	16
Dobson Chapel	Wilbur Carr, P.O. Box 417A, Kenansville 28349	7	4	2	12	0	0	0	0	0	16
Evergreen	Madison Lane, Rt. 1, Rose Hill 28458	3	5	2	0	0	0	0	0	0	25
Faison	D.R. Matthews, Faison 28341	11	14	2	32	0	0	0	1	0	39
Garland	Wilbert Davis, Box 147, Garland 28441	7	0	2	40	0	0	0	0	0	14
Garner's Chapel	None	0	0	0	0	0	0	0	1	0	0
Grove Park	David Jones, 710 Stewart Ave., Clinton 28328	10	0	2	20	0	0	0	0	23	45
Immanuel	Charles Adams, Rt. 1, Box 234, Clinton 28328	11	9	4	0	0	0	0	1	0	64
Ingold	None	0	0	0	0	0	0	0	0	0	0
Island Creek	Linwood Hanchey, Rt. 2, Rose Hill 28458	3	7	2	0	0	0	0	3	0	33
Johnson											
Kenansville	Amos Brinson, Jr., Box 8, Kenansville 28349	12	2	4	11	20	0	0	0	0	30
Magnolia	None	0	6	0	0	12	0	2	0	0	22
Mount Olive											
Mount Vernon	None	0	0	6	0	0	0	0	1	0	0
Mount Gilead	Evans Puryear, Rt. 4, Box 280, Clinton 28328	6	0	1	12	0	0	0	0	0	6
New Hope	Danny Johnson, Rt. 1, Turkey 28393	0	0	0	11	0	0	0	1	0	19
Piney Grove	None	0	3	0	0	0	0	0	0	0	4
Poplar Grove	None	0	0	0	0	0	0	0	0	0	0
Poston	John Braswell, Watha 28471	5	5	2	0	0	0	0	1	0	0
Rose Hill	Weldon A. Clack, Rt. 2, Box 55, Clinton 28328	12	0	0	8	0	0	0	1	0	39
Rowan	None	8	8	5	26	12	0	0	3	0	0
Sharon	None	10	1	3	0	0	0	0	0	0	31
Shiloh	None	0	0	0	0	0	0	0	1	0	19
Siloam	None	0	0	0	0	0	0	0	0	0	22
Teachey	George Pinyatello, Rt. 1, Turkey 28393	4	6	1	0	0	0	0	0	0	0
Turkey	None	24	10	0	8	0	0	0	2	0	21
Union Grove	J.B. Herring, 307 Walnut St., Warsaw 28398	4	0	4	26	0	0	0	0	0	0
Warsaw	E.B. Thornton, Rt. 1, Willard 28478	5	0	2	0	0	0	0	1	0	65
Wells Chapel	None	0	0	0	0	0	0	0	0	0	19
TOTALS		**186**	**94**	**52**	**255**	**50**	**10**	**15**	**23**	**23**	**700**

TABLE G TOTAL RECEIPTS, LOCAL EXPENDITURES & STEWARDSHIP — 1982

Association: EASTERN
State: NORTH CAROLINA
Associational Treasurer: WALTER THOMASSON
Address / P.O. Box: Clinton, North Carolina 28328

CHURCHES / TREASURERS & ADDRESSES (INCLUDE ZIP CODE)	21 Number of tithers	22 Cooperative Program goal as percent of undesignated receipts	23 Associational missions goal as percent of undesignated receipts	124 Undesignated gifts, offerings, etc.	125 Designated gifts, offerings, etc.	126 Total tithes, all offerings, and special gifts	127 All other receipts	128 Total receipts	129 Money borrowed during the year	130 Church staff salaries	131 Money paid out on new construction during the year	132 Debt retirement during the year	133 Church literature	134 All other local expenditures	135 Total local expenditures
Albertson — Ruth Outlaw, Rt. 1, Mt. Olive 28365	8	3	1	11274	3784	15057		15057		7800			631	9336	17767
Alum Springs — Donnell Bell, Rt. 5, Mt. Olive 28365	3	3		26929	1932	28861		28861		17480			1200	4757	23437
Bear Marsh — Milton Massey, Turkey 28393	11	7	1	23337	5026	28363	2650	31013	6500	6400	38068		1410	8147	54026
Beulah — Marie J. Pope, 305 Inverness Rd., Clinton 28328	17	2	13	23644	647	24291		24291		13325		4381	1316	4352	18993
Browns — Johnny Chestnut, Rt. 2, Warsaw 28398	15	11	3	25498	3900	29398	300	29698		11180		2000	939	4939	31439
Calvary — Blanton Barwick, Box 165, Calypso 28325	7	3	1	25498	3900	29398	300	29698		11120			582	2052	31316
Calypso — Barbara Smith, Rt. 1, Garland 28441	10	3	3	15988	1637	17547		17547		10400	3583	77550	608	4024	18625
Center — J.S. Eakins, 417 LaFayette St., Clinton 28328	8	15	2	15888	133	17547		17547					643	2070	
Clinton — Ethelene Usher, Rt. 1, Box 72, Rose Hill 28458	310	10	2	265071	53720	298791	18280	337071		62196	8875	77550	6550	140900	297196
Concord —	2	7	2	12505	8524	21029		21029		8987			643	2070	20575
Corinth — Bobby Bryan, Rt. 2, Rose Hill 28458	50	93	29	38506	5376	43882	2021	45903		11062		2121	1588	33253	45903
Dobson Chapel — Lucille Brown, Rt. 2, Rose Hill 28458	1	7	3	21126	1283	22410		22410		12599			1528	11480	25607
Evergreen — Floyd Sutton, Rt. 1, Magnolia 28453		2	1	22632	4295	26927		26927		9244			1369	6722	19456
Faison — Hazel Kelly, Faison 28341	12	2	2	1222	29063	30285		30285		10913			2854	14484	28251
Garland — Dorothy Hart, Box 187, Garland 28441	38	11	3	24887	6466	41353	39	41392		19693	5325		2283	6585	33886
Garner's Chapel — Durham Grady, Rt. 1, Mt. Olive 28365	5	10		16810	2639	19449	226	19675		9678			442	3797	13917
Grove Park — Charles Warren, 110 Underwood St., Clinton 28328	100	12	16	125172	4022	129194	1665	130859		35596	78795	35090	6170	32998	109854
Immanuel — Martha King, 114 Harmon St., Clinton 28328		75	35	96764	205776	302540	7907	310447		50617			12038	18777	160227
Ingold — Betsy M. Carter, Box 2, Harrells 28444		6	2	25163	1500	26663		26663		12240			1374	9252	22866
Island Creek — Garland King, Rt. 1, Teachey 28464	40	46		40510	4471	44721		44721		17650			1200	8221	27071
Johnson — Violette Phillips, Hwy. 24, Kenansville 28349	20	10	2	37428	9951	47379	384	47763		18683	4363		3955	10208	37209
Kenansville — A.F. Oakley, Box 216, Kenansville 28349		10	3	35246	3825	39071	696	39767		14300			1629	14138	30067
Magnolia — Alma Martino, Magnolia 28453		10	3	23068	5348	28416		28416		8394			637	10735	17185
Mount Olive — Miss Margaret Martin, 500 W. Main St., Mt. Olive 28365	70	9	9	109568	37741	147809	4528	147334		41175		21527	6484	40779	122547
Mount Vernon — Ruby A. Pope, Rt. 5, Clinton 28328	12	10	3	26366	600	22486		27486		8394				7578	12155
Mount Gilead — Larry Wiggins, Rt. 2, Box 128A, Clinton 28328		10	3	42619	1805	44424	460	44884		19010			2684	10600	32294
New Hope — R.L. Leonard, Rt. 1, Turkey 28393	13	5	3	17623	667	18290	190	18480		14019		4154	914	1780	16713
Piney Grove — Marion Darden, Rt. 2, Faison 28341	10	19	12	26645		36970		36970		13478		1619	1664	14679	33975
Poplar Grove — Mrs. Billie King, Rt. 1, Faison 28341	6	3	1	16127	10125	16127		16127		12018	6000		1313	8936	29886
Poston — Althea Blanton, Rt. 3, Wallace 28466	140	10	2	66615		69505	344	69850		15572	7389	10542	3680	20586	50381
Rose Hill — John Moore, 313 W. Main St., Rose Hill 28458			14	68130	3191	71321		71321		20824	5747	47363	3057	13800	45070
Rowan — Donald Pope, Box 411, Clinton 28328	19	9	3	48378	51100	99477		99477	5000	21568	13856		5335	18434	98447
Sharon — Homer James, Rt. 2, Wallace 28466	25	14	3	37468	1607	39075		39075		17000			7741	4950	4354?
Shiloh — Mrs. Camelia Brown, Rt. 1, Chinquapin 28521	45	5	3	34760	4278	39638	1381	41018		8320		8760	1132	13228	31440
Siloam — R.O. Sanderson, Rt. 1, Harrells 28444	10	3	19	17960	5971	23931		23931		9026			1007	6779	16812
Teachey — Elwood Fussell, P.O. Box, Teachey 28464	12	13	15	28783	18312	47095	1944	49038		16800			1041	7061	24902
Turkey — Louise Allen, Box 223, Turkey 28393	20	10	.007	30000	4635	34635		34635		17810			1732	12708	32250
Union Grove — Louise Carter, Rt. 4, Box 301, Warsaw 28328	7	.007		10816	3446	14262	351	14613		4800	534		747	4542	10624
Warsaw — W.G. Britt, 301 N Front St., Warsaw 28398	78	64	16	107693	18345	126038		126038		37202		21559	4000	58822	121583
Wells Chapel — Brenda Bowen, Rt. 1, Wallace 28466		11	21	28681	6975	35656	386	36042		17020		5180	1478	7903	31581
TOTALS	**1124**			**2148706**	**536274**	**2181631**	**43752**	**2245389**	**11500**	**688984**	**172535**	**241846**	**95709**	**619402**	**1828480**

TABLE H MISSION EXPENDITURES — 1982

Association: EASTERN — NORTH CAROLINA
Associational Clerk: PHILLIP BILLINGS
Address: Route 1, B.J x 19 — Harrells, North Carolina 28444

CHURCHES	CHURCH CLERKS & ADDRESSES (INCLUDE ZIP CODE)	136 Money paid out on new construction during the year	137 All other church sponsored mission expend.	138 Total church sponsored mission expenditures	139 Cooperative Program	140 Associational missions program	141 State missions	142 SB Home Missions (incl. Annie Armstrong Easter offering)	143 SB Foreign Mis. (incl. Lottie Moon Chr.tmas offering)	144 S3 Christian education (schools, etc.)	145 SB Children's homes (cash plus goods)	146 SB Hospitals	147 SB Homes for the aged	148 All other (Bible Society, Temperance League, etc.)	149 Total other mission cause expenditures	150 Grand Total Mission expenditures
Albertson	Marie K. Harper, Rt. 2, Box 281, Mt. Olive 28365	0	0	0	1000	300	1100	136	219	0	0	0	0	0	1755	2755
Alum Springs	E.G. Hatch, Jr., Rt. 5, Box 468, Mt. Olive 28365	0	0	0	750	300	0	469	395	0	957	0	0	49	2121	2871
Bear Marsh	Denise Hedley, 107 Oakland Terrace, Clinton	0	50	50	1673	1653	0	27	93	0	0	0	0	70	869	2552
Beulah	Shaun Carr, Rt. 3, Box 97, Clinton 28328	0	0	0	300	350	300	346	301	0	0	0	0	0	1367	1667
Browns	Linda Savage, Rt. 2, Box 95R, Warsaw 28398	0	0	0	2098	792	55	0	0	0	0	0	0	0	946	3044
Calvary	Henderson D. McCullen, Box 75, Calypso 28325	0	0	0	540	280	453	434	99	0	0	0	0	0	1667	2207
Calypso	Leona Blackburn, Rt. 1, Box 175, Garland 28441	0	0	0	902	527	0	0	500	0	0	0	0	0	592	1494
Center	Sue Miller, 504 Allen St., Clinton 28328	0	113	113	22500	4300	3000	3000	53	0	0	0	0	9397	27308	49808
Clinton	Mary Lee Usher, Rt. 1, Box 86, Rose Hill 28458	0	0	0	1382	637	91	52	7611	0	0	0	0	0	873	873
Concord	Betty Butts, Rt. 1, Teachey 28464	0	0	0	4709	1440	1200	548	933	0	0	0	0	1600	1296	2255
Corinth	Julia Brock, Rt. 2, Box 146, Rose Hill 28458	0	0	0	1740	746	646	96	1826	0	0	0	0	309	6614	11323
Dobson Chapel	Mrs. Noah Todd, Rt. 1, Box 321, Magnolia 28453	0	0	0	380	434	55	0	146	0	0	0	0	60	1270	3036
Evergreen	Helen Britt, Faison 28341	0	0	0	470	470	288	301	0	0	0	0	0	661	1787	1650
Faison	Evelyn Davis, Box 147, Garland 28441	0	0	0	3516	970	0	510	300	0	0	0	0	991	4261	2257
Garland	Annie B. Albertson, Rt. 1, Box 437, Mt. Olive 28365	0	0	0	800	150	383	415	1502	0	0	0	0	1621	2841	7777
Garner's Chapel	Jeanne Pope, 904 Raleigh Rd., Clinton 28328	0	0	0	15017	2045	1100	1134	655	0	0	0	0	925	6067	3641
Grove Park	Martha Tart, Box 652, Clinton 28328	0	0	0	7350	4371	500	1029	1580	0	0	0	0	838	8838	21084
Immanuel	Sara W. Pope, Rt. 4, Box 92, Clinton 28328	0	0	0	840	360	0	175	1500	0	0	0	0	410	1735	16188
Ingold	Mrs. Frank Caldwell, P.O. Box 293, Wallace 28466	0	0	0	1680	749	0	250	761	0	0	0	0	0	1771	2575
Island Creek	Dennis Kirby, Box 475, Kenansville 28349	0	0	0	3807	390	600	555	624	0	0	0	0	0	1327	3451
Johnson	Edna E. Brinson, Box 8, Kenansville 28349	0	0	0	1080	675	95	171	650	120	1200	400	350	219	4379	5735
Kenansville	Betty R. Chesnutt, Rt. 1, Box 277, Warsaw 28398	0	0	0	2200	2875	1086	2481	404	0	34	0	0	283	1662	5499
Magnolia	Dr. T.E. Shaver, Box 496, Mt. Olive 28365	0	0	0	9284	1400	0	454	2923	0	0	0	0	301	9667	3862
Mount Olive	Girlie Quinn, 301 Fairfax St., Clinton 28328	0	0	0	3569	1071	575	301	350	551	492	400	350	0	4353	18952
Mount Vernon	Catherine Peterson, Rt. 2, Box 104, Clinton 28328	0	0	0	1100	885	150	228	359	0	205	551	555	0	2876	4353
Mount Gilead	Shelby Blanchard, Rt. 1, Turkey 28393	0	0	0	500	300	175	316	788	0	150	150	150	0	2072	6445
New Hope	Blanche D. Casey, Rt. 5, Box 56, Clinton 28328	0	0	0	500	398	0	0	50	0	0	0	0	0	1579	3172
Piney Grove	Velsa L. Spencer, Rt. 1, Faison 28341	0	0	0	6980	1500	0	626	714	0	0	0	0	55	503	2079
Poplar Grove	Louise Hardison, 201 S. Teachey Rd., Wallace 28466	0	0	0	12377	1204	685	3045	5490	0	188	0	0	175	3015	1003
Poston	Dr. Larry Price, Box 638, Rose Hill 28458	0	0	0	4000	1645	283	306	979	150	0	0	0	930	10604	9995
Rose Hill	Barbara Briggs, 717 SW Blvd., Clinton 28328	0	0	0	3600	860	272	571	668	0	0	0	0	689	4293	22981
Rowan	Madeline Norris, Rt. 1, Box 2E, Chinquapin 28521	0	0	0	2466	990	33	212	455	0	0	0	0	103	2371	8293
Sharon	Cathy Jarosewicz, Rt. 2, Box 250B, Wallace 28466	0	0	0	600	380	145	449	942	0	0	0	0	550	2379	5971
Shiloh	Louise Maynard, Rt. 2, Box 124, Harrells 28444	0	0	0	3878	580	1511	1109	4653	0	0	0	0	111	2019	4845
Siloam	Mrs. I. Ferrell Hall, 502 W. Westbrook St., Wallace 28466	0	0	0	3024	997	329	710	1200	0	0	0	0	0	8403	12281
Teachey	Lettie Phipps, Box 96, Turkey 28393	0	0	0	196	997	0	103	100	0	164	190	0	550	257	2619
Turkey	Louise Carter, Rt. 4, Box 301, Clinton 28328	0	0	0	6995	1455	834	2343	2360	0	0	0	0	329	664	12281
Union Grove	Peggy Grice, 309 E. Pollock St., Warsaw 28398	0	0	0	2914	961	185	351	466	0	0	0	0	44	7321	6281
Warsaw	Luola P. Rivenbark, Rt. 1, Box 221, Willard 28478	0	0	0											2007	850
Wells Chapel		0	0	0												14316
TOTALS		0	163	163	136677	38829	16129	24116	42783	821	3390	1291	1055	20720	149319	286048

71

TABLE I SPECIAL INFORMATION — 1982

Association: EASTERN
State: NORTH CAROLINA
Moderator: JOHN FLAKE
Address — P.O. Box / **City:** Clinton / **State:** North Carolina / **Zip:** 28328

Column legend (headers 29–53):

29	No. church-type missions started during the year
30	No. church-type missions currently operating
31	No. other-type missions started during the year
32	No. other-type missions currently operating
33	No. New Sunday School Members
34	No. persons completing witness training
35	$ Annie Armstrong Offering
36	Kindergarten enrollment
37	N=none TV=TV R=radio B=both
38	Number of revivals
39	Number S.S. Members / Not church members
40	No. of college students baptized
41	Deaf Sunday School enrollment
42	No. of persons who served in a missions evangelism project in U.S.
43	No. of persons who served in a missions evangelism project overseas
44	N=none V=volunteer P=paid
45	Number of families signing Bible Study Commitment Cards
46	Begin weekly workers meet?
47	New Baptist Hymnal '75
48	Begin visitation program
49	History committee
50	Baptist Men's Day
51	Seminary degree
52	Christian Literature Day
53	State paper in budget

Does church have, observe, plan, use etc.? Y=YES N=NO

CHAIRMEN OF DEACONS & ADDRESSES (INCLUDE ZIP CODE)

Church	Chairman of Deacons & Address
Albertson	Sam Wallar, Rt. 2, Mt. Olive 28365
Alum Springs	Elbert J. Davis, Rt. 2, Mt. Olive 28365
Bear Marsh	L.A. Pope, Rt. 2, Box 409B, Clinton 28328
Beulah	Joseph Powell, Rt. 3, Clinton 28328
Browns	Russell Killette, Rt. 1, Warsaw 28398
Calvary	Don Guy, Box 163, Calypso 28325
Calypso	Ray Allen Cannon, Rt. 1, Garland 28441
Center	Tom Blount, 504 Beaman St., Clinton 28328
Clinton	Gatha Drew, Rt. 1, Box 386, Magnolia 28453
Concord	Charles Knowles, Rt. 1, Box 123, Wallace 28466
Corinth	Wilbur Carr, P.O. Box 417A, Kenansville 28349
Dobson Chapel	Billy Chestnutt, Rt. 1, Magnolia 28453
Evergreen	Henry Brown, Faison 28341
Faison	Gene Hart, Box 187, Garland 28441
Garland	Varner Garner, Rt. 1, Mt. Olive 28365
Garner's Chapel	Franklin Lindsay, Rt. 1, Box 21B, Clinton 28328
Grove Park	Jeff Honeycutt, 1232 Sunset Ave., Clinton 28328
Immanuel	Bobby H. Lamb, Rt. 1, Box 138, Garland 28441
Ingold	Linwood Hanchey, Rt. 2, Rose Hill 28458
Island Creek	Amos Brinson, Jr., Box 8, Kenansville 28349
Johnson	Kenneth Baker, Magnolia 28453
Kenansville	Dr. T.E. Shaver, Box 486, Mt. Olive 28365
Magnolia	Reboyd Warwick, Rt. 5, Clinton 28328
Mount Olive	Lonnie J. Bass, Rt. 2, Box 110A, Clinton 28328
Mount Vernon	Raymond Blanchard, Sr., Rt. 1, Turkey 28393
Mount Gilead	DeWitt King, Rt. 2, Faison 28341
New Hope	Doug Blackmon, Rt. 1, Faison 28341
Piney Grove	John Braswell, Wetta 28471
Poplar Grove	Byron Teachey, Box 6, Rose Hill 28458
Poston	Edward Byrd, Rt. 2, Box 221, Clinton 28328
Rose Hill	W.L. Brant, Chinquapin 28521
Rowan	David Maready, Rt. 1, Chinquapin 28521
Sharon	George McGill, Rt. 2, Box 23, Harrells 28444
Shiloh	Linwood Brinkley, Rt. 2, Rose Hill 28458
Siloam	H.J. Register, Rt. 1, Turkey 28393
Teachey	I.K. Carter, Jr., Rt. 4, Box 300, Clinton 28328
Turkey	James F. Strickland, Box 783, Warsaw 28398
Warsaw / Wells Chapel	I.C. Ennis, Rt. 1, Wallace 28466

Data (columns 29–45)

Church	29	30	31	32	33	34	35	36	37	38	39	40	41	42	43	44	45
Albertson	0	0	0	0	8	0	469	0	N	1	11	0	0	0	0	N	0
Alum Springs	0	0	0	0	5	0	0	0	N	1	2	0	0	0	0	N	0
Bear Marsh	0	0	0	0	4	0	155	0	N	1	8	0	0	0	0	N	0
Beulah	0	0	0	0	9	0		0	N	1	14	0	0	0	0	N	0
Browns	0	0	0	0	21	0	434	0	N	2	10	0	0	0	0	N	0
Calvary	0	0	0	0	4	0	13	19	N	1	6	0	0	0	0	P	0
Calypso	0	0	0	0	27	2	3000	25	R	2	8	0	0	0	0	P	25
Center	0	0	0	0	4	10	52	0	N	2	5	0	0	1	0	N	0
Clinton	0	0	0	0	0	0	548	0	N	1	0	0	0	0	0	V	0
Concord	0	0	0	0	6	0	96	0	N	1	5	0	0	0	0	V	0
Corinth	0	0	0	2	9	0	435	0	N	1		0	0	0	0	V	0
Dobson Chapel	0	0	0	0	0	0	286	0	N	1	15	0	0	4	0	V	0
Evergreen	0	0	0	0	10	0	510	0	N	2	30	0	0	1	0	N	0
Faison	0	0	0	0	0	0	415	0	R	2	0	0	0	0	0	V	0
Garland	0	0	0	0	0	0	1134	0	N	2		0	11	0	0	V	0
Garner's Chapel	0	0	0	0	0	0	1044	0	N	2	10	0	0	0	0	N	0
Grove Park	0	0	0	0	3	0	175	0	N	2	6	0	0	0	0	V	0
Immanuel	0	0	0	0	15	0	650	70	R	2		0	0	0	0	N	0
Ingold	0	0	0	0	12	0	555	0	N	1	19	0	0	0	0	V	0
Island Creek	0	0	0	0	10	0	600	0	R	2		0	0	0	0	N	0
Johnson	0	0	0	0	9	0	171	0	N	2	8	0	0	0	0	N	0
Kenansville	0	0	0	0	0	0	2481	0	N	2	6	0	0	2	0	N	0
Magnolia	0	0	0	0	0	0	350	0	N	1	23	0	0	0	0	V	0
Mount Olive	0	0	0	0	10	0	301	0	R	2	10	40	0	0	0	N	0
Mount Vernon	0	0	0	0	19	0	228	0	N	1	4	0	0	2	0	V	0
Mount Gilead	0	0	0	0	0	0	316	0	N	1		0	0	0	0	V	0
New Hope	0	0	0	0	0	0	55	0	N	2	5	0	0	0	0	N	0
Piney Grove	0	0	0	0	0	0	627	0	N	2	1	0	0	0	0	V	0
Poplar Grove	0	0	0	0	31	0	685	0	N	2	3	0	0	0	0	V	0
Poston	0	0	0	0	12	7	306	0	N	1	4	0	0	0	0	V	0
Rose Hill	0	0	0	0	13	0	571	0	N	2		0	0	0	0	V	0
Rowan	0	0	0	0	4	0	212	0	N	1	5	0	0	0	0	V	0
Sharon	0	0	0	0	0	0	449	0	N	2		40	0	0	0	N	0
Shiloh	0	0	0	0	5	0	1108	0	N	2	7	0	0	0	0	V	0
Siloam	0	0	0	0	7	0	710	0	N	2	22	0	0	0	0	V	0
Teachey	0	0	0	0	0	0	103	26	R	1		0	0	2	0	N	0
Turkey	0	0	0	0	12	0	905	0	N	1		0	0	0	0	V	0
Union-Grove / Warsaw / Wells Chapel	0	0	0	0	0	0	351	0	N	1		0	0	0	0	Y	0
TOTALS					283	19	20500	70		58	234	40	11	8	3		25

Data (columns 46–53, Y/N)

Church	46	47	48	49	50	51	52	53
Albertson	N	Y	N	N	N	N	N	Y
Alum Springs	N	N	N	Y	Y	Y	N	N
Bear Marsh	N	Y	N	N	N	N	N	Y
Beulah	N	N	N	N	N	N	N	Y
Browns	Y	N	N	N	Y	Y	N	N
Calvary	N	Y	N	N	Y	N	Y	Y
Calypso	Y	Y	Y	Y	Y	Y	Y	Y
Center	N	Y	N	N	Y	N	Y	Y
Clinton	N	N	N	N	Y	Y	N	Y
Concord	N	N	N	N	Y	Y	Y	Y
Corinth	N	Y	N	N	Y	Y	Y	Y
Dobson Chapel	N	N	N	N	N	N	N	N
Evergreen	N	Y	N	N	Y	Y	Y	Y
Faison	N	Y	N	N	Y	Y	Y	Y
Garland	N	N	N	N	Y		N	Y
Garner's Chapel	N	Y	N	N	Y	Y	N	Y
Grove Park	N	N	N	N	Y	N	c	N
Immanuel	N	N	N	N	N	N	N	N
Ingold	N	N	N	N	Y	Y	N	Y
Island Creek	N	N	N	N	Y	Y	Y	Y
Johnson	N	N	N	N	Y	Y	Y	Y
Kenansville	N	N	N	N	Y	Y	Y	Y
Magnolia	N	Y	Y	Y	Y	Y	Y	Y
Mount Olive	N	Y	N	N	Y	Y	Y	Y
Mount Vernon	N	N	N	N	Y	N	Y	Y
Mount Gilead	N	N	N	N	Y	Y	Y	Y
New Hope	N	N	N	N	Y	Y	N	Y
Piney Grove	N	Y	Y	Y	Y	Y	Y	Y
Poplar Grove	N	N	N	N	Y	Y	Y	Y
Poston	N	N	N	N	N	N	N	Y
Rose Hill	Y	Y	Y	Y	Y	N	Y	Y
Rowan	N	N	N	N	N	N	N	Y
Sharon	N	N	N	N	Y	N	N	Y
Shiloh	N	N	N	N	N	N	N	Y
Siloam	N	N	N	N	N	N	N	Y
Teachey	N	Y	N	N	N	N	N	Y
Turkey	N	Y	N	N	Y	N	Y	Y
Union-Grove / Warsaw / Wells Chapel	N	Y	N	N	N	N	N	Y

Minutes * Church Histories * Church Directories * Sermon Books * Genealogies
A Division of Henington Publishing Co., Inc.

SOUTHERN BAPTIST
Wolfe City, Texas 7
214 496-2226

For as the heaven is high above the earth,
so great is his mercy toward them that fear him.

Psalms 103:11

NORTH CAROLINA EASTERN BAPTIST ASSOCIATION

ONE-HUNDRED FIFTY-SIXTH ANNUAL

SESSION
1827 - 1983

3
hurch
ting)

SECOND DAY
October 25, 1983
Turkey Baptist Church
(Beulah - New Hope Assisting)

THEME
'THAT YE MAY GROW IN GRACE''

CLERK
Philip Billings

NEXT ANNUAL MEETING
First Day
Piney Grove Baptist Church
(Mount Vernon Assisting)
Monday, October 29, 1984
Second Day
Sharon Baptist Church
Shiloh Assisting
Tuesday, October 30, 1984

TABLE OF CONTENTS

CHURCH	PASTOR	ADDRESS	TELEPHONE
Albertson	Caleb Goodwin, Jr.	P.O. Box 37, Albertson 28508	568-951
Alum Springs	Shelton Justice	Rt. 1, Box 38A-2, Warsaw 28398	293-7524
Bear Marsh	E.C. Mattocks	Rt. 2, Box 52, Mount Olive 28365	658-6133
Beulah	Willie O. Carr	Rt. 5, Box 50, Clinton 28328	C-592-6530 / H-592-3789
Brown	Joseph W. Moss, Sr.	Rt. 6, Box 389, Clinton 28328	C-564-6060 / H-592-5642
Calvary	Andy Wood	103 Wade Street, Warsaw 28398	293-7458
Calypso		Box 248, Calypso 28325	
Center	Robert E. Hill	P.O. Box 153, Clinton 28328	C-532-2118 / H-592-4910
Clinton	James Pardue	P.O. Box 837, Clinton 28328	C-592-8124
Concord	Eddie Wetherington	Rt. 5, Box 39-A, Clinton 28328	592-2898
Corinth	Dennis Knight	Rt. 1, Box 329-B, Rose Hill 28458	289-3928
Dobson Chapel	Ernest L. Johnson, Jr.	Rt. 1, Box 118-A, Magnolia 28453	296-1473
Evergreen	Donald Ailsworth	Rt. 1, Rose Hill 28458	532-4757
Faison	Charles Kirkland	P.O. Box 426, Faison 28341	267-2591
Garland	Raleigh Carroll	P.O. Box 367, Garland 28441	C-529-5201 / H-529-2531
Garner's Chapel	William Shipp	Rt. 1, Mount Olive 28365	658-3503
Grove Park	Davis Benton	605 N.E. Blvd., Clinton 28328	C-592-3937 / H-592-3513
Hickory Grove	E.P. Warren	Rt. 1, Box 122, Clinton 28328	592-2159
Immanuel	A.L. McGee (Interim)	Sunset Avenue, Clinton 28328	592-3854
Ingold	Jake Robert Carroll	P.O. Box 5265, Ingold 28446	529-4181
Island Creek	James L. Hartsell	Rt. 2, Box 349, Rose Hill 28458	289-2606
Johnson	Kenneth Durham	Rt. 2, Box 71, Warsaw 28398	C-293-4757 / H-293-4980
Kenansville	Lauren R. Sharpe	P.O. Box 517, Kenansville 28349	C-296-0659 / H-296-1389
Magnolia	A.R. Teachey	702 Hall Street, Rose Hill 28458	C-289-2217 / H-289-3850

Church	Minister	Address	Phone
Mount Gilead	Oliver Skerrett	Rt. 2, Box 106, Clinton 28328	592-6533
Mount Olive	Anthony Z. Gurganus	301 N. Chestnut St., Mount Olive 28365	C-658-2062 H-658-2351
Mount Vernon	Willie O. Carr	Rt. 5, Box 50, Clinton 28328	533-3789
New Hope	Paul Rose	Rt. 1, Box 355, Turkey 28393	C-533-3089 H-685-4600
Piney Grove	Farrell H. Miller	Rt. 2, Box 122-A, Faison 28341	C-533-3532 H-533-3232
Poplar Grove	Donald R. Coley	Rt. 1, Box 77½, Faison 28341	C-285-2439 H-285-2476
Poston		Rt. 1, Box 347-B, Wallace 28466	
Rose Hill	Jerry D. Kinlaw	P.O. Box 459, Rose Hill 28458	H-289-2250 H-289-3882
Rowan	Michael Shook	202 Reedsford Road, Clinton 28328	C-592-7508 H-592-7268
Sharon	Phillip R. Denton	P.O. Box 126, Chinquapin 28521	C-285-4391 H-285-3062
Shiloh	Eugene Hardin	Rt. 1, Box 347, Chinquapin 28521	285-7403
Siloam	W. Phil Billings	Rt. 1, Box 19, Harrells 28444	C-532-4077 H-532-4444
Teachey	Larry G. Blount	P.O. Box 38, Teachey 28464	285-2788
Turkey	Larry D. Padgett	P.O. Box 216, Turkey 28393	C-592-5562 H-592-2416
Union Grove	L.L. Barnes	Rt. 2, Box 584, Elizabethtown 28337	588-4422
Warsaw	John A. Johnson (Interim)	108 Plank Street, Warsaw 28398	293-4236
Wells Chapel	Freddie Harris	Rt. 1, Wallace 28466	C-532-4210 H-532-4528

MINISTERS NOT PASTORS

Church	Minister	Address	Phone
Bear Marsh	Homer Bumgardner (OM)	Rt. 2, Warsaw 28398	293-7072
Clinton	T.N. Cooper (OM)	P.O. Box 55, Clinton 28328	592-2293
	J.A. Crowe, Sr. (OM)	190 Jasper Street, Clinton 28328	592-8758
	Waldo Early (OM)	207 Dixie Circle, Clinton 28328	592-2704
	Jasper Hinson (OM)	Rt. 6, Box 161, Clinton 28328	592-2088
	M.M. Johnson (OM)	P.O. Box 1093, Clinton 28328	592-2296

Church	Representative	Address	Telephone
Island Creek	William M. Jones (OM)	110 Forest Drive, Clinton 28328	592-2472
Poston	Clyde Davis (OM)	Rowan Road, Clinton 28328	592-5313
Rose Hill	Albert Rivenbark (OM)	Rt. 1, Willard 28478	532-4553
	Hal Bilbo (OM)	507 N. College, Wallace 28466	285-5888
	Evon Johnson (LM)	Jacksonville	
Rowan	Bi ly Todd (OM)	107 Dee Street, Clinton 28328	592-3441
Union Grove	Paul Barefoot (OM)	Rt. 4, Box 210, Clinton 28328	592-5572
Warsaw	D.W. Branch (OM)	515 E. College St., Warsaw 28398	293-4986
	Mitchell Rivenbark (OM)	509 E. Hill St., Warsaw 28398	293-7496
	John A. Johnson (LM)	108 E. Plank St., Warsaw 28398	293-4958

EXECUTIVE BOARD REPRESENTATIVES

CHURCH	REPRESENTATIVE	ADDRESS	TELEPHONE
Albertson	Nathan Kelly	Rt. 1, Albertson 28508	
Alum Springs	Larry Harper	Rt. 2, Box 281, Mount Olive 28365	658-3614
Bear Marsh	Stanley Byrd	Rt. 2, Mount Olive 28365	
Beulah	George Cox	Rt. 1, Turkey 28393	533-3427
Brown	Curtis Pope	305 Inverness Road, Clinton 28328	592-5209
	Mark McPherson	Rt. 3, Clinton 28328	
Calvary	Russell Killette	Rt. 1, Warsaw 28398	293-7674
	James Arnette	310 Wards Bridge Road, Warsaw 28398	293-7226
Calypso			
Center			
Clinton	Charles Lee Pope	P.O. Box 514, Clinton 28328	592-2469
	Graham Butler	1016 Jasper Street, Clinton 28328	592-7580
Concord	Gary Bell	P.O. Box 725, Rose Hill 28458	289-3226
	Francis Usher	Rt. 1, Box 86, Rose Hill 28458	289-2681
Corinth	Price Knowles	115 E. Main, Rose Hill 28458	289-3741
	George Jones	Rt. 1, Rose Hill 28458	289-2554
Dobson Chapel	James P. Brown, Jr.	Rt. 2, Rose Hill 28458	289-3463
	Russell Brown	Rt. 2, Rose Hill 28458	289-2228
Evergreen	Jerry Todd	P.O. Box 20, Harrells 28444	532-2271
	Dwight Grady	Rt. 1, Rose Hill 28458	

Faison	Clement R. Shine	Rt. 2, Faison 28341	267-2676
	David Allsbrook	105 E. Hill St., Warsaw 28398	293-4863
Garland	Gene Hart	P.O. Box 187, Garland 28441	529-4311
Garner's Chapel	Morris Rose	Rt. 1, Mount Olive 28365	658-5425
Grove Park	Gordon & A ede Powell	1002 Raleigh Road, Clinton 28328	592-3982
Hickory Grove	Miss Joyce Warren	Rt. 1, Box 131, Clinton 28328	564-6241
	Mrs. Jean Warren	Rt. 1, Box 122, Clinton 28328	564-2159
Immanuel	Dick Pope	621 NW Blvd., Clinton 28328	592-4221
Ingold	Wilbert Massey	1001 Naylor Street, Clinton 28328	592-2642
	Norwood Carter	P.O. Box 2, Harrells 28444	529-1921
Island Creek	Henry L. Blackburn	Rt. 4, Clinton 28328	529-3891
Johnson	Mr. & Mrs. Edward Teachey	210 E. Boney Street, Wallace 28466	285-
	Robert Southerland	Rt. 2, Warsaw 28398	293-4690
Kenansville	Violette Phillips	P.O. Box 727, Kenansville 28349	296-1038
	Amos Brinson	Box 8, Kenansville 28349	296-0749
	O.R. Blizzard	Rt. 1, Kenansville 28349	289-2568
Magnolia	Jack Joyner	Magnolia 28453	289-2766
	Clifton Chesnutt	Magnolia 28453	592-4074
Mount Gilead	Lonnie Bass	Rt. 2, Box 110-A, Clinton 28328	592-6737
	Max Peterson	Rt. 2, Box 152, Clinton 28328	658-4191
Mount Olive	W.K. Lewis	W. Steel St., Mount Olive 28365	658-
	W.B. Murray, Jr.	W. Main St., Mount Olive 28365	592-5852
Mount Vernon	Reboyd Warwick	Rt. 5, Clinton 28328	533-3586
New Hope	R.W. Blanchard, Jr.	Rt. 1, Turkey 28393	533-3639
	Robert Frederick	Rt. 1, Turkey 28393	533-3420
Piney Grove	Oscar Thornton	Rt. 2, Box 116-B, Faison 28341	
	Wayne Thornton	Rt. 2, Box 115, Faison 28341	
Poplar Grove	Garland Britt	Rt. 2, Box 176, Faison 28341	
Poston	Jimmy Jordan	Rt. 1, Faison 28341	267-6961
Rose Hill	Aileen Moore	Rt. 3, Wallace 28466	
Rowan	Donald Pope	P.O. Box 411, Clinton 28328	592-3437
	Barbara Briggs	717 S.W. Blvd., Clinton 28328	592-7228
Sharon	Phillip R. Denton	Chinquapin 28521	285-3062
Shiloh	P.A. Maready	Rt. 2, Wallace 28466	285-2726
	G.C. Raynor	Rt. 2, Wallace 28466	532-4211
Siloam	R.O. Sanderson	Rt. 1, Harrells 28444	532-4497
	C.P. Eakins	Harrells 28444	

Turkey	Creson Ezzell	Rt. 1, Turkey 28393	533-3368
	H.J. Register	Rt. 1, Turkey 28393	533-3845
Union Grove	George G. Fryar	Rt. 4, Box 27, Clinton 28328	592-4830
	Morris Ezzell	Rt. 4, Box 351-A, Clinton 28328	592-2280
Warsaw	John A. Johnson	108 E. Plank St., Warsaw 28298	293-4830
Wells Chapel	John W. Johnson	Rt. 1, Wallace 28466	285-
	Jim Moody	Rt. 1, Box 130, Wallace 28466	285-

GENERAL ASSOCIATIONAL OFFICERS

Moderator	Donald Coley	Rt. 1, Box 347-B, Wallace 28466	285-2476
Vice Moderator	Lucille Yancey	P.O. Box 711, Clinton 28328	592-3080
Clerk	Phil Billings	Rt. 1, Box 19, Harrells 28444	532-4444
Associate Clerk	E.C. Mattocks	Rt. 2, Box 52, Mount Olive 28365	658-6133
Treasurer	Martha Pierce	103 Denton Avenue, Clinton 28328	592-6967
Associate Treasurer	Jo Robinson	Rt. 2, Box 269, Clinton 28328	592-3044

CHURCH PROGRAM OFFICERS

Brotherhood:
Director   Charles Kirkland (See Pastors)
Pioneer Director
Crusader Director

Church Music:

Director	Jean Hatch	P.O. Box 837, Clinton 28328	592-8124
Council Members:	Janet Register	Rt. 2, Rose Hill 28458	289-3367
	Vivian Kirkland	P.O. Box 426, Faison 28341	267-2591
	Curtis Pope	(See Executive Board Representatives)	

Church Training:

| Director | Mary Carter | P.O. Box 334, Garland 28441 | 529-4121 |

Age-Group Directors:

Adult	Phyllis Durham	Rt. 2, Box 71, Warsaw 28398	293-4980
Youth	Rose Pleasant	Box 203, Mount Olive 28365	658-3036
Children	Rene' Carroll	P.O. Box 367, Garland 28441	529-2531
Pre-School			

Sunday School:

Director	James Hartsell	(See Pastors)	
8.5 x '85	Larry Padgett	(See Pastors)	
VBS Director			
Adults	Charlotte Hartsell	Rt. 2, Box 349, Rose Hill 28458	289-2606
Youth	Sue Padgett	P.O. Box 216, Turkey 28393	592-2416
Older Children	Barbara Shook	202 Reedsford Road, Clinton 28328	592-7268
Middle Children	Dennis Knight	(See Pastors)	
Younger Children	Sylvia Knight	Rt. 1, Rose Hill 28458	289-3928
Pre-School	Tempie Wood	103 Wade St., Warsaw 28398	293-7458

Woman's Missionary Union:

Director	Helen Register	Rt. 1, Turkey 28393	533-3845
Assistant Director	Mary Carter	Garland 28441	529-4121
Secretary/Treasurer	Lillian Pope	P.O. Box 411, Clinton 28328	592-3437
Baptist Women Director	Linda Billings	Rt. 1, Box 19, Harrells 28444	532-4444
BYW Director & YBW	Glenda Todd	107 Dee Street, Clinton 28328	592-3441
Acteens Director	Gloria Lockerman	Rt. 3, Box 394-H, Clinton 28328	592-4121
Girls in Action Dir.	Paula Matthis	Rt. 4, Clinton 28328	592-5802
Mission Friends	Tempie Wood	103 Wade St., Warsaw 28398	293-7458
Mission Action Dir.	Connie Carlton	Rt. 1, Warsaw 28398	293-7106

DENOMINATIONAL REPRESENTATIVES

American Bible Society	H.J. Register (See Executive Board Representatives)
Children's Home	John A. Johnson (See Ministers not Pastors)
Homes For Aging	Millard M. Johnson (See Ministers not Pastors)
Christian Education	Anthony Gurganus (See Pastors)
Cooperative Program	Albert Pope (See Ministers not Pastors)
Annuity Board	Waldo Early (See Ministers not Pastors)

Hospital
Christian Literature/Biblical Recorder

Gerald Quinn, Wards Bridge Road, Warsaw 28398   293-4579
T.N. Cooper (See Ministers not Pastors)

COMMITTEES

Trustees:
Larry Harper (1986)   Rt. 2, Box 281, Mount Olive 28365   658-3614
Carroll Turner (1985)   604 N. Center St., Mount Olive 28365   658-6337
Wayne Wilson (1984)

Committee on Committees:
Ken Durham, Chairman   (See Pastors)
Florence Hoover   Rt. 2, Box 18, Harrells 28444   532-4336
R.O. Sanderson   (See Executive Board Representatives)
Shelton Justice   (See Pastors)
W.K. Lewis   (See Executive Board Representatives)

Evangelism:
Dennis Knight (1986)   (See Pastors)
*Anthony Gurganus (1985)   (See Pastors)
*Freddie Harris (1984)   (See Pastors)

Mission:
Davis Benton, Chairman (1986)   (See Pastors)
Kenneth Goodson (1985)   Rt. 4, Box 289, Mount Olive 28365   658-9817
Mitchell Rivenbark (1984)
(Includes Following Chairpersons):
Florence Hoover (1985) (Literacy)
Carol Todd (1985) (Mentally Handicapped)
Sylvia Knight (1985) (Deaf)
Ken Durham (1985) (Senior Adult)
Andy Wood (1985) (Migrant)

- 9 -

Media Library:
Joyce Braswell, Chairman (1985)   Rt. 1, Box 53-A, Watha 28471   285-7133
Margaret Goodson (1984)   Rt. 4, Box 389, Mount Olive 28365   658-9817
Joyce Lucas (1986)   606 Blaney Street, Clinton   592-3610

Pastoral Support:
Phillip Denton, Chairman (1986)   P.O. Box 126, Chinquapin 28521   285-3062
R.O. Sanderson (1984)   (See Executive Board Representatives)
W.K. Lewis (1985)   (See Executive Board Representatives)

Program Committee:
Freddie Harris, Chairman (1985)   (See Pastors)
Gene Hardin (1986)   (See Pastors)
*Larry Harper (1984)   (See Executive Board Representatives)

Historical Committee:
Charlotte Hartsell, Chairman (1984)   (See Sunday School)
Marsha Lewis (1986)
Waldo Early (1986)   (See Ministers not Pastors)

Stewardship Committee:
Gene Hart, Chairman (1985)   (See Executive Board Representatives)
Mitchell Rivenbark (1985)   (See Ministers not Pastors)
John Braswell (1985)   Rt. 1, Box 53-A, Watha 28471   285-7133
Florence Hoover (1984)   (See Committee on Committees)
Donald Pope (1984)   (See Executive Board Representatives)
Davis Benton (1984)   (See Pastors)
Ed Colwell (1986)   Rt. 1, Turkey 28393   533-3372
Priscilla McGill (1986)   Harrells 28444
Jimmy Strickland (1986)   P.O. Box 783, Warsaw 28398   293-4289
Martha Pierce (Treasurer)   (See Associational Officers)

Ordination Committee:
Don Coley, Chairman (1986)   (See Pastors)
Millard Johnson (1986)   (See Ministers not Pastors)
*Michael Shook (1985)   (See Pastors)
Amos Brinson (1985)   (See Executive Board Representatives)
William Jones (1985)   (See Ministers not Pastors)
Jerry Kinlaw (1984)   (See Pastors)

Literacy Committee:
Florence Hoover, Chairperson (1985)   (See Committee on Committees)
*Mavis Pigford (1984)   501 Forrest Road, Warsaw 28398   293-7952
Faye Gaddy (1986)   Rt. 6, Clinton 28328   592-3270

Senior Adult Ministries:
*Ken Durham, Chairperson (1985)   (See Pastors)
Sue Padgett (1984)   (See Sunday School)
Joyce Warren (1986)   (See Executive Board Representatives)

Ministries to the Mentally Handicapped:
Carol Todd, Chairperson (1985)   (See Missions Committee)
Clara Huffman (1984)   Rt. 1, Box 16, Chinquapin 28521   285-3585
Randy Kight (1986)   Kenansville 28349

Deaf Ministries:
*Sylvia Knight, Chairperson (1985)   (See Sunday School)
Mary Boney (1984)   Rt. 3, Box 72, Wallace 28466
Mary Lee Jones (1986)   Warsaw 28398

Migrant Ministries:
Andy Wood, Chairman (1985)   (See Pastors)
Gail Naylor (1985)   607 Thornton Street, Clinton 28328   592-2944
Francis Clifton (1984)   Rt. 1, Faison 28341   267-2551
Betty Carr (1984)   505 Carolina Ave., Clinton 28328   592-4860
Betty Rose (1986)   Rt. 1, Box 355, Mount Olive 28365   658-4600
Wilson Spencer (1986)   Rt. 1, Faison 28341   267-0931

Nominating Committee:
John Braswell, Chairman (1984)   (See Stewardship Committee)
Millard Johnson (1984)   (See Ministers not Pastors)
Farrell Miller (1985)   (See Pastors)
George McGill (1985)   Rt. 2, Box 23, Harrells 28444   532-4276
H.J. Register (1986)   (See Executive Board Representatives)
Charles Lee Pope (1986)   (See Executive Board Representatives)

*Filling Unexpired Term

- 11 -

ALBERTSON:
ALUM SPRINGS: Larry W. Harper, Carolyn Sanderson, Dill Sanderson,
    Larry Herring, Sam Waller
BEAR MARSH: L.B. Southerland, E.J. Davis, E.C. Mattocks
BEULAH: George Cox, Adell Creech, Callie Call, Willie Carr,
    Milton Massey
BROWN: Joe Powell, Edna Powell, Herbie Jordan, Randall Spiva,
    Effie Bass, Curtis Pope
CALVARY: Ethel Batts, Hannah Farmer, Nancy Smith
CALYPSO: Frances Powell, Louise Turner, Charles Rivenbark
CENTER: Louis Register, David Blackburn, Doris Hill, Robert
    Hill
CLINTON: L.E. Williamson, Waldo Early, Tom Cooper, Jasper Hinson,
    Eleanor Early, Everette Peterson, Cleone Cooper, Martha Pierce
CONCORD: G.R. Brice, Grace Brice, Mary Lee Usher
CORINTH: Betty Butts, Fay Fussell, Thelma Dempsey, Annie Ruth
    Hall, J.C. Savage, Jr., Maggie Johnson
DOBSON'S CHAPEL: Ruby Rouse, Kate Kilpatrick, Naomi Brock, Julia
    Brock, Betty Brown, Elna Grey Bostic
EVERGREEN: Jerry Todd, Mrs. Jack Stuart, Mrs. Billy Chestnutt
FAISON: Lucy Custer, Stella Sutton, Annie Brown, Charles Kirkland
GARLAND: Gene Hart, Raleigh Carroll, Anna Belle McLelland, Rene'
    Carroll, Mary Carter, Mary Ethel Smith
GARNER'S CHAPEL: Theron Garner, Randolph Garner, Joyce Shipp
GROVE PARK:
HICKORY GROVE: Jean Warren, Joyce Warren, Egbert Strickland,
    Lumis Strickland, Geneva Strickland, Elsie Strickland
IMMANUEL: Dick Pope, Katherine Pope, Bevie Melson, Mercedes
    Floyd, Christine Massey, Mildred Honeycutt, Martha King,
    Magdalene Moore, Rossie Mattocks, M/M James Goff, M/M Thomas
    Merritt
INGOLD: M/M Henry L. Blackburn
ISLAND CREEK: Charlotte Hartsell, Centelle Hanchey, Edward
    Teachey, Daphne Teachey
JOHNSON: Robert Southerland, R.A. Best, Kenneth Durham
KENANSVILLE: Macy Brinson, Margaret Oakley, Lorena Vestal,
    Wilma Pate, Rose Swain, Sally Tyndall
MAGNOLIA: Mrs. A.R. Teachey, Carlton Smith, Charles Bowman
MOUNT GILEAD: Pearl Merritt, Gertrude Powell, Pauline Wiggins,
    Steve Bass, Lonnie Bass.
MOUNT OLIVE: Helen Bell, Virginia Lindsay, Pearl Cherry, Kenneth
    Goodson, Margaret Goodson, Alma Anderson, Eunice Landin, Rose
    Pleasant, Teva Draughon, Rose Lewis
MOUNT VERNON: Gladys Martin, Evelyn Tew, Norene Royal, Delores
    Quinn, Franklin Barber, Minnie Lou Gainey, Thelma Gainey,
    Milton Gainey, Lou Pearl Simmons
NEW HOPE: Shelby Blanchard, Paul Rose, Ed Colwell, Robert
    Frederick, Thelma Ware, Esther Hines, Buck Blanchard
PINEY GROVE: Irene Darden, Dot Boyette, Eloise Clifton, Carol
    Miller, Farrell Miller, DeWitt King
POPLAR GROVE:
POSTON: Mary Boney, Lula Dixon, Laura Ramsey, Thelma Murray,
    Annette Henderson
ROSE HILL: Annie L. Rouse
ROWAN: Kathy Bailey, James Yancey, Dixie Yancey, Mozzelle Jones,
    Richard Hairr, Cooper Hairr
SHARON: Margaret Brinley, Annie Cavenaugh, Louise Southerland,

Jim Southerland, Clara Huffman, T.G. Huffman
SHILOH: Virginia Aycock, Pauline Mobley, David Maready, May Lee
Raynor, Rifton Raynor
SILOAM: Priscilla McGill, Alma Futrell, Linda Billings, Norma
Johnson, Edna King, Louise Maynard
TEACHEY: Joe Ward, Manley Teachey, Leland McGill
TURKEY: Helen Register, Ruth Ellis, Sue Padgett, Creson Ezzell
UNION GROVE: M/M George G. Fryar, Rodela Batts, Evelyn Fryar,
Marilyn Carter, Cathy Matthis
WARSAW: Nancy Herring, Helen Ann Straughan, Gerald Quinn, Rita
Quinn, Doris Chestnutt, Robert Chestnutt, Blanche Draughan,
Dot Rollins
WELLS CHAPEL: Catherine Thornton, Florence Hoover, Freddie Harris,
Alma Highsmith, Luola P. Rivenbark

PROCEEDINGS

1. Vice-Moderator, Don Coley, called to order the 156th Annual
   Session of the Eastern Association at 3:15 P.M., October 24,
   1983, in Siloam Baptist Church; Harrells, North Carolina.
2. The Association sang "Amazing Grace".
3. Eugene Hardin read II Corinthians 8:1-12 and led in prayer.
4. Clyde Davis, substituting for the associate clerk, reported
   registration representing 38 churches and moved that the
   messengers present constitute a quorum. Passed.
5. Clyde Davis, substituting for chairman of Program Committee,
   presented the order of the service and moved its adoption as
   the order of business. Passed.
6. Tony Gurganus, Nominating Committee Chairman, presented for
   nomination Phil Billings as Clerk and E.C. Mattocks as
   Associate Clerk. Both were elected.
7. No petitionary letters were received for this Annual Session.
8. The Vice-Moderator appointed the following committees:
   A. Resolution
      Raleigh Carroll, Chairman
      Kenneth Goodson
      Helen Register
   B. Time, Place and Preacher
      Andy Wood, Chairman
      David Maready
      Mozzelle Jones
   C. Memorials
      Eddie Wetherington, Chairman
      Ken Durham
      Jake Carroll
9. Jo Robinson, for the Treasurer, presented the Treasurer's
   Report which was adopted.
10. Phil Billings, Clerk, presented the Associational Council
    Report. Action was deferred to the second day's session,
    pending clarification of a new committee created during the
    year and its title name. It was also noted that no Constitu-
    tion Committee was appointed during July 25, 1983's Execu-
    tive Board Meeting.
11. Miscellaneous Business
    Gene Hart, Chairman of the Stewardship Committee, pre-
    sented the 1983-84 Budget for information purposes. Action
    will be taken during the second day's session.
12. "In Loving Kindness Jesus Came" was sung.

13. Agency Reports were given as follows:
    A. Annuity Board   Waldo Early
    B. Christian Literature/Biblical Recorder   Tom Cooper
    C. Baptist Foundation   Ken Durham
    D. American Bible Society   H.J. Register
14. Garland Hendricks brought a message.
15. Phil Billings, Host Pastor, gave greetings from the host church, Siloam.
16. The Association sang, "We Have Heard the Joyful Sound".
17. Reports of the Social Service Institutions were given as follows:
    A. Baptist Home for Aging   Millard Johnson
    B. Baptist Children's Home   Clyde Davis
    C. Baptist Hospital   Clyde Davis
18. Dr. Michael C. Blackwell, President of North Carolina Baptist Children's Homes, Inc., gave a message from the Homes of North Carolina.
19. Clyde Davis, Director of Missions, presented the following churches certificates of recognition for their advancements in baptisms, local church budget increases, Cooperative Program giving increases, and Associational giving increase:
    Teachey, New Hope, Brown, Shiloh, Mount Gilead, Island Creek, Ingold, Dobson's Chapel, Rowan, Corinth, Poston, Calvary, Sharon, Turkey, Garner's Chapel, Beulah, Evergreen, Concord, Alum Springs, Immanuel, Johnson, Union Grove, and Faison.
20. New Pastors and Church Staff Members were recognized by Clyde Davis:
    1. E.C. Mattocks, Pastor, Bear Marsh
    2. Dennis Knight, Pastor, Corinth
    3. Ernest (Ed) Johnson, Pastor, Dobson Chapel
    4. Raleigh Carroll, Pastor, Garland
    5. Jake Carroll, Pastor, Ingold
    6. A.R. Teachey, Pastor, Magnolia
    7. Eugene Hardin, Pastor, Shiloh
    8. E.P. Warren, Pastor, Hickory Grove
    9. Hal Bilbo, Youth and Educational Minister, Poston
    10. Gary Chadwick, Youth Director, Grove Park
21. The Association sang, "My Jesus, I Love Thee".
22. Gary Chadwick sang a solo of inspiration.
23. Dr. Delos Miles delivered the Doctrinal Message based on Jeremiah 9:23-24 and I Corinthians 1:26.
24. Phil Billings led in prayer of thanksgiving and blessing for the evening meal.

FIRST DAY - EVENING SESSION

1. Vice-Moderator, Don Coley, called the Association to order at 7:10 P.M., October 24, 1983.
2. Jean Hatch led in the singing of "Blessed Assurance, Jesus Is Mine".
3. Raleigh Carroll read John 15:15 and led in prayer.
4. Paula Clayton presented Eastern Association's Christian Social Ministries' Activities of the past year. Five new committees were created during the past year. Their chairmen explained the programs:
    A. New Committee Reports:
       Deaf Ministries   Mary Boney

Literacy Ministries   Florence Hoover
  Mentally Handicapped Ministries   Carol Todd
  Senior Adults Ministries   Ken Durham
 B. Ongoing Social Committee Reports:
  Migrant Ministries   Andy Wood
5. Jean Hatch led in the singing of "I Love to Tell the Story".
6. Steve Bass brought a special medley of inspirational music.
7. Cecil Etheridge, Home Mission Board, Atlanta, brought the Missionary Message.
8. The Vice-Moderator adjourned the session with prayer of benediction by Michael Shook.

SECOND DAY - OCTOBER 25, 1983

1. Vice-Moderator, Don Coley, called the Association to order at 9:30 A.M. in Turkey Baptist Church, Turkey, North Carolina.
2. Jean Hatch led the Association in singing "Stand Up For Jesus".
3. Dennis Knight read Acts 1:8 and led in prayer.
4. Clyde Davis, substituting for the Associate Clerk, reported registration representing 35 churches and moved that the messengers present constituted a quorum. Passed.
5. Miscellaneous Business
 A. Phil Billings, Clerk, moved that the Executive Council Report be accepted as read yesterday. Passed.
 B. Michael Shook moved that the committee, Ministry to Mentally Retarded be renamed Ministry to Mentally Handicapped. Passed.
 C. Paula Clayton submitted her verbal resignation as part-time Christian Social Ministries Director, effective December 31, 1983. Her resignation was regretfully accepted.
6. Larry Padgett, host Pastor, extended greetings and welcome from Turkey Baptist Church, to the Association.
7. Eugene Warrick, Home Mission Board, presented opportunities to Pioneer Missions in West Virginia.
8. Standing Committee Reports:
 A. Missions Committee   Michael Shook
 B. Stewardship   Gene Hart
 C. Evangelism   Not Given
 D. Media Library   Thelma Davis
 E. Pastoral Support   Clyde Davis
9. Clyde Davis, Director of Missions, challenged the Association with his Missions Sermon, "A Look at Our Mission".
10. Gene Hart, Chairman of Stewardship Committee moved that the 1983-84 budget be approved as submitted in the first day session. Mr. Hart answered questions of clarification. Motion passed.
11. Tony Gurganus called for recognition of College and University representatives. None responded. Mr. Gurganus moved the report of Christian Higher Education be approved. Passed.
12. Tony Gurganus moved that the Nominating Committee Report be approved. Passed.
13. Ken Durham moved that the Committee on Committees be approved. Passed.
14. Reports of Appointed Committees:
 A. Resolutions   Raleigh Carroll, Chairman
 B. Time, Place and Preacher   Andy Wood, Chairman

October 29, 1984, Piney Grove/Mount Vernon
October 30, 1984, Sharon/Shiloh
Preacher: Farrell Miller - Alternate: Dennis Knight
C. Memorials   Eddie Wetherington, Chairman
15. Jean Hatch led in the singing of "Our Best".
16. Church Program Organizational Reports:
    A. Departments: Directors:
       Brotherhood   Charles Kirkland
       Church Music   Jean Hatch
       Church Training   Phil Billings
       Sunday School   James Hartsell
       Vacation Bible School   James Hartsell
       WMU   Betsy Carter
    B. The following certificates were presented for achieve-
       ments in Sunday School Program:
       1. Certificate of Recognition
          James Hartsell
          Charlotte Hartsell
       2. Certificate of Appreciation
          Sue Padgett
          Tim Bass
          Andy Wood
          Tempie Wood
          Timmy Mercer
          Greg Thornton
          Larry Padgett
17. Robert Stewart, Director, North Carolina Baptist Convention
    Sunday School Department, brought a message.
18. Jean Hatch led in the singing of "Take My Life and Let it
    Be".
19. Dean Padgett brought special music with an inspirational
    song.
20. Jerry Kinlaw read Matthew 28:16-20.
21. Larry Padgett brought the Annual Sermon based on Matthew
    28:16-20.
22. Vice-Moderator, Don Coley adjourned the 156th Annual Session
    of the Eastern Baptist Association with a prayer.

                ASSOCIATIONAL EXECUTIVE BOARD REPORT

    The Executive Board met the Association's constitutional re-
quirements of four quarterly meetings for the purpose of acting
for the Association between Annual Meetings. Following is a
summary of actions taken:

November 29, 1982 - Rowan Baptist Church
    John Flake moderated with thirty-three churches in attendance.
    Department and committee reports were given.
January 24, 1983 - Johnson Baptist Church
    John Flake moderated with thirty churches in attendance.
    Hickory Grove Baptist Church, Route 1, Clinton, submitted a
    letter of admittance into Eastern Baptist Association. Hickory
    Grove was extended membership after motion and vote. Donald
    Coley, Chairman of Committee on Committees, moved that five
    new standing committees be established. The motion passed.
    The new committees are Literacy Ministries, Ministry to
    Mentally Handicapped, Deaf Ministries, Senior Adult Minis-
    tries, and Migrant Ministries. Other committee and department
    reports were given.

                            - 16 -

April 25, 1983 - New Hope Baptist Church
  John Flake moderated with twenty-eight churches in attendance.
  Department and committee reports were given.
July 25, 1983 - Poplar Grove Baptist Church
  Vice-Moderator, Donald Coley, moderated with twenty-four
  churches in attendance. A motion was made by Michael Shook,
  Chairman of the Missions Committee that Eastern Baptist Associ-
  ation request $8,000.00 from the Cooperative Missions Fund,
  North Carolina Baptist State Convention for Christian Social
  Ministry and four student summer workers. Motion passed. De-
  partment and committee reports were given. Donald Coley ap-
  pointed the following for Moderator, John Flake:
  COMMITTEE ON COMMITTEES: Ken Durham, Chairman
                               Shelton Justice
                               R.O. Sanderson
                               W.K. Lewis
                               Florence Hoover
August 29, 1983 - Warsaw Baptist Church
  Moderator, John Flake, called the Executive Board into a
  special session. Thirty-three churches were in attendance.
  A motion was made that the Eastern Baptist Association in-
  crease it's request to the North Carolina State Convention
  from $8,000.00 to $18,000.00 for a full time Christian Social
  Ministries Director. The motion was approved. This special
  session was adjourned after this action.

                          Respectfully submitted,
                          Phil Billings, Clerk

                RESOLUTION COMMITTEE REPORT

    Whereas: the Eastern Baptist Association's Migrant Ministries
Committee has completed its first year as a standing committee
and has experienced two years of fruitful ministry in the geographical area of Eastern Association,
    Be it resolved: that the 156th session of Eastern Baptist
Association expressed its appreciation to the following:
    1. To God for leadership and blessings experienced throughout
       the migrant ministry programs for 1981-82 and 1982-83
    2. To the churches and individuals within our Association who
       have contributed to the ministry project over and above
       regular contributions.
    3. To the churches, organizations and individuals outside of
       Eastern Association, whose significant contribution in the
       form of time, monetary gifts, Bibles, clothing, shoes,
       and/or supplies added greatly to the scope of our migrant
       ministry.
    We move the adoption of this resolution and that it be mailed
to the following:
Mt. Zion Baptist Church of Snellville, Georgia
Woman's Missionary Union of Pullen Memorial Baptist Church
  of Raleigh, North Carolina
Cedar Fork Baptist Church of Beulaville, North Carolina
First Baptist Church of Jacksonville, North Carolina
Mrs. Nita Anderson of Raleigh, North Carolina
Acteens of Providence Church of Holly Ridge, North Carolina
Clayton Baptist Church of Clayton, Georgia
Watts Street Baptist Church of Durham, North Carolina

GA Campers from Camp Mundo Vista in care of the Woman's
    Missionary Union of North Carolina
Southern Pines Baptist Church of Southern Pines, North
    Carolina
Bennie Travel Mission Action Group of Swansboro, North
    Carolina
Whereas: the North Carolina Eastern Baptist Association held
its one hundred and fifty-sixth annual session in the spirit of
Christ and to the glory of God,
Be it resolved:
1. That we express our deepest appreciation to the officers
   of the Eastern Baptist Association for their splendid
   planning and the execution of this 156th meeting and
   especially to our Vice-Moderator, Don Coley.
2. That we express our deep appreciation to the host churches,
   Siloam, assisted by Evergreen, and Turkey assisted by
   Beulah and New Hope, for the bountiful meals prepared for
   us and the excellent manner in providing for our comfort.
3. That we express our appreciation to the Rev. Clyde Davis,
   Director of Missions, for all his efforts in making this
   annual meeting a huge success.
4. That we resolve to encourage individuals TO BE MORE
   "others oriented" so that others might see the reality,
   the greatness and goodness of God!
5. We resolve that our association of 41 churches shall be
   known for its commitment to Jesus Christ, the Head of the
   Church and the proclamation of His Word "That Ye May Grow
   in Grace".
6. To remember in prayer our Moderator, John Flake, during
   his illness, and also the families of our service men who
   gave their supreme sacrifice in Lebanon.
7. Finally, that we strongly support our Christian Social
   Ministries which include the deaf, literacy, mentally
   handicapped, senior citizens, and migrants. Included is
   the preceding resolution given from the Christian Social
   Ministries Committee.

                        Respectfully submitted,
                        Raleigh F. Carroll, Chairman
                        Kenneth W. Goodson
                        Helen P. Register

WMU SEVENTY-FOURTH ANNUAL SESSION MINUTES

    The 74th Annual Session of Eastern Association met April 21,
1983, with Rowan Baptist Church. Mrs. Norwood Carter, WMU Director, presided. Meeting was opened with singing "We Are Called
to be God's People". Mrs. Coleman Carter, WMU Assistant Director,
had our prayer calendar. Devotion was taken from Galatians 5:22
. . . We as Christians should have our bags packed at all times
(just as we prepare for a long journey) . . . in that bag should
be Love, Joy, Peace, Patience, Kindness and Faith. Only then
will we be ready to go and witness for our Lord.
    Welcome was extended by Lillian Pope, who pointed out that
when Rowan last hosted the Annual Session (1969) 300 people were
registered.
    At the business session, Jackie Stroud, Baptist Women Director
for two years, stated her willingness and availability if needed

to help. Paula Clayton, CSM Director for Eastern Association thanked the WMU for their support of the Migrant Ministry; she reported 9 churches having visited camps, provided refreshments, Bibles, clothing and health kits, and requested our help again this year. Frances Tew, Mission Action Director, reported that 349 bottles of lotion were sent to the Woman's Correctional Unit (500 having been requested). She informed that the Sampson County Handicap Program needs volunteers. Mrs. Andy Wood, Mission Friends Director, stressed the need for Sunday School teachers, mission leaders to lay groundwork for our heirs of tomorrow; through our teaching today, and expressions of love, we strive for a great harvest. Helen Register, Enlistment and Enlargement Director, stated that our WMU depends on our "decision to grow" . . . take a look at ourselves and see if we have enthusiasm for WMU. Get excited about WMU . . . enroll prospects and have training sessions.

Mrs. Edward Thornton extended invitation for the 75th Annual Session to be held with Wells Chapel Church with Siloam as co-host. Invitation accepted.

Afternoon speaker was Mrs. Carol Todd, regarding the Mentally Handicapped. She emphasized the spiritual as well as basic needs, suggesting that we minister to these persons through Sunday School classes, birthday parties, Christmas caroling, camps and retreats.

Rev. Clyde Davis, Director of Missions, introduced a new WMU (Hickory Grove Church) to the association, extending a welcome to them.

Blessings were asked on our food, and meeting adjourned for the evening meal.

The night session was opened with singing of hymn "We've A Story to Tell". The following reports were heard:

Baptist Young Women's Director - Glenda Todd reported one new BYW organization.

Acteens Director - Gloria Lockerman, reported a retreat at Wells Chapel in December for Acteens and GA's during which Foreign Mission study was taught. This year a similar meeting will be at First Baptist, Clinton, December 3 for Acteens, GA's and RA's.

GA Director - Paula Matthis told of Day Camp, April 9, in which the Home Mission study was taught, along with crafts and music. 101 GA's and Acteens attended. She reported two churches re-organized GA's and one new GA organization was started.

Jane Kaleel presented the 1983-84 WMU officers for election:

Director	Helen Register
Assistant Director	Mary Carter
Secretary	Lillian Pope
Baptist Women Director	Linda Billings
BYW Director & YBS	Glenda Todd
Acteens Director	Gloria Lockerman
Girls-in-Action Director	Paula Matthis
Mission Friends Director	Tempie Wood
Mission Action Director	Connie Carlton

Motion made, and passed, accepting these officers. Officers were installed by Mrs. Waldo Early.

Rowan Ladies' Ensemble brought message in music.

Evening message brought by Rev. Ken Wellmon, missionary to the Leeward Islands.

Benediction by Lucille Yancey.

125 people were registered for this meeting.

OUR BELOVED DEAD

ALBERTSON: Deacon Edwin Holt
ALUM SPRINGS: Mrs. Ethel M. Kornegay
BEAR MARSH: Mrs. Betty Pate, Mrs. Virginia Kornegay, Mrs. Rederick Vernon
BEULAH: (None)
BROWN: Haywood Pope, Mrs. Bessie Dudley
CALVARY: Mrs. Pearl Graham, Deacon Maurey Lanier, Mrs. Georgia Stevens, Mrs. Ethel Sutton
CALYPSO: Mrs. May Guy, Mrs. Mary A. Nunn, Mrs. Lonnie Joyner, Hugh G. Kennedy, Vance Bland
CENTER: Willie Edge
CLINTON: Mrs. Davis Peterson, Mrs. Paul Crumpler, Mrs. R.B. Wilson, Buck Draughon, Mrs. Bernice Bradshaw, Mrs. Lee Hobbs, Mrs. Annie Brice, Joe McClanahan, Wade Warren, Deacon L.C. Boney, J. Paul Parker, Mrs. J.E. Cook, Willie B. Sneed, Mrs. Virginia Strickland, Harvey Royal, Edwin Peterson, W.T. Underwood, Martin Carter, Mrs. Jessie Hilliard
CONCORD: M.L. Brinson
CORINTH: Deacon Robert J. Johnson, Mrs. Katie Fussell, James Albert Hollingsworth
DOBSON CHAPEL: Deacon Wilbur W. Brock, Mrs. Exie Brock, Harry L. Brown
EVERGREEN: Mrs. Norman Bennett, Mrs. Alpheus Carter, Mrs. Grady Marley
FAISON: Mrs. Frank Kelly
GARLAND: Mrs. Florrie M. Matthews, Mrs. Inez B. Johnson
GARNER'S CHAPEL: Mrs. Catherine Goodson
GROVE PARK: Mrs. Annie Laura Jones, E.E. Norris, Durwood Lee, Deacon Walter Crumpler, Mrs. Nellie Cannady, Wesley Williamson
HICKORY GROVE: Deacon Darrol Hairr, Billy Warren
IMMANUEL: Artie Feck
INGOLD: Bernie H. Oliver, W. James Parker, Preston R. Bradsher
ISLAND CREEK: Mrs. Norma Rivenbark, Mrs. Betty Brinson, Mrs. Ethel Gray Hanchey, Tate Hanchey, Claude Rivenbark, Levi Duff
JOHNSON: Mrs. Jennie Mae Boyette
KENANSVILLE: Lee T. Blanton, Eva Williams, William Quinn, Margaret Dail
MAGNOLIA: Mrs. Fred Johnson, Mrs. Lila Wilson, Mrs. Genevieve Tucker, Warren Bostic, Ernest Pope
MOUNT GILEAD: Mrs. Lillie Bowling, Mrs. Alma Bryant
MOUNT OLIVE: R.R. Hines, Felix Bell, Elwood Rivenbark, Mrs. Janie Sullivan, Mrs. D.R. Benton, Mrs. George Flowers, William Kelly, Elmer Brock, Mrs. Vivian Brogdon
MOUNT VERNON: Larry Pope
NEW HOPE: Deacon J.D. Johnson, Claude E. Smith, Deacon Raymond W. Blanchard, Mrs. Virginia Blanchard
PINEY GROVE: Deacon Floy Darden, Mrs. Louise Peterson, Mrs. Eula Thornton, Mrs. Anna Butler
POPLAR GROVE: None
POSTON: Mrs. Pauline Register, Mrs. Inez Merritt, Mrs. Loucille Carter, Vernon Salmon, Johnnie Stallings
ROSE HILL: Mrs. Edith Brown, Mrs. Lucian Scott, Retire Missionary Miss Katie Murray, Mrs. P.G. Blanton
ROWAN: Charles Malpass, Jr., Mrs. Myrtie Bell, Robert Lynn Matthis, Harold Clack, Mrs. Keron Robinson
SHARON: Mrs. Sudie Pickett, Billy Brinkley, William Woodward, Ethel Sanderson

SHILOH: Mrs. Macy Batchelor, Roscoe Henderson
SILOAM: Mrs. Sadie Bowen, Mrs. Pauline Peterson, Mrs. Verna
  Carawan
TEACHEY: Deacon Linwood C. Brinkley
TURKEY: Fred Meyer, Owen McGee, Chancey Howard
UNION GROVE: Mrs. Doris Saunders, William B. Fryar
WARSAW: Mrs. Reba Carlton, Mrs. Elizer Barnette, Mrs. Rosa
  Williams, Mrs. Louise Jones, Forest Martin, Thurston Ketch-
  side, Arnold Jones, Deacon Paul Potter
WELLS CHAPEL: Deacon William H. Tatum, Pearly J. Moore, R.A.
  Bland, Jr., Charles Johnson

BAPTIST HOSPITAL REPORT

Baptist Hospital has celebrated its sixtieth anniversary
during 1983 by continuing to expand and improve its services.
During the year the hospital has installed a nuclear magnetic
resonance machine in the Department of Diagnostic Radiology. With
the use of radio waves, this machine produces pictures as good as
or better than standard x-rays and can also provide valuable
information based on the body's chemistry without posing any
radiation hazard.
Baptist Hospital is also providing a new treatment aimed at
finding and removing the cause of heart attacks. The procedure
attempts to dissolve clots in the coronary arteries feeding
blood to the heart muscle by injecting a clot-dissolving drug
through a catheter.
During the past year a survey team from the North Carolina
Department of Human Resources designated the hospital's Emergency Department as a Level I trauma center which indicates
that the department offers all major services for serious injuries twenty-four hours a day seven days a week.
Because of these and other services provided by the hospital,
a total of 23,903 patients were admitted to its approximately
700 beds during the year for a total of 213,021 days of patient
care. An additional 66,039 persons visited the hospital's emergency room and outpatient clinics.
The Department of Pastoral Care provided more than 14,000
hours of pastoral service to hospital patients, their families,
and the Medical Center staff besides leading at least four worship services each week in the Davis Memorial Chapel. The
Pastoral Counseling division provided 14,493 hours of counseling
to persons who had individual or family problems or concerns.
The Clinical Pastoral Education division provided training at
some level for more than 100 students. During the past year Dr.
Mahan Siler, who has been with the department for ten years,
resigned as its director in order to return to the pastorate.
In order to provide adequate care of its patients, Baptist
Hospital employs approximately 3,500 people and has buildings
and equipment valued at more than $100,000,000. The operating
budget for 1983 was $101,000,000.
During the past year the hospital trustees have reviewed
plans for another major capital expansion program to begin when
construction funds are available.
Careful management with continuing emphasis on cost-contain-
ment projects has made it possible for the hospital to operate
in the black with only a 4 percent room rate increase during the
past year.

- 21 -

During the 1982 fiscal year the hospital received from the churches of the Baptist State Convention a total of $497,019 through the Cooperative Program and $343,665 through the North Carolina Missions Offering. Cooperative Program funds helped to underwrite the budget of the Pastoral Care Department and the gifts received through North Carolina Missions Offering assist financially needy patients in paying their hospital bills.

The hospital administration and staff are deeply grateful to the Baptist State Convention and all its constituents whose leadership and support make it possible for the hospital to provide these ministries.

Respectfully submitted,
Gerald Quinn, Chairman

CHRISTIAN HIGHER EDUCATION REPORT

NEW COLLEGE PRESIDENTS

Wingate College and Wake Forest University have elected new presidents. Dr. Paul R. Corts took office on July 1, 1983. Dr. Thomas K. Hearn, Jr., assumes the presidency of Wake Forest on October 1, 1983.

Dr. Corts has been a college teacher and administrator in Kentucky and Oklahoma. A graduate of Georgetown College and Indiana University, he is an experienced leader and author in the fields of communications and fund-raising.

Dr. Hearn, an ordained Baptist Minister, is a graduate of Birmingham Southern College, Southern Baptist Theological Seminary and Vanderbilt University. He has served one pastorate in Indiana. He is an experienced college teacher and administrator in Virginia and Alabama.

Congratulations to Wingate and Wake Forest! These qualified leaders join Presidents Fred B. Bentley, John E. Weems, Norman A. Wiggins, Bruce E. Whitaker and Craven E. Williams as leaders in Christian higher education for North Carolina Baptists.

SEEKING THE BAPTIST STUDENT

All of the seven North Carolina Baptist colleges want to serve more of the students from the churches. Pastors and lay leaders can help by recommending Baptist colleges to Baptist young people.

CALLING THE ROLL IN GRATITUDE

North Carolina has been a leader among Baptists in Christian higher education for 149 years. Moral and financial support from the churches has made possible the ministry of our colleges. The Cooperative Program continues to provide health for the colleges and opportunity for young people.

Campbell, Chowan, Gardner-Webb, Mars Hill, Meredith, Wake Forest and Wingate are grateful to North Carolina Baptists. Please continue to favor us with your young people, your gifts and your prayers.

Respectfully submitted,
Anthony Gurganus, Chairman

BAPTIST FOUNDATION REPORT

Have you ever received a "Mrs. Pig Letter"? We want our 1983 report to be such a thank you note to North Carolina Baptists.

When our children were tots they, like other children, had their favorite story book that never was read enough to suit them. Even today, as adults, they agree that POSTMAN OF BAYBERRY LANE was their favorite book. The gist of the story centered around Mrs. Pig who every day met the postman at her mail box but to no avail. The postman felt "sorry" for Mrs. Pig because her box was always empty so he suggested she have a party and invite all other ladies in the community, such as Mrs. Cow, Mrs. Horse, Mrs. Sheep, etc. The party was planned, the ladies came, and for days afterward thank you notes were delivered by Mr. Postman to Mrs. Pig. So, at our house, when thank you notes are written or received, we chuckle and remember with nostalgia that these are "Mrs. Pig letters".

We of the Foundation are indeed thankful for what Baptists of North Carolina are doing to guarantee support for the multitude of Christian missions and ministries carried on by Baptists. To serve in the Trustee role as managers of trust funds established by gifts from individuals, both living and through Will, is an exciting experience.

During the past year increased interest has been shown by individuals attending estate planning seminars sponsored by the Foundation and through personal visits by Foundation staff. Greater numbers are committing a tithe of what they leave at death, when they no longer need it, to Christian causes.

The asset value of trusts held at the end of last fiscal year totalled $8,214,696. Designated new additions to trusts were $276,815. Income from investments of trust assets totalled $523,140. Investment asset market value gain during the year was $398.812.

We are thankful for the facilities in the new Baptist Building making it possible to have the staff in one suite of offices. It has been pleasant to welcome many adult church groups who have visited the new building.

We welcome other visits or opportunities to discuss with individuals effective estate planning alternatives involving wills and trusts which could provide sustained support for Baptist cause(s) even beyond lifetime.

Respectfully submitted,
Ken Durham, Chairman

NORTH CAROLINA BAPTIST HOMES, INC., REPORT

Through North Carolina Baptists, God continues to bless our North Carolina Baptist Homes with meaningful blessings, and we are grateful!

One of the most significant blessings that we have received during the year has been a 31% increase in the percentage used for distribution of funds through the Cooperative Program. This percentage change, along with strong Cooperative Program support during the first five months of 1983, has meant an increase of $29,079.73 over the same period in 1982. Total Cooperative Program funds for the period totalled $135,647.39.

For the first five months of 1983, undesignated support through the North Carolina Missions Offering provided $74,087.47 toward the Homes' benevolent care needs. Designated gifts of $42,274.58 brought the total NCMO support to $116,362.05.

Through these mission gifts of $252,009.44, we were able to provide care for over 50% of the residents in the five Homes and Nursing Care who have limited resources. Even with this mission support, benevolent care exceeded the resources by $132,975.00 for the five-month period. This gap must be bridged, and we must continue to receive more through the Cooperative Program and the North Carolina Missions Offering if we are to meet the needs of residents in the Homes. This still leaves the many who are waiting to enter the Homes, but do not have sufficient funds to pay the cost of care.

The Baptist Homes have been and continue to be a benevolent care ministry throughout the 32 years of caring. Because of the over-extended benevolent care ministry, the Trustees have had to put a hold on admissions of persons who cannot demonstrate the resources to pay the cost of care for their life expectancy. Let's change this picture as rapidly as possible. The only way that it can be changed is through a concerted effort of increased giving through the Cooperative Program and the North Carolina Missions Offering.

Another step forward during May of this year was the approval by the Homes' Trustees of a Capital Funds Campaign of $2,500,000 for the meeting of needs on the Hayes Home Campus, Winston-Salem. This challenge will meet some of the very vital needs of updating the Nursing Care Unit. Included in this updating will be a physical therapy room, patient dining room/activity area, and other vital needs related to food service. A second area of need includes the building of additional rooms at Hayes Home. These rooms are desperately needed to make possible additional beds in the Nursing Care Unit. This expansion will require additional money beyond the current Capital Funds Campaign. The upcoming campaign will be the first major capital funds effort that the Baptist Homes have undertaken. We covet your prayers for a successful effort.

The needs of older persons in our nation and state become more and more acute with each passing day. It is imperative that we focus more on the needs and that we provide as wisely as we can for them in the family of our North Carolina Baptist Homes, now and for the future.

We believe that the future of the Homes' ministry is in God's hands. We shall continue to trust Him for our needs, and urge you to join Him and us as we strive to meet the needs of this vital ministry to older persons.

Respectfully submitted,
Millard M. Johnson, Chairman

BAPTIST CHILDREN'S HOMES REPORT

The Pembroke Family Services Center serves nine Southeastern counties: Robeson, Bladen, Sampson, Cumberland, Harnett, Hoke, Scotland, Richmond, and Columbus. The central office is located on the campus of Odum Home in Pembroke, North Carolina.

The Pembroke Area Family Services Center continues to serve the nine county area with quality care and full staff of social

- 24 -

workers, child care workers, and administrative personnel. The on-campus facilities offer residential group care, emergency care and co-planning to families. All other services offered by the Baptist Children's Homes may be accessed through the office.

Due to the support of several local churches and groups, a complete wood shop is now available to be used by the children being served in group care and a ceramics shop is nearing completion. These facilities increase the opportunities that can be offered to the children in care.

On July 1, 1983, the Baptist Children's Home welcomed its new President, Dr. Michael C. Blackwell, a native of Gastonia. Dr. Blackwell becomes the eighth President of the Baptist Children's Homes of North Carolina and follows in a noble tradition of excellence established by the seven men who preceded him in this position. In making the announcement of Dr. Blackwell's selection, Dr. William Brown, Chairman of the Board of Trustees, said that "we firmly believe that Dr. Blackwell will continue to lead this vital ministry in an exemplary manner. His unique talents, personality and commitments will assure that this ministry remains at the vanguard of excellence in child care in meeting the challenge of resolving the hurts of children and families in need."

Dr. Blackwell served churches in both North Carolina and Virginia before assuming the Presidency of the Baptist Children's Homes.

Respectfully submitted,
John A. Johnson, Chairman

ANNUITY BOARD REPORT

"Nineteen hundred eighty-two has proven to be an epochal year for all of us at the Annuity Board. Even in the midst of varying interest rates, unemployment, recession and denominational unrest, the Annuity Board has continued to develop, market and service the retirement and insurance plans for the associations, churches and agencies of the Southern Baptist Convention," said Annuity Board President Darold H. Morgan.

Key statistical highlights in 1982 included"
1. A 10 percent 13th Check was mailed to annuitants who retired before 1980. Those annuitants who retired in 1980-82 received their 13th Check bonus in their monthly checks.
2. A total of $30,663,412 was paid in retirement benefits.
3. Total assets administered by the board as of Dec. 31, 1982 $1,057,947,515 compared to $896,535,999 on Dec. 31, 1981.
4. Relief funds from the Cooperative Program totalled $455,009.
5. Membership records indicated that 18,111 persons were enrolled in Plan A, 65,855 in Plan B and 4,256 in Plan C.
6. Earnings on retirement and related funds for 1982 totaled $108,923,263. This compares to $46,068,904 for 1981 or an increase of $62,854,359.

STATISTICAL HIGHLIGHTS 1983

Retirement Plans	Member Accounts and Benefits	Insurance	Members
Plan A (church-agency)	16,383	*Health Insurance	25,796
Fixed Fund (church-agency)	52,952	Group Life (church)	18,279
Balanced Fund (church-agency)	8,365	Group Life (agency)	18,102
Variable Fund (church-agency)	4,256	**Life Benefit Plan	2,047
Benefits Paid (Retirement and Relief)	$30,663,412	Seminarian Life	1,705
Relief Recipients	392	Seminarian Medical	4,513

*Includes churches and agencies
**Closed to new members

Respectfully submitted,
Waldo Early

THE BIBLICAL RECORDER

The BIBLICAL RECORDER is celebrating 150 years of service to North Carolina Baptists. Founded by Thomas Meredith while he was pastor of the Edenton Baptist Church, the RECORDER is the fourth oldest among the 34 state Baptist papers in the Southern Baptist Convention, exceeded in age only by the Georgia, Kentucky and Virginia papers.

The past twelve months have been a time of transition for the RECORDER. R.G. Puckett became editor upon the retirement of Marse Grant in September, 1982. Lawrence E. High came as managing editor of the RECORDER from the editorship of THE MARYLAND BAPTIST. Puckett is the only man in Southern Baptist life to have served four different state Baptist papers. High and Puckett are the only team of editors who have both served as editors of other state papers before coming to North Carolina.

The cost of second-class postage threatened the very survival of the state Baptist papers in 1982, including the RECORDER. However, with the faithful support of subscribers, assistance from the state convention and tight management of finances, the paper is now stable and as secure as possible under present economic conditions. Future costs for second-class postage are unknown and greatly feared. Your prayerful concern at this point is earnestly requested.

The format of the paper was changed to tabloid from the magazine style which had served for approximately 40 of the 150 years of the RECORDER. Economy of production and increased space by approximately 50 percent were the deciding factors. Those readers who preferred the magazine style have generally accepted the tabloid because of the money saved and the added amount of news coverage of North Carolina and Southern Baptists.

In March, the directors of the RECORDER approved a plan to make circulation the highest priority in 1983. Churches are urged to put the paper in the budget so that every resident family receives a copy. Club plans are available for interested persons and key leadership in the church.

The editors and staff of the RECORDER are grateful for the opportunity to have this ministry among North Carolina Baptists. We invite your news items, letters to the editor and items of interest to all North Carolina Baptists. Most of all, the staff requests your prayer support and faithful reading of the BIBLICAL RECORDER, one of the largest and most influential Baptist papers in the history of Baptists in the United States.

Respectfully submitted,
T.N. Cooper

CHRISTIAN LITERATURE

The task is great and many people in our land need to know the facts in the printed word and pictures to enhance the romance of the Bible.

"Response to Gospel makes heavy demand on publication work. Publication Ministries relate to Baptists overseas printed an awesome quantity and diversity of materials to reach people and develop believers through Bible teaching, Christian nurture and Bible distribution.

Total Publications Overseas in 1983 - "Christian Books 723 titles, periodicals 446 titles, tracts 18,000,000 copies". (The Foreign Mission Board, Richmond).

Dr. N.C. Brook, Raleigh, states, "State Missions cannot flourish without information getting out to the people. It's a long way from Manteo to Murphy. These are fields white unto harvest at both ends of the state. Mountaineers will hardly hear about Resort Ministries along the Carolina Coast without speakers and literature to inform. Baptists cannot afford NOT TO inform the people".

President W. Randall Lolley, Southeastern Seminary, states, "Our Seminary believes in importance of doctrinally sound and decision-challenging literature to be used in our churches. Our professors regularly serve as writers of Christian literature, and we give serious instruction to our students on the value of Christian literature as they now serve and will serve as minister in our churches."

Respectfully submitted,
T.N. Cooper

CHURCH TRAINING REPORT

The year was off to a good start with 189 persons attending "M" (Mobilization) Night at Rowan in November, 1982. Michael Shook delivered the theme message on family involvement; Clyde Davis interpreted the curriculum for 1982-83; Barbara Shook produced and presented a fashion show to introduce the literature; age level directors presented challenges.

Church training officers received instruction at the Enablers Conference at Caraway for the Developing Believers Workshop held at Rowan in May for all local church officers and other workers. This was to train local churches for implementation of a Developing Believers emphasis to begin in October, including promotion of doctrine, belief and behavior.

Twelve children were winning participants in the state
Children's Bible Drill, with Amy Matthews achieving her 3-year
award. We had two state winners in the Youth Bible Drill.
Mary Carter conducted the Church Training session at the Key
Leaders Conference on August 29, 1983.
All of us are challenged to equip, to develop and to serve.
Church Training is the program for this Bold Growth in Disciple-
ship.

Respectfully submitted,
Lucille Yancey

MISSIONS COMMITTEE REPORT

The Missions Committee is charged with the responsibility
of working with the Christian Social Ministries director in
discovering, analyzing, and presenting to the Association opportunities for mission action. Changes in the constitution last
year brought committees into being for the purpose of ministering to persons with special needs such as migrants, deaf, senior
adults, mentally handicapped and the illiterate.
The Executive Board approved a request for $18,000.00 from
the North Carolina Baptist State Convention for the purpose of
securing a full time Director of Christian Social Ministries.
The focus of attention in the past year has been on migrant
ministries. The Ministries to Mentally Handicapped Committee is
functioning well under the capable leadership of Mrs. Carol Todd.
Greater attention is needed to develop the work in other areas.
The key to having a successful Christian Social Ministries
program is an open line of communication between the associational personnel, the Missions Committee and the volunteer leadership in the local churches. An effective missions program can
be conducted through prayer, hard work, and commitment to the
tasks.

Respectfully submitted,
Michael Shook, Chairman

LIBRARY/MEDIA COMMITTEE REPORT

The Library/Media Committee has met regularly to discuss
needs, set goals and plan actions during the year. These have
been represented by the following:
    Telephone contacts with pastors or key persons in churches
        that do not have Library/Media Centers or whose centers
        are inactive
    Classifying and cataloguing media and books in Associational
        Office.
    Key Leadership Conference at Warsaw was used for promotion
    Observance of National Library Week in churches
    Individual Conference with media directors
    Library/Media Week at Ridgecrest by one member of the committee
    Started a new center at Alum Springs Church.

Respectfully submitted,
Thelma Davis, Chairman

SUNDAY SCHOOL REPORT

To see a renewed interest in Sunday School is exciting and there seems to be a genuine renewed interest among our Sunday Schools of the Eastern Baptist Association. More and more Sunday Schools are calling upon the ASSISTeam to come and do leadership and organizational training. Let's Pray that God will now give growth to our Sunday Schools.

One or more members of the ASSISTeam have been into at least twelve of our churches, at their invitation, to work individually with their Sunday School. Already, dates for the coming year are being scheduled for more leadership training in a one or two church setting.

Plans were begun this year for one of the most exciting events in Sunday School work. An Enrollment/Enlargement Campaign for our association has been planned for February 25 - March 4, 1984. We are praying that this event will yield many new members and regain some old members who have dropped away from our Sunday Schools.

Our goals for the coming year are to see at least a 5% or more growth in membership, to work individually with at least 25% of our Sunday Schools, to see at least 10% of our Sunday Schools reported as Standard, 10% of our Sunday School leaders earning leadership study credits, and to maintain a weekly average attendance of 50% or more in our schools.

Matthew 28:19-20 gives us Jesus's instructions, God's intentions, and the Holy Spirit's inspiration. Let's do a super job in winning people to Christ and teaching them in Sunday School!

Respectfully submitted,
James Hartsell, Chairman

DEAF MINISTRIES COMMITTEE REPORT

It has been the directive of the Deaf Ministries Committee to encourage churches to become more aware of the needs of the hearing impaired in their communities and to minister to them. They are a very lonely people.

Poston Church held a Retreat, November 1983 from 5 - 9 P.M., beginning with worship led by Jack Marshburn, Wilmington, N.C., followed by a fellowship meal, and recreation. There were 50 people in attendance.

Respectfully submitted,
Mary Boney, Chairman

MIGRANT MINISTRIES COMMITTEE REPORT

Eastern Association's Migrant Ministries Committee strives to provide ministry to migrant and seasonal farmworkers during the harvest season in the geographical area of the Association. By meeting spiritual, physical, educational, and awareness needs, the committee aims toward the purpose as stated above.

Our first year as a standing committee of the Association, and our second year into a concentrated effort at meeting migrant needs, proved to be a positive year.

Twenty-three churches participated actively in our ministry in one form or another. Close to cne hundred volunteers were honored at the end of the summer for giving of their time in our summer efforts. Assistance was received from eleven churches and organizations outside our Association.

The aspects of the ministry included three churches adoptic camps - Grove Park, New Hope, and Mount Olive, weekly worship services in Spanish and Creole (a new addition this year), the sponsorship of two Mission Youth Groups at Immanuel and Warsaw Churches; the continuation of the child supervision program at Tri-County Community Health Center, volunteer operation of the clothing closet; support of the Sampson County Migrant Shelter, and providing emergency travel and food monies when needs arose.

Excellent leadership was provided in the summer ministry by summer staffers Rhonda Gainey, James Garrison and Brenda Nowell. Part-time leadership came from Wilfred and Andree Lubin and Mario Vargas. Also, our cooperation with the Duplin Hispanic Ministries Committee provided shared ministry with Rev. Jimmy Creech and Revs. Thom and Debbie McCloud along with the use of their facility.

Our ministry expanded into as many as twenty labor camps plus individual family residents this associational year. Five decisions were made as a result of our ministry with two baptisms being completed.

Special recognition should be awarded to the Committee members, Betty Carr, Francis Clifton, Gaily Naylor, Paul Rose and Walter Thomasson for their efforts. God has indeed blessed our ministry, and for that we are most grateful!

Respectfully submitted,
Andy Wood, Chairman

LITERACY MINISTRIES COMMITTEE REPORT

One of every five Americans cannot read or write. There are increasing numbers of foreign-born whose lack of English is much more obvious. They face life in the United States economically, physically, and spiritually handicapped by the lack of ability to use English.

Being shut out of the world of words is to be in poverty. Not having direct access to God's Word limits one spiritually. Not having the capacity to read or write English condemns those in our land to live lives of unfulfilled dreams. Some are very good workers but their lack of English blocks communications and keeps them from getting better jobs.

Twenty percent of the nations workers are unable to read or write and count adequately - thus hurting the ability of the U.S. business to compete with international firms. One out of five workers is functionally illiterate (unable to participate in even entry-level training) - without remedial instruction in the "Three R's". Many people in our land cannot write their own name, so they use the "X".

This Christian ministry needs to be developed. Volunteers are needed to teach English, reading, writing, and conversational skills - particularly in our Association. Literacy Ministry is

ended to both adult non-readers and school age children.
efully structured workshops prepare volunteers to work with
-readers.
Within every community, neighborhood and church, there are
ple who have never told anyone that they cannot read or write.
The Bible is clear about the responsibility of the poor among
 Giving the gift of the common language is one of the best
s to remove barriers. It also provides a means of sharing
ist. "Discipline (instruct) your son while there is hope,
not set your heart on his destruction". (Proverbs 19:18 RSV).
istance to youth in formative years through Literacy Ministry
 mean the difference between destruction and hope.
Literacy Ministry is a response to Biblical mandates: (1)
w the love of God for the total person (2) Provide fertile
nessing environment (3) Be obedient to the example of Christ.
Literacy Ministry provides encounters to meet physical, emo-
nal, mental and spiritual needs, and is most effective when
unded in the local church and carried out by program organi-
ions. Support by the minister and church members encourages
wth and continuation of ministry. Mission action through
therhood and WMU provides excellent framework for the minis-
. The church Missions Committee can have a particularly im-
tant role in developing this ministry.
The Literacy Ministry Volunteer
1. Is called of God to serve in a literacy ministry
2. Has completed a 16-hour Home Mission Board approved
   Literacy Mission Workshop
3. Is committed to teaching for at least one year
4. Understands, speaks, reads and writes English
Specific objectives of this ministry are to:
1. Discover people who do not understand, speak, read or
   write English
2. Tutor school-age youth who need training apart from the
   classroom
3. Assist adults in improving skills in understanding, speaking, reading, or writing English
4. Teach people to read and understand the Bible
5. Help people discover and become what God wants them to be
6. Help churches fulfill God's command to minister and witness
7. Help people to help themselves
8. Provide welcome, freindship and fellowship for students
9. Teach American culture and customs to non-English-speaking
   people
0. Assist students in meeting every day needs such as cooking,
   acquiring medical attention, filing income tax, obtaining
   citizenship, passing drivers license test, shopping, en-
   rolling in school, banking, exchanging money and completing job application forms.
BE A VOLUNTEER! HELP SOMEONE TO SEE THE LIGHT!

                         Respectfully submitted,
                         Florence Hoover, Chairman

                    CHURCH MUSIC REPORT

The goals of our Association and in each church have been
 to aid others in worship through music (2) to teach people
read music (3) to train key leaders to nurture their God-

given talent and to witness the good news of Jesus Christ to lost souls.

On January 17, 1983, the first Associational Adult Choir Festival was held at Clinton First. Ten churches were represented. Seven choirs participated with a total attendance of 250. On March 15, 1983, the Regional Adult Choir Festival was held at Elizabethtown Baptist Church. Each region in our state consists of ten associations, and for this festival, 9 choirs were present and 5 of these were from the Eastern Association.

I attended the Key Leadership Conference in Ridgecrest and led a conference in our Association, in August. I personally feel that the churches in our association not only just want music - they want good music and good music leadership. This is obvious by the very fact that Poston and Mount Gilead have called a minister of music within the past year.

In the coming year, let us set even higher goals for our churches, seek the leadership that is needed, and work so that even more people will be singing a new song of Zion.

Respectfully submitted,
Jean Hatch

PASTORAL SUPPORT COMMITTEE REPORT

The Pastoral Support Committee, consisting of Davis Denton, Chairman, W.K. Lewis, and R.O. Sanderson, took the theme of "Strengthen the Pastor's Family Relationship" as our theme and goal for 1982-83.

We have welcomed eight new pastors who have begun their ministry in Eastern Association during the year.

Two Family Counseling and Guidance meetings were held in conjunction with the Eastern Baptist Association Pastors Conference. The first was a film and discussion entitled "Greater Than Gold"", held on March 14, 1983. The second was September 19, 1983. A seminar on counseling was held on May 16, 1983, and was led by Dr. Christopher Schooley of the Fayetteville Family Life Center.

Our purpose and aim is to support and strengthen the pastors and their families of the Eastern Baptist Association. May we always be aware of the needs of others!

Respectfully submitted,
Davis Benton, Chairman

MINISTRY TO THE MENTALLY HANDICAPPED

A new area of the Christian Social Ministry to emerge in the past year was that of ministering to those that are mentally handicapped. In August, a day retreat was held at Harrells for the residents of the four group homes in our area. A memorable time was enjoyed by those who attended as they participated through a devotional time, made some crafts, and dined on grilled hamburgers and home made ice cream. It was a day of seeing old friends for some; while for others it was a time for making new acquaintances.

A Christmas dinner for the residents of the group homes is being eagerly anticipated by both the residents and volunteers. At this time, stuffed animals donated by churches will be wrapped by the residents for children in the Child Development Center in Clinton.

Plans are being made for Sunday School classes in certain churches which will be geared toward the mentally handicapped. These classes will endeavor to meet the special needs of this population.

We are grateful for the support we have received during the year, and we hope to even better meet the needs of this population with your continued prayer and support.

Respectfully submitted,
Carol Todd, Chairman

BROTHERHOOD REPORT

Nineteen hundred eighty-three has been a year of training and planning to prepare our associational brotherhood leaders for a process of exercising Bold Mission Thrust for 1984. During the Key Leadership Conference in May special training was given to provide our Baptist Men (BM) and Royal Ambassador (RA) leaders with adequate information and knowledge to carry forth the purpose of their organizations - to teach Missions and encourage Mission Service.

This year we were fortunate in having leaders from the N.C. Brotherhood Department come to a training session at Warsaw Baptist Church and encourage B.M. and R.A. organizations to use SBC printed materials and programs as an aid in planning and presenting weekly and monthly programs. Several churches which did not have B.M. groups indicated a desire to begin such work.

Again, this summer our B.M. worked with Christian Social Ministries in a combined effort to provide playground equipment and picnic tables for migrant children at the Tri-county Health Clinic at Newton Grove.

During the winter months of 83-84, B.M. hope to construct several pieces of playground equipment for this same playground.

Goals for Brotherhood for 83-84
1. Train or retrain 3 Assn. Brotherhood Officers
2. Involve B.M. Officers and R.A. Leaders in leadership training
3. Involve Associational men in inspiration and promotion
4. Provide individual assistance for 3 church B.M. groups
5. Involve Crusaders from 10 churches in fellowship and sports
6. Involve R.A.'s in sports activities
7. Assist churches that desire to improve existing R.A. Chapters
8. Assist in training 10 persons to teach Foreign & Home Study books.

The Associational Brotherhood Department exists for the sole purpose of bringing men and boys to a saving knowledge of Jesus Christ. Our desire is to assist you in any way.

Please call us. To Him Be the Glory.

Respectfully submitted,
Charles P. Kirkland

REPORT OF THE AMERICAN BIBLE SOCIETY

"You wanted to kill people by the power of the gun; here is the Bible. Now go and face people with the power of the Word."

With these words, a prison guard in Kenya gave a convict a copy of the Bible which had been supplied by the Bible Society in Kenya. As a result of his reading it, the prisoner committed his life to Christ and is now beginning a new life with hope and faith.

Similar miraculous conversions are taking place daily all around the world and the American Bible Society is grateful for the support of the Southern Baptist Convention in helping to win these people to the Lord. Through the ministry of the ABS and the Bible Societies with which it is associated, men, women and children in record numbers and in over 150 nations and territories are receiving the Scriptures that often lead to such personal encounters with the living Christ. Bible Societies around the world distributed a total of 484,633,537 Bibles, Testaments, Portions and Selections in 1982. This represents a 9.1 percent increase over 1981's figures, and includes 10,883,159 Bibles, 12,177,593 Testaments, 32,575,846 Portions and 428,996,939 Scripture Selections.

Good News for New Readers Scriptures, a graded approach to Scriptures for first readers are now available in languages spoken in 70 different countries around the world.

HOW YOU HELPED IN LATIN AMERICA!

In the streets and plazas of Caracas, thousands of Venezuela's poor people and beggars wander about seeking surcease and crowds of tourists mingle with them in the public plazas. The Bible Society in Venezuela has organized a special team of volunteers from many of the local churches to distribute Scriptures among these masses of people. One of the participants reports: "Both beggars and travelers walk with their heavy burden of worry and pre-occupation. This is why we go and meet them in the streets, plazas and stations of Caracas to put the Word of God into their hands. Hopefully, our efforts will touch the lives and hearts of all those who come across this army of volunteer distributors of the Word of Life."

AND YOU HELPED HERE AT HOME!

Millions of men, women and children in the United States, patients in hospitals, members of the armed forces, people in Christian congregations and schools, even visitors to the Southern Baptist Pavilion, and other exhibits at the WORLD'S FAIR in Knoxville, Tennessee - received Scriptures supplied by the American Bible Society. One especially important program involved the distribution of New Testaments among prisoners in the United States.

THE CHALLENGE:

Scripture shortages are growing worldwide. Even though Bible Societies are working harder than ever to provide enough Scriptures for the people of the world, millions may yet have to go without the comfort and guidance of God's Word in the coming year. But the American Bible Society is beginning 1984 with a renewed determination to further increase its ministry both in the United States and throughout the world. Scriptures MUST be made available to the millions of people who are eagerly seeking His Word. We pray that our joint ministries will grow in strength and that our witness together will provide others with the comfort, guidance and faith promised by our Lord: "Come to me, all of you who are tired from carrying heavy loads, and I will give you rest." (Matthew 11:28).

Respectfully submitted,
H.J. Register, Chairman

NOMINATING COMMITTEE REPORT

The Nominating Committee places in nomination, the following persons to serve in positions as indicated for the 1983-84 Associational year:

Moderator - Donald Coley   Vice Moderator - Lucille Yancey
Clerk - Philip Billings   Assistant Clerk - E.C. Mattocks
Treasurer - Martha Pierce   Assistant Treasurer - Jo Robinson
     Trustee - Larry Harper (Term Expires 1986)

SUNDAY SCHOOL
Director - James Hartsell
8.5 x '85 - Larry Padgett
VBS Director - Greg Thornton
Age-Group Leaders:
    Adults - Charlotte Hartsell
    Youth - Sue Padgett
    Older Children - Barbara Shook
    Middle Children - Dennis Knight
    Younger Children - Sylvia Knight
    Preschool - Tempie Wood

BROTHERHOOD
Director - Charles Kirkland
Pioneer Director -
Crusader Director -

MUSIC
Director - Jean Hatch
Council Members:
    Janet Register
    Vivian Kirkland
    Curtis Pope

WOMAN'S MISSIONARY UNION
Director - Helen Register
Assistant Director - Mary Carter
Secretary - Lillian Pope
Baptist Women Director - Linda Billings
BYW Director and YBW - Glenda Todd
Acteens Director - Gloria Lockerman
Girls in Action Director - Paula Matthis
Mission Friends Director - Tempie Wood
Mission Action Director - Connie Carlton

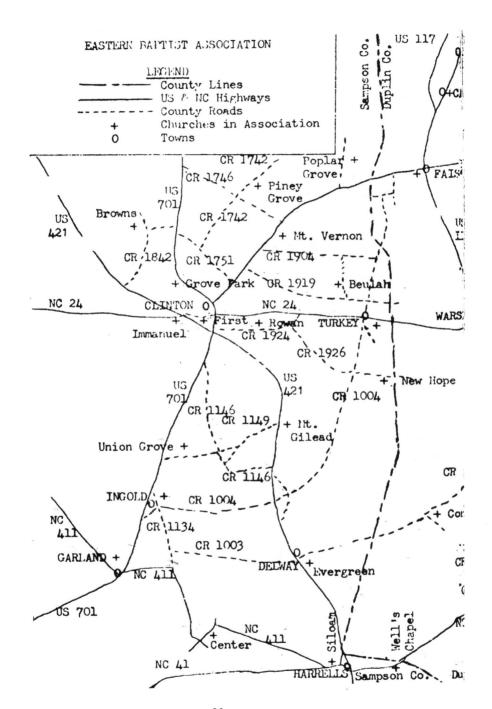

EASTERN BAPTIST ASSOCIATION

LEGEND
———— ·— County Lines
———— US & NC Highways
- - - - - - County Roads
+ Churches in Association
O Towns

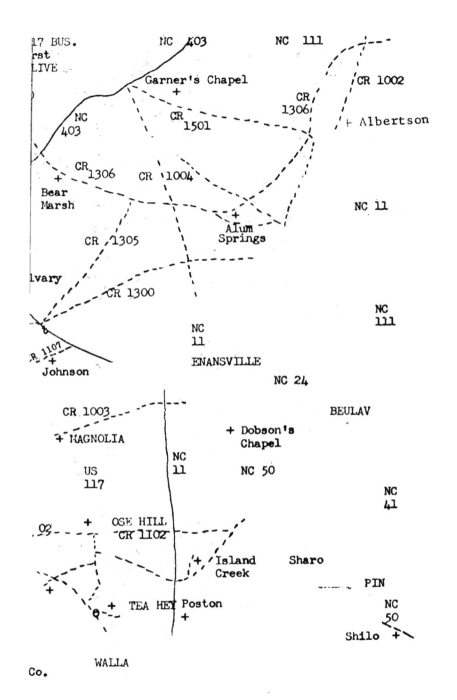

17 BUS.
rst
LIVE

NC 403

NC 111

Garner's Chapel
+

CR 1002

NC
403

CR
1501

CR
1306

+ Albertson

CR 1306
+

CR 1004

NC 11

Bear
Marsh

CR 1305

Alum
Springs

lvary

CR 1300

NC
111

R 1107
+
Johnson

NC
11

ENANSVILLE

NC 24

CR 1003

BEULAV

+ MAGNOLIA

+ Dobson's
Chapel

US
117

NC
11

NC 50

NC
41

.02
+

OSE HILL
CR 1102

+ Island
Creek

Sharo

+

PIN

+

+ TEA HEY Poston
+

NC
50

Shilo +

WALLA

Co.

CHURCH TRAINING
Director - Mary Carter
Age-Group Directors:
    Adult - Phyllis Durham
    Youth - Rose Pleasant
    Children - Rene' Carroll
    Pre-school -

                        Presented by:
                        Nominating Committee,
                        Anthony Gurganus, Chairman
                        Larry Harper
                        John Braswell
                        Millard Johnson
                        Farrell Miller
                        George McGill

            COMMITTEE-ON-COMMITTEES REPORT 1983-84

EVANGELISM   MEDIA LIBRARY
*Anthony Gurganus, Chairman 1985   Joyce Braswell, Chairman 1985
Dennis Knight 1986   Mrs. Margaret Goodson 1984
*Freddie Harris 1984   Joyce Lucas 1986

MISSION   PASTORAL SUPPORT
Davis Benton, Chairman, 1986   Phillip Denton, Chairman 1986
Mitchell Rivenbark 1984   R.O. Sanderson 1984
Kenneth Goodson 1985   W.K. Lewis 1985
(Includes following chairpersons):
Literacy - Florence Hoover 1985
Mentally Handicapped - Carol Todd 1985
Deaf - Sylvia Knight 1985
Senior Adult - Ken Durham 1985
Migrant - Andy Wood 1985

PROGRAM   STEWARDSHIP
Freddie Harris, Chairman 1985   Gene Hart, Chairman 1985
Gene Hardin 1986   Mitchell Rivenbark 1985
*Larry Harper 1984   John Braswell 1985
                                        Florence Hoover 1984
HISTORICAL   Donald Pope 1984
Charlotte Hartsell, Chmn. 1984   Davis Benton 1984
Marsha Lewis 1985   Ed Colwell 1986
Waldo Early 1986   Priscilla McGill 1986
                                        Jimmy Strickland 1986
NOMINATING   Associational Treasurer
John Braswell, Chairman 1984
Millard Johnson 1984
Farrell Miller 1985   ORDINATION
George McGill 1985   Don Coley, Chairman 1986
H.J. Register 1986   Millard Johnson 1986
Charles Lee Pope 1986   *Michael Shook 1985
                                        Amos Brinson 1985
                                        William Jones 1984
                                        Jerry Kinlaw 1984
MINISTRIES TO MENTALLY HANDICAPPED
Carol Todd, Chairperson 1985   LITERACY MINISTRIES
Clara Huffman 1984   Florence Hoover, Chairperson '85
Mrs. Randy (Herman) Kight 1986   *Mavis Pigford 1984
                                        Mrs. Faye Gaddy 1986

                        - 38 -

DEAF MINISTRIES
*Sylvia Knight, Chairperson 1985
Mary Doney 1984
Mary Lee Jones 1986

SENIOR ADULT MINISTRIES
*Ken Durham, Chairperson 1985
Sue Padgett 1984
Joyce Warren 1986

MIGRANT MINISTRIES
Andy Wood, Chairman 1985
Gail Naylor 1985
Francis Clifton 1984
Betty Carr 1984
Betty Rose 1986

*Filling unexpired term

Presented by:
Committee-on-Committees
Ken Durham, Chairman
Florence Hoover
R.O. Sanderson
Shelton Justice,
W.K. Lewis

VACATION BIBLE SCHOOL REPORT

Ninety-three VBS workers from 17 churches received training in the Church VBS Workers Clinic held in Warsaw, April 21, 1983. Associational VBS workers who received training earlier in the STATE VBS CLINIC led the conferences.
At the time of this report, 27 churches reported having had VBS. Those reported are:

Church	Enroll-ment	Avg. Att.	No. Days	Hours Daily	Prof. Faith	Miss. Off.	Achieve-ment
Alum Springs	36	27	5	2.5	0	30.00	*
Beulah	77	69	5	2	0	36.00	Merit
Calypso	53	40	5	2.5	0	51.00	Merit
Concord	72	71	5	2.5	0	40.00	Advanced
Corinth	104	91	5	2.5	0	150.00	Merit
Evergreen	80	64	5	3	0	139.00	Merit
Garland	67	59	5	3	2	73.00	Merit
Garner's Chapel	40	33	5	2	0	53.00	*
Grove Park	135	86	6	2.5	0	81.00	Advanced
Immanuel	111	101	5	3	10	51.00	Merit
Ingold	36	32	5	2	0	17.00	*
Island Creek	104	84	5	2	0	22.00	Merit
Johnson	*	*	11	*	*	16.00	*
Mount Gilead	81	73	5	2	0	69.00	*
Mount Olive	122	105	5	3	0	53.00	Advanced
Mount Vernon	25	24	5	2.5	0	43.00	*
New Hope	33	29	5	2.5	0	35.00	Merit
Piney Grove	139	98	5	2	*	*	*
Poplar Grove	*	42	5	2.5	0	*	*
Poston	160	129	5	3	9	48.00	Merit
Rose Hill	91	77	5	3	0	53.00	Merit
Rowan	106	87	5	3	0	61.00	Advanced
Sharon	103	92	5	3	0	24.00	Merit
Shiloh	65	56	5	3	0	103.00	Advanced
Teachey	33	25	5	2	0	48.00	*
Union Grove	48	46	5	3	0	35.00	Advanced
Warsaw	79	79	5	3	0	38.00	*

*Not indicated on report.

ADMINISTRATIVE SUPPORT MINISTRIES

Director of Missions

1110	Salary	$10,500.00
1120	Housing	5,900.00
1130	Travel	3,600.00
1140	Annuity	829.92
1150	Insurance	1,828.08
1160	Convention and Conferences	600.00
1170	Social Security	2,000.00

Secretary - Part-time

1210	Salary	5,110.00
1220	Social Security	350.00

Office Expense

1310	Repairs	300.00
1320	Copier Service	600.00
1330	Supplies	800.00
1340	Printing	200.00
1350	Postage	600.00
1360	Telephone	600.00

Equipment Purchase

1410	Purchase of Equipment	1,300.00

Associational Minutes

1510	Expense of Minutes	1,200.00

Lending Library

1610	Materials	250.00

Associational General Officers Training

1710	Expenses	100.00
	TOTAL	$36,768.00

CHRISTIAN SOCIAL MINISTRIES

Director of Christian Social Ministries

2110	Salary 3 Months Half-time	1,875.00	
	9 Months Full-time	13,500.00	
	(To be divided as desired by director)		15,375.00
2120	Housing		
2130	Travel		
2140	Insurance		
2150	Conference		100.00

Office Expense

2210	Supplies	400.00
2220	Postage	400.00
2230	Telephone	400.00
2240	Utilities	900.00

Migrant Ministry Summer Workers

2311	Salaries	4,000.00
2312	Social Security	268.00
2313	Travel	600.00
2314	Meals	1,200.00
2315	Speaker Expense	300.00
2316	Hunger Fund	3,350.00
2317	Unforeseen Expenses	200.00

Deaf Ministry

2410	Activities	100.00

2420	Associational Leader Training	50.00
Literacy Ministry		
2510	Activities	100.00
2520	Associational Leader Training	50.00
Senior Adults Ministry		
2610	Activities	100.00
2620	Associational Leader Training	50.00
Mentally Handicapped Ministry		
2710	Activities	300.00
2720	Associational Leader Training	100.00
	TOTAL	

$28,343.00

CHURCH DEVELOPMENT/CHRISTIAN EDUCATION MINISTRIES

Sunday School		
3011	Activities	690.00
3012	Promotion	110.00
3013	Associational Leader Training	225.00
Church Training		
3021	Activities	300.00
3022	Promotion	60.00
3023	Associational Leader Training	400.00
Woman's Missionary Union		
3031	Activities	380.00
3032	Promotion	190.00
3033	Associational Leader Training	645.00
Brotherhood		
3041	Activities	832.00
3042	Promotion	100.00
3043	Associational Leader Training	190.00
Music		
3051	Activities	275.00
3052	Promotion	100.00
3053	Associational Leader Training	25.00
Evangelism		
3061	Activities	-100.00
3062	Promotion	25.00
3063	Associational Leader Training	225.00
Media Library		
3071	Activities	150.00
3072	Promotion	25.00
3073	Associational Leader Training	125.00
Mission		
3081	Activities	200.00
3082	Promotion	30.00
3083	Associational Leader Training	325.00
Pastor Support		
3091	Activities	260.00
3092	Promotion	65.00
3093	Associational Leader Training	25.00
Stewardship		
3101	Activities	260.00
3102	Promotion	65.00
3103	Associational Leader Training	25.00
	TOTAL	

$6,427.00

MISSION ADVANCE MINISTRIES

4100	Mount Olive College Baptist Student Union	200.00

```
4200   Council of Associational Ministries
       "CAM"
       TOTAL                                   _____        200.00
```

FELLOWSHIP MINISTRIES

```
Pastors Conference
5110   Speaker Expense                         150.00
5120   Promotion                               150.00
5130   Associational Leader Training            25.00
Annual Meeting
5210   Expenses                                300.00
Associational Fellowship Meals
5310   Expenses                                400.00
       TOTAL                                                1,025.00
```

MISCELLANEOUS

```
6100   Unforeseen Expenses                     400.00
6110   Baptist Center Fund                      -0-
       TOTAL                                                  400.00
       GRAND TOTAL                                         $73,163.00
```

ANTICIPATED INCOME

```
Church Contributions (Undesignated)                       $43,234.00
Churches for Associational Minutes                          1,200.00
Church Contributions (Designated Migrant)                   4,000.00
Individuals (Designated)                                    1,000.00
Baptist State Convention (CSM Director)                    15,375.00
Baptist State Convention (Summer Workers)                   2,500.00
Home Mission Board (Hunger Fund)                            3,350.00
Copier Fees                                                   250.00
Interest Income:
   Interest from IMMA (Housing)                             2,000.00
   N-O-W Account (Checking)                                   250.00
                                                          $73,163.00
```

TREASURER'S REPORT

October 1, 1982 - September 30, 1983

```
BROUGHT FORWARD                              $ 6,295.68
   Less Employees Tax Withheld                   167.01
   Net Available Funds                                       6,128.67

RECEIPTS
   Undesignated:
      Church Contributions                    36,334.89
      Interest from N-O-W Account                373.68
      Total                                                 36,708.57

   Designated:
      CSM Salary - Baptist State Con-
         vention                               6,875.02
      Migrant Missions                         8,270.42
```

```
Baptist Center Fund                          374.88
Printing - Sale of Minutes                   939.05
Office Equipment                             500.00
Housing - Interst from IMMA                2,105.44
     TOTAL                                             19,064.81

Refunds:
Stewardship Committee                        167.33
Sunday School                                181.15
Missions Committee-Migrant Missions           13.01
Office Supplies - Copier Fees                197.15
N.C. Sales Tax                               264.38
     TOTAL                                                823.02

TOTAL RECEIPTS                                         56,596.40
TOTAL AVAILABLE FUNDS                                  62,725.07


DISBURSEMENTS
Mission Advance:
    Mount Olive College BSU                  200.00
        TOTAL                                            200.00
Association Office:
    Equipment and Repairs                  1,714.39
    Printing                               1,364.47
    Office Supplies                        1,291.74
    Postage                                1,619.38
    Telephone                              1,186.73
        TOTAL                                          7,176.71
Salaries·
    Director of Missions                  11,500.00
    Director, Christian Social Ministry    4,750.00
    Secretary                              4,800.00
        TOTAL                                         21,050.00
Other Personnel Expense:
    Retirement and Insurance               2,657.40
    FICA - Employers Part                    314.70
    Housing:
        Director of Missions               5,900.00
        Director, Christian Social Min.    1,000.00
    Travel.
        Director of Missions               3,600.00
        Director, Christian Social Min.    1,500.00
    Conventions and Conferences              600.00
        TOTAL                                         15,572.10
Education and Promotion.
    General Promotion and Training           773.21
    Sunday School                            581.06
    Church Training                          762.98
    Brotherhood                               91.82
    Woman's Missionary Union                 525.52
    Church Music                               6.58
    Audio-Visuals                            86.00
    Evangelism Committee                      -0-
    Stewardship Committee                    699.96
    Missions Committee:
      Migrant Missions:
          Salaries              3,022.50
          FICA(Employers Part)     65.66
          Travel                1,555.20
```

```
            Supplies              460.03
            Other Expenses      4,420.55
             Total Mig. Min.    9,523.94
    Other Mission Activities     306.08
             TOTAL                         9,830.22
     Pastor Support Committee               346.85
     Library Committee                        2.07
     Pastors Conference                     202.47
     Total Education & Promotion                       $13,926.81

MISCELLANEOUS
  IRS Penalty                               27.49
  North Carolina Sales Tax                 180.92
  Transferred to IMMA                      374.88
TOTAL EXPENDITURES                                     58,508.91
BALANCE September 30, 1983                              4,216.16
  Plus Employee Withholdings                              303.05
NET BALANCE September 30, 1983                          4,519.21
```

FUNDS DEPOSITED IN INSURED MONEY MARKET ACCOUNT

```
BROUGHT FORWARD October 1, 1982                        $30,396.51
RECEIPTS
  Baptist Center Fund                      374.99
  Interest Earned:
    Principal from sale of Missionary
      Home                               2,105.44
    Baptist Center Fund                    426.78
    Reserve Fund                           312.97
  Total                                                 3,220.07

DISBURSEMENTS
Transferred to General Fund                            -2,105.44
BALANCE, September 30, 1983                            $31,511.14
```

SUMMARY

```
GENERAL FUND                                            4,519.21
FUNDS DEPOSITED IN IMMA:
  Principal from Sale of Missionary
    Home                                22,394.00
  Baptist Center Fund                    5,476.80
  Reserve Fund                           3,640.34
  TOTAL                                                31,511.14
TOTAL CASH ASSETS September 30, 1983                  $36,030.35
```

CHURCHES' CONTRIBUTIONS TO ASSOCIATIONAL MISSIONS

CHURCH	1981	1982	1983
Albertson	166.00	150.00	150.00
Alum Springs	250.00	300.00	340.00
Bear Marsh	300.00	300.00	300.00
Beulah	606.42	696.31	611.38
Brown	350.00	350.00	85.00

Calvary	633.96	875.49	809.02
Calypso	280.00	280.00	300.00
Center	387.53	527.76	462.75
Clinton, First	1,900.00	3,350.00	2,675.00
Concord	366.87	636.80	596.79
Corinth	1,440.00	1,440.00	1,440.00
Dobson Chapel	390.18	745.70	635.25
Evergreen	240.00	240.00	180.00
Faison	440.01	470.49	496.95
Garland	939.01	1,036.19	883.26
Garner's Chapel	150.00	150.00	150.00
Grove Park	1,521.63	1,635.96	1,635.96
Hickory Grove (joined EBA January 24, 1983			
from New South River)			
Immanuel	3,329.00	3,332.00	3,622.00
Ingold	400.00	400.00	400.00
Island Creek	240.00	600.00	792.00
Johnson	613.66	748.58	1,136.42
Kenansville	300.00	300.00	300.00
Magnolia	695.20	642.07	707.93
Mount Gilead	1,326.73	825.00	1,376.99
Mount Olive	2,375.00	2,875.00	3,375.00
Mount Vernon	400.00	400.00	530.00
New Hope	550.00	650.00	650.00
Piney Grove	375.00	225.00	375.00
Poplar Grove	398.24	398.24	-0-
Poston	1,000.00	1,500.00	1,600.00
Rose Hill	1,006.00	1,196.00	1,276.00
Rowan	1,110.00	1,385.00	1,571.00
Sharon	766.40	860.00	900.00
Shiloh	624.24	766.47	1,124.19
Siloam	380.00	380.00	400.00
Teachey	450.00	500.00	580.00
Turkey	860.88	907.20	896.64
Union Grove	132.07	197.69	187.16
Warsaw	1,452.00	1,452.00	1,755.00
Wells Chapel	679.66	728.70	778.20
	$29,825.59	$34,453.65	$36,334.89

AUDIT COMMITTEE REPORT

This is to certify that we, the Auditing Committee for the 1982-83 Eastern Association year, have examined the books and supporting records of the Secretary/Treasurer for the said year and affirm our belief that the totals and accounting of receipts and disbursements are in good order and further affirm, to the best of our knowledge and belief, that all totals are accepted as accurate. This the 18th October, 1983.

Respectfully,
Charles E. Pope
Sharon B. Turner
W. Carroll Turner
Mary S. Carter
Gene M. Hart

HISTORY OF TURKEY BAPTIST CHURCH

"75 Years of Serving the Lord Together"

Turkey Baptist Church was organized Nov. 8, 1908, as a circuit church with three other churches.

The first officers were: Y.B. West, deacon; C.E. Shipp, clerk; and S.H. Britt, treasurer. The first service was preached by the Rev. J.M. Page, who was called to serve as Turkey Baptist Church's first pastor, at a salary of $6.00 per month.

In Sept. 1909, a deed for the lot on which the church stands was presented to the church by J.B. and Eva Daniels.

The Rev. Page pledged to give a dollar for each dollar the members raised to build the church. He did, and it is said that he worked side by side with the carpenters for days at a time on the wooden structure, although handicapped by having only one perfect hand.

In January, 1952, the congregation voted to build a new church at the urging of four widowed churchwomen: Rossie Sutton, Maggie Powell, Eva Sutton, and Anna West.

The congregation met for church services in the school auditorium until the building was completed in November. Mr. K.C. West was the foreman over construction and Mrs. Mae West drew the plans for the building.

In 1961, Turkey Baptist withdrew from the three-church field, which then included Beulah and Poplar Grove, and began a full time program.

In Nov. 1965, building plans were accepted for the new educational plant, and on Oct. 23, 1966, the plant was dedicated.

On Monday, Oct. 28, 1968, Mr. George Roberts, Chairman of the Building Fund Committee, Mr. O.R. Phipps, and Mr. Lester Massey, went to the First Citizens Bank and Trust Company in Clinton, N.C., and paid off all the debts against the church, and brought back the bank notes marked "PAID".

The church program today includes: Sunday School, Morning and Evening Worship Services, Church Training, Mid-Week Prayer Service, all of the Mission Organizations, and four choirs. In 1983, the church is privileged to host the 41 churches of the Eastern Baptist Association at Annual Session.

In 1983, we recognize our rich heritage of "75 Years of Serving the Lord Together".

HISTORICAL TABLE

YEAR	PLACE	MODERATOR	CLERK	PREACHER
1827	Beulah	James Matthews	J.L. Britt	J.B. Taylor
1929	South West	James Matthews	V.N. Seawell	W.M. Kennedy
1830	Limestone	James Matthews	J.R. Oliver	C.A. Jenkins
1831	Bull Tail	James Matthews	F.H. Ivey	W.B. Pope
1832	Island Creek	James Matthews	L.T. Carroll	J.B. Harrell
1833	Browns	James Matthews	J.T. Bland	Hiram Stallings
1833	Lisbon	James Matthews		J ha Cornto
1834	Bear Marsh	W.J. Findley	Allen Morriss	Allen Morriss
1835	Limestone	W.J. Findley	Allen Morriss	George Fennell
1836	Beaver Dam	George Fennell	Allen Morriss	H. Swinson
1837	Well's Chapel	W.J. Findley	Allen Morriss	George Fennell
1838	Rowans	W.J. Findley	G.W. Hufham	Hiram Stallings
1839	Johnson's	James Mathis	G.W. Hufham	G.W. Hufham
1840	Concord	James Carroll	G.W. Hufham	George Fennell
1841	Bear Mash	James Carroll	G.W. Hufham	G.W. Hufham
1842	Red Hill	James Carroll	G.W. Hufham	H. Stallings
1843	Beulah	James Carroll	G.W. Hufham	R. McNab
1844	Kenansville	James Carroll	G.W. Hufham	W.J. Findley
1845	Lebanon	Benjamin Oliver	J.G. Dickson	David Rogers
1846	Wilmington	James McDaniel	J.G. Dickson	W.J. Findley
1847	Harriet's Chapel	James McDaniel	J.G. Dickson	David Thompson
1848	White Oak	James McDaniel	J.G. Dickson	James Rogers
1849	Mt. Gilead	James McDaniel	Robert McNab	saac W. West
1850	Bear Marsh	James McDaniel	A.J. Battle	W.J. Findley
1851	Little Creek	Benjamin Oliver	A.J. Battle	A.J. Battle
1852	New Hope	G.W. Wallace	A.J. Battle	D. Furman
1853	Moore's Creek	G.W. Wallace	D. Cashwell	L.F. Williams
1854	Beulah	G.W. Wallace	D. Cashwell	M.R. F reg
1855	Concord	G.W. Wallace	D. Cashwell	W.P. Riddle
1856	Boykin's Chapel	G.W. Wallace	G.W. Wallace	James McDaniel
1857	Warsaw	G.W. Wallace	G.W. Hufham	C.C. Gordon
1858	Bear Marsh	Benjamin Oliver	G.W. Hufham	G.W. Wallace
1859	Beaver Dam	Benjamin Oliver	Amos Royal	W.M. Kennedy
1860	Lebanon	Benjamin Oliver		G.W. Wallace

Year - Location			
1861 - Piney Grove	Benjamin Oliver	J.G. Dickson	Hugh McAlpin
1862 - Mt. Gilead	S.J. Faison	J.G. Dickson	J.B. Taylor
1863 - Beulah	S.J. Faison	J.G. Dickson	J.L. Pritchard
1864 - B ykin's Chapel	Owen Fennell	J.G. Dickson	G.W. Wallace
1865 - Moore's Creek	Owen Fennell	J.N. Stallings	J.S. Wathall
1866 - Union Chapel	W.M. Kennedy	J.N. Stallings	R.F. Marable
1867 - Bear Marsh	W.M. Kennedy	Isham Royal	J.L. Pritchard
1868 - Beulah	Hugh McAlphin	Isham Royal	Hugh McAlpin
1869 - Lisbon	Hugh McAlphin	Isham Royal	W.M. Kennedy
1870 - Well's Chapel	J.L. Stewart	Isham Royal	G.S. Best
1871 - New Hope	Hugh McAlpin	Isham Royal	J.E. King
1872 - Union Lenoir	Hugh McAlpin	Isham Royal	W.M. Kennedy
1873 - Shiloh	Hugh McAlpin	Isham Royal	W.M. Young
1874 - Island Creek	J.N. Stallings	Isham Royal	J.N. Stallings
1875 - Beaufort	J.N. Stallings	Isham Royal	G.S. Best
1876 - Mt. O vᵬ	J.L. Stewart	Isham Royal	J.P. Faison
1877 - Corinth	J.L. Stewart	Isham Royal	J.C. Hiden
1878 - New Bern	J.L. Stewart	Isham Royal	A.D. Cohen
1879 - Piney Grove	J.L. Stewart	Isham Royal	J.N. Stallings
1880 - Bethel	J.L. Stewart	Isham Royal	S.W. Westcot
1881 - Magnolia	J.L. Stewart	J.R. Oliver	J.L. Stewart
1882 - Emma's Chapel	J.L. Stewart	J.R. Oliver	A.C. Dixon
1883 - Bethlehem	J.L. Stewart	J.L. Britt	F.H. Ivey
1884 - Pollocksville	J.L. Stewart	J.L. Britt	J.R. Taylor
1885 - Mt. O vᵬ	J.L. Stewart	J.L. Britt	J.W. Eason
1886 - Clinton	J.L. Stewart	J.L. Britt	J.L. Stewart
1887 - Well's Chapel	J.L. Stewart	J.L. Britt	C.C. Newton
1888 - Warsaw	J.L. Stewart	J.L. Britt	T.H. Pritchard
1889 - Concord	J.L. Stewart	J.L. Britt	F.R. Underwood
1890 - Riley's Creek	J.L. Stewart	J.L. Britt	C.A. Jenkins
1891 - Dobson's Chapel	J.L. Stewart	Oliver Blackburr	O.P. Meeks
1892 - Emma's Chapel	J.L. Stewart	Oliver Blackburr	J.L. Stewart
1893 - J hns a's	J.L. Stewart	Oliver Blackburr	O.P. Meeks
1894 - Lisbon	J.L. Stewart	A.R. Herring	John Mitchell
1895 - Corinth	S.D. Swaim	A.R. Herring	A.A. Butler
1896 - Island Creek	S.D. Swaim	A.R. Herring	C.G. Wells
1897 - Kenansville	J.L. Stewart	A.R. Herring	I.F. B rᴂ
1898 - Harrell's Store	J.L. Stewart	A.R. Herring	J.L. Stewart

1899 - Mount Holly	J.L. Stewart	A.R. Herring	R.H. Gilbert
1900 - Mount Olive	J.L. Stewart	A.R. Herring	N.B. 6b
1901 - Mount Gilead	J.L. Stewart	A.R. Herring	J.M. Alderman
1902 - Hallsville	J.L. Stewart	A.R. Herring	J.L. Stewart
1903 - Rose Hill	J.L. Stewart	A.F. Robinson	V.N. Johnson
1904 - New Hope	C.E. Daniel	A.F. Robinson	J.H. Booth
1905 - Mount Olive	C.E. Daniel	A.F. Robinson	J.L. Stewart
1906 - Lisbon	C.E. Daniel	H.L. Stewart	C.M. Rock
1907 - Clinton	C.E. Daniel	A.R. Herring	J.M. Page
1908 - Warsaw	C.E. Daniel	A.R. Herring	J.M. Alderman
1909 - Corinth	C.E. Daniel	A.R. Herring	P.A. Anth ng
1910 - Bethel	C.E. Daniel	A.R. Herring	E.J. Harrell
1911 - Rowan	C.E. Daniel	A.R. Herring	W.B. Rivenbark
1912 - Bear Marsh	C.E. Daniel	A.R. Herring	J.G. Newton
1913 - Beulaville	C.E. Daniel	A.R. Herring	B.G. Early
1914 - Oak Vale	C.E. Daniel	A.R. Herring	C.H. Cashwell
1915 - Johnson's	C.E. Daniel	A.L. Carlton	W.N. Johnson
1916 - Calypso	C.E. Daniel	A.L. Carlton	B.T. Herring
1917 - Piney Grove	C.E. Daniel	A.L. Carlton	B.T. Vann
1918 - Concord	H.L. Stewart	E.P. Blanchard	D.P. Harris
1919 - Hallsville	H.L. Stewart	E.P. Blanchard	R.W. Cawthon
1920 - Clinton	H.L. Stewart	E.P. Blanchard	L.R. O'Brien
1921 - Siloam	H.L. Stewart	E.P. Blanchard	R.T. Vann
1922 - Sharon	H.L. Stewart	D.J. Middleton	J.M. Duncan
1923 - Corinth	H.L. Stewart	D.J. Middleton	G.W. Rollins
1924 - Dobson's Chapel	T.H. King	D.J. Middleton	T.H. King
1925 - Turkey	T.H. King	C.I. Robinson	S.L. Naff
1926 - Island Creek	H.L. Stewart	C.I. Robinson	J.H. Barnes
1927 - Beulah	H.L. Stewart	C.I. Robinson	W.R. Beach
1928 - Bear Marsh	H.L. Stewart	C.I. Robinson	C.V. Brooks
1929 - Ingold	H.L. Stewart	C.I. Robinson	E.N. Johnson
1930 - Hallsville	H.L. Stewart	C.I. Robinson	R.C. Foster
1931 - New Hope	F.W. McGowen	C.I. Robinson	T.H. Williams
1932 - Kenansville	F.W. McGowen	C.I. Robinson	L.M. Holloway
1933 - Mount Gilead	F.W. McGowen	C.I. Robinson	R.F. Marshburn
1934 - Concord	F.W. McGowen	C.I. Robinson	L.L. Johnson
1935 - Magnolia	F.W. McGowen	C.I. Robinson	W.P. Page
1936 - Rowan	F.W. McGowen	C.I. Robinson	

Year	Place			
1937	Warsaw	F.W. McGowen	C.I. Robinson	J.L. Powers
1938	Beulaville	F.W. McGowen	C.I. Robinson	W.R. Stephens
1939	Rose Hill	F.W. McGowen	C.I. Robinson	J.P. Gulley
1940	Clinton	F.W. McGowen	C.I. Robinson	S.L. Morgan, Jr.
1941	Bear Marsh	F.W. McGowen	C.I. Robinson	J.B. Sessoms
1942	Johnson's	F.W. McGowen	C.I. Robinson	J.L. Jones
1943	Turkey	F.W. McGowen	C.I. Robinson	T.N. Cooper
1944	Mount Olive	F.W. McGowen	C.I. Robinson	G. Van Stephens
1945	Ingold	F.W. McGowen	C.I. Robinson	J.V. Case
1946	New Hope & Mount Vernon	G. Van Stephens	C.I. Robinson	G.W. Lambert
1947	Island Creek & Corinth	G. Van Stephens	C.I. Robinson	Gilmer Beck
1948	Garland & Cedar Fork	G. Van Stephens	C.I. Robinson	A.L. Benton
1949	Rose Hill & Clinton	Thomas L. R ch,l Jr.	Paul L. Cashwell	E.N. Teague
1950	Magnolia & Mt. Gilead	Mack Herring	Paul L. Cashwell	J.C. Conoly
1951	Piney Grove & Warsaw	Mack Herring	Paul L. Cashwell	J.P. Royal
1952	Siloam & Dobson's Chpl.	Mack Herring	Paul L. Cashwell	Elliot B. Stewart
1953	Mount Olive & Turkey	A.W. Greenlaw	Paul L. Cashwell	E.F. Knight
1954	Rowan & Johnson's	Mack Herring	Paul L. Cashwell	T.W. Williams
1955	Sharon & Beulaville	Paul L. Cashwell	Paul T. Mull	Julian Motley
1956	Warsaw & Bear Marsh	J.C. Mitchell	Paul T. Mull	Robert A. Melvin
1957	Immanuel & Kenansville	T.W. Williams	H.M. Baker	M.M. Turner
1958	Rose Hill	C.F. Shipp	Eugene B. Hager	M.M. Johnson
1959	Calypso & Ingold	C.F. Shipp	Eugene B. Hager	Lauren Sharpe
1960	Island Crk. & Grove Pk.	D.E. Parkerson	Paul T. Mull	Jerry DeBell
1961	Clinton, 1st & Magnolia	D.E. Parkerson	Paul T. Mull	L.H. Knott
1962	Mt. Olive & Mt. Gilead	Mack Herring	Paul T. Mull	A. Quakenbush
1963	Siloam & Turkey	Milton Boone	Paul T. Mull	Hugh R. Williams
1964	Piney Grove & Sharon	Milton Boone	Paul T. Mull	D.E. Parkerson
1965	Rowan & Well's Chapel	M.M. Johnson	E.L. Eiland	Wayne Wheeler
1966	Warsaw, 1st & Br. Marsh	Hugh Ross Williams	M.S. McLain	R.H. Kelley
1967	Kenansville & Corinth	Hugh Ross Williams	M.S. McLain	R.A. Thompson
1968	Rose Hill & Immanuel	John R. Johnson	M.S. McLain	Glen Holt
1969	Calypso & Garland	John R. Johnson	M.S. McLain	Norman Aycock
1970	Island Crk. & Grove Pk.	J hn A. Johnson	M.S. McLain	Waldo Early
1971	Clinton, 1st & Magnolia	Norman Ayc ck	M.S. McLain	Anthony Gurganus
1972	Piney Gr. & Mt. Gilead	Vern n Braswell	R.B. Little	J.B yce Brooks
1973	Siloam	Vern n Braswell	R.B. Little	W.M. Jones

SCHEDULE OF MEETING PLACES OF EASTERN ASSOCIATION

1984
1st Day *Piney Grove
         Mount Vernon

2nd Day *Sharon
         Shiloh

1985
1st Day Rowan
2nd Day *Poston
         Wells Chapel

1986
1st Day *Warsaw
         Calvary
2nd Day *Bear Marsh
         Garner's Chapel
         Alum Springs

1987
1st Day *Kenansville
         Albertson
2nd Day *Corinth
         Teachey

1988
1st Day Rose Hill
2nd Day *Immanuel
         Hickory Grove

1989
1st Day *Calypso
         Faison
         Poplar Grove
2nd Day 'Garland
         Ingold
         Center

1990
1st Day *Island Creek
         Dobson's Chapel
2nd Day *Grove Park
         Brown

1991
1st Day Clinton, First
2nd Day *Magnolia
         Concord
         Johnson

1992
1st Day Mount Olive
2nd Day *Mount Gilead
         Union Grove

1993
1st Day *Siloam
         Evergreen
2nd Day *Turkey
         Beulah
         New Hope

*Meeting Place
 Other listed churches assisting with meal on respective days

RULES OF ORDER

1. At the meeting of the Association the Moderator elected at the preceding session shall preside. In the case of his absence, the Vice Moderator shall preside.

2. Each session of the Association shall be opened with religious exercises.

3. At each daily session and previous to proceeding to business the Associate Clerk shall be requested to announce the number of churches represented and the total number of messengers representing these churches. When it is determined that a majority of the churches are represented the Moderator shall declare the Association duly constituted. It shall be necessary for a majority of the churches to be represented for the Association to transact business other than adjournment. The proceedings of the first of the Annual Session shall be read the morning of the second day and the proceedings of the second day shall be read at the first Council of the Association to meet following the Annual Meeting.

4. The members shall observe toward the officers and each other that courtesy which belongs to Christians.

5. Any member wishing to speak shall arise and address the presiding officer and shall confine himself strictly to the question under consideration and avoid personalities.

6. No member shall speak more than twice on the same question without permission.

7. All motions seconded shall be definitely stated by the presiding officer before discussion.

8. No motion shall be withdrawn after discussion.

9. When a question is under discussion, no motion or proposition shall be received except to lay on the table, to adjourn, to amend, to commit, or to postpone to a definite time, which several motions shall have preference in the order in which they are stated.

10. After a motion has been decided, any member having voted in the majority may move a re-consideration.

11. All questions except such as relate to the Constitution shall be decided by a majority vote.

12. The Association shall have the right to decide what subjects shall be admitted to consideration.

13. The rules of order may be altered or amended at any session of the Association by a Majority vote.

CONSTITUTION

PREAMBLE

We, the Missionary Baptist Churches of Jesus Christ, composing the EASTERN BAPTIST ASSOCIATION, convinced of the necessity of an association of churches in order to promote fellowship, missions, education, Christian service, the preaching of the gospel, and to cooperate with the Baptist State Convention of North Carolina and the Southern Baptist Convention in their work, do hereby agree and subscribe to the following articles.

- 53 -

ARTICLE I. NAMES

This association shall be known and denominated as the North Carolina EASTERN BAPTIST ASSOCIATION.

ARTICLE II. PURPOSE

The purpose of this association shall be the promotion of Christ's Kingdom among men, and the means of accomplishing this shall be in strict conformity to the New Testament.

ARTICLE III. AUTHORITY

This association claims to be independent and sovereign in its own sphere, but shall never attempt to exercise any authority over the internal affairs of the churches.

ARTICLE IV. COMPOSITION

This association shall be composed of all ordained ministers who are members or pastors of member churches, the general offic of the association, the director of missions, and three messenge from each church with one additional messenger for every one-hundred members over the first one-hundred, no church being al-lowed more than ten messengers.

ARTICLE V. MEETINGS

The Annual Session of the Association shall commence on Monday after the fourth Lord's Day in October. The church year for the churches of the association shall commence on October 1, and end on September 30.

ARTICLE VI. OFFICERS

The officers of the association shall be a moderator, a vice moderator, a clerk, and associate clerk, the chairman of the Historical Committee, a treasurer and an associate treasurer. All officers shall be elected annually except the chairman of the Historical Committee who is the senior member of the Historical Committee. The moderator shall not be elected to serve more than two full years at one period and shall assume office at the close of the annual session at which he is elected.

ARTICLE VII. TRUSTEES

The association shall have three (3) trustees who shall serve three-year terms in rotation, the replacement to be elected by the association annually.

ARTICLE VIII. EXECUTIVE BOARD

The association shall have an Executive Board consisting of th general officers of the association; the director of missions, the director of Christian Social Ministries; the directors of as-sociational Brotherhood, Church Music, Church Training, Sunday School, and Womans Missionary Union; the chairpersons of associational standing committees; each active and retired pastor in the association; and two lay persons (men or women) from each church to be elected by the church and whose name shall be included in the church letter to the association.

ARTICLE IX. ASSOCIATIONAL COUNCIL

The association shall have an Associational Council consisting of the officers of the Executive Board; the directors of associational Brotherhood, Church Music, Church Training, Sunday School and Womans Missionary Union: the chairpersons of Evangelism, Media Library, Missions, Pastoral Support, and Stewardship; the director of missions, and the director of Christian Social Ministries.

ARTICLE X. COMMITTEES

The association shall have such committees as may be deemed necessary for orderly and efficient achievement of the association's purpose. Members on standing committees shall be on the rotating basis with one-third of the members rotating off each year. Members completing a three year term shall not be eligible for re-election until one year has passed. A member elected to fill an unexpired term shall be eligible for election to a full term following the completion of the unexpired term.

ARTICLE XI. CHURCH PROGRAMS

The association shall organized groups of officers for the five (5) church programs: Sunday School, Church Training, Women's Missionary Union, Brotherhood, and Music.

ARTICLE XIII. MISCELLANEOUS

The association shall not maintain fellowship with any church which neglects to observe gospel order.

ARTICLE XIV. CONSTITUTIONAL CHANGES

This constitution may be amended on the second day of any annual session by a vote of two-thirds of the messengers present provided the proposed changes have been presented on the first day of the annual session.

BY-LAWS

ARTICLE I. DUTIES OF OFFICERS

A. MODERATOR - The moderator on the first day of each Annual Session of the Association shall appoint the following committees to function during the session: Place and Preacher; Resolutions; and Memorials. At the last regular meeting of the Executive Board before the Annual Session of the Association, the moderator shall appoint a Constitutional Committee to serve during the Annual Session, and a Committee on Committees.

It shall be the duty of the moderator to enforce an observance of the constitution, preserve order, decide all questions of order, vote in case of a tie, and act as chairman of the Executive Board

B. VICE MODERATOR - It shall be the duty of the vice moderator to preside in the absence or at the request of the moderator, to give other appropriate assistance to the moderator, and to succee to the office of moderator, if and when during his tenure of office the office of moderator becomes vacant.

C. CLERK - It shall be the duty of the clerk to record the proceedings of each Annual Session, superintend their printing and distribution, and serve as secretary of the Executive Board and the Associational Council.

It shall be his duty to report the actions of the Executive Board to the Annual Session of the Association. He shall report the actions of the Associational Council to the next meeting of the Board or to the Annual Session of the Association, which-ever comes first.

D. ASSOCIATE CLERK - It shall be the duty of the associate clerk to register the messengers, to report upon request the number of churches represented and the total number of messengers representing these churches, and to perform such other duties as are usually performed by an associate clerk.

E. TREASURER - It shall be the duty of the treasurer to receive all funds contributed by the churches or collected during the Annual Session of this body, to distribute all funds received as ordered by the association, and to make to the Association an annual report of the condition of the treasury.

F. ASSOCIATE TREASURER - It shall be the duties of the associa treasurer to assist the treasurer in the performance of his dutie as directed by the treasurer.

ARTICLE II. DUTIES OF TRUSTEES

The trustees shall be the representatives of the Association in legal matters, and shall perform such duties as the Association or the Executive Board may prescribe.

ARTICLE III. EXECUTIVE BOARD

A. OFFICERS - The officers of the Executive Board shall be: moderator, vice moderator, clerk, associate clerk, treasurer, and associate treasurer. The corresponding officers of the Association elected during the last Annual Session of the Association shall serve in these positions on the Executive Board.

B. DUTIES - The Executive Board shall cooperate with the Baptist State Convention of North Carolina in its program for the furtherance of the work fostered by the body within the bounds of the Association; it shall act for the Association on any matters requiring attention between Annual Sessions of the Association; and it shall have power to fill any vacancies on the Board during the year. The clerk shall make a report of the work of the Executive Board at the Annual Session of the Association. The director of missions or other workers employed by the Association shall make a quarterly report to the Executive Board in order that the said Board shall be prepared to make a full report to this body.

C. MEETINGS - The Executive Board shall meet at least once each quarter at a time and place designated by the Board after the first meeting which will be called by the moderator who shall

serve as chairman of the Board. With proper notice being given
to all members of the meeting, and when it is determined that a
majority of the churches are represented the chairman shall declare the Board duly constituted.

ARTICLE IV. COMMITTEES

A. STANDING COMMITTEES - A majority shall constitute a quorum
for each committee.
1. ELECTION OF COMMITTEES: All committee members shall be
persons who have demonstrated talent for performing the work of
the committee, or who have stated a willingness to receive training to equip them for the work of the committee.
Standing Committees shall be formed from a slate of persons
selected, notified, secured to serve, and nominated by the Committee on Committees. The nominees, then, must be elected by the
Association in its annual session. Special committees shall be
recommended when deemed appropriate to perform the business and
ministry of the Association, and are subject to the approval of
the Executive Board. These committee posts shall be filled by the
Committee on Committees from a slate of persons selected, notified,
secured to serve nominated, and presented to and elected by the
Executive Board. These committees shall have definitely prescribed
duties and a definite term of service before they are established.
2. MISSIONS COMMITTEE: The Missions Committee shall be composed of three (3) at-large members, the chairpersons of standing
committees whose duties relate to Christian Social Ministries,
the director of Christian Social Ministries, and the associational
directors of Brotherhood and Womans Missionary Union. The rotation
system shall apply to the three at-large members only. Chair persons from other committees shall be rotated from within their
individual committees. The Missions Committee shall work with the
director of Christian Social Ministries in discovering, analyzing,
and presenting to the Association opportunities for mission action;
and in coordination of the association's mission activities. Upon
determining that new committees are needed to direct specific
social ministries, the Missions Committee shall bring to the attention of the Executive Board the need for such committees. The
Missions Committee shall work with the director of Christian
Social Ministries in writing the prescription as required by
ARTICLE IV of the By-Laws.
3. STEWARDSHIP COMMITTEE: The Stewardship Committee shall
be composed of nine (9) members. This committee shall be responsible for recommending a budget to the Association in its Annual
Session, for the distribution of all associational funds, and for
devising plans for raising such funds as are necessary for carrying on the associational programs. The Stewardship Committee shall
lead a program of Biblical stewardship education and promotion
among the churches and on the associational level. The associational treasurer shall be a member of this committee. The Stewardship Committee shall have the financial records of the association audited annually.
4. EVANGELISM COMMITTEE: The Evangelism Committee shall be
composed of three (3) members. It shall be the duty of this committee to promote evangelism both in the local church and on an
associational level. It shall serve to link the Association with
state and south-wide departments of evangelism and shall use every
available means for fostering the cause of winning the lost to
Christ.

5. MEDIA LIBRARY COMMITTEE: The Media Library Committee shall be composed of three (3) members duly elected by the Association and resource personnel as appointed by the moderator whose duty it shall be to encourage the establishing and promotion of libraries in churches.

6. PASTORAL SUPPORT COMMITTEE: The Pastoral Support Committee shall be composed of three (3) members whose duties shall be to provide an ongoing continuing program of help to pastors and church staff members in areas of need. The program shall include guidance for those who are just beginning to prepare for church related vocations; career assessment; spiritual, emotional, and physical needs of pastors and church staff.

7. PROGRAM COMMITTEE: The Program Committee shall be composed of three (3) members. It shall be their duty to arrange the program of the annual session of the Association and for all other sessions which may be called.

8. ORDINATION COMMITTEE: The Ordination Committee shall be composed of six (6) members (Pastors and Deacons). This committee shall offer to any church, upon request, advice and assistance in the examination and ordination of deacons and ministers.

9. HISTORICAL COMMITTEE: The Historical Committee shall consist of three (3) members. The committee shall obtain and edit the histories of two churches each year to be included in the minutes, and shall maintain an up-to-date history of the Association. The senior member of the committee shall be the chairman.

10. NOMINATING COMMITTEE: The Nominating Committee shall be composed of six (6) members. It shall be the duty of this committe to submit nominations to the Association in session for the associational general officers (with the floor open for nominations) as well as for representatives to denominational agencies and interests for the following year and to fill any vacancies which may occur during the year.

This committee shall also be responsible for forwarding to the Executive Board at their third meeting for approval and to the Association for election, the directors of Brotherhood, Sunday School, Woman's Missionary Union, Church Training, and Church Music. The Church Program Organizations directors shall then become members of the Nominating Committee. The Nominating Committee shall present to the Executive Board at their fourth meeting a complete slate of officers for the five Church Program Organizations.

11. DEAF MINISTRIES COMMITTEE: The Deaf Ministries Committee shall be composed of three (3) members whose duties shall be to plan, promote, and evaluate mission ministry projects in consultation with the Missions Committee for deaf persons across the Association. The committee shall enlist, train and guide volunteers in its ministry.

12. LITERACY MINISTRIES COMMITTEE: The Literacy Ministries Committee shall be composed of three (3) members. The duties of the committee shall be to identify needs of the non-readers in the Association and to plan, promote and evaluate mission ministry projects in consultation with the Missions Committee to meet the identified needs. The committee shall also be responsible for enlisting, training and guiding volunteers involved in its ministry.

13. MINISTRIES TO MENTALLY HANDICAPPED COMMITTEE: The Ministries to Mentally Retarded Committee shall be composed of three (3) members whose duties shall be to identify, plan, promote, and

evaluate mission ministry programs in consultation with the
Missions Committee, for mentally retarded persons. The committee shall enlist, train, and guide volunteers in its ministry.
14. MIGRANT MINISTRIES COMMITTEE: The Migrant Ministries
Committee shall be composed of six (6) members. The members of
the committee shall be responsible for planning, promoting, and
evaluating the migrant mission ministries of the Association
in consultation with the Missions Committee. Its duties shall
include enlisting, training, and guiding volunteers in Migrant
Mission Ministries.
15. SENIOR ADULT MINISTRIES COMMITTEE: The Senior Adult
Ministries Committee shall be composed of three (3) members
whose duties shall be to plan, promote, and evaluate mission
ministries to senior adults, in consultation with the Missions
Committee. The Committee shall enlist, train, and guide volunteers in its ministry.
B. APPOINTED COMMITTEES:
1. CONSTITUTION AND BY-LAWS COMMITTEE: This committee shall
be composed of three (3) members, whose duty it shall be to study
and recommend changes in the Constitution and By-Laws and bring
reports as necessary to the Association.
2. PLACE AND PREACHER COMMITTEE: This committee shall be
composed of three (3) members, whose duty it shall be to make the
Association aware of the rotating system of meeting places, and
to recommend to the Association in Annual Session a place or
places for meeting, along with a preacher and alternate for the
sermon for the following year.
3. RESOLUTIONS COMMITTEE: This committee shall be composed
of three (3) members whose duty it shall be to study all resolutions referred to it by the Association or the Executive Board
and report suitable resolutions at the Annual Session.
4. MEMORIALS COMMITTEE: This committee shall be composed of
(3) members whose duty it shall be to prepare and present at the
Annual Session an appropriate program of memorial for those of
our number who have died during the preceeding year. These names
may be secured from the letters to the Association from the
member churches.
5. COMMITTEE ON COMMITTEES: This committee shall be composed
of six (6) members whose duty it shall be to select and nominate
persons for the standing committees and shall appoint successors
when vacancies occur during the year.

ARTICLE V. DUTIES OF CHURCH PROGRAM DIRECTORS

A. The ASSOCIATION SUNDAY SCHOOL DIRECTOR shall promote and
supervise the Sunday School Program of the Association, and shall
be responsible for the direction of Vacation Bible School work
of the Association in cooperation with the director of missions.
B. THE ASSOCIATIONAL CHURCH TRAINING DIRECTOR shall promote
and supervise the Church Training Program of the Association in
cooperation with the director of missions.
C. The ASSOCIATIONAL WOMAN'S MISSIONARY DIRECTOR shall promote
and supervise the Woman's Missionary Union Program of the Association cooperating with the director of missions and in keeping
with the Constitution and By-Laws of the Woman's Missionary Union
of the EASTERN BAPTIST ASSOCIATION.

D. The ASSOCIATIONAL BROTHERHOOD DIRECTOR shall promote and supervise the Brotherhood Program of the Association in cooperation with the director of missions.

E. THE ASSOCIATIONAL MUSIC DIRECTOR shall promote and supervise the Church Music Program of the Association in cooperation with the director of missions.

ARTICLE VI. ASSOCIATIONAL COUNCIL

A. Purpose - The Purpose of the Associational Council shall be to provide a consultative, advisory, and coordinative service to the Association and its various programs and committees.

B. Duties - The duties of the Associational Council shall be: provide for communication between associational officers, organizations, and committees; study church needs in the association and needs of the people in the area of the Association; propose long-range and short-range goals for the Association; prepare and recommend plans for involving organizations and committees appropriately in attaining goals; review and coordinate plans made by the organizations and committees and relate these to the attainment of goals; evaluate the use of resources; and report through appropriate channels progress made toward attainment of associational goals. The Council shall exercise general supervision of the work of the director of missions. In the event the position of director of missions becomes vacant, the Council shall recommend to the Association or the Executive Board for approval a search committee whose duties shall be to seek prayerfully a person to fill the position.

C. Officers - The officers of the Associational Council shall be the chairman and the secretary. The moderator shall serve as chairman.

The associational clerk shall be the secretary. In the absence of the secretary, the chairman shall appoint a temporary secretary

ARTICLE VII BY-LAWS CHANGES

These by-laws may be amended on the second day of any Annual Session by a vote of the majority of the messengers present and voting provided the proposed changes have been presented on the first day of the annual session.

STATISTICAL TABLES

Association

EASTERN

State

NORTH CAROLINA

Director of Associational Missions

CLYDE L DAVIS, SR

Address	**City**	**State**	**Zip**
P O Box 712	Warsaw	North Carolina	28398

TABLE B SUNDAY SCHOOL — 1983

Association: EASTERN
State: NORTH CAROLINA
Associational Sunday School Director: JAMES HARTSELL
Address: Rt. 2, Box 349 **City:** Rose Hill **State:** North Carolina **Zip:** 28458

CHURCHES	SUNDAY SCHOOL DIRECTORS & ADDRESSES (INCLUDE ZIP CODE)	54 Cradle Roll enrollment (Birth to 2 years)	55 Preschool enrollment (Birth through 5 years)	56 Children enrollment (6-11 years or grades 1-6)	57 Youth enrollment (12-17 years or grades 7-12)	58 Young Adult enrollment Single (18-29 yrs or H.S. grad through 29 yrs)	59 Young Adult enrollment Married (18-29 yrs or H.S. grad through 29 yrs)	60 Adult enrollment (30-59 years)	61 Senior Adult enrollment (60 and over)	62 Adults Away enrollment	63 Homebound enrollment	64 General officers enrollment	65 Enrollment of mission(s) of church	66 Total ongoing Sunday School enrollment	67 Bible Study Groups enrollment	68 Total enrolled in Bible Study	69 Average Weekly Sunday School Attendance	70 Number ethnic Sunday School members	71 Church V.B.S. enrollment	72 Mission V.B.S. enrollment	73 Backyard Bible Club enrollment
Albertson	Marshall Stroud, R-1, Albertson 28508	3	7	10	10	0	2	11	15	0	0	9	0	76	0	76	46	0	38	0	0
Alum Springs	Larry Herring, R-2, Mt. Olive 28365	3	7	18	6	4	10	24	31	0	0	3	0	76	0	76	46	0	31	0	0
Bear Marsh	Timothy Bell, R-5, Mt. Olive 28365	0	9	21	18	8	7	19	32	0	0	0	0	110	0	110	70	0	66	0	0
Beulah	Lonnie Carter, R-2, Clinton 28328	3	5	7	14	11	0	7	6	0	0	7	0	61	15	76	5	0	55	0	0
Brown	Miss Renee Pope, 305 Inverness Road, Clinton 28328	0	14	12	20	4	7	27	15	0	0	3	0	104	0	104	76	0	72	0	0
Calvary	Bill Savage, R-1, B-35R, Warsaw 28398	2	10	16	14	4	8	22	10	0	3	9	9	96	0	96	46	0		0	0
Calypso	A.D. Johnson, Box 27, Calypso 28325	7	5	16	13	9	27	22	32	0	0	0	0	115	0	115	55	0	49	0	0
Center	Ray Allen Cannady, R-1, B-184, Garland 28441	7	8	9	12	4	0	32	0	0	0	3	0	76	0	76		0	65	0	0
Clinton	Keith Jones, 109 Raiford St., Clinton 28328	0	66	90	87	30	38	254	127	33	3	9	0	734	7	741	336	12	143	0	0
Concord	Rary Bell, P.O. Box 725, Rose Hill 28458	5	15	20	12	23	12	16	0	0	0	4	0	77	0	77	65	0	72	0	0
Dobson Chapel	Ray Fussell, R-1, B-82, Teachey 28464	5	15	21	12	8	8	86	32	0	0	3	0	190	0	190	97	0	110	0	0
Evergreen	James P. Brown, R-2, Rose Hill 28458	7	7	20	21	8	0	22	18	0	0	3	0	99	0	99	53	0	53	0	0
Faison	Jerry Todd, Box 20, Harrells 28444	7	7	8	10	8	14	30	13	0	0	3	0	95	0	95	49	0	86	0	0
Garland	Henry Brown, Faison 28341	0	13	12	12	0	4	23	16	0	0	14	0	108	0	108	25	0	130	0	0
Garners Chapel	Gene M. Hart, Box 187, Garland 28441	3		5	12	14	6	23	26	0	0		0	104	0	104		0	69	0	0
Grove Park	Albert Britt, R-1, Mt. Olive 28365	0	31	25	4	10	6	132	54	0	0	4	0	54	307	307	164	0	32	32	0
Hickory Grove	Ronnie Warren, 202 Fox Lake Dr., Clinton 28328	0	31	20	35	6	0	4	25	0	25	2	0	307	0	307	25	0	133	32	0
Immanuel	Larry Strickland, R-1, Clinton 28328	0	23	53	10	53	39	35	31	0	0	4	0	127	375	375	259	0	81	0	0
Ingold	Wilbert Massey, 1001 Naylor St., Clinton 28328	0		14	6	14	16	109	13	10	10	0	0	375	0	375	52	0	18	0	0
Island Creek	J. Gordon Cashwell, Box 5212, Ingold 28446	0	11	18	15	7	0	34	0	0	0	8	0	96	0	96	52	0	45	0	0
Johnson	George Brown, R-3, Wallace 28466	3	8	16	18	8	21	25	32	0	25	8	0	160	0	160	111	0	104	0	0
Kenansville	Mavis Pigford, 501 Forrest Rd., Warsaw 28398	7	7	7	15	14	0	12	29	0	0	3	0	100	0	100	65	0	81	0	0
Magnolia	F.F. Oakley, Box 216, Kenansville 28349	0	3	40	9	9	16	30	18	0	0	2	0	99	0	99	60	0	60	0	0
Mt. Gilead	Kenneth Baker, Magnolia 28453	0		11	34	16	10	25	38	0	0	3	0	105	0	105		0	45	0	0
Mt. Olive	Lonnie Bass, R-2, B-110, Clinton 28328	0	30	62	59	5	78	75	36	0	10	7	0	257	0	257	124	0	79	0	25
Mt. Vernon	Richard Blackwelder, Box 91, Mt. Olive 28365	0	26	9	16	8	16	105	100	0	0	23	0	455	0	455	203	0	122	0	0
New Hope	Tony Rackley, R-2, Clinton 28328	0	6	11	7	5	10	15	29	0	0	2	0	106	0	106	75	0	38	0	0
Piney Grove	C. Ed Colwell, R-1, Turkey 28393	0	3	2	2	4	0	41	34	0	0	4	0	90	0	90		0	30	0	0
Poplar Grove	Dewitt King, R-2, B-111, Faison 28341	0	9	16	14	12	19	47	33	0	0	4	0	152	0	152	104	0	139	0	0
Poston	Jane Bradshaw, R-2, Faison 28341	0	5	14	4	4	0	24	17	0	0	6	0	67	0	67	40	0	43	0	0
Rose Hill	Sherry Padgett, R-3, Wallace 28466	1	54	33	34	12	23	100	26	1	3	3	0	290	0	290	140	0	160	0	13
Rowan	J.T. Kelly, Box 122, Rose Hill 28458	8		23	22	13	20	35	89	0	0	3	0	230	0	230	118	0	91	0	0
Sharon	Jo N. Robinson, R-2, B-269, Clinton 28328	0	37	21	25	24	22	87	95	0	0	4	0	305	0	305	173	0	106	0	0
Shiloh	Jimmy Mercer, Chinquapin 28521	7		23	15	3	12	56	41	0	0	0	0	156	0	156	91	0	103	0	0
Siloam	Ray Likens, R-1, Chinquapin 28521	0	15	19	9	7	10	22	0	0	0	2	0	132	0	132	93	0	65	0	0
Teachey	Wayne Cannady, Box 13, Harrells 28444	0	8	15	12	10	0	20	28	0	0	3	0	96	0	96	45	0	33	0	0
Turkey	Jerry Dempsey, R-1, B-125A, Teachey 28464	0	8	28	8	7	6	26	17	2	0	2	0	80	0	80	54	0	33	0	0
Union Grove	H.J. Register, R-1, Turkey 28393	0	24	28	14	8	9	29	33	0	0	5	0	149	0	149	83	0	70	0	0
Warsaw	Raeford H. Carter, R-4, B-349A, Clinton 28328	0	20	25	17	7	18	40	10	0	0	15	0	142	0	142	110	0	49	0	0
Wells Chapel	Lawton Kitchin, 502 Curtis Rd., Warsaw 28398	0	20	45	45	10	18	83	67	0	0	5	0	289	0	289	140	0	79	0	0
	Florence Hoover, R-2, B-17, Harrells 28444	11	6	11	13	10	0	44	32	0	6	3	0	155	0	155	97	0	62	0	0
TOTALS		50	583	792	330	383	567	1883	1325	36	57	185	9	6695	22	6717	3282	12	3030	32	38

- 63 -

Association
EASTERN

State
NORTH CAROLINA

Associational Church Training Director
MARY S. CARTER

Address	City	State	Zip
P O Box 334	Garland	North Carolina	28441

TABLE D MUSIC MINISTRY — 1983

Association: EASTERN
State: NORTH CAROLINA
Associational Music Director: JEAN HATCH
Address: P.O. Box 837 — City: Clinton — State: North Carolina — Zip: 28328

CHURCHES	MUSIC DIRECTORS & ADDRESSES (INCLUDE ZIP CODE)	87 Preschool enrollment (4-5 years)	88 Children enrollment (6-11 years or grades 1-6)	89 Youth enrollment (12-17 years or grades 7-12)	90 Adult enrollment (18 and over)	91 Handbell ringers enrollment	92 Vocal ensembles enrollment	93 Instrumental ensembles enrollment	94 General music leaders enrollment	95 Enrollment of mission(s) of church	96 Total ongoing church music enrollment	97 Church Music Average Weekly Ongoing Attendance	98 Senior adult choir enrollment
Albertson	Laurel Stroud, Rt. 1, Albertson 28508	0	8	0	0	0	0	0	2	0	10	8	0
Alum Springs	Connie Jones, Rt. 1, Mt. Olive 28365	0	7	1	16	0	0	0	2	0	26	18	0
Bear Marsh	Kaye Warren, 120 E. John St., Mt. Olive 28365	0	14	0	23	0	0	0	5	0	42	35	8
Beulah	Joyce Creech, Rt. 1, Box 724, Faison 28341	0	0	4	8	0	0	0	1	0	13	12	8
Brown	Curtis W. Pope, 305 Inverness Rd., Clinton 28328	6	7	8	20	0	0	0	1	0	44	30	0
Calvary	Russell Killette, Rt. 1, Warsaw 28398	0	0	0	10	0	0	0	3	0	10	10	0
Calypso		0	0	0	20	0	0	0	3	0	23	15	0
Center		0	0	0	15	0	0	0	4	0	18	12	0
Clinton	Jean Hatch, 309 Fairfax St., Clinton 28328	18	60	32	51	0	12	14	2	0	191	123	0
Concord		0	0	1	10	0	0	0	2	0	13	10	0
Corinth	Allene Knowles, Rt. 1, Rose Hill 28458	0	0	12	20	0	0	0	3	0	36	15	0
Dobson Chapel	Janet Register, Rt. 2, Rose Hill 28458	0	0	20	18	0	0	0	3	0	41	20	0
Evergreen	Carol Todd, P.O. Box 20, Harrells 28444	3	1	0	11	0	5	0	6	5	24	13	0
Faison	Henry Brown, Faison 28341	0	11	0	20	0	0	0	3	0	47	16	20
Garland	Sarah M. Tingle, P.O. Box 206, Garland 28441	0	0	4	14	0	0	0	3	0	21	15	14
Garners Chapel		0	0	0	6	0	0	0	2	0	21	6	0
Grove Park	Stan Benton, 1108 Bass Dr., Clinton 28328	0	10	12	32	0	0	0	4	0	56	35	0
Hickory Grove		0	0	20	20	0	0	0	2	0	26	12	0
Immanuel	Dan Arnold, 1000 Naylor St., Clinton 28328	7	22	13	35	0	10	0	10	0	97	70	0
Ingold	Bobby H. Lamb, Rt. 1, Box 138, Garland 28441	0	0	0	0	0	0	0	0	0	0	0	0
Island Creek	Johnnie Norris, Rt. 2, Rose Hill 28458	3	3	11	17	0	5	0	4	0	40	25	0
Johnson	John W. Boyette Jr., Rt. 2, Warsaw 28398	3	4	9	22	0	0	4	6	0	44	14	0
Kenansville	Henry M. West Jr., Rt. 2, Warsaw 28398	3	7	0	8	0	5	0	2	0	20	10	1
Magnolia		3	10	1	16	0	0	0	2	0	16	10	0
Mt. Gilead	Rhonda Gainey, 209 Glendale Dr., Clinton 28328	3	3	18	3	0	0	0	4	0	43	32	0
Mt. Olive	Jim Strickland, RFD 4, Mt. Olive 28365	9	24	7	18	0	10	0	2	0	66	60	0
Mt. Vernon	Phyliss Lindley, Blaney St., Clinton 28328	0	0	7	18	0	0	0	5	0	27	16	15
New Hope	Nell Corbett, Rt. 1, Turkey 28393	0	0	0	13	0	0	0	5	0	18	12	0
Piney Grove	Ruth King, Rt. 2, Box 111, Faison 28341	0	1	14	23	0	0	0	5	0	43	26	0
Poplar Grove	Elaine S. Jordan, Rt. 1, Faison 28341	8	8	10	10	0	0	0	1	0	29	20	0
Poston	Annette Henderson, Rt. 3, Box 63, Wallace 28466	12	12	7	45	0	0	4	10	0	73	15	15
Rose Hill	Linda Murphy, RFD 2, Rose Hill 28458	6	0	0	20	0	26	0	10	0	56	24	0
Rowan	Lucille Yancey, P.O. Box 711, Clinton 28328	0	7	6	24	0	4	4	6	0	53	23	0
Sharon	Betty Brant, Chinquapin 28521	0	0	0	24	0	0	0	4	0	24	15	0
Shiloh	Rifton Raynor, Rt. 2, Wallace 28466	0	0	2	17	0	0	0	3	0	22	15	0
Siloam	Angelyn Burgess, Rt. 1, Harrells 28444	0	4	7	8	8	0	1	3	0	23	7	8
Teachy		0	0	3	8	0	3	0	4	0	18	9	0
Turkey	Sue Padgett, P.O. Box 216, Turkey 28393	10	13	8	15	0	4	0	8	0	45	20	0
Union Grove	Roger Wells, Rt. 4, Box 357-D, Clinton 28328	10	10	10	20	0	3	0	5	0	53	30	0
Warsaw	Catherine Vestal, P.O. Box 453, Warsaw 28398	0	15	15	12	0	0	0	2	0	70	56	0
Wells Chapel	Geraldine Johnson, Rt. 1, Box 8, Harrells 28444	0	0	0	0	0	0	0	4	0	19	10	0
TOTALS		90	263	242	696	8	84	23	143	5	1552	914	66

- 65 -

Association
EASTERN

State
NORTH CAROLINA

Associational WMU Director
HELEN REGISTER

Address	City	State	Zip
Rt. 1, Box 401	Turkey	North Carolina	28393

Church	Director / Address
Albertson	Laurel Stroud, R-1, Albertson 28508
Alum Springs	Marie Harper, R-2, Mt. Olive 28365
Bear Marsh	Hazel Pipkin, R 5, Mt. Olive 28365
Beulah	Betty Jackson, Clinton 28328
Brown	Doris Sinclair, R-3, B-9J, Clinton 28328
Calvary	Virginia Hines, Box B6, Calypso 28325
Calypso	Joyce Hudson, R-1, Harrells 28441
Center	
Clinton	
Concord	Mary Lee Usher, R-1, B-86, Rose Hill 28458
Corinth	Sharon Matthews, R-1, Rose Hill 28453
Dobson Chapel	Betty Brown, R-2, Rose Hill 28458
Evergreen	Daisey Chesnutt, R 1, Magnolia 28453
Faison	Helen Flowers, Faison 28341
Garland	Mrs. Hosea W. Cain, R 1, B-33A, Garland 28441
Garners Chapel	Dobbie Row, Rt. 1, Mt. Olive 28365
Grove Park	Velva Lindsay, H-1, B-21B, Clinton 28328
Hickory Grove	Carolyn Medlin, R-1, Clinton 28328
Immanuel	Lynn Adams, R-1, B-23X, Clinton 28328
Ingold	Winnie M. Matthis, R-4, Clinton 28328
Island Creek	Charlotte Hartsell, R-2, B-349, Rose Hill 28458
Johnson	Samme Southerland, R-2, Warsaw 28398
Kenansville	Lorena Vestal, P.O. Box, Kenansville 28349
Magnolia	Mrs. Jack Joyner, Magnolia 28453
Mt. Gilead	Parnell Matthis, R-4, B-327, Clinton 28328
Mt. Olive	Mrs. Joe Caveness, John St., Mt. Olive 28365
Mt. Vernon	Gail Gainey, R-5, Clinton 28328
New Hope	Thelma Ware, R-1, Turkey 28393
Piney Grove	Dot Boyette, 707 Underwood St., Clinton 28328
Poplar Grove	
Poston	Martha Teachey, R-3, Wallace 28466
Rose Hill	Linda Hawes, R-2, B-7, Rose Hill 28458
Rowan	Ruby Peterson, R-2, B-377, Clinton 28328
Sharon	Clara Huffman, Chinquapin 28521
Shiloh	Donas Hardin, R-1, B-34J, Chinquapin 28521
Siloam	Betty Sanderson, R-1, Harrells 28444
Teachy	Elwood Futrell, Box 1, Teachey 28464
Turkey	Sue Padgett, Box 216, Turkey 28393

- 66 -

TABLE F BROTHERHOOD — 1983

Association: EASTERN
State: NORTH CAROLINA
Associational Brotherhood Director: CHARLES KIRKLAND
Address: P.O. Box 426 **City:** Faison **State:** North Carolina **Zip:** 28341

CHURCHES	BROTHERHOOD DIRECTORS & ADDRESSES (INCLUDE ZIP CODE)	114 Crusaders (6-11 years or grades 1-6)	115 Pioneers (12-17 years or grades 7-12)	116 RA director and committee	117 Baptist Men enrollment—Basic	118 Baptist Men enrollment—Prayer	119 Baptist Men enrollment—Mission Action	120 Baptist Men enrollment—Witnessing or Lay Renewal	121 Brotherhood director and other general Brotherhood officers	122 Enrollment of mission(s) of church	123 Total ongoing Brotherhood enrollment
Albertson		0	0	0	0	0	0	0	0	0	0
Alum Springs		0	0	0	0	0	0	0	0	0	0
Bear Marsh		0	0	0	0	0	0	0	0	0	0
Beulah		0	0	0	0	0	0	0	0	0	0
Brown	Herbie Jordan, Rt. 3, Box 97, Clinton 28328	7	6	3	15	0	0	0	1	0	32
Calvary	James Baker, Greenwood Terrace, Mt. Olive 28365	8	0	2	0	0	0	0	4	0	0
Calypso	Louis Register, Rt. 1, Box 17-A, Rose Hill 28458	0	0	5	0	0	0	0	1	18	42
Center		0	0	0	0	0	10	0	1	0	1
Clinton	Gene Pierce, 103 Denton Ave., Clinton 28328	12	0	0	60	0	25	0	6	25	133
Concord		0	0	0	0	0	0	0	0	0	0
Corinth	Wilbur Carr, Rt. 2, Rose Hill 28458	2	10	2	7	0	0	0	1	0	12
Dobson Chapel	Howard McKenzie, Rt. 1, Rose Hill 28458	3	2	2	15	0	0	0	0	0	14
Evergreen	Donald R. Matthews, Faison 28341	0	5	2	16	0	0	0	4	0	25
Faison	Wilbert Davis, P.O. Box 147, Garland 28441	8	0	2	12	0	0	0	1	0	20
Garland		0	0	0	0	0	0	0	0	0	23
Garners Chapel	David Jones, 710 Stewart Ave., Clinton 28328	11	0	2	30	0	0	0	1	0	0
Grove Park		0	0	4	30	0	0	0	1	0	44
Hickory Grove		11	0	0	0	0	0	0	0	0	0
Immanuel	Charles Adams, Rt. 1, Box 23X, Clinton 28328	0	9	4	40	0	0	0	1	0	64
Ingold		0	0	0	0	0	0	0	0	0	0
Island Creek	Johnny Blanton, Rt. 2, Rose Hill 28458	2	6	2	18	20	0	0	2	0	30
Johnson		5	2	1	0	0	0	0	1	0	29
Kenansville	Amos Brinson, Box 392, Kenansville 28349	12	6	4	15	0	0	0	1	0	22
Magnolia		0	0	0	0	0	0	0	0	0	0
Mt. Gilead	Herbert Ballance, Rt. 2, Box 120, Clinton 28328	8	5	1	0	4	0	0	1	0	19
Mt. Olive		16	7	4	0	0	0	0	0	0	20
Mt. Vernon		0	0	2	0	0	0	0	0	0	9
New Hope		0	0	0	0	0	0	0	0	0	0
Piney Grove		0	0	0	0	0	0	0	0	0	0
Poplar Grove		0	0	0	0	0	0	0	0	0	0
Poston	John Braswell, Rt. 1, Box 53-A, Watha 28471	0	0	0	0	5	0	0	1	0	6
Rose Hill	Weldon Clack, Rt. 2, Box 55, Clinton 28328	5	4	2	15	0	0	0	0	0	6
Rowan		0	0	1	0	0	0	0	1	0	27
Sharon	David Maready, Rt. 1, Chinquapin 28521	14	25	0	0	0	0	0	0	0	40
Shiloh		0	0	0	0	0	0	0	0	0	0
Siloam	George Pinyatello, Rt. 1, Turkey 28393	0	0	3	15	4	3	4	3	0	22
Teachy	Glendell Fryar, Rt. 4, Box 27, Clinton 28328	2	3	1	0	15	0	2	1	1	0
Turkey	J.B. Herring, 307 Walnut St., Warsaw 28398	7	5	4	8	0	1	1	5	0	28
Union Grove	Kalton Newkirk, Rt. 1, Box 205, Willard 28478	24	10	4	25	3	0	0	1	0	61
Warsaw		6	0	4	26	0	0	0	2	0	65
Wells Chapel		0	0	4	10	0	0	0	0	0	22
TOTALS		163	105	53	312	51	39	7	36	44	810

Association

EASTERN

State

NORTH CAROLINA

Associational Treasurer

MARTHA PIERCE

Address	City	State	Zip
103 Denton Ave.	Clinton	North Carolina	28328

		Undesignated gifts offerings, etc.	Designated gifts offerings, etc.	All other receipts	Total receipts
Albertson	Johnnie P. Harper, Rt.1, Albertson 28508	17193	1364		
Alum Springs	Ruth Outlaw, Rt.1, Mt. Olive 28365	13659	2191		
Bear Marsh	Donnell Bell, Rt.5, Mt. Olive 28365	30408	2724		
Beulah	Milton Massey, Rt.1, Box 12, Turkey 28393	26071	1996		
Brown	Marie J. Po e 305 Inverness Rd. Clinton 28328	23331	450		
Calvary	y 8398	26908	3349		
Calypso	in o 28325	28475	9396		
Center	a 11	15219	2835		
Clinton	r Clinton 28328	244147	21856		
Concord	n e Hill 28458	13578	7434		
Corinth	ryan, Rt.2, Rose Hill 28458	39786	4278		
Dobson Chapel	rown, Rt.2, Rose Hill 28458	21310	9305		
Evergreen	rtton, Rt.1, Magnolia 28453	20306	8091		
Faison	lly, Faison 28341	1005	43101		
Garland	C. Hart P.O. Box 187 Garland 28441	30895	5040		
apel			5000		

TABLE H MISSION EXPENDITURES — 1983

Association: _____ State: _____ Associational Clerk: _____

CHURCHES	CHURCH CLERKS & ADDRESSES (INCLUDE ZIP CODE)	136 Money paid out on new construction during the year	137 All other church sponsored mission expenditures	138 Total church sponsored mission expenditures	139 Cooperative Program	140 Associational missions program	141 State missions	142 SB Home Mission (incl. Annie Armstrong Easter offering)	143 SB Foreign Mis. (incl. Lottie Moon Christmas offering)	144 SB Christian education (schools, etc.)	145 SB Children's homes (cash plus goods)	146 SB Hospitals	147 SB Homes for the aged	148 All other (Bible Society, Temperance League, etc.)	149 Total other mission cause expenditures	150 Grand Total Mission expenditures
Albertson	Marshall Stroud, R-1, Albertson 28508	0	0	0	0	150	86	546	433	86	138	301	86	40	1866	1866
Alum Springs	Marie K. Harper, R-2, Mt. Olive 28365	0	0	0	1000	340		300	448	1100	907	0	0	0	2238	3188
Bear Marsh	E.G. Hatch Jr., R-5, B-68, Mt. Olive 28365	0	0	0	750	300	35	307	782	0	0	0	0	0	1581	2331
Beulah	Linda Creech, 508 Raleigh Rd., Clinton 28328	0	0	0	1207	517				0	0	0	0	50	567	1794
Brown	Sharon S. Carr, R-3, B-97, Clinton 28328	0	0	0	200	185	150	150	200	0	0	0	0	200	735	935
Calvary	Linda Savage, R-1, B-95R, Warsaw 28398	0	0	0	2037	833	150	75	100	0	0	0	0	1158	2316	4353
Calypso	Henderson D. McCullen, B-75, Calypso 28325	0	0	0	600	370	426	442	488	0	0	0	0	0	1726	2326
Center	Leona Blackburn, R-1, B-175, Garland 28441	0	0	0	771	463		25	61	0	0	0	0	0	574	1345
Clinton	Sue Miller, 504 Allen St., Clinton 28328	0	0	0	21000	2400	150	2600	6101	1000	0	0	0	25	13101	34101
Concord	Mary Lou Usher, R-1, B-86, Rose Hill 28458	0	0	0	1433	597	67	30	284	0	0	0	0	0	978	2411
Corinth	Betty P. Butts, R-1, B-115, Teachey 28464	0	0	0	6567	1440	1200	553	1059	0	0	0	0	0	4252	10819
Dobson Chapel	Julia Brock, R-2, B-146, Rose Hill 28458	0	0	0	1482	635		81	65	0	0	0	0	52	833	2315
Evergreen	Mrs. Forrest Daniels, R-1, B-202, Rose Hill 28458	0	5419	5419	789	300	321	568	1159	0	0	0	0	100	2448	8656
Faison	Helen Britt, Box 212, Faison 28341	0	0	0	497	497	257	224	298	0	0	0	0	0	1276	1773
Garland	Evelyn D. Davis, Box 147, Garland 28441	0	0	0	3534	964		298	1089	0	0	0	0	0	2333	5867
Garners Chapel	Annie G. Albertson, R-1, B-437, Mt. Olive 28365	0	0	0	953	150	270	335	635	0	0	0	0	673	2063	3016
Grove Park	Jeanne Pope, 904 Raleigh Rd., Clinton 28328	0	0	0	14193	2045	557	1132	1500	0	150	0	150	349	5583	19976
Hickory Grove	Joyce Warren, R-1, B-131, Clinton 28328	0	0	0	1200	600	549	393	813	0	0	0	0	0	2665	3865
Immanuel	Martha Tart, Box 652, Clinton 28328	0	0	0	7868	3622	1210	2452	2612	0	0	0	0	10	9896	17764
Ingold	Sara W. Pope, R-4, B-92, Clinton 28328	0	0	0	840	400		175	250	0	0	0	0	0	1825	2665
Island Creek	Kathaleen Caldwell, Box 293, Wallace 28466	0	0	0	1836	792	175	641	1000	0	0	0	0	1000	4125	5961
Johnson	Dennis L. Kirby, Box 475, Kenansville 28349	0	0	0	4258	1136	555	806	732	120	1200	0	0	1517	3481	7739
Kenansville	Edna Brinson, Box 8, Kenansville 28349	0	0	0	1080	600	600	450	650	0	0	400	350	252	4380	5460
Magnolia	Betty Chestnutt, R-1, B-277, Warsaw 28398	0	0	0	2376	675	104	286	640	0	21	0	0	210	2228	4604
Mt. Gilead	Catherine Peterson, R-2, Box 104, Clinton 28328	0	0	0	3770	1131	404	353	841	400	230	0	0	502	3686	7456
Mt. Olive	Dr. Tom Shaver, Box 486, Mt. Olive 28365	0	0	0	10303	3375	1261	3158	3859	0	0	0	0	327	12353	22656
Mt. Vernon	Gurley Quinn, 301 Fairfax St., Clinton 28328	0	0	0	0	530		657	390	1580	457	1573	1526	700	6713	6713
New Hope	Shelby Blanchard, R-1, B-269, Turkey 28393	0	1434	1434	1100	650		157	275	0	160	150	150	0	1542	4076
Piney Grove	Blanche Casey, R-5, B-56, Clinton 28328	0	0	0	500	300	207	355	1098	0	0	0	0	0	1960	2460
Poplar Grove	Ann Miller, R-2, Faison 28341	0	0	0	0	0				0	0	0	0	0		
Poston	Louise Hardison, 201 S. Teachey Rd., Wallace 28466	0	0	0	7554	1600	474	773	813	0	450	0	0	0	3886	11440
Rose Hill	Dr. Larry E. Price, Box 638, Rose Hill 28456	0	0	0	13763	1176	944	4655	6150	0	0	0	0	226	13375	27138
Rowan	Barbara Briggs, 717 S.W. Blvd., Clinton 28328	0	0	0	4200	1571	351	526	1113	0	0	0	0	695	4256	8456
Sharon	Madelene Norris, R-1, B-2E, Chinquapin 28521	0	0	0	3600	900	262	345	953	0	0	0	0	264	2724	6324
Shiloh	Cathy Jarosewicg, R-2, B-250B, Wallace 28466	0	0	0	1874	1124	34	227	379	0	151	168	0	86	1850	3724
Sloam	Louise Maynard, R-2, B-124, Harrells 28444	0	0	0	600	400	188	249	644	0	0	0	0	0	1481	2081
Teachy	Mrs. Harrell Hall, 502 W. Westbrook St., Wallace 28466	0	0	0	4100	580	1347	1144	4670	0	0	0	0	512	8253	12353
Turkey	Lettie Phipps, Box 96, Turkey 28393	0	0	0	2989	897	253	201	1375	0	151	168	0	0	2725	5714
Union Grove	Louise Carter, R-4, B-301, Clinton 28328	0	0	0	239	187		100	103	0	0	0	0	0	709	948
Warsaw	Peggy Grice, 309 E. Pollock St., Warsaw 28398	0	0	0	7080	1755	2370	844	2388	0	0	0	0	1287	8644	15724
Wells Chapel	Luda P. Rivenbark, R-1, B-221, Willard 28478	0	0	0	3104	778	212	557	1016	0	0	0	0	282	2845	5949
TOTALS		0	6853	6853	141247	36765	15869	27152	47466	4286	3864	2592	2262	10517	150772	298872

State
NORTH CAROLINA
Moderator
DONALD COLEY
Address
Rt. 1, Box 347-8   City   State
Wallace   North Carolina

⊃

type mission
perating
_____

ng the year

Annie Armstrong Offering

mber Church
cations Volunteers
=none   TV=TV
R=radio   B=both
o. of Families Signing Bible
tudy Commitment Cards

umber S S Members
ot church members

No of college
students baptized

=growing S=stab
=declining

NOTES

NOTES

NORTH
CAROLINA
EASTERN BAPTIST
ASSOCIATION

1984

NORTH CAROLINA
EASTERN BAPTIST
ASSOCIATION
RED FIFTY-SEVENTH ANNUAL
SESSION

1827 - 1984

PTIST CHURCH Assisting	SECOND DAY October 30, 1984 SHARON BAPTIST CHURCH SHILOH, Assisting

THEME

"LABORERS TOGETHER"

CLERK
E. C. Mattocks

NEXT ANNUAL MEETING
First Day

ROWAN BAPTIST CHURCH
Monday, October 28, 1985

Second Day

POSTON BAPTIST CHURCH
(Wells Chapel Assisting)
Tuesday, October 29, 1985

TABLE OF CONTENTS

ASSOCIATIONAL DIRECTORY
PASTORS

CHURCH	PASTOR	ADDRESS	TELEPHONE
Albertson	Caleb Goodwin, Jr.	P.O. Box 37, Albertson 28508	568-3951
Alum Springs	Shelton Justice	Rt. 1, Box 38-A-2, Warsaw 28398	293-7524
Bear Marsh	E.C. Mattocks	Rt. 2, Box 52, Mount Olive 28365	658-6133
Beulah	Eddie Wetherington	Rt. 5, Box 25-A, Clinton 28328	C-592-6530 H-592-2898
Brown	Joseph W. Moss, Sr.	Rt. 6, Box 389, Clinton 28328	C-564-6060 H-592-5642
Calvary	Andy Wood	103 Wade Street, Warsaw 28398	293-7458
Calypso	Thomas H. Hupp	P.O. Box 406, Calypso, 28325	658-5223
Center	Robert E. Hill	P.O. Box 153, Clinton 28328	C-532-2118 H-592-4910
Clinton	James Pardue	P.O. Box 837, Clinton 28328	C-592-8124 H-592-8220
Concord			
Corinth	Dennis Knight	Rt. 1, Box 329, Rose Hill 28458	289-3928
Dobson Chapel	Ernest L. Johnson, Jr.	Rt. 1, Box 118-A, Magnolia 28453	296-1473
Evergreen	Jasper Hinson(Interim)	Rt. 6, Box 161, Clinton 28328	592-2088
Faison	Charles Kirkland	P.O. Box 426, Faison	267-2591

Immanuel	Tony Wilson	P.O. Box 52, Clinton, 28328	C-592-3854
Ingold	Jake Carroll	P.O. Box 5252, Ingold 28446	529-4181
Island Creek	James L. Hartsell	Rt. 2, Box 349, Rose Hill	289-2606
Johnson	A.L. McGee(Interim)	Rt. 2, Box 71, Warsaw 28398	C-293-4757
Kenansville	Lauren R. Sharpe	P.O. Box 517, Kenansville 28349	C-296-0659
			H-296-1389
Magnolia	A.R. Teachey	702 Hall Street, Rose Hill 28458	C-289-2217
			H-289-3850
Mount Gilead	Oliver Skerrett	Rt. 2, Box 106, Clinton 28328	592-6533
Mount Olive	Anthony Gurganus	301 N. Chestnut Street, Mount Olive 28365	C-658-2062
			H-658-2351
Mount Vernon	Waldo Early(Interim)	307 Dixie Circle, Clinton 28328	592-2704
New Hope	Henry Simpson(Interim)		
Piney Grove	Farrell Miller	Rt. 2, Box 122-A, Faison 28341	C-564-6061
			H-564-4848
Poplar Grove	Gerald Garris	Rt. 5, Box 314, Dudley 28333	736-1825
Poston	Donald Coley	Rt. 1, Box 347-B, Wallace 28466	C-285-2439
			H-285-2476
Rose Hill	Jerry D. Kinlaw	P.O. Box 459, Rose Hill 28458	C-289-2250
			H-289-3882
Rowan	Michael Shook	202 Reedsford Road, Clinton 28328	C-592-7508
			H-592-7628
Sharon	Raymond Futch	P.O. Box 126, Chinquapin 28521	C-285-4391
Shiloh	Eugene Hardin	Rt. 1, Box 347, Chinquapin 28521	285-7403
Siloam	Timothy Register	Rt. 1, Box 19, Harrells 28444	C-532-4077
			H-529-2411
Teachey	Henry Herring	P.O. Box 158, Teachey 28464	285-2788

Turkey	Mack Musselwhite	P.O. Box 148, Turkey 28393	C-592-5562 H-592-2056
Union Grove	L.L. Barnes	Rt. 2, Box 584, Elizabethtown 28337	588-4422
Warsaw	David Moore	202 E. College Street, Warsaw 28398	C-293-4236 H-293-7479
Wells Chapel	L.D. Munn(Interim)	Friendly Acres, Wallace 28466	C-532-4210

MINISTERS NOT PASTORS

Bear Marsh	Homer Bumgardner (OM)	Rt. 2, Warsaw 28398	293-7072
Beulah	Willie Carr (OM)	105 Don Street, Clinton 28328	592-
Brown	Joseph P. Powell (LM)	Rt. 3, Clinton, 28328	592-4298
Clinton	T. N. Cooper(OM)	P.O. Box 55, Clinton 28328	592-2293
	J.A. Crowe, Sr. (OM)	190 Jasper Street, Clinton 28328	592-8758
	Waldo Early(OM)	307 Dixie Circle, Clinton 28328	592-2704
	Jasper Hinson(OM)	Rt. 6, Box 161, Clinton 28328	592-2088
	M.M. Johnson(OM)	P.O. Box 1093, Clinton 28328	592-2296
	Bob Doan (OM)	Rt. 6, Clinton 28328	564-6145
	William M. Jones(OM)	110 Forest Drive, Clinton 28328	592-2472
	Clyde Davis(OM)	Rowan Road, Clinton 28328	592-5313
	Jean Hatch(OM)	309 Fairfax Street, Clinton 28328	592-6215
	L.E. Williamson(OM)	512 Nicholson Street, Clinton 28328	592-0202
Garland	Tim Register(OM)	Rt. 1, Box 19, Harrells 28444	529-2411
Island Creek	Albert Rivenbark(OM)	Rt. 1, Willard 28478	532-4553
	Harvey Blanton(OM)	Rt. 2, Rose Hill 28458	289-2639
			592-2091

Albertson		
Alm Springs	Larry ...ler, Rt. 2, Box 281, Mount Olive, NC 28365	658-3614
	Larry Herring, Rt. 2, Mount Olive 28365	658-5182
Bear Marsh	Leslie B. Southerland, Rt. 2, Mount Olive 28365	658-4512
Beulah	Tex Cline, 205 Dogwood Drive, Warsaw 28398	293-4285
	Bill Herring, Rt. 2, Box 186A, Faison 28341	533-3765
	Curtis Pope, 305 Inverness Road, Clinton 28328	592-5209
B · ·en	Jmes R. Blackman, Rt. 3, Clinton 28328	564-4207
Calvary	Russell Killette, Rt. 1, Warsaw 28398	293-7674
	Lynn Hilton, 805 North Center Seet, Warsaw, 28398	293-4856
Calypso	Charles Rivenbark, Box 5, Calypso 28325	658-2019
Center		
Clinton	Charles .de Pope, P.O. Box 514, Clinton 28328	592-2469
	Graham t. Br, 1016 Jasper Avenue, Clinton 28328	592-7580
Concord	Gary Bell, P.O. Box 725, Rdse Hill 28458	289-3226
Corinth	Francis Usher, Rt. 1, Box 86, Rose Hill 28458	289-2681
	Price ds, 115 E. Main, Rose Hill 28458	289-3741
Dobson Chapel	ge Jones, Rt. 1, Box 317, Bse Hill 28458	289-2733
	Jmes P. Brown, Jr, Rt. 2, Rose Hill 28458	289-3463
Evergreen	Russell · Ben, Rt. 2, Rose Hill 28458	289-2228
	Dwight t5y, Rt. 1, Rose Hill 28458	532-4034
Falson	Jerry Todd, P.O. Box 21, Harrells 28444	532-2271
	Clement R. Shine, P.O. Box 96, Faison 28341	267-2676
Garland	David Allsbrook, D5 E. Hill Street, Warsaw 28398	293-4863
Garner's Chapel	Gene Hart, P.O. Box 187, Garland 28441	529-4311
	Cecil Rose, Rt. 1, Mount Ole 28365	658-5425
	Mark Best, Rt. 1, Mount Olive, 28365	658-3327
Grove Park	Gordon & Alene Powell, 1002 Raleigh Road, Clinton 28328	592-3982
Hickory Grove	Joyce Warren, Rt. 1, Box 131, Clinton 28328	564-6241
	Jean Warren, Rt. 1, Box 122, Clinton 28328	564-2159
Immanuel	Jeff Honeycutt, 1232 Sunset Avenue, Clinton 28328	592-4295
	John Mey, Rt. 4, Box 118, Clinton 28328	592-5376
Ingold	Henry L. Blackburn, Rt. 4, Box 257, Clinton 28328	529-3891
	Norwood Carter, P.O. Box 2, Harrells 28444	529-4112
Island Creek	Mr. & Mrs. Harvey Blanton, Rt. 2, Rose Hill 28458	289-2639

4

Johnson		
Kenansville	Amos Brison, Box 8, Kenansville 28349	296-1519
	O.R. Blizzard, Rt. 1, Kenansville 28349	296-0749
Magnolia	Jack Joyner, Magnolia 2853	289-2568
	Clifton Chesnutt, Magnolia 28453	289-2766
Mount Gilead	Nathan Gay, Rt. 4, Box 166-B, Clinton 28328	592-4846
	Lonnie J. Bass, Rt. 2, Box 110-A, Clinton 28328	592-4074
Mnt Olive	W.K. Lewis, 128 N. Center Street, Mount Olive 28365	658-9507
	W. B. Ndy, Box 348, Mnt Olive 28365	658-2146
Mount Vernon	old Warwick, Rt. 5, Clinton 28328	658-2529 or
New Hope	R.W. Blanchard, Jr., Rt. 1, Box 269, Turkey 28393	592-5852
	Robert Frederick, Rt. 1, Turkey 28393	533-3586
Piney Grove	Irene Darden, Rt. 2, Box 122, Falson 28341	533-3639
	Jimmy Thornton, Rt. 2, Box 147, Falson 28341	533-3382
Poplar Grove	Garland Britt, Rt. 2, Box 176, Falson 28341	533-3449
	Jimmy den, Rt. 1, Falson 281	
Poston	Alleen Moore, Rt. 3, Wallace 28466	267-6961
	Margaret Stafford, Rt. 3, Wallace 28466	285-3436
Rose Hill	Ww Teachey Rt. 3, Wallace 28466	285-4739
Rowan	Gin Bradshaw, P.O. Box, Rose Hill 28458	285-2959
	Dald ope, P.O. Box 411, Clinton 28328	289-2464
Sharon	Barbara Briggs, 717 SW Rd., Clinton 28328	592-3437
	T.G. Huffman, Chinquapin 28521	592-7228
Shiloh	Earnest Gray, Chinquapin 28521	285-3585
	P.A. Maready, Rt. 2, Box 126, Wallace 28466	285-3704
Siloam	Wilton Aycock, Rt. 1, Chinquapin, 28521	285-3062
	R.O. Sanderson, Rt. 1, Box 62, Harrells 28444	285-3833
Teachey	C.P. Eakins, Harrells, 28444	532-4211
Turkey		532-4497
	Creson Ezzell, Rt. 1, Box 262, Turkey 28393	533-3368

GENERAL ASSOCIATIONAL OFFICERS

Director of Missions	Clyde Davis, P.O. Box 263, Clinton 28328	293-7077
Associational Secretary		
Moderator	Jo Neal Robinson, Rt. 2, Box 269, Clinton 28328	592-5313
	Donald H. Coley, Rt. 1, Box 347-B, Wallace 28466	592-3044
Vice Moderator		285-2439
Clerk	Lucille Yancey, P.O. Box 711, Clinton 28328	285-2476
Associate Clerk	E.C. Mattocks, Rt. 2, Box 52, Mount Olive 28365	592-3080
	Farrell Miller, Rt. 2, Box 122A, Faison, 28341	658-6133
		564-4848
Treasurer	Bill Boyette, P.O. Box 467, Warsaw 28398	564-6061
		293-7141
Associate Treasurer	Jo Neal Robinson, Rt. 2, Box 269, Clinton 28328	293-3173
Trustee		592-3044

CHURCH PROGRAM OFFICERS

Brotherhood		
Director	Woody Brinson, P.O. Box 43, Kenansville 28349	296-0784
Church Music:		
Director	Jean Hatch, 309 Fairfax Street, Clinton 28328	592-6215
		592-8124
Sunday School:		
Director	James Hartsell, Rt. 2, Box 349, Rose Hill 28458	289-2606
Adult	Charlotte Hartsell, Rt. 2, Box 349, Rose Hill 28458	289-2606
Older outh	L.E. Williamson, 512 Nicholson Street, Clinton 28328	592-0202
Younger Youth		
der Children	Naomi de, 205 E. Chelly et, Warsaw, 28398	293-7479
Younger Children	Cathy Hopkins, P.O. Box 712, Warsaw 28398	293-7077
Older Preschool	Temple d, 103 Wade Street, Warsaw 28398	293-7458
Middle Preschool	Jenny Strickland, Rt. 1, Box 145, Clinton 28328	564-4502
Mentally dicapped	Margaret Musselwhite, P.O. 148, Turkey 28393	592-2566
VBS	Dennis ght, Rt. 1, Box 329, Rose Hill 28458	289-3928
D tr, Teacher &	David e, 202 Coll ge Street, w 28398	293-4236
Training Improvement		

6

Church Training		
Adult Dir	Hal Bilbo, Rt. 3, Box 67, Wallace 28466 (DIRECTOR)	285-5888
Youth Dir	Phyllis Durham, Rt. 2, Box 71, Warsaw 28398	293-3474
Children	Rose Pleasant, 123 E. James, Mount Olive, 28365	658-3036
Preschool	Rene' Carroll, P.O. Box 367, Garland 28441	529-2531

Womans' Missionary Union:

Dir	Helen Regi te, Rt. 1, Box B, Turkey 28393	533-3845
Assistant Dir	Mary Evelyn Wells, Box 66, oe Hill 28458	289-2691
Secretary-Treasu er	Edith Lee, 503 dow Street, Clinton 28328	592-4484
BYW Dir	thia Price, P.O. Box 638, oe Hill 28458	289-3837
Baptist Women Director	Donas Hardin, Rt. 1, Box 347, Chihquapin 28521	285-7403
Ass't. BW Dir	Shelby Blanchard, Rt. 1, Box 269, Turkey 28393	533-3586
Ass't. BYW Dir	Glenda Tdd, 107 De Street, Clinton 8328	592-3441
Acteens Dir	Gloria Lockerman, Rt. 3, Box 3H, Clinton 28328	592-6356
Ass't. Acteens Dictor	oDna aBs, Rt. 2, Box 101-A, Clinton 28328	592-6289
GA Dir	Msa Mr, Box 84, ason 8341	298-3370
Ass't. GA Di ter	Ruth King, Rt. 2, Box 111, aon 28521	564-6697
Mission Friends Di e.	Temple oWd, 103 aWe Street, dw 28398	293-7485
Ass't MF Dir	Bunnie Wson, 408 Est Rd, Ww 28398	293-3143
Mission Action Dictor	Ge Carlton, Rt. 1, Box 257, sw 28398	293-7106
Cent rdal Chairman	Inez h, Rt. 6, Clinton 28328	592-4537

DENOMINATIONAL REPRESENTATIVES

American Bible Society	H.J. Register, Rt. 1, Box 401B, Turkey 28393	533-3845
Childrens' Homes	John A. Johnson, 108 E. Plank Street, Warsaw 28398	293-4958
Baptist Retirement Homes	Millard M. Johnson, P.O. Box 1093, Clinton 28328	592-2296
Christian Education	David Moore, 202 E. College Street, Warsaw 28398	293-4236

Missions Council:

Davis Benton, Director	605 NE Blvd. Clinton 28328	592-3937
Kenneth Goodson	Rt. 4, Box 389, Mount Olive 28365	658-9817
James Pardue	P.O. Box 837, Clinton 28328	592-8124
Florence Hoover	Rt. 1, Box 18 (Chairman, Literacy Committee)	532-4336
Kenneth Durham	Rt. 2, Box 71, Warsaw (Chairman, Senior Adult Committee)	293-3474
Andy Wood	103 Wade Street, Warsaw 28398 (Chairman, Migrant Ministries Committee)	293-7458
Sylvia Knight	Rt. 1, Box 329, Rose Hill 28458 (Chairman, Deaf Ministries Committee)	289-3928
Woody Brinson	P.O. Box 43, Kenansville, 28349 (Associational Brotherhood Director)	296-0784
Connie Carlton	Rt. 1, Box 257, Warsaw 28398 (ASsociational WMU Mission Action Director)	293-7106

Deaf Ministries:

Sylvia Knight, Chairman	Rt. 1, Box 329, Rose Hill 28458	289-3928
Mary Lee Jones	502 E. Hill Street, Warsaw 28398	293-4616
Phyllis Durham	Rt. 2, Box 71, Warsaw 28398	293-3474

Migrant Ministries:

Andy Wood, Chairman	103 Wade Street, Warsaw 28398	293-7458
Gail Naylor	607 Thornton Street, Clinton 28328	592-2944
Wilson Spencer	Rt. 1, Faison 28341	267-0931
Lynn Hilton	805 N. Center Street, Warsaw 28398	293-4856
Charles Adams	Rt. 1, Box 23X, Clinton 28328	564-6517
Jane Kaleel	401 Pineview Road, Clinton 28328	592-2043

Literacy Ministries:

Florence Hoover, Chairman	Rt. 2, Box 18, Harrells, 28444	532-4336
Faye Gaddy	Rt. 6, Clinton 28328	592-3270
Mavis Pigford	50† Forrest Road, Warsaw 28398	293-7952

Mentally Handicapped Ministries:

Carol Todd	P.O. Box 21, Harrells 28444	532-2271
Hannah Farmer		
Margaret Musselwhite	P.O. Box 148, Turkey 28393	592-2056
Judith Pardue	803 Raleigh Road, Clinton 28328	592-8220

Senior Adult Ministries:

Kenneth Durham, Chairman	Rt. 2, Box 71, Warsaw 28398	293-3474
Joyce Warren	Rt. 1, Box 131, Clinton 28328	564-6241
Henry Herring	P.O. Box 158, Teachey 28464	285-2788

COMMITTEES

Trustees:

(1987)			
(1986)	Larry Harper	Rt. 2, Box 281, Mount Olive 28365	658-3614
(1985)	Carroll Turner	604 N. Center Street, Mount Olive 28365	658-6337

Committee on Committees:

Lucille Yancey, Chairman	P.O. Box 711, Clinton 28328	592-3080
W.K. Lewis	128 N. Center Street, Mount Olive 28365	658-9507
Mack Musselwhite	P.O. Box 148, Turkey 28393	592-2056
Lonnie Bass	Rt. 2, Box 110A, Clinton 28328	592-4846
R.O. Sanderson	Rt. 1, Box 62, Harrells 28444	532-4211
Shelton Justice	Rt. 1, Box 38-A-2, Warsaw 28398	293-7524

JOYCE LUCAS(1986) 606 Blaney Street, Clinton 28382 592-3610
THELMA DAVIS (1987) P.O. Box 263, Clinton 28328 592-5313

PROGRAM COMMITTEE:
Raleigh Carroll (1985) P.O. Box 367, Garland 28441 529-2531
Eugene Hardin (1986) Rt. 1, Box 347, Chinquapin 28521 285-7403
Larry Harper (1987) Rt. 2, Box 281, Mount Olive 28365 658-3614

HISTORICAL:
Martha Lewis (1985) 307 Dixie Circle, Clinton 28328 592-2704
Waldo Early (1986)
Shelton Justice, Chairman (1987) Rt. 1, Box 38-A-2, Warsaw 28398 293-7524

STEWARDSHIP:
Gene Hart, Chairman (1985) P.O. Box 187, Garland 28441 529-4311
Mitchell Rivenbark (1985) 509 E. Hill Street, Warsaw 28398 293-7496
John Braswell (1985) Rt. 1, Box 53-A, Watha 28471 285-7133
Ed Colwell (1986) Rt. 1, Turkey 28393 533-3372
Pricilla McGill (1986) Rt. 2, Box 23, Harrells 28444 532-4276
Jimmy Strickland (1986) P.O. Box 783, Warsaw 28398 293-4289
Michael Shook (1987) 202 Reedsford Road, Clinton 28328 592-7268
Tony Curganus (1987) 301 N. Chestnut Street, Mount Olive 28365 658-2062
Tony Wilson (1987) P.O. Box 52, Clinton 28328 592-3854
Bill Boyette(Associational Treasurer) P.O. Box 467, Warsaw 28398 293-7141

ORDINATION:
Farrell Miller, Chairman (1985) Rt. 2, Box 122-A, Clinton 28328 564-4848
George McGill (1985) Rt. 2, Box 23, Harrells 28444 532-4276
H.J. Register (1986) Rt. 1, Box 401-B, Turkey 28393 533-3845
Charles Lee Pope (1986) P.O. Box 514, Clinton 28328 592-2469
Jane Kaleel (1987) 401 Pineview Road, Clinton 28328 592-2043
Lois Colwell (1987) Rt. 1, Turkey 28393 533-3372

PROPERTIES:
Mrs. Elwood Fussell (1985) P.O. Box 1, Teachey 28464 285-3180
J.B. Herring (1986) 307 Walnut Street, Warsaw 28298 293-4956
Raleigh Carroll, Chairman (1987) P.O. Box 367, Garland 28441 529-2531

10

ALBERTSON - Rev. Caleb Goodwin, Mrs. Francis Kelly
ALUM SPRINGS- Larry W. Harper, Carolyn Sanderson, F
Eugene Outlaw, Sam Waller
BEAR MARSH - E.G. Hatch, Elbert Davis, Leslie South
Pipkin
BEULAH - T.M. Creech, Adell Creech
BROWN - Rev. Joe Moss, Stacy Thigpen, Robert Crisp, James
CALVARY -
CALYPSO - Mrs. Louise Turner, Mrs. Frances Powell, Charle
Clanton Barwick, Rev. Tom Hupp
CENTER - Rev. Robert Hill, Doris Hill, Mrs. Leona Blackburn
CONCORD- Mr. & Mrs. Francis Usher, G.R. Brice
CORINTH - Mrs. Betty Butts, Price Knowles, Mrs. Ruth K
Wells Kay Johnson, Rebecca Jackson
DOBSON CHAPEL- Julia Brock, Betty Brown, Lucille Bro
Sanderson, Ruby Rouse, Naomi Brock
EVERGREEN - Esther Stuart, Jerry Todd, Billy Chestnutt, Ver
FAISON- Henry Brown, Annie Brown, Ruby Allsbrook
CLINTON -James Pardue, Jean Hatch, L.E. Williamson, Char
Florence Pope, Graham Butler, Everette Peterson, Martha
Johnson, T.N. Cooper
MOUNT OLIVE - Helen Bell, Pearl Cherry, Margaret Go
Anderson, Eunice Landon, Rose Pleasant, Kenneth Goods
Cooke, Teva Draughon
GARLAND - Rene' Carroll, Hugh Hobbs, Mary Carter, Gene H
GARNER'S CHAPEL -- Mark Best, Varner Garner, Nina L. Ga
HICKORY GROVE - Jean Warren, Joyce Warren, Geneva Strick
IMMANUEL - Rev. Tony D. Wilson, Caroline Mercedes F
Mattocks, Martha King, Gene Butler, Dick Pope, Chris
Mildred Honeycutt
INGOLD - Henry L. Blackburn, Mrs. Henry L. Blackburn
ISLAND CREEK - Centelle Hanchey, Charlotte Hartsell,
George Brown
JOHNSON - Robert Southerland, Katie Mae Kirby
KENANSVILLE - Macy Brinson, Margaret Oakley, Sally Eva T
Pate, Amos Brinson, O.R. Blizzard, Woody Brinson
MAGNOLIA - Mildred Teachey, Nellie M. Burns, Charles Bo
M. Tucker, Carlton Smith, A.R. Teachey
MOUNT GILEAD- Nita Rackley, Max Peterson, Mary Lillie Pe
Crea Warren
MOUNT VERNON - Minnie Lou Gainey, Ruby Pope, Gurley Q
Hall, Della Barber
NEW HOPE - Ed. Colwell, Shelby Blanchard, Lewis Johnson,
R.W. Blanchard, Celestial Colwell
PINEY GROVE -
POPLAR GROVE -
POSTON - Annette Henderson, Lula Dixon, Effie Kenne
Teachey, Thelma Teachey, Thelma Murray
ROWAN - Kathy Bailey, Ruby Peterson, Gertrude Marsl
Yancey, James Yancey, Dicy Pittman, Cooper Hairr
ROSE HILL - Jerry Kinlaw, Mrs. E.G. Murray, Irene Edwar
Hawes, Annie Rouse, Albert Pope, Ruth Pope

11

SHARON - Margaret Brinkley, Annie Cavenaugh, Louise Padgett, Jim Southerland, Louise Southerland

SHILOH - Wilton Aycock, Alton Mobley, Nolie James, Eugene Hardin, Donas Hardin

SILOAM - Betty Sanderson, Louise Maynard, Mourine Carter, Elizabeth McGill, Julia Peterson, Pauline Hall

TEACHEY-

TURKEY - Creson Ezzell, Della Ezzell, Ollie Ray Phipps, Lettie Phipps, Ruth Ellis, Olivia Ellis

UNION GROVE - Rodella Batts, Kathy Mattis, Evelyn Fryar, Gail Carter, Brenda Saunders, Mr. & Mrs. Glenwood Fryar, Mr. & Mrs. Anthony Carter

WARSAW - Nancy Herring, Helen A. Straughan, Blanche Draughan, Mary H. Powell, Geral Quinn, Rita Quinn, James Page, Harriett Page

WELLS CHAPEL - Florence Hoover, Alma Highsmith, I.C. Ennis, Mary Johnson, Mary Bland, Laura Moore.

PROCEEDINGS

1. Moderator, Don Coley, called to order the 157th Annual Session of the Eastern Baptist Association at 3:10 P.M., October 29, 1984 in Piney Grove Baptist Church, Clinton, North Carolina.
2. The Association sang "All Hail the Power of Jesus Name"
3. Mack Musselwhite read I Corinthians 3:6-9 and led in prayer.
4. Raleigh Carroll, Chairman of Program Committee, presented the order of the service and moved to adoption as the order of business. Passed.
5. E.C. Mattocks, associational clerk, reported registration representing 36 churches and moved that the messengers present constitute a quorum. Passed.
6. Charles Lee Pope, Nominating Committee Chairman, presented for nomination E.C. Mattocks as clerk and Farrell Miller as Associate Clerk. Both were elected.
7. The moderator appointed the following committees:

    A. Resolution
        1. Ed. Johnson, Chairperson
        2. Raymond Futch
        3. Jean Hatch
    B. Time, Place, Preacher
        1. Michael Shook, Chairperson
        2. Henry Herring
        3. Jake Carroll
    C. Memorials
        1. A.R. Teachey, Chairperson
        2. William Shipp
        3. Jerry Kinlaw

8. Clyde Davis, substituting for the associational treasurer, presented the Treasurer's report.
9. E.C. Mattocks, Clerk, presented the associational Executive Board report and moved for its adoption. Passed.
10. Miscellaneous Business

    Davis Benton, speaking for the Stewardship Committee, presented the 1984-85 Budget for information purposes. Action was deferred to a later session.

11. David Moore, Constitution Committee Chairman, p
amendment to the constitution and moved for its adoption
deferred to the second day's session.
12. The Association sang "Wonderful Words of Life".
13. Agency Reports were given as follows:
    A. Christian Literature/Biblical Recorder   Tom
    B. Baptist Foundation   Ken Dur
    C. American Bible Society   H. J. Re
    D. Annuity Board   Clyde Da
14. Alvin F. Butters brought a message.
15. Farrell Miller, host pastor, gave greetings from the
Piney Grove.
16. The Association sang "God of Grace and God of Glory".
17. Reports of the Social Service Institutions were given as t
    A. Baptist Childrens' Homes   David
    B. Baptist Hospital   David Mc
    C. Baptist Home for the Aging   Millard
18. James M. Sauls, Jr. brought a message.
19. New Pastors were recognized by Clyde Davis:

    1. Thomas Hupp, Calypso
    2. Tony Wilson, Immanuel
    3. Gerald Garris, Poplar Grove
    4. Raymond Futch, Sharon
    5. Henry Herring, Teachey
    6. Mack Musselwhite, Turkey
    7. David Moore, Warsaw
20. Dennis Knight read John 17:28-26 and led in prayer.
21 Gary Chadwick sang a solo of inspiration.
22. Farrell Miller brought the Annual Sermon based on John
23. Moderator Don Coley led in prayer of thanksgiving and t
the evening meal

FIRST DAY - EVENING SESSION
1. Jean Hatch led in a singspiration.
2. Moderator, Don Coley, called the Association to order at 7
October 29, 1985.
3. Clyde Davis recognized three more new pastors:
    1. James Pardue, Clinton, First
    2. Tim Register, Siloam
    3. Henry Simpson, Interim at New Hope
4. The Association sang "Send the Light".
5. Thomas Hupp read Ephesians 3:14-19 and led in prayer.
6. Missions Ministries Director, Cathy Hopkins, presented th
Ministries Development Program committees and they reported
    Deaf Ministry   Sylvia Knight
    Literacy Ministry   Florence Hoover
    Mentally Handicapped Ministry   Carol Todd
    Senior Adult Ministry   Ken Durham
    Migrant Ministry   Andy Wood
7. The Migrant Ministry Committee recognized the following c
individuals for their participation: Bear Marsh, Calypso, Cal
Clinton, Corinth, Dobson Chapel, Faison, Garland, Grove Par
Johnson, Magnolia, First Mount Olive, Hickory Grove, Mount
Hope, Piney Grove, Poplar Grove, Poston, Rose Hill, Rowan,
Siloam, Turkey, Warsaw and Wells Chapel.

13

Also recognized were Jane Kaleel, Mary H. Powell, Clyde Davis, Thelma Davis, John Flake and Mary Lee Jones.

8. The Association sang "O Zion Haste".

9. The choir of Clinton, First brought our special music.

10. Anthony Gurganus brought the Annual Doctrinal message on the "House hold of God".

11. Moderator, Don Coley, adjourned the session with prayer.

SECOND DAY - OCTOBER 20, 1984

1. Moderator, Don Coley, called the Association to order at 9:30 A.M., in Sharon Baptist Church, Chinquapin, North Carolina.

2. The Association sang "Stand Up, Stand Up for Jesus".

3. Henry Herring read I Corinthians 1:10 and Romans 15:5 and led in prayer.

4. E.C. Mattocks, Clerk, reported registrations representing 35 churches and moved that the messengers present constitute a quorum. Passed.

5. Paul Mull from New River Baptist Association, brought greetings.

6. David Moore, speaking for the Constitution Committee, moved that the previously presented amendments be adopted. Passed.

7. Raymond Futch, host pastor, extended greetings and welcome from Sharon Baptist Church.

8. Standing Committee Reports:
   - A. Historical Committee .... Don Coley
   - B. Missions .... Andy Wood
   - C. Ordination .... Don Coley
   - *D. Stewardship .... Davis Benton
   - E. Evangelism .... Anthony Gurganus
   - F. Media Library .... Thelma Davis

* (It was moved that the budget be adopted). Passed.

9. Clyde Davis, Director of Missions, submitted a letter of intent to retire.

10. Clyde Davis, Director of Missions, presented "On Mission Together".

11. Davis Benton moved that a "Long Range Task Force" be appointed by the moderator to report annually to the Association. Thomas Hupp moved to amend the motion with "15 persons to serve". Passed.

12. Woody Brinson moved that 9 people of the Long Range Task Force be lay-persons. Passed.

13. Anthony Gurganus moved that the report on Christian Higher Education be accepted. Passed.

14. Rob Pierce of Campbell University brought a message.

15. Charles Lee Pope gave the report of the Nominating Committee and moved that it be adopted. Passed.

16. Lucille Yancey moved that the report of Committee on Committees be accepted with stated changes. Passed.

17. Report of Appointed Committees:
   - A. Resolutions .... Ed Johnson, Chairperson
   - B. Time, Place Preacher .... Michael Shook, Chairperson
     - October 28 1985 .... Rowan Baptist Church
     - October 29 1985 .... Poston/Wells Chapel
     - Preacher - Jerry Kinlaw - Alternate, A.R. Teachey
   - C. Memorials .... A.R. Teachey, Chairperson

18. Ed Johnson gave the Resolutions Committee Report ar
the adoption. **Passed.**
19. The Association **sang** "The Church's One Foundation".
20. Church **Program Organizational** Reports:

Church Music	Jean Hatch
Church Training	Don Coley
Sunday School	Don Coley
VBS	Dennis Knight
WMU	Helen Register
Brotherhood	Woody Brinson

21. The following were presented certificates for ac
Standard Sunday School work:
Dennis Knight, L.E. Williamson, Tempie Wood, Ba
Sylvia Knight, Clyde Davis.
22. Eddie Pettie brought a message based on Matthew 9:35
23. The Association sang "Hark, the Voice of Jesus Calling"
24. Jean Hatch brought a solo of inspiration.
25. Ed Bullock of the Foreign Mission Board brought
missionary message on Isaiah 6:1-8.
26. Moderator Don Coley adjourned the 157th Annual S
Eastern Baptist Association with prayer.

RESOLUTIONS COMMITTEE REPORT

Whereas: the North Carolina Eastern Baptist Association
one-hundred and fifty-seventh annual session in the Spirit c
to the glory of God,
Be it resolved:

1. That we express our deepest appreciation to the o
Eastern Baptist Association for their splendid planning
of this 157th session and especially to our moderator, Dor
2. That we express our deepest appreciation to the h
Piney Grove, assisted by Mount Vernon, and Sharor
Shiloh, for the scrumptious meals prepared in bountiful
the excellent manner in providing for our comfort.
3. That we express our appreciation to the Rev
Director of Missions, for all his efforts in making this
session a huge success.
4. That we resolve to encourage unity of the fellowship
as admonished by our Lord Jesus "That they may all
as Thou, Father, art in Me, and I in Thee, that they a
Us; that the world may believe that Thou didst send
there be respect for the Doctrine of the Priesthood of
and that our unity comes in the midst of diversity ar
infinite love for us is the cement of that unity.
5. That we resolve to express that unity of spirit
mutual uplifting of our sister churches to God in pra
power of God may lead us all to fulfill the Kingd
spreading the gospel to all mankind.
6. To continue to support the Missions Development Pr
the resources, talents and abilities that God has given r
our fervent prayers.

15

7. That we resolve to continue to work as laborers together to develop our churches, our association, our mission outreach, and our denominational ties for the ongoing of the Kingdom of God on this earth.

Respectfully submitted,
Ed Johnson, Chairman
Jean Hatch
Raymond Futch

WMU SEVENTY-FIFTH ANNUAL SESSION MINUTES

The seventy-fifth WMU Annual Session of Eastern Association met April 26, 1984 with Wells Chapel and co-hosted by Siloam Church. Mrs. Helen Register, Director, presided. Meeting was opened with singing of hymn "Jesus Saves". Opening prayer by Rev. L.D. Munn. Welcome was extended by Mrs. Edward Thornton.

Business: Minutes read and approved. Nominating committee for 1984-85 is made up of Frances Tew, Daisy Chestnutt and Charlotte Hartsell. Each church was reminded to send in mid-year reports to director. New zone coordinators are Joyce Warren, Janie Strickland, Virginia Hines, Katie Johnson and Linda Hawes. We had a good collection of socks and ties for the seminary students in Nigeria. Thanks were given to Lucille Yancey for designing program covers. Assistant director, Mrs. Coleman Carter was absent due to illness of her husband.

Program theme - MANY FACES OF PRAYER AND MINISTRY - was given by word and by poster.

WMU Watchword	Mrs. Donald Pope
Associational Missions	Mrs. Andy Wood
North Carolina Missions	Mrs. Steve Matthis & Clinton First G A' S
Cooperative Program	Mrs. Ted Lockerman & Piney Grove Acteens
Home Missions "God Shed His Grace on Thee, America"	
	Mrs. Leonard Yancey
Foreign Missions	Mrs. Billy Todd
Mission Action	Mrs. Johnny Carlton

This was summed up with posters with many FACES of prayer and ministry being paraded down the aisles to remind us of all the places mission action is applied. We were reminded of health kits and first-aid kits for the Migrant Program. Once again, we will participate in the Womens Correctional Program.

Hymn: "Christ For the Whole Wide World"

Grace for meal, by Mrs. Norwood Carter

Adjourned for supper

The night session was begun with singing of "Serve the Lord with Gladness"

Prayer and meditation by Mrs. Ken Durham. Special music by Martha Pierce accompanied by Jean Hatch.

Invitation was extended for the 76th session to be at Grove Park in Clinton.

Mrs. Lucille Yancey presented the 1984-85 WMU Officers for election:

Director	Mrs. H.J. Register
Assistant Director	Mrs. W.S. Wells, Jr.
Secretary	Mrs. Erwin Lee
Baptist Women Director	Mrs. Eugene Hardin
Assistant Baptist Women Director	Mrs. W. W. Blanchard, .
Baptist Young Women Director	Mrs. Cynthia Price
Assistant Baptist Young Women Dr.	Mrs. Billy Todd
Acteens Director	Mrs. Ted Lockerman
Assistant Acteens Director	Mrs. Byron Bass
GA Director	Mrs. Maressa Mercer
Assistant GA Director	Mrs. DeWitt King
Mission Friends Director	Mrs. Andy Wood
Assistant Mission Friends Director	Mrs. Bunnie Hardison
Mission Action Director	Mrs. Johnny Carlton
Centennial Committee Chairman	Mrs. Inez Peterson

Motion was made to accept these officers. Officers w
with prayer of dedication by Mrs. Katie Johnson.
Hymn: "Our Best"

ATTENDANCE REPORT -- 186 registered   -- 27 churche

Mrs. Inez Peterson reported Centennial Celebration
each church choose chairman and gather history of that WML
are to be sent to Mrs. Peterson. The September Leadershi
will give instructions to these chairmen, as well as a chall
next 100 years.
Program was presented by the BYW of Campbell Un
topic, "Christian Higher Education in North Carolina"
Hymn: "Here Am I, Send Me"

Benediction by Rev. Clyde Davis

Respectfully Submitted,
Lillian Pope, Secretary

17

OUR BELOVED DEAD

ALUM SPRINGS: Lucy Taylor

BEAR MARSH: Faye Bumgardner, Sceanie Brock, Linda Land, Gene Brogden, Fred Brock, Paul King

BEULAH: George Carter

BROWN: Marie Blackman, E.B. Bass, J.G. Dickinson

CALYPSO: Jerry Mercer, Floyd Sutton, Carl Morgan

CENTER: Jeanie Smith, Annie Pearl Blackburn, James Harrell

CLINTON: Clarence Bennett, Thelma Lovell, Mary Davis, Carroll Oliver, L.D. Dixon, Betsy Harris, Ruth Wooten, James Herring, Forest Hargrove, Lydia Allardyce, Raymond Boykin, Lula Gregory

CONCORD: Deacon Vasser Spearman, Mattie Williams

CORINTH: Deacon Raymond Bryant, Ray Johnson, Jennie DeVane, Geneva Thomas Merritt, Mary Weise Johnson

DOBSON'S CHAPEL: Otis Parker, Deacon Henry L. Sanderson, Jr., Lillie Belle Teachey, Joseph C. Brock

EVERGREEN: Pearl Chestnutt

GARLAND: Sarah M. Tingle

GROVE PARK: Lillie Sandy, Dallas Woody, Deacon Arthur Northcutt

HICKORY GROVE: Annie Belle Bass, Maggie Lockamy

IMMANUEL: Ira Smith, Bertha Smith, Minister of Music Dan Arnold

INGOLD: Annie F. Blackburn, Frank Bordeaux

ISLAND CREEK: Marion Brown, Clyde Rivenbark, Raymond Bradshaw, Ethel McCullen, Raeford Brown, Ronnie Bond, Dallas Teachey

JOHNSON: Rachel B. Stroud

KENANSVILLE: Virginia Dixon Holland, Maurice Brinson, Marie D. Cannady

MAGNOLIA: Deacon Tom Kissner, Deacon Fred Johnson, Bill Williamson

MOUNT GILEAD: Agnes Powell, Oscar Peterson, Margaret Matthis, Eva McCul

MOUNT OLIVE: Lillian Potter, Nora Jones, H.J. Skipper, Frances Lowe, Lou Holliday, Daisy Cook, Mary Brinwon, Mrs. O.E. Cannon, Rodney Knowles Francis Reaves, Mrs. Brookie O. Robertson, Joe Gray Whitted

MOUNT VERNON: Mrs. Ottie Gainey, Ruby Jones, Rowena Pope, Fulton Pope, Ben Allen

NEW HOPE: Claude Colwell

PINEY GROVE: Lucy Muriel King

POPLAR GROVE: Nida Miller

POSTON: Roger Johnson, Juanita Moore

ROWAN: John Paul Daughtry, Henry Bordeaux, Kizzie McCullen, Eva Tew, Louise Baldwin, Armaitha Jordan, Rosa Quick, Kittie Marshburn

SHARON: Corbet Pierce, Earnest Easter, Alton Lanier, Carol Cottle Futreal

SHILOH: George Sholar, Jr., Levirah Whaley

SILOAM: Bertamae Powell, Bessie Sawyer, Francis Ennis

TURKEY: Deacon Linwood King, Deacon Leslie Roberts, Wrenville O'Quinn

UNION GROVE: Eva P. Fryar, Justice W. Fuller

WARSAW: Virginia Phillips, Dora Ketchside, Ruby Revelle, Rev. D.W. Branc Carrie Mae Brock, Mamie L. Branch

WELLS CHAPEL: Carrie Barnhill, Donna Johnson, Deacon E.M. Tatum

Piney Grove Baptist Church was constituted March 13, received into the Union Association (now Eastern) in October church records prior to 1868 have been lost. Brother Bryan an oral history. The church was first organized by Rev. Ro a Free Will Baptist, and was called Brush Yard.

In 1841 William Darden suggested to Brother Elmore tha be reorganized as a Missonary Baptist. On March 13, 1 accomplished with the guidance of three ministers: Rev. Rev. William Dupree and Rev. George Wallace. In changing much confusion existed and many members left, leaving 19 men and 13 women.

From the records preserved from 1868, it showed 174 w and 37 Negroes, making Piney Grove one of the largest me rural Sampson County and covering territory from Great Co Faison.

In 1880, 28 members left to organize a church to be knc Grove and in 1885, 9 members left to constitute a church at l

A Womens Missionary Aid Society was organized in Ma November, 1929 a Ladies Aid was formed with Josephine Ha Darden) as first president. In October, 1946 it was re Woman's Missionary Union with Mrs. Hazel Skipper as the firs

In the spring of 1946 the church decided to go half-tim Vernon and saw the need of a parsonage. In 1947 land for t was given by Theron Askew and John R. Darden. The pa completed in the fall of 1947. In September, 1975, the church new house and lot to be used as the parsonage and the old p sold.

According to the old minutes the old church buildir around 1856. In the early fall of 1949 it was torn down a Ground-breaking for the new church was held October 22, foundation laid October 28, 1948 and completed in five months (April, 1949). The new church building was dedica 1951 with the "Sealing of the Cornerstone" held during t program.

In July, 1904 a motion was made to purchase an acre (cemetery, but there is no record of when the cemetery established. Additional land was donated to the cemetery in 1 Mrs. H. Emmett Powell. A perpetual care fund was establis 1973.

In 1956-58 plans were made for an educational plant. N Whit Darden and John R. Darden donated additional land an 12, 1958 ground-breaking ceremonies were held and the exte was completed in 1961.

Piney Grove Church accepted, as a memorial gift for Thornton, a beautiful steeple which was installed April 1 dedicated June 21, 1981.

The church became a full-time pastorate in 1966 and pr membership of 227 members under the spiritual leadership Farrell Miller, Sr.

A goal of Piney Grove is to lift up Jesus so that many n to HIM (John 12:32).

HISTORY OF SHARON BAPTIST CHURCH

On Saturday, March 17, 1860, Brother Alfred Guy and Brother William M. Kennedy, along with other brothers and sisters in Christ from Island Creek met to organize a church at Chinquapin. At the eleven o'clock hour, Brother Guy preached from Revelation 2:17. After preaching, Brother Guy was called upon to act as moderator over the motion that a church be duly constituted on this site.

The church covenant was read and adopted. A declaration of faith was also read and unanimously adopted. All who wished to become members of this new church came forward and signed the constitution.

At that meeting the church was legally constituted as a Baptist Church. The newly formed church membership consisted of ten male and thirty-seven female members.

It was not until some time later that Dr. Pritchard named it the Sharon Baptist Church.

The first sanctuary was built about one-half mile west of the present site on the old Wallace road. The original sanctuary burned and land was purchased from Thomas Thigpen in 1890. The present structure was built by Tom Horne, beginning in 1890 and completing it in 1900. The educational sections were added in 1948 and 1950.

The block structure, known as Denton Hall, which is used solely for fellowship meals and community senior citizens clubs, was dedicated May 1, 1983 in honor of Rev. Phillip Denton, Sr., who was the pastor and coordinator of the construction. Almost all the labor involved in the raising of this structure was a volunteer labor of love by the members of the church and community.

On December 24, 1961, Rev. Robert L. Bowen was called as the first full-time pastor.

In the past, Sharon has had as pastor, Dr. Van Murrell, Dr. John I. Durham, and Dr. James H. Blackmore.

Rev. Raymond Futch, present pastor, began his work August 1, 1984.

CHRISTIAN HIGHER EDUCATION REPORT

YOUR NORTH CAROLINA BAPTIST COLLEGES. . . CAMPBELL - CHOWAN - GARDNER- WEBB - MARS HILL - MEREDITH - WAKE FOREST - WINGATE -

WHY BAPTIST COLLEGES?

In a special study adopted by the Council on Christian Higher Education, the Baptist college was described as a place for study; a place for growing in spiritual and intellectual maturity; and a place where life continues and futures are shaped.

That same report says Baptist colleges are worth what they cost because they offer:

1. A good comprehensive educational experience.
2. An atmosphere of Christian trust and loving concern.
3. The challenge to think and to distinguish among values.
4. An understanding of the place of faith, and the scope and limitations of reason.
5. Acceptance into a person-centered community where spiritual personal and intellectual growth are encouraged.
6. The opportunity to become familiar with the great idease and cultures of the past.

20

7. The motivation to develop a Christian world view
    uncertainties of the future and for resisting the
    to Christian thought.

The choice of a college has a life-shaping impac'
people are encouraged at attend Baptist colleges. It will
difference in their lives.
    The ministry of our Baptist colleges has prospered
because of the prayers and gifts of churches, and becau
continue to attend.

Please continue to send your young people, youi
prayers to our Baptist colleges.

Repectfu
Anthony

ASSOCIATIONAL EXECUTIVE BOARD REPORT

The Executive Board met the Association's constituti(
of four quarterly meetings for the purpose of acting fo
between Annual Meetings. Following is a summary of acti
    November 21, 1983 - CALVARY BAPTIST CHURCH
    Don Coley moderated with. twenty-six churches
Director of Missions, Clyde Davis, requested that a sear
formed to enlist a full time Christian Social Minister. '
made a motion and passed. A motion was also made tl
dollars be allocated from the reserve fund to cover the p
a minister. It too passed. Department and committee re

January 30, 1984 - GROVE PARK CHURCH
    Don Coley moderated with twenty-two churches in
Christian Social Minister Search Committee presented C
their choice and moved she be accepted. Motion passe
then shared her testimony and then a period of ques1
followed. By standing vote, she was called. In other bu
was made that the moderator appoint a committee to stud'
the "Tel-Net" program for our association. The motio(
department and committee reports were given.
    April 9, 1984 - WARSAW BAPTIST CHURCH
    Don Coley moderated with twenty-four churche$
Moderator announced the Tel-Net Committee as cons
Pardue, Chairperson, Dennis Knight, Gene Hart and Mi(
missions committee made a motion that a special non-mand
taken during Associational Emphasis Week for the support
Social Ministry. Motion passed. The Nominating Com
nomination names for five Church Program directoi
unexpired term of clerk. Motion passed. Other departme
reports were given.
                    July 30, 1984 - DOBSON'S CHAPEL B
    Don Coley moderated with twenty-eight churches in
two summer student missionaries, Brenda Nowell and Rita
their work in Migrant Ministry. It was announced that (

Sunday School team had achieved the level of a Standard Sunday School. The nominating committee submitted their report for the 1984-85 associational year. A motion was made to accept the report and it passed. The Evangelism Committee made a motion that our association participate in the "GOOD NEWS AMERICA - GOD LOVES YOU" simultaneous revival of March 9 - 16, 1986. Motion passed. Motion was made that a properties committee be made a standing committee. This committee would be delegated responsibility for associational equipment and property. Motion passed. Moderator Coley announced the Constitutional Committee members as well as the Committee-on-Committees members. Other department and committee reports were given.

Respectfully submitted.
E. C. Mattocks, Clerk

AMERICAN BIBLE SOCIETY REPORT

Reports are now in from over 180 locations worldwide where the Bible Societies are at work and we praise God for the encouraging advances being made on almost all fronts. More than 700 translation projects were underway on all continents last year designed to make the Good News more widely known and understood. For many of these, it is the first time any portion of Scripture has been translated into the language of the people. In addition, through the close cooperation of churches and missions worldwide, many of the Southern Baptist churches, more than 497 million copies of Scripture. . . from whole Bibles to single Selections. . .found their way into the hearts and homes of men and women in nearly every country on earth. None of this would have been possible without the prayerful support of your people both as individuals and as congregations.

In Zaire, translation projects have progressed well during the past year, and seven of the twelve current projects are for very first Bibles in Zairean languages: Ebeonbe, Giphende, Kisongye, Kituba, Lendu, Mashi and Uruund. The Ebeonbe Old Testament is nearing completion, and the manuscript will probably be ready during 1984. Scripture distribution in Zaire has shown a large increase in 1983: 74.7% higher than 1982 distribution figures.

A special need in Zaire during 1984 is support for the free distribution of New Reader Scriptures for the people of the Bateke plateau, until recently an area closed to the outside world. Now that this area has opened, many adults and children are learning to read, and the Bible Society has received numerous requests from churches in the area to provide them with materials to introduce people to Scripture reading. "New Reader Scriptures" specially translated and graded, are a critical first step toward the eventual ability to read the entire Bible for oneself.

In Kenya, orders are being processed for the new translation of the New Testament in the Maasai language. The Turkana New Testament was completed in 1983, a major achievement, in that this is the very first New Testament in this important language, spoken by nearly a quarter of a million people in Kenya. Kenyans are thirsty for God's Word. . .one consignment of 15,000 Bibles came and went in three days! Scripture distributions rose appreciably in 1983, and a further leap is anticipated for 1984. particularly in New Testament and New Reader Scriptures.

In Brazil, recent developments indicate steady progress
God's Word to nearly 122,000,000 men, women and children
country. Now that Bibles are being produces for the first ti
manufactured in Brazil itself, costs saved from importing pap
even greater potential for distribution in the future.

Literacy is still a prime concern of the government in
the Bible Society is making Scripture available to many thous
readers. In 1984 there is a special need for support of the di
290,000 Scriptures to new-literates in a style of language adap
who have just learned to read.

Here in the United States, distribution by the ABS in 19
total of over 126 million Bibles, Testaments, Portions and
Members of the armed forces, prisoners, patients in he
students in Christian schools were among the recipient
Scriptures. Many churches, who receive Scripture supplies
have reported great forward strides in their evangelism a
programs.

An especially intensive program of ministry to ethnic gr
country is expected to accelerate rapidly during 1984. There
people who have come to our country from foreign lands seek
and new hope, and ABS is eager to assist the churches
God's Word to our new compatriots in their first languages -
Cambodian, Laotian, French, Haitian, Creole and Spanish, an
In addition, churches will be helping these new Americans
language through New Reader Scriptures in English. The
translated Biblical texts are designed for those just
read...either in their mother tongue or in a new language.

Respectfully subr
H. J. Register, (

BAPTIST FOUNDATION REPORT

In the midst of our attention to space exploration, a
science fiction personalities, and the real-life exploits of as
lovable character, "E.T." was born. He became the object of
and affection, as well as the source of revenue for his crea
North Carolina Baptist foundation, the letters "E.T." ha
another and especially significant meaning during the year
most exciting new idea was the creation of the Endowm
Everybody's Trust. It is now possible for practically every
churches to participate in sustained support of Baptist wo
perpetual trust. Each of us wishes we could continue our wit
We know that we should plan for such continuing witness.,
of us can participate in permanent support of our parti
interest.

The Endowment Trust you create may be started with a
as $25.00. You may add a tax deductible gift to it as often
in whatever amount you wish. When the principal attains a m
you predetermine (usually $1,000), then the income earned i
to the Baptist cause which you have also predetermined. Th
be paid every year, after year, after year - forever!

The potential? If friends of just one-half the members of our churches who die each year should place their memorial gifts in Endowment Trusts to honor those persons, we could increase the support base of Baptist work by six million dollars each year!

If trose of us who shop and search for a meaningful gift for parent or other loved one should give them, instead, a trust in their name, we would instantly make available millions of dollars for mission outreach!

One example is worth a million descriptive words. Just a few months ago, a widow in Thomasville created an Endowment Trust in memory of her husband. Her initial gift was $100. At Christmas, she and her children added to the Trust. As this report is being written, five checks totaling $300. to be placed in the Trust have arrived from this family "in memory of him on Father's Day". Surely a more loving and significant gesture is difficult to find. Each of us has equal access to such joy'

The impact of the E.T. Trust, and the increasing awareness that we each have a responsibility for the eternal use of our material resources, has caused Baptists of North Carolina to give this past year through new trusts, designated additions to existing trusts, and through increase value of assets managed by the Foundation a total of $953,000, an increase of almost a million dollars each year! Income earned by trusts - income which is all paid out to Baptist causes or annuitants - was over $534,000 last year. A half-million dollars distributed, much of it in the name of persons no longer living here on earth!

Rapidly increasing, and very evident in this past year, is the service rendered as executor of estates and through exercising power of attorney. This is a service which the Foundation happily affords and which will soon be expanded when a staff person will be assigned this responsibility.

No author of science fiction generates more excitement than you who make commitment of self and substance for the Lord's work - forever! The Foundation exists to help you discover ways to demonstrate your own commitment through planned stewardship of those resources which you leave after life on earth ceases.

Respectfully submitted,
Ken Durham, Chairman

LITERACY MINISTRIES COMMITTEE REPORT

During the summer ELIZABETH McGILL and FLORENCE HOOVER worked with a Spanish girl, MARIA, helping her with beginning English on Thursday mornings, weekly. Maria was eager to learn and was learning rapidly. Her most difficult sound was the "Y". She called it a "J". BRENDA NOWELL, the interpreter for us, was so helpful in communicating with Maria, not only in the language, but also providing transportation to the medical center for her sick child, JOEY.

How can we communicate JESUS unless we speak or understand the same language? The literacy ministry needs expansion from many volunteers. Even this year the migrant women who worked in the fields during the day wanted to learn English at night and there was no one to teach them.

We need your help with language missions! BE A VOLUNTEER!

Respectfully submitted,
Florence Hoover, Chairman

MENTALLY HANDICAPPED MINISTRIES COMMITTEE REPOI

Realizing our privilege and responsibility as Chris members within our association have strived to minister to nandicapped this year. One way that members of the chui CLINTON area were able to show their love and concern for population was by providing the residents of the four local with a holiday dinner at Christmas. No only was the dir ROWAN with REV. MICHAEL SHOOK bringing the devotional, of that church, along with IMMANUEL, GROVE PARK ANI FIRST provided delicious food which was enjoyed by all who a

Many children at the Child Development Center in Clint blessed at Christmas by the generosity of many WMU womer the association. As the gifts were opened, and the you handicapped children saw the stuffed toys at the Christma: expressions on the children's faces would have let each wom of her time so generously, know how much their though appreciated.

This summer our association provided its first Vacation for the Adult Mentally Handicapped. REV. ANDY WOOD ar BAPTIST CHURCH graciously provided their church facilil special ministry. Through Bible study, crafts, music, fellowsI puppet shows, the gospel was proclaimed. Many thanks to SILOAM, JAMES EZZELL OF EVERGREEN BAPTIST CHURCH, KIGHT of KENANSVILLE BAPTIST CHURCH for providing for this three day Bible School.

We are also indebted to CALVARY BAPTIST CHURCH for Sunday School Class for the mentally handicapped under leadership of Hannah Farmer. Other churches within our as in the process of developing classes for this special populatioi

Special thanks and recognition should go to CLARA H RANDY KIGHT for all their work as members of this committe thankful for all the support we have received this year.

Respectfully submitted,
Carol Todd, Chairman

DEAF MINISTRIES COMMITTEE REPORT

The Deaf Ministries Committee has been busy trying ' how best to minister to deaf persons in our area. We have n during the past year and have had some very rewarding planning with deaf friends the kinds of activities that would i and help to meet their spiritual and social needs.

POSTON CHURCH sponsored an evening Thanksgiving November 19. This worship service was followed by a fellov and recreation time for all who attended.

On April 21, the association sponsored a hearing-imp service which was held at CORINTH church. The ladies of provided a snack supper for every one following the meanin worship.

Our last activity of the associational year was a fun ti and recreation at WARSAW RECREATIONAL PARK on August : of meditation was led by several deaf persons. Everyone enjo' which the WARSAW CHURCH provided for supper.

25

These times of sharing with our deaf friends were rewarding experiences for every one who participated.

Our MAJOR GOAL for the future is to be able to begin a weekly Sunday School class and time of worship for the deaf in our association.

Respectfully submitted,
Sylvia S. Knight, Chairman

WOMAN'S MISSIONARY UNION REPORT

Nineteen hundred eighty-four has been an exciting year for WMU. Our emphasis for the year "Partnership in Prayer and Ministry" has helped us to understand the partnership nature of missions in relation to prayer and ministry. During the State Leadership Workshop in August, specific training was given to provide each WMU leader with adequate information and knowledge to carry forth the purpose of her organization. Those officers, in turn, taught church WMU leaders from our association. We were delighted that 93 leaders attended the training conference held at the WARSAW BAPTIST CHURCH in September. Forty of our forty-one churches have at least one WMU organization.

The WMU associational officers met quarterly for planning and evaluation.

An associational Mission Study for Acteens and Girls-in-Action was held on December 3, at FIRST BAPTIST, CLINTON. It was well-attended. Our appreciation to all who helped to make this a success.

Our 75th Annual Session was held on April 26 at WELLS CHAPEL Church, with SILOAM and Wells Chapel providing a warm reception and a fantastic meal. Their hospitality was superb! There were 192 women, girls and men in attendance.

GOALS FOR WMU - 1984-85:

To train or retrain 9 associational WMU officers
To train 125 church WMU officers
To assist in training 4 persons to teach the Foreign Mission and Home Mission books(jointly sponsored with Baptist Men)
To provide inspiration and information to 250 women and girls
To involve women and girls from 41 churches in Mission Action and personal witnessing.

The purpose of WMU is to promote and support missions by providing missions organizations for women, girls, and perschoolers; leadership and plans for special projects for the church, involving the family and individuals in mission.

Our WATCHWORD for the year has been a constant reminder that the Lord does not expect us to witness in our own strength nor does he expect us to minister without a well-defined strategy. "BE PERSISTENT IN PRAYER, AND KEEP ALERT AS YOU PRAY, GIVING THANKS TO GOD. BE WISE IN THE WAY YOU ACT TOWARD THOSE WHO ARE NOT BELIEVERS, MAKING GOOD USE OF EVERY OPPORTUNITY YOU HAVE.(Colossians 4:2, 5 TEV).

Respectfully submitted,
Helen Register, WMU Director

BAPTIST HOSPITAL REPORT

During the past year Baptist Hospital admitted 24,577 p
total of 218,735 days of patient care. There were 211,547 out
visits and 31,930 visits to the emergency room. Surgica
totaled 11,816 including 700 open heart operations anc
transplants.

Several clinical advances during the past year serve as
the hospital's quality care. (1) Neurosurgeons have deve
procedure for treating head injuries which has resulted in ou
lowest mortality rate for patients with this type of injury
medical center in the world. (2) Improvements in perinat
special emphasis on prevention of preterm labor have resul
infant mortality rate and in a 15% reduction in the number
Forsythe County needing to be admitted to the intensive care
A new treatment offers relief without surgery for many pati
from ruptured vertebral discs. (4) Many patients with k
should benefit from the use of new equipment being acq
Section on Urology. It uses ultrasound to break up stones o
tract so that, in many instances, surgery is not necessary.

The School of Pastoral Care during the past year pro
pastoral education to 276 ministers through 47 clinical-pastor
Chaplains in the Department of Pastoral Care made more than
to patients, families of patients, and hospital staff. The dep
provided more than 20,000 hours of pastoral counseling at
centers in Winston-Salem, Fayetteville, Raleigh, Morc
Charlotte. This program was supported in part from gifts
Cooperative Program which amounted to $515,556 during th
Dr. J. Dewey Hobbs began his work on Mary 15 as the nev
the Department of Pastoral Care.

The hospital received $351,801 through the North Caro
offering during the fiscal year. A total of 418 patients recei
assistance on their bills through this fund. These bills ra
from $20 to $21,000.

The trustees, staff and especially the patients at Bap
are deeply grateful to the Baptist churches for their continui

Respectfully submittec
Gerald Quinn, Chairm

SENIOR ADULT MINISTRIES COMMITTEE REPORT

So often, society accepts us as we grow older as an
furniture, too good to discard but lacking the beauty and st
with everything around us. Even worse, those who consider
old, willingly allow themselves to be pushed back to a corner.
learning that the Senior Adults of Eastern Baptist Association
old furniture whose usefulness has seen its day, but are l
antiques which grow more priceless as age progresses.

The Senior Adult ministry of Eastern Baptist As
endeavoring to accentuate the value of our Senior ADults.
musical we enjoyed, proved that age brings with it special
opportunities. The fall Awareness Conference emphasized th
Senior Adults to the future work of our Lord.

27

Plans are being made for 1984-85 Senior Adult Ministries to touch more of our churches through our Senior Adults. The associational Senior Adult Ministry committee stands ready to help our churches build a Senior Adult Program to more fully appreciate and capitalize on the talent and value of the Senior Adults with whom God has blessed our churches.

Senior Adults can add to every church - LET US HELP!

Respectfully submitted,
Senior Adult Committee

BAPTIST RETIREMENT HOMES OF NORTH CAROLINA, INC., REPORT

Through many special individuals, blessings of great significance are coming to the Baptist Retirement Homes.

Some of the events and activities that are blessing the lives of residents through the special people who are giving unselfishly of themselves to the ministry of the Baptist Retirement Homes. From October, 1983 - April, 1984, you gave 26.3% of the Homes total income through your Cooperative Program, North Carolina Missions Offering and special gifts. This support covered 77% of the Homes' benevolent care ministry. Benevolent care projections for the fiscal year ending September 30, 1984, are running at about $1,000,000. Mission gifts, it appears will fall short of the need by some $250,000. During the 1983 fiscal year, mission support was $306,000 less than the need. Currently, approximately 40% of the residents in the five Homes are able to cover their full cost of care. Ten percent of the Nursing Care residents underwrite their full cost of care. The 1983 change in the Homes' Cooperative Program allocation greatly added to the support which you have given. Your prayer support, your personal encouragement and visits are also greatly appreciated because they mean so much to the residents, staff, and to the ongoing effective ministry of the Homes.

To effectively operate a $3.2 million ministry takes a diverse group of individuals looking from many different perspectives. ONe special group of these individuals are the Trustees whom you have elected. They are your voice in the overall operations of the Homes' ministry. Numerous major decisions have launched a Capital Funds Campaign--"A Call To Remember...," revised admission policies, secured consulting services to review the total operations of the Homes. Members of the Trustees are comprising a Search Committee to locate a successor to the president upon his retirement in October, 1985.

In an effort to more effectively depict the ministry which the Homes are rendering, the Trustees voted to change the Homes' name to the Baptist Retirement Homes of N.C., Inc.

Operating expenses for the Homes' ministry increased approximately 3% during the 1983 fiscal year. Currently, expenses are running 3.6% ahead of the same period last year. The 220 Baptist Homes' employees are responsible for such a modest increase.

During the past months, another group of important people have come together for a special purpose and work in the life of the Retirement Homes. For the first time in the Homes' history, a state-wide Capital Funds Campaign has been undertaken. Fred Lovette, retired President and Chairman of the Board for Holly Farms, is working to pull together key leaders across North Carolina to formulate an Advisory Team and leadership people to raise $2½ million through the "A Call To Remember..." Campaign. Gifts to the "A Call To Remember..." Campaign

28

are going to be used to renovate and update the Hayes H
Plans include a new kitchen facility, support facilities for
Care Unit, and improvements to the grounds of the Hayes Hor
    Life expectancy figures indicate that the Homes ca
providing approximately 8 years of care for 80 year old resi
the growing segment of our population is the 65 plus grou
your support and encouragement will grow in proportion to th
we have as a ministry with older persons. Please let us he
that together we might work to be an effective ministry for ou

Respectfully submitted,
Millard M. Johnson, Chair

CHILDRENS' HOMES REPORT

    Odum Home has experienced some very positive program
the addition of two positions that will greatly enhance our
hurting children and their families. These are an education
and a recreation coordinator. The positions are filled by t
people who have already extended the scope of what we are al
    We are in the process of renovating the Main building at
to give us a greater office space and a small area to
overnight guests. We will have a combination library/resource
will house material for both children and staff, as well as
these are used for small group meetings such as a paren¹
group and communication workshop.
    Odum Home is the site of a pilot project that will link th
areas of the Baptist Childrens' Home by computer. This syst
office automation, telecommunications and electronic filing to c
efficient operation.
    We continue to praise the Lord for the faithfulness of the
North Carolina who have supported this child care ministry
one-hundred years with their prayers, concern, underst
financial resources.

Respectfully submitted,
John A. Johnson, Chairman

NOMINATING COMMITTEE REPORT

    The Nominating Committee places in nomination the na
following persons to serve in positions as indicated for the A
Year, 1984-85:

GENERAL OFFICERS

Moderator	Don Coley
Vice-Moderator	Lucille Yancey
Clerk	E.C. Mattocks
Associate Clerk	Farrell Miller
Treasurer	Bill Boyette
Associate Treasurer	Jo Robinson
Trustee	

29

CHURCH PROGRAM OFFICERS
Brotherhood

Director	Woody Brinson

Church Music

Director	Jean Hatch

Sunday School

Director	James Hartsell
Adult	Charlotte Hartsell
Older Youth	L.E. Williamson
Younger Youth	Cathy Hopkins
Older Preschool	Tempie Wood
Middle Preschool	Jenny Strickland
Mentally Handicapped	Margaret Musselwhite
VBS	Dennis Knight
Director of Teacher & Training Improvement	David Moore

Church Training

Director	Hal Bilbo
Adult	Phyllis Durham
Youth	Rose Pleasant
Children	Rene' Carroll
Preschool	

Womans Missionary Union

Director	Helen Register
Assistant Director	Mary Evelyn Wells
Secretary-Treasurer	Edith Lee
BYW Director	Cynthia Price
Baptist Women Director	Donas Hardin
Ass't Baptist Women Director	Shelby Blanchard
Ass't BYW Diurector	Glenda Todd
Acteens Director	Gloria Lockerman
Ass't Acteens Director	Donna Bass
GA Director	Maresa Mercer
Ass't GA Director	Ruth King
Mission Friends Director	Tempie Wood
Ass't Mission Friends Director	Bunnie Hardison
Mission Action Director	Connie Carlton
Centennial Chairman	Inez Peterson

Presented by : John Braswell, Chairman
Millard Johnson
Farrell Miller
George McGill
H.J. Register
Charles Lee Pope

COMMITTEE ON COMMITTEES REPORT

STEWARDSHIP
Gene Hart, Chairman	1985
1985 Mitchell Rivenbark	1985
John Braswell	1985
Ed Colwell	1986
Priscilla McGill	1986
Jimmy Strickland	1986
Michael Shook	1987
Tony Gurganus	1987
Tony Wilson	1987

The Associational Treasurer

EVANGELISM
E.C. Mattocks	1985
Dennis Knight, Chairman	1986
Oliver Skerrett	1987

MEDIA LIBRARY
Barbara Shook, Chairman	1985
Joyce Lucas	1986
Thelma Davis,	1987

NOMINATING
Farrell Miller, Chairman	1985
George McGill	1985
H.J. Register	1986
Charles Lee Pope	1986
Jane Kaleel	1987
Lois Colwell	1987

* LITERACY MINISTRY
Florence Hoover, Chairman	1985
Faye Gaddy	1986
Mavis Pigford	1987

* MENTALLY HANDICAPPED MINIS.
Carol Todd	1985
Hannah Farmer	1986
Margaret Musselwhite	1987
Judith Pardue	

* SENIOR ADULT MINISTRIES
Kenneth Durham, Chairman	1985
Joyce Warren	1986
Henry Herring	1987

* Changed to MISSIONS DEVELOPMENT
  PROGRAM by constitutional amendment.

PROGRAM
Raleigh Carroll Ch
Eugene Hardin
Larry Harper

PROPERTIES
Mrs. Elwood Fusse
J.B. Herring
Raleigh Carroll, C

HISTORICAL
Martha Lewis
Waldo Early
Shelton Justice, C

ORDINATION
Michael Shook
Amos Brinson
Millard Johnson
Donald Coley, Cha
Mack Musselwhite
Shelton Justice

MISSIONS
Kenneth Goodson
Davis Benton, Cha
James Pardue
Florence Hoover, Cl
Co

Chr.
Handicapped
Ken Durham, Chr.
Adult Commi
Andy Wood, Chr. M
Ministry Commit
Sylvia Knight, Cha
Ministries Comm

*DEAF MINISTRIES
Sylvia Knight, Cha
Mary Lee Jones
Phyllis Durham

*MIGRANT MINISTR
Andy Wood, Chairn
Gail Naylor
Wilson Spencer
Lynn Hilton
Charles Adams
Jane Kaleel

Submitted by: Lucille Yancey, Chairman
               W.K. Lewis
               Mack Musselwhite
               Lonnie Bass
               R.O. Sanderson
               Shelton Justice

CHURCH TRAINING REPORT

The task of discipleship is one that is often left undone, resulting in impotent believers. In the Great Commission, we are given the responsibility to disciple all converts. That is the reason for Church Training, and our challenge for every church to offer a Church Training program.

The EASTERN ASSOCIATION is indebted to Mary Carter for her years of faithful service with Church Training. From this foundation that has been laid, I pray that Church Training will continue to move forward to better assist churches in discipling believers.

Phyllis Durahm(Adult), Rene' Carrol(Children), and I received training at Caraway in August, 1983. Rose Pleasant(Youth and Masterlife) received a week of intensive training in the Masterlife program at Ridgecrest. We shared our ideas in the Key Leadership Conference in August.

We are proud of the children and youth from Eastern Association who participated in the State Bible Drills. I hope this coming year will be even more exciting as First Baptist, Clinton will host one of the State Childrens' Bible Drills, May 4, 1985.

First Baptist, Mount Olive, served as host to the "M" Night program in November, 1983. One of the largest attendance in recent years enjoyed an excellent program.

Resources for helping local churches expand or begin their Church Training is greater than ever with specially trained resource persons and resource kits. "Ask and it shall be given unto you" . . . .

Respectfully submitted,
Hal Bilbo

MEDIA LIBRARY COMMITTEE REPORT

Work through the associational committee has centered in four major areas:

I. A workshop at Warsaw. Four tables were set up for participation in one or all areas of interest that covered the f o l l ow-ing topics:
    A. How to Begin a New Unit
    B. Book Selection - major emphasis on childrens' books
    C. Samples of displays and promotional aids
    D. Classification and cataloging media
II. Key Leadership Conference focused on encouragement and fellow-ship for media workers. Discussions included responsibility of the library media center in providing media for church leaders.
III. Beginning new centers - Alum Springs. Encouraging churches to activate neglected centers has been an on-going effort.

32

IV. Classifying and cataloging media in associational office
exciting project. These are ready for use and you are er
make good use of these that include personal and gro⌐
missions and missions update that keeps information curre

A. Books
B. Films
C. Filmstrips and cassette tapes
D. Equipping Center
E. Video cassettes
F. Projection equipment

Respectfully submitted,
Thelma Davis

SUNDAY SCHOOL REPORT

"Gather the people together, men, women and childr⌐
stranger that is within thy gates, that they may hear, and tl
learn, and fear the Lord your God, and observe to do all {
this law:" Deuteronomy 31:12. There is no doubt that God
growing Sunday Schools.

This has been a very exciting and profitable year in
Schools of Eastern Baptist Association. The ASSISTeam, or
team, had the privilege of working with at least 15 of the Su⌐
of this association.

The Association had 10 churches participating in a Su
Enrollment/Enlargement Campaign. These ten churches had a⌐
265 workers in a four-night training series. An average of
per church per night. They had 1867 people in attendance
following the training. That attendance was 76% of the enrollm
10 churches. Almost 1000 new prospects were discovere
churches. This Campaign brought one of the most exciting ⌐
our Sunday Schools this past year.

Another exciting happening with the Sunday School
Association was becoming a Standard Associational Sunday
ASSISTeam of 1983-84 is to be commended for this
accomplishment.

The future is now, and the 1984-85 ASSISTeam i
accomplish many things to improve our Sunday Schools. Our
see 5% membership growth over last year, to see an average a
50% or more, also to see at least 10% of our Sunday Schoo
standard Sunday Schools. Leadership training is also on a t
with our ASSISTeam this year.

"Great Day in The Morning" was our theme this ye
Attendance Day on October 28. Together let's make our the
Year in 1984-85". Consider seriously adopting the "REAGI
outreach ideas in each Sunday School.

Respectfully submitted,
James Hartsell, Director

33

MISSIONS COMMITTEE REPORT

The two main functions of the Missions Committee is to help coordinate the work of the various Christian Social Ministries Committees, and work with the CSM director in discovering, analyzing, and presenting opportunities to the Association for mission action.

During 1983-84 the various committees have been very active in mission action. The Literacy Committee, Florence Hoover Chairperson, is teaching English as a second language; the Mentally Handicapped Committee, Carol Todd Chairperson, has worked with this group in our association on several major projects, the Deaf Committee, Sylvia Knight Chairperson, has an ongoing program for the deaf; the Senior Adult Committee, Ken Durham Chairperson, has led seminars during the year; the Migrant Committee, Andy Wood Chairperson, has done another outstanding job this year working with migrants in our area. The chairperson of each of these committees, the CSM Director, Mrs. Cathy Hopkins, the DOM, Mr. Clyde Davis, the Associational WMU Director, Mrs. Helen Register, and the Associational Brotherhood Director, Mr. Woody Brinson, serve on the Missions Committee.

The following are just a few of the achievements of the Missions Committee efforts during the past year:

-Presented Cathy Hopkins to the Executive Board January 30, 1984 to be voted on as full-time Director of Christian Social Ministries, pending the Home Mission Board appointment. The salary is a joint effort of the Baptist State Convention and the Home Mission Board.

-Establishment of a Food Closet Ministry. Hunger Funds received from the Home Mission Board through the Baptist State Convention totaled $3,500.

-Establishment of a Clothes Closet Ministry in Grove Park Church Chapel building. Jane Kaleel serves as coordinator.

-Total Disaster Relief Funds dispersed $85,617.19[Funds from BSC and gifts to the Association Office designated "disaster relief"]. Poplar Grove Church received $23,817.20 and 28 families received $61,799.99.

-Special CSM offering totaled $1,518.30 from 19 churches.

-An Inter-faith Witness Project was the showing of "The Godmakers", an expose' of Mormonism. GrovePark and Poston hosted the movie.

-Made plans with BSC and Clinton, First to take a census of Hispanic people living in our area to discover the potential for starting a Hispanic Mission in our association.

Respectfully submitted,
Davis Benton, Chairman

MIGRANT MINISTRIES COMMITTEE REPORT

Eastern Association Migrant Ministries Committee strives to provide ministry to migrants and seasonal farmworkers during the harvest season and to those who stay year-round in the geographical area of the association. Meeting the spiritual, physical, social and educational needs of the migrants and making Eastern Baptist Association aware of the needs is our purpose.

34

EASTERN BAPTIST ASSOCIATION
LEGEND

— – — County Lines
——— US & NC Highways
- - - - - - County Roads
+ Churches in Association

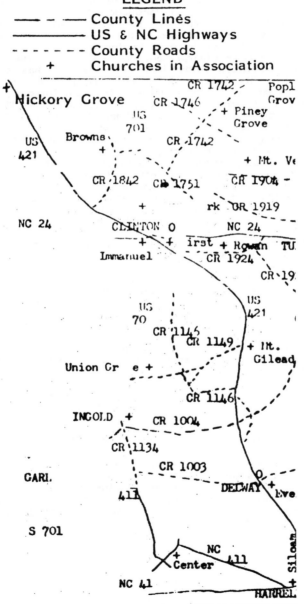

CR 1742 — Popl
Hickory Grove   CR 1746   Grov
+ Piney
US   Grove
701
Browns   CR 1742
US
421   +
+ Mt. Ve
CR 1842   CR 1751   CR 1904 —
+   rk CR 1919
NC 24   CLINTON O   NC 24
+ + irst + Rowan TU
Immanuel   CR 1924
CR 19

US   US
70   421
CR 1146
CR 1149 + Mt.
Gilead
Union Gr e +
CR 1146
INGOLD +   CR 1004
CR 1134
CR 1003
GARL.
DELWAY + Eve
411
S 701
NC
+ 411 Siloam
+ Center
NC 41   HARREL

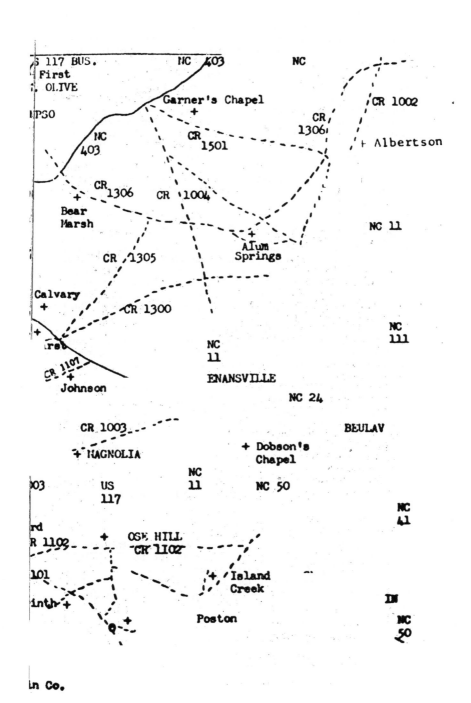

Each year we have expanded our ministry. Migr
Teams were formed by First Baptist, Clinton, Grove F
Baptist, Mount Olive to minister to Hispanics and teams fr
and Faison to minister to Haitians. These ministry tear
fellowship and worship in the camps.

On Tuesday nights, Hispanic worship services w
success. Churches from across our association led i
services and served refreshments. Those churches w
Poplar Grove, Calvary, Grove Park, Bear Marsh, Mag
Warsaw and Poston. Transportation to the services wa
Calvary, Clinton First and by John Flake. We appreciate
Methodist Church and the shared ministry we had wi
Creech and the Revs. Thom and Debbie McCloud.

Two youth groups led three Backyard Bible Clubs
They were First Baptist Church, Raeford and First E
Wallace. The facilities of Warsaw and Piney Grove wer
Raeford group.

Four Christian Service Corps volunteers serve
Association, giving two weeks each of their time. 1
Williams, Raleigh; Mary A. Grizzard, Emporia, Virginia;
Nancy Harrell of Brunswick, Ga. Mr. & Mrs. Clyde I
Hester Powell of Warsaw provided housing for the volunte

Our summer missionaries provided excellent leaders
in ministry opportunities as they served and told ot
migrant ministry work. The students were Brenda N
Maynor. They spoke in 13 different Eastern Bapt
churches.

Over 200 people from our association actively particip
ministry this past summer. 125 volunteers were honored
at the end of the summer. 14 of our churches became d
in migrant ministry and 19 churches indirectly, givir
financial aid, Bibles, etc.

Special recognition should be awarded to the comr
Wilson Spencer, Gail Naylor, Betty Rose, Betty Carr and
for their efforts. God has blessed our ministry and for t
the praise, honor and glory!

Many other nice things were done by so many (
people and we thank every one of you and the many chu
it a success.

Respectfully submitted
Andy Wood, Chairman

THE BIBLICAL RECORDER REPORT

History was made last year when the Biblical R
oldest of the 35 state Baptist papers in the Southern Bap
celebrated 150 years of Baptist papers in North Carolina. /
made again in 1984 when for the first time in more thar
Recorder moved into its own building, becoming the fourth
have its own building.

In February, 1912, the Recorder moved into its own building in the heart of Raleigh. In July, 1984, the paper moved into its own building in the middle of one of the fastest growing areas of the Captial City. Coming to Raleigh in 1838 from New Bern, the Recorder is the oldest business in Raleigh and exceeded in terms of operations in Raleigh only by Brown-Wynne Funeral Home which began in 1836.

The business of the Biblical Recorder is the Lord's business! Since it was founded by Thomas Meredith, the Baptist paper of North Carolina has been committed to the advancement of the Kingdom of God as Baptists coordinate their resources to spread the Gospel to the ends of the earth. The purpose of the Recorder is to inform, indoctrinate, enlist, inspire and provide a forum for unity in the fellowship as we fulfill the Great Commission.

For the third consecutive year, subscription rates will NOT be raised. In 1982 a gigantic increase in the cost of second-class postage (260 per cent) necessitated the increase in subscription rates but now that the rates have moderated some(they are still 80 per cent higher than 1981) and the new Biblical Recorder Building was entered debt-free, the paper will hold the line on subscription rates. We want to make it as easy as possible for churches to send the paper to every family.

Never has there been a greater time than now when Baptists needed to be well-informed. Ther is so much misinformation, exploitation and manipulation in our time that Baptists need a source of news that can be trusted to present facts as they are available and apply them to the betterment, not the harm, of Baptists.

There are tensions in the Baptist family, partly produced by the world conditions in which we operate, and Baptists need a forum where differing views can be expressed. Many so-called Baptist papers provide only one point of view; they do not permit an exchange of ideas and perspectives. The Biblical Recorder does and must always serve all Baptists of our fellowship.

"Every true Baptist believer a faithful Recorder reader" sounds like an impossible dream but we have set that as a goal for the ministry of the paper which from its beginning was designed to serve the cause of Christ by serving all of His people, not just a limited few. We are grateful for the support we have received across the years and request your continued prayers, support and readership. We continue our march toward making the Biblical Recorder the best state Baptist paper in the Southern Baptist Convention. Tar Heel Baptists deserve no less!

Respectfully submitted,
T. N. Cooper

ANNUITY BOARD REPORT

The Annuity Board sends a retirement benefit check to over 13,000 Southern Baptist annuitants each month. This means that this number of Southern Baptist homes receive help each month in meeting their obligations. Unfortunately, most of these retired servants receive less than adequate retirement incomes.

The Annuity Board is the Southern Baptist Agency that the retirement and insurance program for the Southe Convention and helps meet the daily living needs for so ma servants who have given their lives to the cause of Christ in Baptist Church. For a moment, try to imagine yourself liv than $200 per month. This is hard to conceive in today's ec hard fact is that approximately 80% of the retired ministe widows in the Southern Baptist Convention try to live on t Approximately 50% of them get less than $100 per month. Tl Baptist Convention average for all annuitants is $142 per mon

Let's bring this message a little closer home. In Noi there are some 1,321 annuitants. Out of this number, 681 rec less per month. Around 415 of this number receive from $' This leaves 225 annuitants receiving over $200 per month!

The Annuity Board and the Baptist State Convention w hand in trying to improve this situation. One improvemer effect January 1, 1988...whereas the Baptist State contributes $200 per year to your pastor's retirement program January, 1988, the convention will contribute $410 per yea mean that $210 will be going into actually building a retire for our ministerial career church staff personnel. This will vast improvement.

One of the great needs is planning for retirement y recent survey it was revealed that the average Baptist pastor time each year planning his vacation than for the ap one-fourth of his life which he will spend in retirement years

Respectfully submitted,
Waldo Early, Chairman

CHURCH MUSIC REPORT

The Music Program of every church exists to tell other saving love of our Lord and Saviour, Jesus Christ through of music... both instrumental and vocal. Our association enc growth of the individual church music programs, seeks to directors aware of new materials and upcoming events, and ai during special emphases, such as revivals and homecomings.

Our second Associational Adult Choir Festival was held 1984 at First Baptist, Clinton. Six choirs participated (tota 189). It was a good service of praise and fellowship among th and perhaps in 1985 we can have one festival in the winter in the summer.

KEY LEADERSHIP CONFERENCE held in August had number of choir directors in several years, and dates were 1984-85 calendar, mutual concerns were shared and possible enlisting new choir members, keeping regular choir member: attendance, and beginning new music groups in the chur discussed.

Let us continue singing about the love of Jesus. His us, and of our service for Him until He comes again.

Respectfully submitte
Jean Hatch, Director

VACATION BIBLE SCHOOL REPORT

Eighty-nine VBS workers from 23 churches attended the VBS Workers Clinic for specialized training, March 27, 1984. Associational VBS workers who received training earlier in the State VBS Clinic, led the conferences:

The following 27 churches reported having had VBS:

Church	Enroll ment	Avg. Att.	No Days	Hours Daily	Prof. Faith	Miss. Off.	Achieve - ment Level
Alum Springs	24	21	5	2	0	34.	Merit
Bear Marsh	29	21	5	2	0	0	Merit
Brown	88	75	5	2½	0	45.	*
Calvary	99	86	6	2	1	*	Advanced
Center	65	59	6	2½	*	*	Merit
Clinton	71(Backyard Bible Club Only)						
Concord	62	51	6	2½	0	50.	Distinguished
Corinth	98	84	6	2½	0	85.	Advanced
Evergreen	47	43	5	2½	0	*	Merit
Garland	63	52	5	3	0	77.	*
Garner's Chapel	36	34	5	1	*	36.	Merit
Grove Park	139	86	6	2½	0	108.	Merit
Hickory Grove	100	80	5	3	*	*	*
Ingold	35	30	5	2½	0	*	*
Island Creek	71	53	5	1½	0	21.	Merit
Johnson	64	58	5	3	0	30.	Merit
Mount Gilead	74	64	5	2	*	40.	*
Mount Olive	71	65	5	3	0	55.	Merit
New Hope	32	27	5	2½	0	48.	Advanced
Piney Grove	136	97	5	2½	*	*	*
Poston	90	79	5	3	5	30.	Advanced
Rose Hill	66	59	5	3	0	28.	*
Rowan	113	90	5	3	0	55.	Distinguished
Shiloh	67	61	5	3	2	100.	Merit
Turkey	79	62	5	2½	*	34.	Merit
Union Grove	46	44	5	2	0	36.	*
Warsaw	86	86	5	1½	0	53.	Merit
Wells Chapel	69	50	5	2½	*	49.	Merit

*Not Indicated

SCHEDULE OF MEETING PLACES OF EASTERN ASSO(

1985

1st Day   Rowan

2nd Day   *Poston
            Wells Chapel

1986
1st Day   *Warsaw
            Calvary

2nd Day   *Bear Marsh
            Alum Springs

1987
1st Day   *Kenansville
            Albertson

2nd Day   *Corinth
            Teachey

1988
1st Day   Rose Hill

2nd Day   *Immanuel
            Hickory Grove

1989
1st Day   *Calypso
            Faison
            Poplar Grove

2nd Day   *Garland
            Ingold
            Center

1990
1st Day   *Island
            Dobso

2nd Day   *Grove
            Browr

1991
1st Day   Clintor

2nd Day   *Magno
            Conco
            Johns

1992
1st Day   Mount

2nd Day   *Mount
            Union

1993
1st Day   *Siloam
            Evergr

2nd Day   *Turke
            Beulah
            New H

1994
1st Day   *Piney
            Moun

2nd Day   *Sharo
            Shilol

*Meeting Place
Other listed churches assisting with meal on respective

BUDGET 1984-85
EASTERN BAPTIST ASSOCIATION

Account Number	ITEM	AMOUNT
	ADMINISTRATIVE SUPPORT MINISTRIES	
	Director of Missions	
1110	Salary	11,500.00
1120	Housing	7,250.00
1130	Travel	4,000.00
1140	Annuity	830.00
1150	Insurance	2,651.00
1160	Conventions and Conferences	600.00
1170	Social Security Offset	2,300.00
	Secretary, Part-time	
1210	Salary	5,400.00
1220	Social Security(Employer)	378.00
	Office Expense	
1310	Repairs	300.00
1320	Copier Service	600.00
1330	Supplies	900.00
1340	Printing	100.00
1350	Postage	800.00
1360	Telephone	800.00
	Equipment Purchase	
1410	Purchase of Equipment	1,000.00
	Associational Minutes	
1510	Expense of Minutes	1,200.00
	Lending Library	
1610	Materials	200.00
	Associational General Officers Training	
1710	Expenses	100.00
	TOTAL	40,909.00
	MISSION DEVELOPMENT PROGRAM	
	Mission Ministries Director	
2110	Salary	14,050.00
2120	Housing	-0-
2130	Travel	3,600.00
2140	Annuity	1,200.00
2150	Conferences	100.00
	Office Expense	
2210	Promotion	400.00
2220	Postage	400.00
2230	Telephone	400.00
2240	Hunger Fund	3,500.00*
	Migrant Ministry	
	Summer Workers	
2311	Salary	2,000.00
2312	Social Security(Employer)	210.00

42

2313	Travel	600.
2314	Meals	1,200.
2315	Housing	500.
2316	Speakers Expense	300.
2317	Supplies	300.
2318	Film Rental	270.
2319	Associational Leader Training	50.
2320	Unforeseen Expenses	200.
	Deaf Ministry	
2410	Activities	300.
2420	Associational Leader Training	50.
	Literacy Ministry	
2510	Activities	100.
2520	Associational Leader Training	50.
	Senior Adult Ministry	
2610	Activities	300.
2620	Associational Leader Training	125.
	Mentally Handicapped Ministry	
2710	Activities	300.
2720	Associational Leader Training	100.
	TOTAL	

CHURCH DEVELOPMENT/CHRISTIAN EDUCATION MINIS

	Sunday School	
3011	Activities	400.
3012	Promotion	90.
3013	Associational Leader Training	211.
	Church Training	
3021	Activities	200.
3022	Promotion	40.
3023	Associational Leader Training	100.
	Womans Missionary Union	
3031	Activities	400.
3032	Promotion	125.
3033	Associational Leader Training	690.
	Brotherhood	
3041	Activities	100.
3042	Promotion	50.
3043	Associational Leader Training	50.
	Music	
3051	Activities	100.
3052	Promotion	50.
3053	Associational Leader Training	25.
	Evangelism	
3061	Activities	100.
3062	Promotion	25.
3063	Associational Leader Training	150.
	Media Library	
3071	Activities	100.
3072	Promotion	25.
3073	Associational Leader Training	100.

	Mission		
3081	Activities	200.00	
3082	Promotion	30.00	
3083	Associational Leader Training	100.00	
	Pastor Support		
3091	Activities	60.00	
3092	Promotion	65.00	
3093	Associational Leader Training	25.00	
	Stewardship		
3101	Activities	60.00	
3102	Promotion	65.00	
3103	Associational Leader Training	50.00	
	TOTAL		3,786.00

MISSION ADVANCE MINISTRIES

	Mount Olive College		
4100	Baptist Student Union	200.00	
	TOTAL		200.00

FELLOWSHIP MINISTRIES

	Ministers Conference		
5110	Speaker Expense	100.00	
5120	Promotion	150.00	
5130	Associational Leader Training	50.00	
	Annual Meeting		
5210	Expenses	200.00	
	Associational Fellowship Meals		
5310	Expenses	600.00	
	TOTAL		1,100.00

MISCELLANEOUS

6100	Unforeseen Expenses	400.00	
	TOTAL		400.00
	GRAND TOTAL		$77,000.00

SPECIAL ACCOUNTS

7100   Causes arising after Budget is adopted will be assigned account numbers in this number series [Example: Disaster Relief following tornado].

*Subject to approval of request for $3,500.00 from HMB.

ANTICIPATED INCOME

CHURCH CONTRIBUTIONS	
CHURCHES(For Associational Minutes)	46,380.00
BAPTIST STATE CONVENTION	1,200.00
HOME MISSION BOARD-HUNGER FUND	23,420.00
COPIER FEES	3,500.00
INTEREST INCOME:	250.00
Interest from IMMA(Housing)	2,000.00
N-O-W Account(Checking)	250.00
TOTAL	$77,000.00

TREASURER'S REPORT - GENERAL FUND

RECEIPTS

FISCAL YEAR ENDED SEPTEMBER 30, 1984

FUND BALANCE - OCTOBER 1, 1983

    Less: Fiscal Year 1983 Payroll Tax Liability Paid in
ADJUSTED FUND BALANCE - October 1, 1983

Contributions
    Undesignated
        From churches $ 39,394
    Designated
        CSM Salaries - BSC $13,826.59
        Migrant Missions
            From churches   1,753.70
            From individuals   290.00
            HMB Hunger Fund 3,500.00
            Summer Workers 2,000.00   7,543.70
        Tornado Relief   83,122.19 104,492
Total Contributions $143,886

REVENUES & REFUNDS

    Sales Tax Refund   236.69
    Sunday School   1,184.10
    Copier Fees   176.44
    Printing Assoc. Minutes   1,001.50
    N-O-W Interest   532.19   3,13

FUND TRANSFERS

    From IMMS Sale of Missionay Home 1,845.45
    From Reserve Fund   1,682.95   3,52

TOTAL RECEIPTS

TOTAL AVAILABLE FUNDS

DISBURSEMENTS
ADMINISTRATIVE SUPPORT MINISTRIES

Director of Missions
    Salary   10,500.00
    Housing   5,900.00
    Travel   3,600.00
    Annuity   829.92
    Insurance   2,445.06
    Conferences   303.25
    Self-Employment Tax   2,000.00
                        $25,578.23

Secretary
    Salary $ 5,109.99
    Social Security   353.87
                             5,463.86

Office Expense
    Repairs   245.88
    Copier Service   381.47
    Supplies   1,535.42
    Printing   427.79
    Postage   1,253.43
    Telephone   1,070.24
    Sales Tax   266.80
                             5,181.03
Equipment Purchases   1,732.00
Printing of Assoc. Minutes   1,235.64
Lending Library   202.78
Associ. Gen. Officer Training   54.79
Total Administrative Support Ministries $39,448.33

CHRISTIAN SOCIAL MINISTRIES
Director of Ministries
    Salary   10,951.59
    Housing   249.99
    Travel   2,541.00
    Annuity   500.00
    Social Security   762.86
                       $15,005.41

Office Expense
    Supplies   259.53
    Postage   115.94
    Telephone   243.66
                          619.13
Miscellaneous   30.00
Rent   990.35
Conferences   24.57
Migrant Ministry
    Salaries   2,000.00
    Social Security   140.00
    Travel   1,119.80
    Meals   400.00
    Speakers   300.00
    Hunger Fund   371.09
    Unforeseen Expense   38.57
                        4,369.46
Literacy Ministry   -0-
Deaf Ministry   60.00
Senior Adults Ministry   66.45
Mentally Handicapped Ministry 179,66
Total Christian Social Ministries $21,345.06

CHURCH DEVELOPMENT/CHRISTIAN EDUCATION
Sunday School   2,092.75
Church Training   639.93
Woman's Missionary Union   479.68
Brotherhood   101.60
Church Music   77.62

Evangelism	42.30	
Media Library	24.93	
Mission	326.16	
Pastor Support	-0-	
Stewardship	303.87	4,088.84

MISSION ADVANCE MINISTRIES
Mount Olive College BSU	200.00

FELLOWSHIP MINISTRIES
Pastors Conference	168.81	
Annual Meeting	261.27	
Fellowship Meals	372.39	
		802.47

UNFORESEEN EXPENSES   250.26

TORNADO RELIEF   83,117.19

TOTAL DISBURSEMENTS
FUND BALANCE INCLUDING RESTRICTED FUNDS
                          September 30, 1984
    Less: Restricted Funds - Hunger Fund
UNRESTRICTED FUND BALANCE- September 30, 1984

STATEMENT OF CASH ASSETS

GENERAL FUND
    Restricted
    Unrestricted

FUNDS FROM SALE OF MISSIONARY HOME
    Beginning Principal Balance
    Interest Revenue
    Interest Revenue transferred to General Fund
    Ending Balance: Interest
                       Principal

BAPTIST CENTER FUND
    Beginning Balance
    Interest Balance
    Ending Balance

RESERVE FUND
    Beginning Fund Balance
    Interest Revenue
    Principal & interest transferred to General Fund
    Ending Balance

(1) Footnote: Interest of $38.73 is being withheld by IRS

47

I have compiled this Statement of Cash Assets and the accompanying Statement of Receipts and Disbursements of Eastern Baptist Association for the fiscal year ended September 30, 1984.

A compilation is limited to presenting in the form of financial statements information that is the representation of management. I have not audited the accompanying statements and, accordingly, do not express an opinion on them.

David A. McLemore, C.P.A.

October 26, 1984

CHURCHES' CONTRIBUTIONS TO ASSOCIATIONAL MISSIONS

	1982	1983	1984
Albertson	150.00	150.00	150.00
Alum Springs	300.00	340.00	360.00
Bear Marsh	300.00	300.00	300.00
Beulah	696.31	611.38	705.01
Brown	250.00	85.00	100.00
Calvary	875.49	809.02	1,116.22
Calypso	280.00	300.00	300.00
Center	527.76	462.75	433.38
Clinton	3,350.00	2,675.00	3,975.00
Concord	636.80	596.79	499.79
Corinth	1,440.00	1,440.00	1,470.98
Dobson Chapel	745.70	635.25	648.75
Evergreen	240.00	180.00	300.00
Faison	470.49	496.95	399.45
Garland	1,036.19	883.26	861.53
Garner's Chapel	150.00	150.00	150.00
Grove Park	1,635.96	1,635.96	2,124.96
Hickory Grove (joined EBA 1-24-83 from New South River ASSoc.			520.00
Immanuel	3,332.00	1,622.00	3,434.00
Ingold	400.00	400.00	500.00
Island Creek	600.00	792.00	792.00
Johnson	748.58	1,136.42	1,130.61
Kenansville	300.00	300.00	300.00
Magnolia	642.07	707.93	682.00
Mount Gilead	825.00	1,376.99	900.00
Mount Olive	2,875.00	3,375.00	3,875.00
Mount Vernon	400.00	530.00	530.00
New Hope	650.00	650.00	350.00
Piney Grove	225.00	375.00	225.00
Poplar Grove	398.24	-0-	500.00
Poston	1,500.00	1,600.00	1,980.00
Rose Hill	1,196.00	1,276.00	1,100.00
Rowan	1,385.00	1,571.00	1,785.00
Sharon	860.00	900.00	1,200.00
Shiloh	766.47	1,124.19	1,299.51
Siloam	380.00	400.00	400.00

Teachey		500.00	58
Turkey		907.20	·89
Union Grove		197.69	18
Warsaw	.	1,452.00	.1,75
Wells Chapel		728.70	77
TOTALS		$34,453.65	$36,33

SPECIAL CSM OFFERING FROM THE CH

Calvary	55.85	Island Creek	81.7
Corinth	69.00	Johnson	107.2
Dobson Chapel	26.00	Kenansville	300.0
Evergreen	30.00	Magnolia	26.0
Grove Park	49.00	Mt. Gilead	30.0
Hickory Grove	35.00	Poston	300.0
Immanuel	18.00	TOTAL	

HISTORICAL TABLE

YEAR	PLACE	MODERATOR	CLERK	PREACHER
1827 –	Beulah	James Matthews	J.L. Britt	J.B. Taylor
1828 –	South West	James Matthews	V.N. Seawell	W.M. Kennedy
1929 –	Limestone	James Matthews	J.R. Oliver	C.A. Jenkins
1830 –	Bull Tail	James Matthews	F.H. Ivey	W.B. Pope
1831 –	Island Creek	James Matthews	L.T. Carroll	J.B. Harrell
1832 –	Browns	James Matthews	J.T. Bland	Hiram Stallings
1833 –	Lisbon	James Matthews		Jha Cornto
1834 –	Bear Marsh	W.J. Findley	Allen Morriss	Allen Morriss
1835 –	Limestone	W.J. Findley	Allen Morriss	George Fennell
1836 –	Beaver Dam	George Fennell	Allen Morriss	H. Swinson
1837 –	Well's Chapel	W.J. Findley	G.W. Hufham	George Fennell
1838 –	Rowans	W.J. Findley	G.W. Hufham	Hiram Stallings
1839 –	Johnson's	James Mathis	G.W. Hufham	G.W. Hufham
1840 –	Concord	James Carroll	G.W. Hufham	George Fennell
1841 –	Bear Mash	James Carroll	G.W. Hufham	G.W. Hufham
1842 –	Red Hill	James Carroll	G.W. Hufham	H. Stallings
1843 –	Beulah	James Carroll	G.W. Hufham	R. McNab
1844 –	Kenansville	James Carroll	G.W. Hufham	W.J. Findley
1845 –	Lebanon	Benjamin Oliver	J.G. Dickson	David Rogers
1846 –	Wilmington	James McDaniel	J.G. Dickson	W.J. Findley
1847 –	Harriet's Chapel	James McDaniel	J.G. Dickson	David Thompson
1848 –	White Oak	James McDaniel	J.G. Dickson	James Rogers
1849 –	Mt. Gilead	James McDaniel	J.G. Dickson	Isaac W. West
1850 –	Bear Marsh	James McDaniel	Robert McNab	W.J. Findley
1851 –	Little Creek	Benjamin Oliver	A.J. Battle	A.J. Battle
1852 –	New Hope	G.W. Wallace	A.J. Battle	D. Furman
1853 –	Moore's Creek	G.W. Wallace	D. Cashwell	L.F. Williams
1854 –	Beulah	G.W. Wallace	D. Cashwell	M.R. Forey
1855 –	Concord	G.W. Wallace	D. Cashwell	W.P. Riddle
1856 –	Boykin's Chapel	G.W. Wallace	D. Cashwell	James McDaniel
1857 –	Warsaw	G.W. Wallace	G. W. Wallace	C.C. Gordℴ
1858 –	Bear Marsh	Benjamin Oliver	G. W. Hufham	G.W. Wallace
1859 –	Beaver Dam	Benjamin Oliver	G. W. Hufham	W.M. Kennedy
1860 –	Lebanon	Benjamin Oliver	Amos Royal	G.W. Wallace

50

Year	Church		
1861	Piney Grove	Benjamin Oliver	J.G. Dickson	Hugh McAlpin
1862	Mt. Gilead	S.J. Faison	J.G. Dickson	J.B. Taylor
1863	Beulah	S.J. Faison	J.G. Dickson	J.L. Pritchard
1864	Boykin's Chapel	Owen Fennell	J.G. Dickson	G.W. Wallace
1865	Moore's Creek	Owen Fennell	J.G. Dickson	J.S. Wathall
1866	Uni a Chapel	W.M. Kennedy	J.N. Stallings	R.F. Marable
1867	Bear Marsh	W.M. Kennedy	J.N. Stallings	J.L. Pritchard
1868	Beulah	Hugh McAlphin	Isham Royal	Hugh McAlpin
1869	Lisbon	Hugh McAlphin	Isham Royal	W.M. Kennedy
1870	Well's Chapel	J.L. Stewart	Isham Royal	G.S. Best
1871	New Hope	Hugh McAlpin	Isham Royal	J.E. King
1872	Union Lenoir	Hugh McAlpin	Isham Royal	W.M. Kennedy
1873	Shiloh	Hugh McAlpin	Isham Royal	W.M. Young
1874	Island Creek	J.N. Stallings	Isham Royal	J.N. Stallings
1875	Beaufort	J.N. Stallings	Isham Royal	G.S. Best
1876	Mt. Olive	J.L. Stewart	Isham Royal	J.P. Faison
1877	Corinth	J.L. Stewart	Isham Royal	J.C. Hiden
1878	New Bern	J.L. Stewart	Isham Royal	A.D. Cohen
1879	Piney Grove	J.L. Stewart	Isham Royal	J.N. Stallings
1880	Bethel	J.L. Stewart	Isham Royal	S.W. Westcot
1881	Magnolia	J.L. Stewart	J.R. Oliver	J.L. Stewart
1882	Emma's Chapel	J.L. Stewart	J.R. Oliver	A.C. Dixon
1883	Bethlehem	J.L. Stewart	J.L. Britt	F.H. Ivey
1884	Pollocksville	J.L. Stewart	J.L. Britt	J.R. Taylor
1885	Mt. Olive	J.L. Stewart	J.L. Britt	J.W. Eason
1886	Clinton	J.L. Stewart	J.L. Britt	J.L. Stewart
1887	Well's Chapel	J.L. Stewart	J.L. Britt	C.C. Newton
1888	Warsaw	J.L. Stewart	J.L. Britt	T.H. Pritchard
1889	Concord	J.L. Stewart	J.L. Britt	F.R. Underwood
1890	Riley's Creek	J.L. Stewart	J.L. Britt	C.A. Jenkins
1891	Dobson's Chapel	J.L. Stewart	Oliver Blackburr	O.P. Meeks

Year		Location	Name	Name	Name
1899	–	Mount Holly	J.L. Stewart	A.R. Herring	N.B. Cobb
1900	–	Mount Olive	J.L. Stewart	A.R. Herring	R.H. Gilbert
1901	–	Mount Gilead	J.L. Stewart	A.R. Herring	N.B. Bb
1902	–	Hallsville	J.L. Stewart	A.R. Herring	J.M. Alderman
1903	–	Rose Hill	J.L. Stewart	A.R. Herring	J.L. Stewart
1904	–	New H pe	C.E. Daniel	A.F. Robinson	V.N. Johnson
1905	–	Mount Olive	C.E. Daniel	A.F. Robinson	J.H. Booth
1906	–	Lisbon	C.E. Daniel	A.F. Robinson	J.L. Stewart
1907	–	Clinton	C.E. Daniel	H.L. Stewart	C.M. R ck
1908	–	Warsaw	C.E. Daniel	A.R. Herring	J.M. Page
1909	–	Corinth	C.E. Daniel	A.R. Herring	J.M. Alderman
1910	–	Bethel	C.E. Daniel	A.R. Herring	P.A. Anthony
1911	–	Rowan	C.E. Daniel	A.R. Herring	E.J. Harrell
1912	–	Bear Marsh	C.E. Daniel	A.R. Herring	W.B. Rivenbark
1913	–	Beulaville	C.E. Daniel	A.R. Herring	J.G. Newton
1914	–	Oak Vale	C.E. Daniel	A.R. Herring	B.G. Early
1915	–	Johnson's	C.E. Daniel	A.L. Carlton	C.H. Cashwell
1916	–	Calypso	H.L. Stewart	A.L. Carlton	W.N. Johnson
1917	–	Piney Grove	H.L. Stewart	A.L. Carlton	R.H. Herring
1918	–	Concord	H.L. Stewart	E.P. Blanchard	B.T. Vann
1919	–	Hallsville	H.L. Stewart	E.P. Blanchard	D.P. Harris
1920	–	Clinton	H.L. Stewart	E.P. Blanchard	R.W. Cawthon
1921	–	Siloam	H.L. Stewart	E.P. Blanchard	L.R. O'Brien
1922	–	Sharon	H.L. Stewart	D.J. Middleton	R.T. Vann
1923	–	Corinth	T.H. King	D.J. Middleton	J.M. Duncan
1924	–	Dobson's Chapel	T.H. King	D.J. Middleton	G.W. Rollins
1925	–	Turkey	H.L. Stewart	C.I. Robinson	T.H. King
1926	–	Island Creek	H.L. Stewart	C.I. Robinson	S.L. Naff
1927	–	Beulah	H.L. Stewart	C.I. Robinson	J.H. Barnes
1928	–	Bear Marsh	H.L. Stewart	C.I. Robinson	W.R. Beach
1929	–	Ingold	H.L. Stewart	C.I. Robinson	C.V. Brooks
1930	–	Hallsville	H.L. Stewart	C.I. Robinson	E.N. Johnson
1931	–	New H pe	H.L. Stewart	C.I. Robinson	R.C. Foster
1932	–	Kenansville	F.W. McGowen	C.I. Robinson	T.H. Williams
1933	–	Mount Gilead	F.W. McGowen	C.I. Robinson	L.M. Holloway
1934	–	Concord	F.W. McGowen	C.I. Robinson	R.F. Marshburn
1935	–	Magnolia	F.W. McGowen	C.I. Robinson	L.L. J hns
1936	–	Rowan	F.W. McGowen	C.I. Robinson	W.P. Page

Year - Church			
1937 - Warsaw	F.W. McGowen	C.I. Robinson	J.L. Powers
1938 - Beulaville	F.W. McGowen	C.I. Robinson	W.R. Stephens
1939 - Rose Hill	F.W. McGowen	C.I. Robinson	J.P. Gulley
1940 - Clinton	F.W. McGowen	C.I. Robinson	S.L. Morgan, Jr.
1941 - Bear Marsh	F.W. McGowen	C.I. Robinson	J.B. Sessoms
1942 - Johnson's	F.W. McGowen	C.I. Robinson	J.L. Jones
1943 - Turkey	F.W. McGowen	C.I. Robinson	T.N. Cooper
1944 - Mount Olive	F.W. McGowen	C.I. Robinson	G. Van Stephens
1945 - Ingold		C.I. Robinson	J.V. Case
1946 - New Hope & Mount Vernon	G. Van Stephens	C.I. Robinson	G.W. Lambert
1947 - Island Creek & Corinth	G. Van Stephens	C.I. Robinson	Gilmer Beck
1948 - Garland & Cedar Fork	G. Van Stephens	C.I. Robinson	A.L. Benton
1949 - Rose Hill & Clinton	Thomas L. Rich, Jr.		E.N. Teague
1950 - Magnolia & Mt. Gilead	Mack Herring	Paul L. Cashwell	J.C. Conoly
1951 - Piney Grove & Warsaw	Mack Herring	Paul L. Cashwell	J.P. Royal
1952 - Siloam & Dobson's Chpl.	Mack Herring	Paul L. Cashwell	Elliot B. Stewart
1953 - Mount Olive & Turkey	A.W. Greenlaw	Paul L. Cashwell	E.F. Knight
1954 - Rowan & Johnson's	Mack Herring	Paul L. Cashwell	T.W. Williams
1955 - Sharon & Beulaville	Paul L. Cashwell	Paul T. Mull	Julian Morley
1956 - Warsaw & Bear Marsh	J.C. Mitchell	H.M. Baker	Robert A. Melvin
1957 - Immanuel & Kenansville	T.W. Williams	Eugene B. Hager	M.M. Turner
1958 - Rose Hill	C.F. Shipp	Eugene B. Hager	M.M. Johns a
1959 - Calypso & Ingold	C.F. Shipp	Paul T. Mull	Lauren Sharpe
1960 - Island Crk. & Grove Pk.	D.E. Parkerson	Paul T. Mull	Jerry DeBell
1961 - Clinton, 1st & Magnolia	D.E. Parkerson	Paul T. Mull	L.H. Knott
1962 - Mt. Olive & Mt. Gilead	Mack Herring	Paul T. Mull	A. Quakenbush
1963 - Siloam & Turkey	Milton Boone	Paul T. Mull	Hugh R. Williams
1964 - Piney Grove & Sharon	Milton Boone	E.L. Eiland	D.E. Parkerson
1965 - Rowan & Well's Chapel	M.M. Johnson	M.S. McLain	Wayne Wheeler
1966 - Warsaw, 1st & Br. Marsh	Hugh Ross Williams		R.H. Kelley

Year – Place			
1974 – Mt. Olive & Bb. Chpl.	Vernon Braswell	R.B. Little	Huber Dixon
1975 – Rowan & Sth	John Flake	R.B. Little	R.B. Little
1976 – Warsaw & Bear Marsh	John Flake	R.B. Little	Willie O. Carr
1977 – Kenansville-Corinth	Anthony Gurganus	ard Whitley	Vernon Braswell
1978 – Rose Hill-Immanuel	Anthony Gurganus	Charles Jolly	Michael Shook
1979 – Island Crk. & Calypso	Gene Hart	Lucille Yancey	Joseph Willis
1980 – Garland & Grove Park	Gene Hart	Lucille Yancey	Paul Rose
1981 – Clinton - Magnolia	L. Mack Thompson	Lucille Yancey	Donald Coley
1982 – Mt. Ole & Mt. Gilead	L. Mack Thompson	Philip Billings	Lauren Sharpe
1983 – Siloam & Turkey	Donald ley	Philip Billings	Larry Padgett
1984 – Piney Grove – Sharon	Donald Coley	E.C. Mattocks	Farrell Miller

RULES OF ORDER

1. At the meeting of the Association the moderator preceding session shall preside. In case of his abse Moderator shall preside.

2. Each session of the Association shall be opened exercises.

3. At each daily session and previous to proceeding t associational clerk shall be requested to announce t churches represented and the total number of messenger these churches. When it is determined that a majority o are represented the moderator shall declare the A: constituted. It shall be necessary for a majority of the represented for the Association to transact busines adjournment. The proceedings of the first day of the shall be read the morning of the second day and the pro second day shall be read at the first Council of the Ass following the Annual Meeting.

4. The members shall observe toward the officers and c courtesy which belongs to Christians.

5. Any member wishing to speak shall arise and address officer and shall confine himself strictly to the c consideration and avoid personalities.

6. No member shall speak more than twice on the same q permission.

7. All motions seconded shall be definitely stated by officer before discussion.

8. No Motion shall be withdrawn after discussion.

9. When a quesion is under discussion, no motion nor p be received except to adjourn, to lay on the table, to am or to postpone to a definite time, which several moti preference in the order in which they are stated.

10. After a motion has been decided, any member havin majority may move a re-consideration.

11. All questions except such as relate to thc Consti decided by a majority vote.

12. The Association shall have the right to decide what si admitted to consideration.

13. The rules of order may be altered or amended at any Association by a majority vote.

CONSTITUTION

PREAMBLE

We, the Missionary Baptist Churches of composing the EASTERN BAPTIST ASSOCIATION, cor necessity of an association of churches in order to prom missions, education, Christian service, the preaching of to cooperate with the Baptist State Convention of North C Southern Baptist Convention in their work, do here subscribe to the following articles.

ARTICLE I. NAMES

This association shall be known and denominate Carolina EASTERN BAPTIST ASSOCIATION.

ARTICLE II. PURPOSE

The purpose of this association shall be the promotion of Christ's Kingdom among men, and the means of accomplishing this shall be in strict conformity to the New Testament.

ARTICLE III. AUTHORITY

This association claims to be independent and sovereign in its own sphere, but shall never attempt to exercise any authority over the internal affairs of the churches.

ARTICLE IV. COMPOSITION

This association shall be composed of all ordained ministers who are members or pastors of member churches, the general officers of the association, the director of missions, and three messengers from each church with an additional messenger for every one-hundred members over the first one-hundred, no church being allowed more than ten messengers.

ARTICLE V. MEETINGS

The Annual Session of the Association shall commence on Monday after the fourth Lord's Day in October. The church year for the churches of the Association shall commence on October 1, and end on September 30.

ARTICLE VI. OFFICERS

The officers of the Association shall be a moderator, a vice moderator, a clerk, an associate clerk, the chairman of the Historical Committee, a treasurer and an associate treasurer. All officers shall be elected annually except the chairman of the Historical Committee who is the senior member of the Historical Committee. The moderator shall not be elected to serve more than two full years at one period and shall assume office at the close of the Annual Session at which time he is elected.

ARTICLE VII. TRUSTEES

The Association shall have three (3) trustees who shall serve three-year terms in rotation, the replacement to be elected by the Association annually.

ARTICLE VIII. EXECUTIVE BOARD

The Association shall have an Executive Board consisting of the general officers of the Association; the director of missions, the Mission Ministries Director; the directors of associational Brotherhood, Church Music, Church Training, Sunday School, and Womans Missionary Union; the chairpersons of associational standing committees; each active and retired pastor in the Association; and two lay persons (men or women) from each church to be elected by the church and whose name shall be included in the church letter to the Association.

ARTICLE IX. ASSOCIATIONAL COUNCIL

The Association shall have an Associational Counc
officers of the Executive Board; the directors
Brotherhood, Church Music, Church Training,
Development Program, Sunday School, and Womans Mis
chairpersons of Evangelism, Media Library, Pasto
Stewardship; the director of missions and the M
director.

ARTICLE X. MISSIONS DEVELOPMEN

The Association shall have a Missions Dev
organization consisting of three(3) at-large members,
be the Mission Development Program director; the co
representing all mission ministries conducted by the
Mission Ministries director; a representative of Br
representative of Womans Missionary Union.

ARTICLE XI. COMMITTEE

The Association shall have such committees as
necessary for orderly and efficient achievement of
purpose. Members on standing committees shall be on
with one-third of the members rotating off each
completing a three year term shall not be eligible fo
one year has passed. A member elected to fill an unexp
eligible for election to a full term following the
unexpired term.

ARTICLE XII. CHURCH PROG

The Association shall organize groups of officers
church programs: Sunday School, Church Training, W
Union, Brotherhood and Music.

ARTICLE XIII. VISITORS

The Association may invite visiting and correspo
seats and extend to them the privilege of the body
voting.

ARTICLE XIV. MISCELLANE(

The Association shall not maintain a fellowship
which neglects to observe gospel order.

ARTICLE XV. CONSTITUTIONAL (

This constitution may be amended on the second (
Session by a vote of two-thirds of the messengers pre
proposed changes have been presented on the first (
Session.

BY-LAWS

ARTICLE I. DUTIES OF OFFICERS

A. MODERATOR - The moderator on the first day of each Annual Session of the Association shall appoint the following committees to function during the session: Place and Preacher; Resolutions; and Memorials. At the last regular meeting of the Executive Board before the Annual Session of the Association, the moderator shall appoint a Constitutional Committee to serve during the Annual Session, and a Committee on Committees.

It shall be the duty of the moderator to enforce an observance of the constitution, preserve order, decide all questions of order, vote in case of a tie, and act as chairman of the Executive Board.

B. VICE MODERATOR - It shall be the duty of the vice moderator to preside in the absence of or at the request of the moderator, to give other appropriate assistance to the moderator, and to succeed to the office of moderator, if and when, during his tenure of office the office of moderator becomes vacant.

C. CLERK - It shall be the duty of the clerk to record the proceedings of each Annual Session, superintend their printing and distribution, and serve as secretary of the Executive Board and Associational Council.

It shall be the clerks duty to report the actions of the Executive Board to the Annual Sessions of the Association. He shall report the actions of the Associational Council to the next meeting of the Board or to the Annual Session of the Association, which ever comes first.

D. ASSOCIATE CLERK - It shall be the duty of the associate clerk to register the messengers, to report upon request the number of churches represented and the total number of messengers representing these churches, and to perform such other duties as are usually performed by an associate clerk.

E. TREASURER - It shall be the duty of the treasurer to receive all funds contributed by the churches or collected during the Annual Session of this body, to distribute all funds received as ordered by the Association, and to make to the Association an annual report of the condition of the treasury.

F. ASSOCIATE TREASURER - It shall be the duties of the associate treasurer to assist the treasurer in the performance of the treasurers' duties as directed by the treasurer.

ARTICLE II. DUTIES OF TRUSTEES

The Trustees shall be the representative of the Association in legal matters, and shall perform such duties as the Association or the Executive Board may prescribe.

ARTICLE III. EXECUTIVE BOARD

A. OFFICERS - The officers of the Executive Board shall be: moderator, vice moderator, clerk, associate clerk, treasurer, and associate treasurer. The corresponding officers of the association elected during the last Annual Session of the Association shall serve in these positions on the Executive Board.

B. DUTIES - The Executive Board shall cooperate v
State Convention of North Carolina in its program for the
the work fostered by the body within the bounds of the
shall act for the Association on any matters requiring at
Annual Sessions of the Association; and it shall have po
vacancies on the Board during the year. The clerk shall
of the work of the Executive Board at the Annual
Association. The director of missions or other workers er
Association shall make a quarterly report to the Exect
order that the said Board shall be prepared to make a ful
body.

C. MEETINGS - The Executive Board shall meet once
other than in the quarter of the Annual Session, at a
designated by the Board. The moderator shall serve as (
Board. With proper notice of the meeting being given 1
and when it is determined that a majority of the
represented the chairman shall declare the Board duly const

ARTICLE IV. COMMITTEES

A. STANDING COMMITTEES - A majority shall const
for each committee.

1. ELECTION OF COMMITTEES: All committee me
persons who have demonstrated talent for performing th
committee, or who have stated a willingness to receive tr
them for the work of the committee.

Standing committees shall be formed from a sl
selected, notified, secured to serve, and nominated by th
Committees. The nominess, then, must be elected by the
its annual session. Special committees shall be recommende
appropriate to perform the business and ministry of the A
are subject to the approval of the Executive Board. T
posts shall be filled by the Committee on Committees f
persons selected, notified, secured to serve nominated ar
and elected by the Executive Board. These committe
definitely prescribed duties and a definite term of servi
are established.

2. STEWARDSHIP COMMITTEE: The Steward
shall be composed of nine (9) members. This comm
responsible for recommending a budget to the Associatior
Session, for the distribution of all associational funds, ar
plans for raising such funds as are necessary for ca
associational programs. The Stewardship Committee shall l
of biblical stewardship education and promotion among th
on the associational level. The associational treasurer sha
of this committee. The Stewardship Committee shall hav
records of the association audited annually.

3. EVANGELISM COMMITTEE: The Evangelism
be composed of three (3) members. It shall be the duty of
to promote evangelism both in the local church and on ;
level. It shall serve to link the Association with state
departments of evangelism and shall use every availa
fostering the cause of winning the lost to Christ.

4. MEDIA LIBRARY COMMITTEE: The Media Library Committee shall be composed of three (3) members duly elected by the Association and resource personnel as appointed by the moderator whose duty it shall be to encourage the establishing and promotion of libraries in churches.

5. PASTORAL SUPPORT COMMITTEE: The Pastoral Support Committee shall be composed of three (3) members whose duties shall be to provide an ongoing continuing program of help to pastors and church staff members in areas of need. The program shall include guidance for those who are just beginning to prepare for church related vocations; career assessment; spiritual, emotional, and physical needs of pastors and church staff.

6. PROGRAM COMMITTEE: The Program Committee shall be composed of three (3) members. It shall be their duty to arrange the program of the Annual Session of the Association and for all other sessions which may be called.

7. ORDINATION COMMITTEE: The Ordination Committee shall be composed of six (6) members (pastors and deacons). This committee shall offer to any church, upon request, advice and assistance in the examination and ordination of deacons and ministers.

8. HISTORICAL COMMITTEE: The Historical Committee shall consist of three (3) members. The committee shall obtain and edit the histories of two churches each year to be included in the minutes, and shall maintain an up-to-date history of the Association. The senior member of the committee shall be the chairman.

9. NOMINATING COMMITTEE: The Nominating Committee shall be composed of six (6) members. It shall be the duty of this committee to submit nominations to the Association in session for the associational general officers (with the floor open for nominations) as well as for representatives to denominational agences and interests for the following year and to fill any vacancies which may occur during the year.

This committee shall also be responsible for forwarding to the Executive Board at their second meeting for approval and to the association for election, the directions of Brotherhood, Sunday School, Womans' Missionary Union, Church Training, Church Music and Missions Development Program. The Church Development Program directors shall then become members of the Nominating Committee. The Nominating Committee shall present to the Executive Board at their third meeting, a complete slate of officers for the five Church Program Organizations and the Missions Development Program.

10. PROPERTIES COMMITTEE: The Properties Committee shall be composed of three (3) members. It shall be the duties of this committee to maintain an up-to-date inventory of all properties and equipment owned by the Association and make recommendations concerning purchase or disposition of properties and equipment.

B. APPOINTED COMMITTEES:

1. CONSTITUTION AND BY-LAWS COMMITTEE: This committee shall be composed of three (3) members, whose duty it shall be to study and recommend changes in the Constitution and By-Laws and bring reports as necessary to the Association.

2. PLACE AND PREACHER COMMITTEE: This committee shall be composed of three (3) members, whose duty it shall be to make the Association aware of the rotating system of meeting places, and to recommend to the Association in the Annual Session a place or places for meeting, along with a preacher and alternate for the sermon for the following year.

3. RESOLUTIONS COMMITTEE: This c
composed of three (3) members whose duty it sha
resolutions referred to it by the Association or the Ex
report suitable resolutions at the Annual Session.
4. MEMORIALS COMMITTEE: This co
composed of three (3) members whose duty it shall
present at the Annual Session an appropriate progra
those of our number who have died during the prece
names may be secured from the letters to the As
member churches.
5. COMMITTEE ON COMMITTEES: This
composed of six (6) members whose duty it shall
nominate persons for the standing committees a
successors when vacancies occur during the year.

ARTICLE V. DUTIES OF CHURCH PROGRAM D

A. THE ASSOCIATIONAL SUNDAY SCHOOL
promote and supervise the Sunday School program o
and shall be responsible for the direction of Vacation
of the Association in cooperation with the director of miss

B. THE ASSOCIATIONAL CHURCH TRAINING
promote and supervise the Church Training Program
in cooperation with the director of missions.

C. THE ASSOCIATIONAL WOMAN's MISSIONARY
shall promote and supervise the Woman's Missionary Uni
Association, cooperating with the director of missions
with the Constitution and By-Laws of the Woman's Mi
the EASTERN BAPTIST ASSOCIATION.

D. THE ASSOCIATIONAL BROTHERHOOD DIRECT
and supervise the Brotherhood Program of the Associat
with the director of missions.

E. THE ASSOCIATIONAL MUSIC DIRECTOR s
supervise the Church Music Program of the Associati
with the director of missions.

ARTICLE VI. MISSIONS DEVELOPMENT PROGR

A. PURPOSE - The purpose of the Missions Dev
shall be to lead the Association to address the priority
the area.

B. ORGANIZATION

1. MISSIONS COUNCIL. The Missions (
composed of the Missions Development
who shall serve as chairperson; the
director; the chairpersons of all compor
Brotherhood director, the Womans
missions action director. The Missions
with the Mission Ministries director
analyzing and presenting to the A
Executive Board new opportunities for
and in coordination of the mission
Missions Development Program. Upon
mission ministry is needed, the Miss
prepare a written description of the (

61

containing its composition and functions. Each new component program shall be presented to the Association or the Executive Board for approval.

2. COMPONENT PROGRAMS
   a. DEAF MINISTRIES - The Deaf Ministries Program shall be composed of three (3) members whose duties shall be to plan, promote, and evaluate mission ministries to hearing-impaired persons. The Deaf Ministries Program shall provide assistance to churches through their missionary education organizations in the development of ministries to hearing-impaired persons in local communities and in the churches' participation in deaf ministries conducted by the association through enlistment, training, and guidance of volunteers in these ministries.
   b. LITERACY MINISTRIES - The Literacy Ministries Program shall be composed of three (3) members whose duties shall be to plan, promote, and evaluate missions ministries designed to assist non-readers, slow readers, and non-English-speaking persons in developing or improving reading skills. The Literacy Ministries Program shall provide assistance to the churches through their missionary education organization in development of literacy ministries conducted by the Association through enlistment, training, and guidance of volunteers in these ministries.
   c. MENTALLY HANDICAPPED MINISTRIES - The Mentally Handicapped Ministries Program shall be composed of three (3) members whose duties shall be to plan, promote, and evaluate ministries to mentally handicapped persons. The Mentally Handicapped Ministries Program shall provide assistance to churches through their missionary education organizations in development of ministries to mentally handicapped persons in the local communities and in the churches participation in mentally handicapped ministries conducted in the association through enlistment, training, and guidance of volunteers in these ministries.
   d. MIGRANT MINISTRIES - The Migrant Ministries Program shall be composed of six (6) persons whose duties shall be to plan, promote, and evaluate the Associations ministries to Migrant farm laborers. The Migrant Ministries Program shall provide assistance to churches through their missionary education organizations in providing ministries to migrant farm laborers in local communities and in the churches' participation in migrant ministries conducted by the Association through enlistment, training, and guidance of volunteers in these ministries.

62

e. SENIOR ADULT MINISTRIES –
Ministries Program shall be com
members whose duties shall be to
evaluate ministries to senior a
Adult Ministries Program shall pi
churches through their mis
organizations in development of ı
adults in local communities and
participation in senior adult mini:
the association through enlistmı
guidance of volunteers in these mir

ARTICLE VII. ASSOCIATIONAL COUN(

A. PURPOSE – The purpose of the Associational ,
provide a consultative, advisory, and coordinativ
Association and its various programs and committees.

B. DUTIES – The duties of the Associational
provide for communication between associational offic
and committees; study church needs in the associatior
people in the area of the association; propose long-ran
goals for the association; prepare and recommend p
organizations and committees appropriately in attaining
coordinate plans made by the organizations and com
these to the attainment of goals; evaluate the use
report through appropriate channels progress made to
associational goals. The Council shall exercise general
work of the director of missions. In the event the pos
missions becomes vacant, the Council shall recommend
or the Executive Board for approval, a search comm
shall be to seek prayerfully a person to fill the positions.

C. Officers – The officers of the Associational C
chairman and the secretary. The moderator shall serve
The Associational clerk shall be the secretaı
of the secretary, the chairman shall appoint a temporary

ARTICLE VIII. BY-LAWS CHANGES

These by-laws may be amended on the second (
Session by a vote of the majority of the messengers p
provided the proposed changes have been presented (
the Annual Session.

TABLE 4. CHURCH MEMBERSHIP AND OTHER INFORMATION — YEAR ENDING SEPTEMBER 30, 1984

Association: EASTERN
State: NORTH CAROLINA
Address: CLYDE L. DAVIS, SR., P.O. Box 712, WARSAW, NORTH CAROLINA 28398

CHURCHES	PASTORS & ADDRESSES (INCLUDE ZIP CODE)	County
ALBERTSON	CALEB GOODWIN, RT. 1, ALBERTSON, NC 28508	DUPLIN
ALUM SPRINGS	SHELTON JUSTICE, RT. 1, B 38A2, WARSAW, NC 28398	DUPLIN
BEAR MARSH	E.C. MATTOCKS, RT. 2, BOX 52, MOUNT OLIVE, NC 28365	DUPLIN
BEULAH	EDDIE WETHERINGTON, RT. 5, BOX 25A, CLINTON, NC 28328	SAMPSON
BROWN	JOSEPH W. MOSS, RT. 6, BOX 389, CLINTON, NC 28328	SAMPSON
CALVARY	ANDY WOOD, 103 WADE STREET, WARSAW, NC 28398	DUPLIN
CALYPSO	THOMAS N. HUPP, P.O. BOX 406, CALYPSO 28325	DUPLIN
CENTER	ROBERT E. HILL, P.O. BOX 153, CLINTON 28328	SAMPSON
CLINTON	JAMES PARDUE, 803 RALEIGH ROAD, CLINTON 28328	SAMPSON
CONCORD		SAMPSON
CORINTH	DENNIS KNIGHT, RT. 1, BOX 329, ROSE HILL 28458	DUPLIN
DOBSON CHAPEL	ERNEST L. JOHNSON JR., RT. 1, BOX 118A, MAGNOLIA	DUPLIN
EVERGREEN (Interim)	JASPER HINSON, RT. 6, BOX 161, CLINTON, 28328	SAMPSON
FAISON	CHARLES KIRKLAND, P.O. BOX 416, FAISON, 28341	DUPLIN
GARLAND	RALEIGH CARROLL, P.O. BOX 367, CARLAND 28441	SAMPSON
GARNERS CHAPEL	WILLIAM SHIPP, RT. 1, MOUNT OLIVE, 28365	DUPLIN
GROVE PARK	DAVIS BENTON, 605 NE BLVD., CLINTON 28328	SAMPSON
HICKORY GROVE	E.P. WARREN, RT. 1, BOX 122, CLINTON 28328	SAMPSON
IMMANUEL	TONY D. WILSON, P.O. BOX 52, CLINTON 28328	SAMPSON
INGOLD	JAKE CARROLL, P.O. BOX 5252, INGOLD 28446	SAMPSON
ISLAND CREEK	JAMES HARTSELL, RT. 2, BOX 349, INGOLD 28458	DUPLIN
JOHNSON		DUPLIN
KENANSVILLE	LAUREN R. SHARPE, P.O. BOX 517, KENANSVILLE 28349	DUPLIN
MAGNOLIA	A.R. TEACHEY, 702 HALL STREET, ROSE HILL 28458	DUPLIN
MOUNT GILEAD	OLIVER SKERRETT, RT. 2, BOX 104, CLINTON 28328	WAYNE
MOUNT OLIVE	ANTHONY GURGANUS, 301 N. CHESTNUT ST., MT. OLIVE.	SAMPSON
NEW HOPE (Interim)	WALDO EARLY, 307 DIXIE CIRCLE, CLINTON 28328	SAMPSON
PINEY GROVE	FARRELL H. MILLER, RT. 2, BOX 122A, FAISON 28341	SAMPSON
POPLAR GROVE	GERALD GARRIS, RT. 5, BOX 31A, DUDLEY 28333	DUPLIN
POSTON	DONALD R. COLEY, RT. 1, BOX 397B, WALLACE 28466	DUPLIN
ROSE HILL	JERRY D. KINLAW, P.O. BOX 859, ROSE HILL, 28458	DUPLIN
ROWAN	C. MICHAEL SHOOK, 202 REEDSFORD RD. CLINTON 28328	SAMPSON
SHARON	RAYMOND FUTCH, P.O. BOX 126, CHINQUAPIN 28521	DUPLIN
SHILOH	EUGENE HARDIN, RT. 1, BOX 347, CHINQUAPIN 28521	DUPLIN
SILOAM	TIMOTHY REGISTER, RT. 1, BOX 19, HARRELLS 28444	DUPLIN
TEACHEY	HENRY HERRING, P.O. BOX 158, TEACHEY 28464	DUPLIN
TURKEY	MACK MUSSELWHITE, P.O. BOX 149, TURKEY 28393	SAMPSON
UNION GROVE	L.L. BARNES, RT. 2, ELIZABETHTOWN 28377	DUPLIN
WARSAW	DAVID MOORE, 202 E. COLLEGE, WARSAW 28398	DUPLIN
WELLS CHAPEL (Interim)	L.D. MUNN, FRIENDLY ACRES, WALLACE 28466	SAMPSON
TOTALS		
PREVIOUS YEAR TOTALS		

Selected totals (columns): Total members reported this year — TOTALS 140,772; PREVIOUS YEAR TOTALS 4,048,504. Total church debt — TOTALS 832,121; PREVIOUS YEAR TOTALS 888,772.

E CARTER, RT.2, BOX 208A, CLINTON 283
WESTBROOK, RT.3, CLINTON, NC 2832L
IE MELTON, RT. 1, WARSAW, NC 28398
MORGAN, RT. 5, BOX 208, Mt OLIVE 283
. CANNON, RT. 1, GARLAND, NC 28441

LL, .O. BOX 725, ROSE ILL, NC 2845I
KM MILES, RT. 1, WALLACE, NC 2866
4ETY ERCUTT, KENANSVILLE, NC 28349
2DD, P.O. BOX 21, HARRELLS, NC 288
RD, FAISON, NC 28341
_ BOX 187, GARLAND,
RT. 1, MOUNT OLIVE 2
SIR CLINTON APT. Cl
UND, RT. 1, BOX 148, I

RDON CASHWELL, P.O. BOX 5212, INGOLD 28448
ORGE BROWN, RT. 2, BOX 180, WALLACE 286NE
VIE PICFORD, 501 FORREST ROAD, WARSAW2839
QS BRUNSON, BOX 392, KENANSVILLE 28391
RL BAKER, MAGNOLIA, NC 28453
NNIE BASS, RT.2, BOX 118A, CLI
CHARD BLACKWELDER, BOX 91, M

COI
COI
DOBSO
EVERG
FAISON
GARLA
CARNE
CROV
HICO

INGOI
ISLAI
JOHN
KENA
MAGNO
MOUNT
MOUNT
NEW HOI

TABLE C CHURCH TRAINING

Association EASTERN

State NORTH CAROLINA

Associational Church Training Director HAL BILBO

Address RT. 3, BOX 67,   City WALLACE   State NORTH CAROLINA 28466

Year ending SEPTEMBER 30, 1984

CHURCHES	CHURCH TRAINING DIRECTORS & ADDRESSES (INCLUDE ZIP CODE)	Preschool enrollment (5 years and under—not in school)	Children enrollment (6-11) (grades 1-6)	Youth enrollment (12-17) (grades 7-12)	Adult enrollment (18 and over)	Equipping Centers	M B M T / Survival Kit	Mastery enrollment	Other enrollment	Total Prep	General officers enrollment	Enrollment of church	Total Church
ALBERTSON		1	2								2		5
ALUM SPRINGS													0
BEAR MARSH										30			30
BEULAH			10										18
BROWN	RANDALL SPIVA, RT. 6, BOX 389, CLINTON, NC 28328			2							1		0
CALVARY													0
CALYPSO													0
CENTER	CHARLES LEE POPE, 801 OAKLAND TERRACE, CLINTON 28328			25	65						2		90
CLINTON			3	119	21				25	16	2		33
CONCORD	J.C. SAVAGE, RT. 1, TEACHEY, NC 28464				10		2			2	2		69
CORINTH	ERNEST L. JOHNSON, RT. 1, BOX 118A, MAGNOLIA, NC 28453					26							36
DOBSON CHAPEL													0
EVERGREEN									12				24
FAISON		3	1	19	20		12						47
GARLAND	WOODROW JARVIS, P.O. BOX—GARLAND, NC 28441												0
CARNERS CHAPEL													0
GROVE PARK													0
HICKORY GROVE	JOHNNY PARKER, 1208 SUNSET AVENUE, CLINTON NC 28328	17	10	11	16				32		1		93
IMMANUEL											7		0
INGOLD													0
ISLAND CREEK													16
JOHNSON													15
KENANSVILLE			18	10	6				33		2		170
MAGNOLIA	KENNETH GOODSON, RT. 4, BOX 389, MOUNT OLIVE NC 28365	8							126		2		20
MOUNT GILEAD													0
MOUNT OLIVE				15					10	10	2		33
MOUNT VERNON	LOIS COLWELL, RT. 1, TURKEY, NC 28393	1	2								1		0
NEW HOPE													0
PINEY GROVE	ELEANOR THOMPSON, RT. 3, WALLACE, NC 28466	12	20	13	72		18		26		5		123
POPLAR GROVE													0
POSTON	MOZELLE JONES, RT. 2, BOX 176AA, CLINTON, NC 28328	5	11	13	35	12			12		3		36
ROSE HILL	LOUISE PADGETT, WALLACE, NC 28466	5	6	1	23								79
ROWAN													35
SHARON													0
SHILOH													0
SILOAM	RICHARD ELLIS, RT. 1, TURKEY, NC 28393	3	6	6	15				4		2		44
TEACHEY													0
TURKEY	BROOKS BOYETTE, 502 FORREST ROAD, WARSAW, NC 28398	6	16	40	25								89
UNION GROVE	E.B. THORNTON, RT. 1, BOX 207, WILLARD, NC 28478	1	4	12	18						3		65
WARSAW													
WELLS CHAPEL													
	TOTALS	64	119	173	395	48	18	0	122	276	38	0	1192
	PREVIOUS YEAR TOTALS	76	180	206	615	25	79	8	185	101	47	2	1202

BSSB 1297 (Rev. 11 83)

66

ALBERTSON
ALUM SPRIN
BEAR MARS
BEULAH
BROWN
CALVA
CALYP
CENTE
C

CORINT
DOBSON
EVERGRE
FAISON
GARLAND
GARNERS
GROVE E/
HICKORY

INGOLD
ISLAND CRI
JOHNSON
KENANSVIL
MAGNOLIA
MOUNT CHLEA
MOUNT OLIVE
MOUNT VERN
NEW HOPE

67

LAUREL STROUD, RT. 1, ALBERTSON, NC 28508
CONNIE JONES, RT. 1, MOUNT OLIVE, NC 28365
KAYE WARREN, 120 J., JOHN STREET, MOUNT OLIVE, NC 28365
MILTON MASSEY, RT. 1, BOX 12, TURKEY, NC 28393
CURTIS W. POPE, 305 INVERNESS ROAD, CLINTON, NC 28328
RUSSELL KILLETTE, RT. 1, WARSAW, NC 28398

JOYCE HUDSON, RT. 1, HARRELLS, NC 2

NA BENTON, RT. 1, TEACHEY, NC 28464
NET REGISTER, RT. 2, ROSE HILL, NC 28458
S. JERRY TODD, P.O. BOX 21, HARRELLS, NC 2866
VIS BRADSHAW, FAISON, NC 28341
E HART, P.O. BOX 387, GARLAND, NC 281

N.BENTON, 510 E. LAURELWOOD APTS, CL
. THOMAS McLAMB, RT. 5, BOX 628, CLIN

BOBBY LAMB, RT. 1, BOX 129, GARLAND, NC
OHNNY NORRIS, RT. 2, BOX 22, ROSE HILL
JOHN W. BOYETTE, JR., RT. 2, WARSAW, NC
HENRY WEST, RT.2, WARSAW, NC 28398
RITA BROWN, RT. 1, MAGNOLIA 28453
RHONDA HOUCHENS, 510 E LAURELWOOD APT...CLINTON 2832
BARBARA STRICKLAND, RT. R, BOX 51A, MOUNT OLIVE 28365
PHYLLIS LINDLY, RT. 2, NEWTON GROVE, NC 28366
NELL CORBETT, RT. 1, TURKEY, NC 28393
ON NC 28341

EASTERN

NORTH CAROLINA

HELEN REGISTER

RT. 1, BOX 401B   TURKEY,   NORTH CAROLINA   28393

CHURCHES	WMU DIRECTORS & ADDRESSES (INCLUDE ZIP CODE)	99	100	101	102	103	104	105	106	107	108	109	110	111	112	113
ALBERTSON	LAUREL STROUD, RT. 1, ALBERTSON, NC 28508	0	0	0	0	0	0	1	0	0	0	0	13	1	0	18
ALUM SPRINGS	MARIE HARPER, RT. 2, MOUNT OLIVE, NC, 28365	0	0	0	0	0	1	1	0	0	0	0	12	1	0	13
BEAR MARSH	HAZEL PIPKIN, RT. 3, MOUNT OLIVE, NC 28365	0	1	0	0	0	1	3	0	2	0	0	33	5	0	43
BEULAH		1	0	0	0	0	0	1	0	0	0	0	11	4	0	16
BROWN	ANN PETERSON, RT. 1, CLINTON, NC, 28328	1	0	0	1	0	1	3	0	0	0	0	15	5	3	27
CALVARY	CLARA MATTHEWS, RT. 1, BOX 78A1, WARSAW, NC 28398	0	0	0	0	0	1	1	0	0	0	0	9	0	0	10
CALYPSO	VIRGINIA HINES, P.O. BOX 66, CALYPSO, NC 28325	0	0	0	1	0	1	3	0	5	0	0	6	3	0	19
CENTER	JOYCE HUDSON, RT. 1, HARRELLS, NC 28444	1	0	1	0	0	0	3	0	0	0	0	12	0	0	15
CLINTON FIRST	JANE KALEEL, P.O. BOX 815 CLINTON, NC 28328	1	1	0	1	2	1	6	0	20	12	0	104	5	0	151
CONCORD	SANDRA ROSE, RT. 1, ROSE HILL, NC 28458	0	0	0	0	0	0	0	0	0	0	0	9	3	0	27
CORINTH	LEONA JOHNSON, RT. 1, ROSE HILL, NC 28458	1	0	1	2	0	2	12	0	16	0	0	32	3	0	27
DOBSON CHAPEL	JULIA BROCK, RT. 2, BOX 146, ROSE HILL 28458	0	1	0	0	1	0	3	0	7	0	0	10	2	0	25
EVERGREEN	MRS. BILLY CHESNUTTE, RT.1 MAGNOLIA, NC 28853	0	0	1	0	0	1	3	0	0	0	0	22	3	0	31
FAISON	STELLA SUTTON, FAISON, NC 28341	1	1	0	0	3	1	3	0	0	2	0	22	3	0	29
GARLAND	MRS. COLEMAN CARTER, P.O. BOX 338,GARLAND, NC 28441	0	0	0	1	0	0	1	0	2	0	0	0	0	0	38
GARNERS CHAPEL	DEBBIE ROSE, RT. 1, MOUNT OLIVE, NC 28365	0	1	0	0	0	0	2	0	0	0	0	22	6	0	31
GROVE PARK	BETTY CARR, 505 CAROLINA AVENUE, CLINTON, NC 28328	0	0	0	1	0	0	1	0	15	0	0	35	0	0	51
HICKORY GROVE	JUDY DAVIS, RT. 3, BOX 331-D, CLINTON, NC, 28328	0	0	1	0	3	0	5	12	13	0	0	15	0	0	50
IMMANUEL	MRS. LYNN ADAMS, RT. 1,BOX 21X, CLINTON, NC 28328	0	0	0	0	1	0	2	0	14	0	0	52	6	0	75
INGOLD	BETSY CARTER, P.O. BOX 2, HARRELLS, NC 28444	1	0	0	0	0	1	1	0	7	0	0	11	2	0	15
ISLAND CREEK	MRS. JAMES HARTSELL, RT. 2, BOX 38,ROSE HILL, NC 28458	0	1	1	1	1	1	6	0	10	0	2	10	2	0	28
JOHNSON	CATHY KIRBY, RT. 2, WARSAW, NC 28398	0	0	0	0	0	0	0	0	0	0	0	20	6	0	52
KENANSVILLE	LORENA VESTAL, RT. 2, BOX 363, KENANSVILLE, NC 28349	0	1	0	1	2	1	4	0	5	15	0	17	3	0	27
MAGNOLIA	SUSAN JOYNER, MAGNOLIA 28453	0	0	0	1	0	0	1	0	0	0	0	2	0	0	40
MOUNT GILEAD	EUNICE BASS, RT. 1,BOX 110A, CLINTON, NC 28328	1	2	1	0	0	1	6	5	13	2	2	35	7	0	61
MOUNT OLIVE	JUDY CAVENESS, 112 E. JOHN STREET, MOUNT OLIVE 28365	1	1	0	1	1	1	6	3	12	2	2	96	7	0	119
MOUNT VERNON	KATHLEEN POPE, RT. 2, CLINTON, NC 28328	0	0	1	0	0	0	3	3	0	0	2	20	3	0	38
NEW HOPE	THELMA WARE, RT. 1, TURKEY, NC 28393	1	1	0	1	0	0	3	2	2	0	0	11	3	0	19
PINEY GROVE	DOT BOYETTE, 207 UNDERWOOD STREET, CLINTON, NC 28328	0	0	0	0	0	0	0	0	0	0	0	0	0	0	0
POPLAR GROVE		1	1	0	1	0	1	5	0	9	0	0	61	7	0	96
POSTON	MARTHA TEACHEY, RT. 1, WALLACE, NC 28466	0	1	1	1	1	0	2	11	6	13	0	67	5	0	101
ROSE HILL	RUBY PETERSON, RT. 3, BOX 317, CLINTON, NC 28328	1	0	0	0	1	1	5	20	7	11	0	31	7	0	68
ROWAN	MARGARET BRINKLEY, CHINQUAPIN, NC 28521	1	1	0	0	0	0	2	7	12	0	0	15	3	0	31
SHARON	DONAS HARDIN, RT. 1, BOX 437, CHINQUAPIN, NC 28521	0	0	0	0	0	0	2	6	6	0	0	16	2	0	29
SHILOH	BETTY SANDERSON, RT. 1, HARRELLS, NC 28444	1	1	1	0	0	0	3	4	4	0	0	0	7	19	16
SILOAM	MRS. WILLARD FUSSELL, P.O. BOX 1,TEACHEY, NC 28464	0	0	0	0	1	0	2	7	7	0	0	11	2	0	41
TEACHEY	DONNA BOYETTE, RT. 1, BOX 401B, TURKEY, NC 28393	1	1	0	0	0	0	3	0	13	16	0	0	6	0	33
UNION GROVE	BRENDA STANCIL, RT. 1, BOX 401B, CLURKEY, NC 28393	1	2	1	1	1	0	6	9	27	0	0	21	3	0	132
WARSAW	MARY HESTER POWELL, 606 N. PINE STREET, WARSAW, NC 28398	1	1	0	1	4	4	8	8	6	18	0	18	6	0	54
WELLS CHAPEL	MARY J. BLAND, P.O. BOX 90, HARRELLS, NC 28444															
	TOTALS	18	28	20	11	39	16	129	130	216	151	107	1035	121	25	1797
	PREVIOUS YEAR TOTALS	19	29	24	11	41	10	135	124	248	152	119	1023	129	33	1850

TOTALS						
PREVIOUS YEAR TOTALS						

68

6556 1797 (Rev. 11 83)

EASTERN

NORTH CAROLINA

WOODY BRINSON

P. O. BOX 43,   KENANSVILLE   NORTH CAROLINA   28349

CHURCHES	BROTHERHOOD DIRECTORS & ADDRESSES (INCLUDE ZIP CODE)	114	115	116	117	118	119	120	121	122	123
		Crusaders 9-11 years or grades 1-6	Pioneers 12-17 years or grades 7-12	RA director and committee	Baptist Men enrollment: Basic	Baptist Men enrollment: Pilot	Baptist Men enrollment: Mission Action	Baptist Men enrollment: Special or Lay Renewal	Brotherhood director and other leaders (brotherhood)	Number of missions	Mission offerings
ALBERTSON		0	0	0	0	0	0	0	0	0	0
ALUM SPRINGS		0	0	0	0	0	0	0	0	0	0
BEAR MARSH		5	0	1	0	0	0	0	0	0	0
BEULAH	JOSEPH W. MOSS, RT. 4, BOX 389, CLINTON, NC 28328	6	6	2	0	0	0	0	0	0	29
BROWN	LYNN HILTON, 805 N. CENTER STREET, WARSAW, NC 28398	0	0	2	13	0	7	0	0	0	25
CALVARY	JAMES BAKER, GREENWOOD TERRACE, MOUNT OLIVE, NC 28365	6	2	2	0	0	0	0	10	0	31
CALYPSO	ROBERT HUDSON, RT. 1, HARRELLS, NC 28441	0	0	4	0	0	0	0	0	0	1
CENTER	WILLIE HOBBS, RT. 3, BOX 143 B, CLINTON 28328	15	0	6	55	10	0	0	0	0	90
CLINTON FIRST											
CONCORD	PRICE KNOWLES, 115 E. MARTIN ST., ROSE HILL, NC 28458	0	0	0	0	0	0	0	0	0	0
CORINTH	MITCH WILLIAMS, RT. 2, ROSE HILL, NC 28458	2	0	2	0	0	0	0	0	0	18
DOBSON CHAPEL	JAMES SPEARMAN, JR., RT. 1, ROSE HILL, NC 28458	2	3	2	7	0	0	0	0	0	14
EVERGREEN	EDWARD MATTHEWS, FAISON, NC 28341	14	0	6	15	0	0	0	0	0	24
FAISON	WILBERT DAVIS, P.O. BOX 187, GARLAND, NC 28441	2	6	2	3	0	0	0	1	0	40
GARLAND		8	6	2	12	0	0	0	0	0	21
GARNERS CHAPEL	FRANKLIN LINDSAY, RT. 1, BOX 218, CLINTON, NC 28328	0	0	2	28	0	0	0	0	0	0
GROVE PARK		8	0	3	0	0	0	0	1	0	43
HICKORY GROVE	J.B. POPE, 621A. N.W. BLVD., CLINTON, NC 28328	0	10	3	15	0	0	0	0	0	01
IMMANUEL		0	0	0	0	0	0	0	0	0	29
INGOLD		0	0	0	0	0	0	0	0	0	0
ISLAND CREEK											
JOHNSON	JOHNNY CARLTON, RT. 1, WARSAW, NC 28398	4	3	1	7	7	0	0	0	0	25
KENANSVILLE	WOODY BRINSON, P.O. BOX 43, KENANSVILLE, NC 28399	9	0	1	15	0	0	0	0	0	25
MAGNOLIA		0	5	1	0	0	0	0	0	0	19
MOUNT GILEAD	HERBERT BALLANCE, RT. 2, BOX 120, CLINTON, NC 28328	6	0	3	0	0	0	0	0	0	9
MOUNT OLIVE		0	0	0	0	0	0	0	0	0	6
MOUNT VERNON		0	0	0	0	0	0	0	0	0	0
NEW HOPE		0	0	0	0	0	0	0	0	0	0
PINEY GROVE											
POPLAR GROVE	JOHN BRASWELL, RT. 1, BOX 53A, MATHA, NC 2871	0	0	0	0	12	0	0	0	0	0
POSTON		0	0	2	0	0	0	0	0	0	0
ROSE HILL	WELDON CLACK, RT. 2, BOX 53, CLINTON, NC 28328	0	0	0	0	0	0	0	0	0	13
ROWAN	EARNEST GRAY, CHINQUAPIN 28521	8	13	4	16	0	0	0	0	0	0
SHARON	DAVID MAREADY, RT. 1, CHINQUAPIN, NC 28521	10	8	2	0	0	0	0	0	0	30
SHILOH		0	0	0	0	0	0	0	0	0	25
SILOAM		0	0	0	0	0	0	0	0	0	0
TEACHEY		0	0	0	0	0	0	0	0	0	0
TURKEY	GEORGE PINYATELLO, RT. 1, TURKEY, NC 28393	0	0	6	8	3	2	0	0	0	0
UNION GROVE	GEORGE C. ERVAR, RT. 1, BOX 13, CLINTON, NC										

69

	Grand Total Mission expenditures
ALBERT — RSHALL STROUD, RT. 1, ALBERTSON, NC 2	2,116
ALUM'SF — RIE HARPER, RT. 2, MOUNT OLIVE, NC 2839	3,262
BEAR M — G. HATCH, JR., RT. 5, BOX 48, MOUNT OLIV	4,122
BEULAH — INDA CREECH, 504 RALEIGH ROAD, CLINTON	2,177
BROWN — HARON CARR, RT. 3, BOX 97, CLINTON, NC	800
CALVA — INGA SAVAGE, RT. 2, BOX 95-R, WARSAW, NC	4,237
CALYPS — ENDERSON McCULLEN, P.O.B. 75, CALYPSO,	3,153
CENTEI — EONA BLACKBURN, RT. 1, BOX 175, GARLAND	1,219
CLINTC	
CORINTH — ARY LEE USHER, RT. 1,	1,291
DOBSON C — ETTY P. BUTTS, RT. 1,	12,696
EVERGREEN — ULIA BROCK, RT. 2, BO;	2,980
FAISON — RS, FORREST L. DANIEL	1,851
GARLAND — IVIAN KIRKLAND, FAISO	2,448
GARNERS CHAP — VELYN DAVIS, P.O. BOX	5,560
GROVE PARK — NNIE G. ALBERTSON, R1	3,480
HICKORY GROVI — EANNE POPE, 301 RALEIG	18,779
IMMANUE — DYCE WARREN, RT. 1, B	4,593
ISLAND CREEK — RS, FRANK CAMPBELL, P.O. BOX 92, CLINTON, NC 28328	2,437
JOHNSON — ENNIS KIRBY, P.O. BOX 475, KENANSVILLE, NC	4,613
KENANSVILLE — DNA BRINSON, BOX 8, KENANSVILLE, NC 2835	9,375
MAGNOLIA — ETTY CHESTNUTT, RT. 1 BOX 277, WARSAW, NC	4,127
MOUNT GILEAD — ATHERINE PETERSON, RT.2, BOX 108, CLINTON, N	4,336
MOUNT OLIVE — R. Y.E. SHAVER, BOX 486, MOUNT OLIVE, NC 283	2,614
MOUNT VERNOI — URLEY QUINN, 301 FAIRFAX STREET, CLINTON, N	20,077
NEW HOPE — HELBY BLANCHARD, RT. 1, TURKEY, NC 28393	7,225
PINEY	
POPLAR GROVE — NN MILLER, RT. 2, BOX 81, FAISON, NC 28341	
POSTON — HELMA TEACHEY, RT. 3, BOX 53, WALLACE, NC	13,444
ROSE HILL — R. LARRY E. PRICE, P.O. BOX 638, ROSE HILL, N	20,750
ROWAN — ABEANA BRIGGS, 717 SW BLVD., CLINTON, NC 2	9,182
SHARON — DELENE NORRIS, RT. 1, BOX 3E, CHINQUAPIN,	7,445
SHILOAH — ATHY JAROSEWICZ, RT. 1, BOX 138, WALLACE,	4,000
SILOAM — OUISE MAYNARD, RT. 2, BOX 148, HARRELLS NC	6,994
TEACHEY — RS, HARRELL HALL, 302 WEST WESTBROOK ST —	13,056
TURKEY — ETTIE PHIPPS, P.O. BOX 94, TURKEY, NC 28393	6,288

71

TABLE I · SPECIAL INFORMATION   YEAR ENDING SEPTEMBER 30, 1984

EASTERN

Moderator DONALD H. COLEY

Address RT. 1, BOX 383-B   City WALLACE   State NORTH CAROLINA   Zip 28328

CHURCHES	CHAIRMAN OF DEACONS & ADDRESSES (INCLUDE ZIP CODE)
ALBERTSON	THURMAN STROUD, RT. 1, ALBERTSON, NC. 28508
ALUM SPRINGS	SAM WALLER, RT. 2, MOUNT OLIVE, N.C., 28365
BEAR MARSH	LESLIE SOUTHERLAND, RT. 2, MOUNT OLIVE, NC 28365
BEULAH	
BROWN	GROVER SINCLAIR, RT. 3, BOX 97, CLINTON, NC 28328
CALVARY	RUSSELL KILLETTE, RT. 1, WARSAW, NC 28398
CALYPSO	WILLIAM BAKER, GREENWOOD TERRACE, MOUNT OLIVE, NC
CENTER	WILLIAM STEEDLY, MOORE STREET, CLINTON, NC 28328
CLINTON, FIRST	CLAY FAYETTE STREET, CLINTON 28328
CONCORD	GARY BELL, P.O. BOX 123, ROSE HILL, NC 28458
CORINTH	DELANA JOHNSON, RT. 1, TEACHEY, N.C. 28464
DOBSON CHAPEL	WILBUR CARR, RT. 2, ROSE HILL, NC 28458
EVERGREEN	NOAH TODD, RT. 1, MAGNOLIA, NC 28453
FAISON	DAVID ALSBROOK, FAISON, NC 28341
GARLAND	HUGH HOBBS, P.O. BOX, GARLAND, NC 28441
CARNERS CHAPEL	CECIL ROSE, RT. 1, MOUNT OLIVE, NC 28365
GROVE PARK	RONNIE WARREN, 202 FOX LAKE DRIVE, CLINTON, NC 28328
HICKORY GROVE	JACKIE TYNDALL, RT. 1, BOX 19A, CLINTON, NC 28328
IMMANUEL	CHARLES ADAMS, RT. 1, BOX 21X, CLINTON, NC 28328
INGOLD	NORWOOD CARTER, P.O. BOX 2, HARRELLS, NC 28444
ISLAND CREEK	GARLAND KING, RT. 1, TEACHEY, NC 28464
JOHNSON	RHODOLPH BEST, WARSAW, NC 28398
KENANSVILLE	DOUGLAS JUDGE, BOX 356, KENANSVILLE, NC 28349
MAGNOLIA	JACK JOYNER, MAGNOLIA, 28453
MOUNT GILEAD	NATHAN KELLY, RT. 1, BOX 166, CLINTON, NC 28328
MOUNT OLIVE	RUSSELL KELLY, 603 BREAZEALLE, MOUNT OLIVE, NC 28365
MOUNT VERNON	WAYNE WILSON, RT. 5, CLINTON, NC 28328
NEW HOPE	ED COLWELL, RT. 1, TURKEY, NC 28329
PINEY GROVE	JAMES THORNTON, RT. 2, BOX 107, FAISON, NC 28341
POPLAR GROVE	DOUGLAS BLACKMON, RT. 1, FAISON, NC 28341
POSTON	
ROSE HILL	E.G. MURRAY, P.O. BOX 636, ROSE HILL, NC 28458
ROWAN	OSCAR CLARKE, 100 E. ROWAN ROAD, CLINTON, NC 28328
SHARON	DAVID WOOD, RT. 1, CHINQUAPIN, NC 28521
SHILOM	DAVID MAREADY, RT. 1, CHINQUAPIN, NC 28521
TEACHEY	R.O. SANDERSON, RT. 1, HARRELLS, NC. 28444
TURKEY	ROY EZZELL, RT. 1, TURKEY, NC 28393
UNION GROVE	LEX CARTER, JR. RT. 1, BOX 300, CLINTON, NC 28328
WARSAW	DOT ROLLINS, 304 WALNUT STREET, CLINTON, NC 28328
WELLS CHAPEL	L.C. ENNIS, RT. 1, BOX 76, WALLACE, NC 28466
	TOTALS
	PREVIOUS YEAR TOTALS

NORTH CAROLINA

EASTERN

BAPTIST

ASSOCIATION

1985

NORTH CAROLINA

EASTERN BAPTIST ASSOCIATION

ONE -HUNDRED FIFTY-EIGHTH ANNUAL

SESSION

1827 - 1985

FIRST DAY
October 28, 1985
Rowan Baptist Church

SECOND DAY
October 29, 1985
Poston Baptist Church

(WELLS CHAPEL Assisting)

THEME

"DEMONSTRATE GOD'S LOVE"

MODERATOR
Donald Coley

CLERK
E.C. Mattocks

NEXT ANNUAL MEETING
First Day

WARSAW BAPTIST CHURCH
(Calvary Assisting)
Monday, October 27, 1986

Second Day

BEAR MARSH BAPTIST CHURCH
(Alum Springs Assisting)
Tuesday, October 28, 1986

NOTES

T A B L E   O F   C O N T E N T S
EASTERN BAPTIST ASSOCIATION
P.O. Box 712, Warsaw, North Carolina 28398
TELEPHONE (919) 293-7077

ASSOCIATIONAL DIRECTORY
PASTORS

CHURCH	PASTOR	ADDRESS	TELEPHONE
ALBERTSON	THOMAS A. JONES	1804 Pink Hill Rd, Kinston 28501	523-1610
ALUM SPRINGS	Shelton Justice	Rt. 1, Box 38A-2, Warsaw 28398	293-7524
BEAR MARSH	E. C. Mattocks	Rt. 2, Box 52, Mount Olive 28365	658-6133
BEULAH	Eddie Wetherington	Rt. 5, Box 29-A, Clinton 28328	592-2898
BROWN	N.J. McManus	Rt. 1, Box 71, Godwin 28344	C-564-6060
CALVARY	Andy Wood	103 Wade Street, allw 28398	293-7458
CENTER		Rt. 1, Box 414, Garland 28441	532-2118
CLINTON	James Pardue	P.O. Box 837, Clinton 28328	C-592-8124
			H- 592-8220
CONCORD	James Parsons	Rt. 1, Box 329-C, Wallace 28466	285-3599
CORINTH	Dennis Knight	Rt. 1, Box 329, dSe Hill 28458	289-3928
DOBSON CHAPEL	Ernest Johnson, Jr.	Rt. 1, Box 118-A, Magnolia 28453	296-1473
EVERGREEN	Jasper Hinson	Rt. 6, Clinton 28328	532-4757
FAISON	Charles Kirkland	P.O. Box 426, Faison 28341	267-2591
GARLAND	Raleigh Carroll	P.O. Box 367, Garland 28441	C-529-5201
			H-529-2531

-4-

INGOLD	Jake Carroll	P.O. Box 5252, Ingold 28446	529-4181
ISLAND CREEK	James Hartsell	Rt. 2, Box 349, Rose Hill 28458	289-2606
JOHNSON	Stephen Moore	Rt. 2, Warsaw 28398	C-293-4757 H-293-4980
KENANSVILLE	Lauren Sharpe	P.O. Box 517, Kenansville 28349	C-296-1137 H-296-1389
MAGNOLIA	A.R. Teachey	702 Hall Street, Rose Hill 28458	C-289-2217 H-289-3850
MOUNT GILEAD	Oliver Skerrett	Rt. 2, Box 106, Clinton 28328	592-6533
MOUNT OLIVE	Anthony Z. Gurganus	301 N. Chestnut St., Mt. Olive 28365	C-658-2062 H-658-2351
MOUNT VERNON	Randall Outland	Rt. 5, Box 50, Clinton 28328	533-3719
NEW HOPE		Rt. 1, Turkey, 28393	
PINEY GROVE	Farrell Miller	Rt. 2, Box 122-A, Faison 28341	C-564-6061 H-564-4848
POPLAR GROVE	Gerald Garris	Rt. 3, Box 314, Dudley 28333	736-1825
POSTON	Donald Coley	Rt. 1, Box 347-B, Wallace 28466	C-285-2439 H-285-2476
ROSE HILL	Jerry Kinlaw	P.O. Box 459, Rose Hill 28458	C-289-2250 H-289-3882
ROWAN	Michael Shook	202 Reedsford Road, Clinton 28328	C-592-7508 H-592-7268
SHARON	Raymond Futch	P.O. Box 126, Chinquapin 28521	C-285-4391
SHILOH	Eugene Hardin	Rt. 1, Box 347, Chinquapin 28521	285-7403
SILOAM	Tim Register	Rt. 1, Box 19, Harrells 28444	C-532-4077 H-532-4444

P.O. Box 158, Teachey 28464

TEACHEY

TURKEY   Mack Musselwhite, P.O. Box 148, Turkey 28393   C-592-5562
H-592-2056

88-4422

UNION GROVE   L.L. Barnes, Rt. 2, Elizabethtown 28337

WARSAW   David Moore, 202 E. College Street, Warsaw 28398   C-293-4236
H-293-7479

WELLS CHAPEL   Ottis King, Rt. 1, Box 128, Wallace, 28466   C-532-4210
H-532-4528

MINISTERS NOT PASTORS

BEAR MARSH	Rev. Homer Baumgardner(OM) Rt. 2, Warsaw 28398	293-7072
CALVARY	Ben Eason(LM) 105 W. Pollock St., W saw 28398	293-7227
	Lynn Hilton(LM), 805 N. Center St., Warsaw 28398	293-4856
CLINTON	T. N. (OM) 211 Park Ave, Clinton 28328	592-2293
	J.A. Crowe, Sr.(OM), 910 Jasper St., Clinton 28328	592-8758
	Waldo Early(OM) 307 Dixie Circle, Clinton 28328	592-2704
	M.M. Johnson (OM)P.O. Box 1093, Clinton 28328	592-2296
	Bob dan, (OM) Rt. 6, Clinton 28328	564 6345
	William M. Jones (OM) 110 Forest Drive, Clinton 28328	592-2472
	Gile aDis (OM) P.O. Box 263, Clinton 28328	592-5313
	lean atch (OM) 309 Fairfax St., Clinton 28328	592-6215
	L.E. Williamson (OM) 512 Nicholson St., Clinton 28328	592-0202
	Ose Wade(LM) Rt. 5, Box 377½, Clinton 28328	592-4328
	Albert Rivenbark(OM)Rt. 1, Box 196, Willard 28478	532-4553
Harvey	(OM) Rt. 2, Rose Hill 28458	289-2639
Samuel Scott	(OM) Rt. 7, Box 34A, Whiteville 28476	
IMMANUEL		
ISLAND CREEK	Caig Hansen(LM) D6 E. College St., Mount Olive 28365	285-5888
MOUNT GILEAD	Hal Bilbo (OM) Rt. 3, Box 67, Wallace 28466	556-2387
MOUNT OLIVE	Age Castles(OM) 339 West Avenue, Wake Forest 27587	532-4746
POSTON	Calhoun Johnson(OM) Rt. 1, Box 315, Magnolia 28453	592-3441
ROSE HILL	Billy (OM) 107 Dee Street, Clinton 28328	
BN		

WARSAW — Mitchell Rivenbark(OM) 509 E. Hill St., Warsaw 28398 — 293-7496
Ken Durham(OM) Rt. 2, Box 71M, Warsaw 28398 — 293-3474

EXECUTIVE BOARD REPRESENTATIVES

ALBERTSON

ALUM SPRINGS — Eugene Outlaw, Rt. 1, Mount Olive 28365 — 658-3458

BEAR MARSH — Larry Harper, Rt. 2, Box 281, Mount Olive 28365 — 658-3614

BEULAH — Leslie Southerland, Rt. 2, Mount Olive 28365 — 658-4512
Tex Cline, 205 Dogwood Drive, Warsaw 28398 — 293-4285

BROWN — Bill Herring, Rt. 2, Box 186A, Faison 28341 — 533-3765
Curtis W. Pope, 305 Inverness Road, Clinton 28328 — 592-5209

CALVARY — Frank Graham, Rt. 3, Clinton 28328
Lynn Hilton, 805 N. Center St., Warsaw 28398 — 293-4856

CENTER — Robert Southerland, Rt. 2, Warsaw 28398 — 293-4690

CLINTON — Charles Lee Pope, 405 Oakland Ter., Clinton 28328 — 592-2469

CONCORD — Graham Butler, 1016 Jasper St., Clinton 28328 — 592-7580
Gary Bell, Rt. 1, Box 238, Rose Hill 28458 — 289-3974

CORINTH — Francis Usher, Rt. 1, Box 86, Rose Hill 28458 — 289-2681
Price Knowles, 115 E. Main, Rose Hill 28458 — 289-3741

DOBSON CHAPEL — George Jones, Rt. 1, Rose Hill 28458 — 289-2733
James Brown Jr., Rt. 2, Rose Hill 28458 — 289-3463

EVERGREEN — Russell Brown, Rt. 2, Rose Hill 28458 — 289-2228
Dwight Grady, Rt. 1, Rose Hill 28458 — 532-4034

FAISON — Jerry Todd, P.O. Box 21, Harrells 28444 — 532-2271
Walter Thomas, Faison 28341 — 267-5801
Fred Wheless, Faison 28341 — 267-2431

GARLAND — Gene Hart, P.O. Box 187, Garland 28441 — 529-4311

GARNER'S CHAPEL — Cecil Rose, Rt. 1, Mount Olive 28365 — 658-5425
Mark Best, Rt. 1, Mount Olive 28365 — 658-3327

GROVE PARK — Jack Parsons, 405 W. Main St., Clinton 28328 — 592-

HICKORY GROVE — Jeannette Benton, 605 NE Blvd., Clinton 28328 — 592-3513
Sara Warren, Rt. 1, Box 130, Clinton 28328 — 564-4252

IMMANUEL	Helen Herring, Rt. 1, Box 124, Clinton 28328	592-4295
I GD	Jeff Honeycutt, 1232 Sunset Avenue, Cl'ton, 28328	592-5376
	John Yancey, Rt. 4, Box 118, Clinton 28328	529 3891
	Henry L. Blackburn, Rt. 4, Box 257, Clinton 28328	289-2639
ISLAND CREEK	Norwood Carter, P.O. Box 2, Harrells 28444	289-2639
JOHNSON	...ey & Tina Blanton, Rt. 2, Rose Hill 28458	296-1038
	Nat Phillips, Rt. 2, ...lle 28349	296-0031
KENANSVILLE	Dennis Kirby, P.O. Box 475, Kenansville 28349	296-1519
	Amos Brinson, Box 8, Kenansville 289	296-0749
MAGNOLIA	O.R. Blizzard, Rt. 1, ...dville 28349	
MOUNT GILEAD	Nathan Gay, Rt. 4, Box 166-B, Clinton 28328	592-4846
	...ie J. Bass, Rt. 2, Box 110-A, Clinton 28328	592 4074
ƏUNT OLIVE	W.K. Lewis, 128 N. Center St., Mount Olive 28365	658-9507
MOUNT VERNON	W.B. Murray, Box 348, Mount Olive 28365	658-2146
	Boyd Warwick, Rt. 5, Clinton 28328	592-5852
	Janice Wilson, Rt. 5, Clinton 28328	533-3596
NEW HOPE	R. W. ...rd, Jr., Rt. 1, Box 269, Turkey 28393	533-3586
	Robert Frederick, Rt. 1, Turkey 28393	533-3639
PINEY GROVE	Irene Darden, Rt. 2, Box 122, Faison 28341	533-3382
	Jimmy Thornton, RT. 2, Box 147, Faison 28341	533-3449
POPLAR GROVE	Garland Britt, Rt. 2, Box 176, Faison 28341	
	Herman Coker, Rt. 1, Faison 28341	
POSTON	Aileen Moore, Rt. 3, Wallace 28466	285-3436
	Margaret Stafford, Rt. 3, Wallace 28466	285-4739

TEACHEY

TURKEY

Creson Ezzell, Rt. 1, Box 262, Turkey 28393   533-3368
H.J. Register, Rt. 1, Box 401-B, Turkey, 28393   533-3845

UNION GROVE

George Fryar, Rt. 4, Box 207, Clinton 28328   592-4830
Roger Wells, Rt. 4, Box 357-D, Clinton 28328   592-4213

WARSAW
WELLS CHAPEL

John A. Johnson, 108 E. Plank St., Warsaw 28298   293-4958
Bland Carr, Rt. 1, Box 207, Willard, 28478   532-4144
E.B. Thornton, Rt. 1, Willard 28478   532-4451

G E N E R A L   A S S O C I A T I O N A L   O F F I C E R S

Eastern Baptist Association
P.O. Box 712, Warsaw, North Carolina 28398
Telephone (919) 293-7077

DIRECTOR OF MISSIONS	William C. Lamb, P.O. Box 712, Warsaw 28398	293-7077
ASSOCIATIONAL SEC'Y.	Jo Neal Robinson, Rt. 2, Box 269, Clinton 28328	592-3044
MODERATOR	Lucille Yancey, P.O. Box 711, Clinton, 28328	592-3080
VICE-MODERATOR	Dennis Knight, Rt. 1, Box 329, Rose Hill 28458	289-3928
CLERK	David Moore, 202 E. College Street, Warsaw 28398	293-7479
TREASURER	Bill Boyette, P.O. Box 467, Warsaw 28398	293-4236
TRUSTEES	DeWitt King, Rt. 2, Box 111, Faison 28341 (1988)	293-3173
		293-7141
	Charles L. Matthis, Rt. 4, Clinton 28328(1987)	533-3365
	Larry Harper(Chairman)Rt. 2, Box 281, Mt. Olive 28365(1986)	592-5197
		658-3614

CHURCH PROGRAM OFFICERS

BROTHERHOOD		
Director	Woody Brinson, P.O. Box 43, Kenansville 28349	296-0784
CHURCH MUSIC		
Director	Raymond Futch, P.O. Box 126, Chinquapin 28521	285-3062

SUNDAY SCHOOL

e**D**or	James Hartsell, Rt. 2, Box 349, Rose Hill 28458	289-2606
Teacher Improvement and Training	David Moore, 202 College Street, Warsaw 28398	293-4236
Outreach Leader	Lynn Hilton, 805 N. Center Street, Warsaw 28398	293-4856
Vacation Bible School	Dennis Knight, Rt. 1, Box 329, Rose Hill 28458	289-3928
Adult		
Younger	Michael Shook, 202 Reedsford Road, Clinton 28328	592-7508
Median Adult	Mack Musselwhite, P.O. Box 148, Turkey 28393	592-2056
Senior Adult	Debbie Futch, P.O. Box 126, Chinquapin 28521	285-3062
Homebound	Charlotte Hartsell, Rt. 2, Box 349, Rose Hill 28458	289-2606
Y utb		
Senior Hi	L.E. Williamson, P.O. Box 837, Clinton 28328	592-8124
Junior Hi	Ric Durham, 202 College Street, Warsaw 28398	293-4236
Children		
Younger	Cathy Hopkins, P.O. Box 712, Warsaw 28398	293-7077
Mi dle	Naomi Moore, 205 E. Chelly St., Warsaw 28398	293-7479
Older	Andy Wood , 103 Wade, Warsaw 28398	293-7458
Pre-School		
Middle	Jenny Strickland, Rt. 1, Box 145, Clinton 28328	564-4502
Older	Temple Wood, 103 Wade Street, Warsaw 28398	293-7458
Special		
Mentally Handicapped	Margaret Musselwhite, P.O. Box 148, Turkey 28393	592-2056

CHURCH TRAINING

Director	Hal Bilbo, Rt. 3, Box 67, Wallace, 28466	285-5888

Baptist Women Director	Donis Hardin, Rt. 1, Box 347, Chinquapin 28521	285-7403
Asst. Bapt. Women Dir	Shelby Blanchard, Rt. 1, Box 269, Turkey 28393	533-3586
Baptist Young Women Dir.	Cynthia Price, P.O. Box 638, Rose Hill 28458	289-3837
Assistant BYW Director	Carrie Bell, 1004 Jasper Avenue, Clinton 28328	592-8884
Acteens Director	Gloria Lockerman, Rt. 3, Box 394-H, Clinton 28328	592-6356
Assist. Acteens Dir.	Donna Bas, Rt. 2, Box 6A, Clinton, 28328	592-6289
GA Director	Phyllis Matthews, 302 Ward's Bridge Road, Warsaw 28398	293-4602
Asst. GA Director	Ruth King, Rt. 2, Box 111, Faison 28341	564-6697
Mission Friends Director	Temple Wd. 103 W, Warsaw 28398	293-7485
Asst. M. F. Director	Frances Tew, 904 Warren Street, Clinton 28328	592-3745
Mission Action Director	Connie Carlton, Rt. 1, Box 257, Warsaw 28398	293-7106
Missi a Action Asst. Dir.	Jane Kaleel, 401 Pineview Rad, Clinton 28328	592-2043
Centennial Chairman	Inez Peterson, Rt. 6, Clinton 28328	592-4537
Area Directors:		
Clinton Area	Louise Strickland, Rt. 1, Clinton 28328	564-4593
Garland & Star Area	Janie Belle Strickland, 404-C Jacob St eet, Clinton 28328	592-5979
Mount Olive Area		
Faison-Warsaw Area	Katie Kirby, Rt. 1, Warsaw, 28398	293-7319
Wallace – Rose Hill	Linda Hawes, Rt. 2, Box 7, Rose Hill 28458	289-3237

SCHEDULE OF MEETING PLACES FOR WMU ANNUAL SESSION

1986	77th Annual Session	Sharon Baptist Church
1987	78th Annual Session	Mount Olive Baptist Church
1988	79th Annual Session	Mount Gilead Baptist Church
1989	80th Annual Session	Johnson Baptist Church

MISSIONS DEVELOPMENT PROGRAM
Cathy Hopkins, Mission Ministries Director
Telephone 293-7077
P.O. Box 712, Warsaw, North Carolina 28398

MISSIONS COUNCIL		
Director	Davis Benton, 605 NE Blvd, Clinton, 28328	592-3937

Kenneth eGn, Rt. 4, Box 389, Mount Olive 28365	658-9817
Margaret Musselwhite, P.O. Box 148, Turkey 28393	592-2056
Doris Carroll, P.O. Box 5252, Ingold 28446	529-4181
James Pardue, P.O. Box 837, Clinton 28328	592-8124
Mary Lee Jones, 502 E. Hill Street, Warsaw 28398	293-4616
Florence Hoover, Rt. 2, Box 17, Wells 28444	532-4336
Andy Wood, 103 Wade, Warsaw, 28398	293-7458
Woody Brinson, P.O. Box 43, Kenansville 28349	296-0784
Connie Carlton, Rt. 1, Box 257, Warsaw 28398	293-7106

DEAF MINISTRIES
Chairman

Mary Lee Jones, 502 E. Hill Street, Warsaw 28398	293-4616
Sylvia Knight, Rt. 1, Box 329, Rose Hill 28458	289-3928
Phyllis Durham, Rt. 2, Box 71, Warsaw 28398	293- 3474

MIGRANT MINISTRIES
Chairman

Ady Wood, 103 Wade St, Warsaw 28398	293-7458
Gail Naylor, 607 Thornton Street, Clinton 28328	592-2944
Wils on Spencer, Rt. 1, Faison 28341	267-0931
Lynn Hilton, 805 N. Center Street, Warsaw 28398	293-4856
Jane Kaleel, 401 Pineview Road, Clinton 28328	592-2043

LITERACY MINISTRIES
Chairman

Florence Hoover, Rt. 2, Box 17, Harrells 28444	532-4336
Faye Gaddy, Rt. 6, Clinton 28328	592-3270
Thelma Davis, P.O. Box 263, Clinton 28328	592-5313

DENOMINATIONAL REPRESENTATIVES

American Bible Society	H.J. Register, Rt. 1, Box 401-B, Turkey 28393	533-3845
Childrens' Homes	John A. Johnson, 108 E. Plank Street, Warsaw 28398	293-4958
Baptist Retirement Homes	Millard M. Johnson, P.O. Box 1093, Clinton 28328	592-2296
Christian Education		
Cooperative Program	Albert Pope, Rt. 1, Box 239, Warsaw 28398	293-4236
Annuity Board	Waldo Early, 307 Dixie Circle, Clinton 28328	592-2704
Baptist Foundation	Ken Durham, Rt. 2, Box 71, Warsaw 28398	293-3474
Baptist Hospital	Gerald Quinn, Wards Bridge Road, Warsaw 28398	293-4579
Christian Literature/		
Biblical Recorder	T. N. Cooper, P.O. Box 55, Clinton 28328	592-2293

COMMITTEES

Committee-On-Committees
Chairman

Anthony Gurganus, P.O. Box 203, Mount Olive 28365	658-2062
Mrs. Elwood Fussell, P.O. Box 1, Teachey 28464	285-3180
David Moore, 202 College Street, Warsaw 28398	293-4236
Temple Wood, 103 Wade Street, Warsaw 28398	293-7458
John Yancey, Rt. 4, Box 118, Clinton 28328	592-5376
Davis Benton , 605 NE Blvd., Clinton 28328	592-3513

Evangelism
Chairman

Dennis Knight, Rt. 1, Box 329, Rose Hill 28458 (1986)	289-3928
Oliver Skerrett, Rt. 2, Box 106, Clinton 28328 (1987)	592-6533
E. C. Mattocks, Rt. 2, Box 52, Mount Olive 28365 (1988)	658-6133

HISTORICAL
Chairman

Shelton Justice, Rt. 1, Box 38-A-2, Warsaw 28398 (1987)	293-7524
Waldo Early, 307 Dixie Circle, Clinton, 28328 (1986)	592-2704
Charlotte Hartsell, Rt. 2, Box 349, Rose Hill 28458 (1988)	289-2606

MEDIA LIBRARY
Chairman

Barbara Shook, 202 Reedsford Road, Clinton 28328 (1988)	592-7268
Joyce Lucas, 606 Blaney Street, Clinton 28328 (1986)	592-3610
Thelma Davis, P.O. Box 263, Clinton 28328 (1987)	592-5313

NOMINATING COMMITTEE
Chairman

Anthony Gurganus, P.O. Box 203, Mount Olive 28365 (1988)	658-2062
H.J. Register, Rt. 1, Box 401-B, Turkey 28393 (1986)	533-3845
Charles Lee Pope, P.O. Box 514, Clinton 8328 (1986)	592-2469
Jane Kaleel, 401 Pineview Road, Clinton 28328 (1987)	592-2043
Lois Colwell, Rt. 1, Turkey, 8293 987)	533-3372
aDis Benton, 605 NE Blvd., Cli tan, 28328 (1988)	592-3513

PASTOR SUPPORT
Chairman

*Randy Outland, Rt. 5, Box 50, Clinton, 28328 (1987)	533-3719
*Raleigh Carroll, P.O. Box 367, Garland 28441 (1986)	529-5201
David Moore, 202 College Street, Warsaw 28398 (1988)	293-4236

PROPERTIES
Chairman

Jake Carroll, P.O. Box 5252, Ingold 28446 (1987)	529-4181
Mrs. Elwood Fussell, P.O. Box 1, Teachey 28464 (1988)	285-3180
J.B. Herring, 307 Walnut Street, Warsaw 28398 (1986)	293-4956

STEWARDSHIP
Chairman

Tony Wilson, P.O. Box 52, Cli tan, 8328 (1987)	592-3854
Ed. Colwell, Rt. 1, Turkey 28393 (1986)	533-3372
Priscilla McGill, Rt 2, Box 23, Harrells 28444 (1986)	532-4276
Jimmy Strickland, P.O. Box 783, Warsaw 8398 (1986)	293-4289
Michael Sbk, 202 Reedsford Road, Clinton 28328 (1987)	592-7508
Anthony Gurganus, P.O. Box 203, Mount Olive 28365 (1987)	658-2062
Ernest Johnson, Rt. 1, Box 118-A, Magnolia 28453 (1988)	296-1473
Francis Clifton, Rt. 1, Faison 28341 (1988)	267-2551

-14-

ORDINATION
Chairman

Don Coley, Rt. 1, Box 347-B, Wallace 28466 (1986)   285-2439
Millard Johnson, P.O. Box 1093, Clinton 28328 (1986)   592-2296
Mack Musselwhite, P.O. Box 148, Turkey 28393 (1987)   592-5562
Shelton Justice, Rt. 1, Box 38-A-2, Warsaw 28398 (1987)   293-7524
Michael Shook, 202 Reedsford Rdd, Clinton 28328 (1988)   592-7508
John A. Johnson, 108 E. Plank Street, Warsaw 28398 (1988)   293-4958

*Serving to fill unexpired terms

ASSOCIATIONAL LONG RANGE PLANING COMMITTEE

James Pardue, Chairman, P.O. Box 837, Clinton, 28328   592-8124
Dennis ight   Rt. 1, Box 329, Rose Hill 28458   289-3928
aDis Be ton   605 NE Blvd., Clinton 28328   592-3513
Tony Wilson   P.O. Box 52, Clinton 28328   592-3854
Dad Moore   202 E. College Street, Warsaw 28398   293-4236
E.C. cks   Rt. 2, Box 52, Mount Olive 28365   658-6133
Gene Hart   P.O. Box 187, Garland 28441   529-4311
Woody Brinson   P.O. Box 43, Kenansville 28349   296-0784
Lucille Yancey   P.O. Box 711, Clinton 28328   592-7061
Florence Hoover   Rt. 2, Box 18, Harrells 28444   532-4336
ndie Bass   Rt. 2, Box 110-A, Clinton 28328   592-4074
Gerald Strickland   Rt. 3, Box 331-B, Clinton 28328   564-6717
Mary Boney   Rt. 3, Box 72, Wallace 28466   285-2932
es L. Pope   P.O. Box 514, Clinton 28328   592-2469
R.O. Sanderson   Rt. 1, Harrells 28444   532-4211

ALBERTSON -
ALUM SPRINGS - Carolyn Sanderson, D.H. Sanderson,
BEAR MARSH - Sam Pipkin, Leslie Southerland
BEULAH - Milton Creech, Tex Cline
BROWN - Stacy Thigpen, Curtis Pope, Mrs. Effie W. Ba
CALVARY - Temple Wood, Hannah Farmer, Ethel Batts,
CENTER - Louis Register, Robert Hudson, Linda Mott
CLINTON - Everette Peterson, Eleanor Early, Inez Pete
          Cleone Cooper, Graham Butler, Jane Kaleel
          Thurston Little
CONCORD - Mrs. Smithie Taylor, Gary Bell
CORINTH - J.C. Savage, Jr., Evelyn Savage, Ray Fuss
          Price Knowles, Betty Butts, Joan Conway
DOBSON CHAPEL - Betty Brown, Julia Brock, Lucille E
          Mildred Register, Isabelle Sanderson
EVERGREEN - Jerry Todd, Betty Ezzell, Edna Johnson
FAISON - Stella Sutton, Helen Flowers, Henry Brown
GARLAND - Renee' Carroll, Gene Hart, Sarah B. Jarvi:
          Annie B. McLelland
GARNER'S CHAPEL - Randolph Garner, Morris Rose, J
GROVE PARK -
HICKORY GROVE - Louise Strickland, Elsie Strickland,
          Egbert Strickland, Geneva Strickland, Lumis S
IMMANUEL - Mercedes Floyd, Dick Pope, Katherine Pop
          Karry Godwin, Frances Tew, Mildred Honeycu
INGOLD - Henry L. Blackburn, Mrs. Henry L. Blackbu
ISLAND CREEK - Centelle Hanchey, Charlotte Hartsell,
          Doris Brown
JOHNSON - Katie Mae Kirby, Ammie Best, Rudolph Bes!
KENANSVILLE - John Matthis, Macy Brinson, Margaret
Wilma Pate, Edna E. Brinson
MAGNOLIA -
MOUNT GILEAD - Willa Crea Warren, Elma Warren, Max
          Lillie Peterson, Pearl Merritt
MOUNT OLIVE - Rose Pleasant, Helen Bell, Pearl Cherr
          Goodson, Kenneth Goodson, Alma And
          Draughon, Madeline Cook
MOUNT VERNON - Gladys Martin, Thelma Hall, Minnie I
          Outland
NEW HOPE - Ed Colwell, Shelby Blanchard, Lewis John:
          Lois Colwell, Buck Blanchard
PINEY GROVE - Irene Darden, Dorothy Boyette, Billie
POPLAR GROVE - Wilbert Massey, Meredith Spencer, M.
POSTON - Annette Henderson, Lula Dixon, Woodrow Te
          Aileen Moore, Margaret Stafford
ROSE HILL - Mr. & Mrs. Albert Pope, Annie Rouse, No
ROWAN - Judy Hairr, Nellie G. Tew, Frances Raynor, I
          Laura Tew, Dorothy Robinson, Monroe Robin:
SHARON - Mr & Mrs. Jim Southerland, Mr. & Mrs. Norv
SHILOH - Donas Hardin, Virginia Aycock, Wilton Aycocl
          Flonnie Hunter

SILOAM - Louise Maynard, Betty Sanderson, Julia Peterson, R.O.
        Sanderson, Maurine Carter
TEACHEY -
TURKEY - H.J. Register, Creson Ezzell, Lettie Phipps
UNION GROVE - Rodella Batts, Aubrey Ezzell, Brenda Hope, Patricia
        Fryar, Peggy Fryar, Mr. & Mrs. George Fryar
WARSAW - Helen Ann Straughan, Gerald Quinn, James Page, Blanche,
        Draughon, Dot Rollins, Rita Quinn, Harriet Page, Mary
        Hester Powell
WELLS CHAPEL - E.B. Thornton, Catherine Thornton, Alma Highsmith,
        I.C. Ennis, Percy Carter

PROCEEDINGS

1. Moderator, Don Coley, called to order the 158th Annual Session of the Eastern Baptist Association at 3:10 P.M., October 28, 1985 in Rowan Baptist Church, Clinton, North Carolina.
2. The Association sang "Love Divine, All Loves Excelling"
3. James Parsons read Ephesians 2:1-10 and led in prayer
4. E.C. Mattocks, Associational clerk, reported registration representing 32 churches and moved that the 120 messengers constituted a quorum. Motion passed.
5. Raleigh Carroll, Chairman of Program Committee, presented the order of service and moved its adoption as the order of business. Motion passed.
6. Farrell Miller, Nominating Committee Chairman, presented for nomination David Moore as clerk and Farrell Miller as Associate clerk. Both were elected
7. The moderator appointed the following committees:
            A. Time, Place & Preacher
               Davis Benton
               Oliver Skerrett, Chairman
               Mack Musselwhite
            B. Resolutions Committee
               Raleigh Carroll, Chairman
               Sylvia Knight
               Ottis King
            C. Memorials Committee
               Michael Shook, Chairman
               Gerald Garris
               Helen Register
8. Jo Robinson, substituting for the associational treasurer, presented the treasurers report and moved its adoption. Motion passed.
9. E.C. Mattocks, Clerk, presented the associational Executive Board Reportand moved its adoption. Motion passed.

10. Miscellaneous Business
    Gene Hart, Stewardship Committee Chairman
consideration the 1985-86 proposed budget, Action
later session.
11. Gene Hart, Director of Missions Search Con
presented for recommendation, Rev. Bill Lamb as ou
missions. Mr. Lamb addressed the Association. Actio
a later session.
12. Waldo Early asked that a letter of remembrance ai
sent to Rev. Willie O. Carr.   Motion passed.
13. Tony Wilson, Constitution Committee Chairma
amendment to the constitution and moved its adop
deferred to the second day's session.
14. The Association sang "There Is A Name I Love To
15. Agency Reports were given as follows:
        A. Christian Literature/Biblical Recorder
        B. Baptist Foundation
        C. American Bible Society
        D. Annuity
16. Edwin Coats brought a message.
17. Michael Shook, host pastor, gave greetings from tl
Rowan.
18. The Association sang "He Keeps Me Singing"
19. Reports of the Social Service Institutions were giv
        A. Baptist Retirement Home.   Millard J
        B. Baptist Hospital   Gerald Q

20. Calvin Knight brought a message
21. New Pastors were recognized by Don Coley:
            James Parsons - Concord
            Steven Moore - Johnson
            Randy Outland - Mount Vernon
            Ottis King - Wells Chapel
            Karry Godwin - Music/Youth Minister -
            Ric Durham - Youth - Warsaw
            Arledge Castle - Deaf Ministry, Poston
            William Ortega - Spanish
            Nathaniel J. McManus - Brown
22. Raymond Futch sang a solo of inspiration
23. A.R. Teachey read the Scripture for the sermon
24. Jerry Kinlaw brought the annual sermon.
25. Moderator Coley led in prayer of thanksgiving and
evening meal.

FIRST DAY EVENING SESSION
1. The Rowan Baptist Choir brought special music.
2. Moderator Coley called the Eastern Association to
October 28, 1985.
3. The Association sang "I Stand Amazed In The Pre
4. Ottis King read Scripture and led in prayer

5. Missions Ministries Director, Cathy Hopkins, presented the Missions Ministries Development Program Committees and they reported as follows:

    Deaf Ministry - Sylvia Knight & Arledge Castles
    Literacy Ministry - Florence Hoover
    Mentally Handicapped Ministry - Margaret Musselwhite
    Senior Adult Ministry - Doris Carroll
    Migrant Ministry - Andy Wood

6. The Association sang "To God Be The Glory"
7. The Rowan Baptist Choir brought special music
8. Rev. Larry Phillips, Missionary to Peru, brought our missionary message
9. Moderator Coley, adjourned the session with prayer

SECOND DAY - OCTOBER 29, 1985

1. Moderator Don Coley, called the Association to order at 9:30 A.M. at Poston Baptist Church, Wallace, North Carolina
2. The Association sang " Blessed Assurance"
3. Randy Outland read Scripture and led in prayer
4. E.C. Mattocks, Clerk, reported registration representing 32 churches and moved that the 124 messengers present constitute a quorum. Motion passed.
5. Miscellaneous Business
    Tony Wilson brought the recommended change to the constitution from the Constitution Committee. Motion passed.
6. Don Coley, host pastor, extended greetings and welcome from Poston Baptist Church
7. Standing Committees Reported:
    History - Waldo Early
    Ordination - Michael Shook
    Stewardship - Gene Hart
    Evangelism - Dennis Knight
    Media - Michael Shook
    Properties - Jake Carroll
8. Gene Hart of the Director of Missions Search Committee recommended William C. (Bill) Lamb as our new director of missions. Motion was seconded and by unanimous standing vote, Rev. Bill Lamb was called. Rev. and Mrs. Lamb addressed the Association and former Director, Clyde Davis, addressed the Association, also.
9. Gene Hart of the Stewardship Committee moved the adoption of the proposed budget. Motion passed.
10. David Moore moved the the report of Christian Higher Education be adopted. Motion passed.

11. Henry Stokes brought a message
12. Ferrell Miller gave the report of the Nominating Committee and moved the adoption. Passed.

13. Tony Gurganus moved that the report of the Committee on Committees by adopted. Passed.
14. Reports of appointed committees
    A. Resolutions Committee – Raleigh Carroll, Chairman
    B. Time, Place, Preacher – Mack Musselwhite, Chairman
       October 27, 1986 – Warsaw Baptist Church
       October 28, 1986 – Bear Marsh Church
       Preacher – E.C. Mattocks, Alternate – David Moore
    C. Memorials Committee; Michael Shook, Chairman
15. The Association sang "Heavenly Sunlight"
16. Church Program Organization Reports
    Church Music – L.E. Williamson
    Church Training – Don Coley
    Sunday School – James Hartsell
    VBS – Dennis Knight
    WMU – Helen Register
17. Nancy Curtis brought a message
18. The Association sang "Footsteps of Jesus"
19. Raymond Futch brought a solo of inspiration
20. David Moore moved the adoption of the Baptist Children's Homes report. Passed
21. E.C. Mattocks, clerk, read a letter to be sent to Rev. Willie O. Carr
22. James Pardue brought our doctrinal message
23. New Moderator Lucille Yancey and Vice-Moderator Dennis Knight were introduced to the Association
24. Lucille Yancey adjourned the 158th Annual Session of Eastern Baptist Association with prayer

RESOLUTIONS COMMITTEE REPORT

Whereas: the North Carolina Eastern Baptist Association has held its one-hundred fifty eighth annual session in the spirit of Christ and to the glory of God, Be it resolved:
   1. that we express our deepest appreciation to the officers of the Eastern Baptist Association for their splendid planning and execution of this 158th session and especially to our moderator, Don Coley for the past three years of dedicated leadership.
   2. That we express our deepest appreciation to the host churches, Rowan and Poston, assisted by Wells Chapel, for providing for our comforts in an excellent manner and for the scrumptious meals so beautifully and lovingly prepared and served.
   3. that we express our appreciation to Brother Clyde Davis and Thelma. They have served our association faithfully and unselfishly for over nine years and the success of this session is largely due to Brother Clyde's efforts. As they are retiring from service in the Eastern Association, we wish them Godspeed in their new mission ministry.

4. that we express our appreciation to Cathy Hopkins, our Missions Ministry Director for her dedication to missions and for the leadership and challenge she has given us.

5. that we commend each of our churches and their missions involvement, especially Poston in their establishing an ongoing deaf ministry and Clinton First in their establishing a Spanish ministry.

6. that in anticipation of the Good News America - God Loves You revivals, we strive together to fulfill our theme to "demonstrate God's love" by being ambassadors for our Lord Jesus Christ here in our association.

7. that we covenant to pray for a unity of spirit in mission within our Southern Baptist Convention that "BOLD MISSION THRUST" might become a reality.

8. that we express our appreciation to the Eastern Baptist Association search committee for their dedication in finding a new Director of Missions, Bill Lamb, and that we pledge to Mr. & Mrs. Lamb our unity and support as he begins his ministry with us on January 1, 1986.

Respectfully submitted,
Raleigh Carroll, Chairman
Sylvia Knight
Ottis L. King

EASTERN BAPTIST ASSOCIATION
P.O. BOX 712
Warsaw, North Carolina 28328

Telephone (919) 293-7077

William C. Lamb, D.O.M.

OUR BELOVED DEAD

ALBERTSON - Deacon Thurman Stroud
ALUM SPRINGS - Kate Herring Williams
BEAR MARSH - Weldon Swinson, Mary Lou King, Ruby
            Best
BEULAH - Rita Register
BROWN - Ruby Hall, Bessie Jackson
CALVARY - Mallard Davis, Henry Jones
CENTER - Deacon David Lee Blackburn
CLINTON - Robert F. Shields, Haywood McLamb, Chris
            Mrs. Robert Shields, Mrs. Jesse Butler, Tor
            Mrs. Art Tenglund, James Butler, Mrs. E. \
CONCORD - Harvey Lane, Raymond Ezzell
CORINTH - Lester Fussell, Maydell Fussell, Mary Young
DOBSON CHAPEL - Deacon Edwin L. Register, Jimmy B
EVERGREEN - Jack Stuart
FAISON - Harold Precythe, Robert Matthews
GARLAND - Thelma Stafford, Lillie Powell, Mary Norris
GARNER'S CHAPEL - Inez Garner, Lola Kornegay
GROVE PARK - Blanche Phillips, Georgia Crumpler, Fra
            Lucille Hollingsworth
HICKORY GROVE - William Strickland, Mary Rhodes Wee
IMMANUEL - Furman Tyndall, James Goff, William Melso
            Michael Register
INGOLD - John H. Burch, Eva R. Smith, Oscar McLamb
            Raymond Bordeaux
ISLAND CREEK - Marshall Walker, Anna Brown, Ruth B
            T. Blanton, Sallie Evans, Deacon Garland K
            Rivenbark, Raymond Fields, Laney Teachey
JOHNSON - Clara Todd, Larry Brown
KENANSVILLE - James D. Kornegay, Allie Williams
MAGNOLIA - Atlas Baker, Deacon Norwood Chestnutt, /
            Gertrude Rouse, Hazel Kissner
MOUNT GILEAD - Cyrus Boney, Laura Ella Smith, Lola
MOUNT OLIVE - Eva E. Brogden, Eloise B. Parker, Sta
            Ethel B. Guy, Gatsie J. Wagstaff
MOUNT VERNON - Arthur Pope, Mary Danzel Warwick,
            Garland Barber
NEW HOPE - Grace Pollock, Thelma C. Bland
PINEY GROVE - Deacon Norman Rackley, Deacon M.L. I
            J.E. Miller, Deacon B. L. Brewer, Billy Bre
            Warrick, Ruth Darden
POPLAR GROVE - David Hinson, Lela Turlington
POSTON - Thelma Murray, Charlie H. Boney
ROSE HILL - Roland Henderson, Annie James, Mary Eth
            Herbert Blanchard
ROWAN - Worth Baldwin, J.M. Burgess, Taft Merritt, [
            Varon Boney

SHARON - Annie Cavenaugh, Marvin Wall, Oscar Homer James,
        Eunice S. Hursey
SHILOH - Hettie Sholar, Emily Houston, John Lanier, Mary R. Lanier,
        Albert James
SILOAM - Callie Jones, Charlie Bass
TEACHEY - None
TURKEY - Grover Westbrook, Linda Naylor, Bromley Jennette,
        Deacon Hubert West
UNION GROVE - Delma George Sutton
WARSAW - Marie Bennett, Deacon Bill Knowles, Sr., Naomi Chambers,
        Deacon Kenneth Rivenbark, Walter Bostic, Estelle Porter
WELLS CHAPEL - Adelle D. Register, Naomi Johnson, Deacon C. Nolan
        Cook

COMMITTEE ON COMMITTEE REPORT

EVANGELISM
Dennis Knight, Chairman 1986
Oliver Skerrett 1987
E.C. Mattocks 1988

PASTOR SUPPORT
*Raleigh Carroll 1986
*Randy Outland, Chairman 1987
 David Moore 1988

HISTORICAL
Waldo Early 1986
Shelton Justice, Chairman 1987
Charlotte Hartsell 1988

STEWARDSHIP
Ed Colwell 1986
Pricilla McGill 1986
Jimmy Strickland 1986
Michael Shook 1987
Anthony Gurganus 1987
Tony Wilson, Chairman 1987
Ernest Johnson 1988
Francis Clifton 1988
John Flake 1988

MEDIA LIBRARY
Joyce Lucas 1986
Thelma Davis 1987
Barbara Shook, Chairman 1988

NOMINATING
H. J. Register 1986
Charles Lee Pope 1986
Jane Kaleel 1987
Lois Colwell 1987
Anthony Gurganus, Chairman 1988
Davis Benton 1988

PROGRAM
Eugene Hardin 1986
Larry Harper 1987
Gene Hart, Chairman 1988

ORDINATION
Millard Johnson 1986
Don Coley, Chairman 1986
Mack Musselwhite 1987
Shelton Justice 1987
Michael Shook 1988
John A. Johnson 1988

* Serving to fill unexpired terms

Respectfully submitted,
Anthony Gurganus, Chairman

MEDIA LIBRARY COMMITTEE REP(

The duty of the Media Library is to encourage promotion of libraries in churches. The committee this reponsibility in several ways.

Members of the committee attended an excl Library Retreat at Caraway.

Two meetings were held in different areas of t with helps being offered for successfully promoting th

The Key Leadership conference in August allow of ideas and a discussion of problems that churches their Media Library.

Respectfully
Barbara Shoc

ASSOCIATIONAL EXECUTIVE BOARD REPORT

The Executive Board met for three quarter purpose of acting for the Association between Ar following is a summary of actions taken:

February 11, 1985 - WARSAW BAPTIST CHURCH

Don Coley moderated with twenty-five churche: Missions Development Program recommended that the the establishment of a deaf ministry at Poston, and endorse the establishment of a Spanish Language Mi from the reserve fund to secure a Spanish pastor. I Henry Herring moved that $1,000.00 be appropriate the Social Security of the Director of Missions Deve and committee reports were given.

April 29, 1985 - MOUNT GILEAD BAPTIST CHURCH

Don Coley moderated with twenty-seven churcl motion was made to send a letter of appreciation for three-hundred dollar gift from the Commodore ar Davis Estate via Hickory Grove Baptist Church. Properties Committee recommended that the trustees given permission to trade a plot of land the Associa Township, with Howard Caroll, and to close the ave properties. Motion passed. Department and committ

July 29, 1985 - TEACHEY BAPTIST CHURCH

Don Coley moderated with thirty-churches Missions Development Council recommended that the from the Cooperative Missions Funds of the Baptist ! the Home Mission Board for 1986 - $35,000.00; for and for 1988 - $33,000.00. Motion passed. The / recommended the following: 1) that a Director Committee be formed; 2) that Mr. Davis be given the amount for July, and that he serve as interim throu if the Search Committee has no nomination by Octob continue as interim at a rate of $610.00 per mor Department and committee reports were given.

Respectfully sub
E.C. Mattacks, (

CHURCH TRAINING REPORT

Church Training is all about developing believers. I am delighted to see how our programs continue to support this goal and I rejoice in the increasing influence of Church Training in the Eastern Baptist Association.

On behalf of the Association, I would like to thank Rene' Carroll and Phyllis Durham for their contribution to our Church Training program. Although they will not be on the team officially, I know that they will continue to be an asset to us. Thanks also to Rose Pleasant, who has served faithfully and energetically with our youth division. Her leadership assured 2 successful youth gatherings this year. We are proud to have her continue on our team.

This past year has been a year of evaluating and re-directing. With the help of pastors who shared their thoughts and perceptions, Mr. Davis and I uncovered many areas where Church Training could benefit our local churches. This year we hope to re-educate the churches to these benefits by helping them discover their equipping needs and supplying the direction to fill the needs. We will also strive to involve every congregation in some kind of Church Training.

The 1985 Children's and Youth Bible Drills were a great success! With Calvary as our host church, many came to watch as 100% of the participants displayed their skills and advanced to the state level. The Association was also honored for Clinton First to host state drills. I challenge more churches to involve their children and youth in this valuable program next year.

The 1984 "M" Night was hosted by Poston Baptist Church. Nine churches were represented with 4 pastors, 17 Church Training directors, and a total attendance of 171. Eugene Warrick spoke on the Home Mission Board's need for people to become personally involved in missions by volunteering their time. The 1985 "M" Night will be held at Grove Park in Clinton, November 25.

Finally, I would like to welcome Randy Outland to our Church Training team. Randy will be our adult consultant and is a certified Masterlife group facilitator. Randy, Rose and I are ready, willing and able to help you with your Church Training needs this coming year as we develop believers for God's glory.

Respectfully submitted,
Hal Bilbo, Director

DEAF MINISTRIES COMMITTEE REPORT

During the past year the Deaf Ministries Committee has tried to reach out in the association in several ways. We have encouraged churches to help us become aware of deaf persons in our area so that we could more effectively reach out to them.

Our major goal for the year was to begin offer
opportunity of a Sunday worship service. On March
was begun at Poston Church. Under the leadership
Coley and the Deaf Ministries Committee, Poston call
become their Minister to the Deaf. This began as a
by June became a weekly ministry. This ministry a
be a growing and vital experience for deaf persons.
We as a committee, do appreciate the many w
other of our churches have served in this m
Association.

Respectfull'
Sylvia Knig

HISTORY OF POSTON BAPTIST CH

As we think of the church "History" of Poston
realize it is "His Story". The story of the blessin
Christ is leading His people in the building of a great

Dr. Eugene Poston, then the Pastor of Wal
saw the need of a mission in Tin City. In the b
1954, Dr. Poston held a revival under a tent wi
starting a mission.

Mrs. Jessie Harrell gave the lot where the
building is now located and later the church bought
adjoining piece of land which gave the mission adec
to build and provide parking space. Dr. Poston s
from 1954 until 1956.

In the year 1956 we called Rev. Claude
During that year a second story was completed and fu

In June 1959 the church was led to call Re
pastor. In the year 1962 the Educational Building
roof was rebuilt. The church parsonage was built in

The church called Rev. Tommy Dees in 196
was purchased from Mrs. Harrell and she willed he
Poston Baptist Church.

In April 1970 the church called Rev. J. Hube
church installed a new heating and air conditioning un

In November 1975 the church was led to a
Willis. Under his leadership our new sanctuary was b

In April 1980 the church was led to call Rev.
pastor. During that year we paid off the indebtednes

In February 1983 Rev. Hal Bilbo was called
Youth and Education..

In October 1984 ground was broken for a new f

Truly God has been with us all the way a
praise His name and give Him the glory!

WMU 76th ANNUAL SESSION MINUTES

The 76th Woman's Missionary Union Annual Session of Eastern Baptist Association was held at Grove Park Baptist Church, Clinton, North Carolina on Thursday, April 25, 1985. At 5 p.m., Mrs. H.J. Register, Director, called the meeting to order with a word of welcome to members and guests. Invocation was given by Rev. Clyde Davis, Director of Missions, and the welcome by Mrs. Delbert Carr. Prayer Calendar was presented by Mrs. James Pardue. The program theme was "By Love Compelled".

The minutes of the previous annual session were read and approved.

The secretary reported an old bank balance of $113.20. Since WMU is now included in the Association budget, the motion was made that a contribution of $113.20 be made to the Fannie E.S. Heck Conference Room Fund at the National Office Complex, WMU, SBC, Birmingham, Alabama. Motion carried.

The following were elected as Nominating Committee 1986-87: Mrs. James Hartsell, Mrs. Norwood Carter and Mrs. Gene Hart.

REPORTS:

The following age-level directors made reports and offered assistance in beginning new organizations: Mrs. Andy Wood-Mission Friends, Mrs. DeWitt King-Girls in Action, Mrs. Ted Lockerman - Acteens, Mrs. Eugene Hardin-Baptist Women, Mrs. Larry Price-Baptist Young Women.

Mrs. W.S. Wells, Jr., Enlistment/Enlargement Director, reported a membership goal of 3300 by 1988(increase of 100%). Group singing of "Come Grow With Us" was led by Baptist Women from Sharon Baptist Church.

Mrs. Edwin Peterson, Centennial Chairman presented goals and information regarding the North Carolina centennial celebration to be held in 1986.

Mrs. Johnny Carlton, Mission Action Chairman, reported contribution of $119.16 toward purchase of hematoflouromet, a lead poisoning detection machine, to be used by the lab at Tri-County Health Center. The machine is the property of the N.C. Baptist State WMU. She also expressed appreciation for the toys and books brought to the annual session by GA's and Acteens for the migrant children.

Mrs. Michael Hopkins, Mission Ministries Director, thanked the group for their continuing support of missions. Mrs. Sylvia Knight gave a report on the Deaf Ministry and led the congregation in singing a song in sign language. Mrs. Zulema Reyes, a member of Faison Baptist Church and the Hispanic Mission, gave her testimony after which she and her five daughters sang songs in English and Spanish.

Rev. Clyde Davis expressed appreciation for Mrs. Hopkins' dedication to missions ministry in the association.

Ms. Carolyn Hopkins, N.C. Acteen Consultant, brought greetings from the State WMU and presented recognition certificate of Merit achievement for 1983-84 to the association. Rose Hill Baptist Church also received certificate for Merit achievement 1983-84.

Mrs. Billy Chesnutt, Chairman, presented the 1985-1986 WMU officers for election. The Nominating Committee report was accepted and the following were elected:

Director	Mrs. H.J. Register
Ass't. Director	
Enlistment/Enlargement	Mrs. W. S. Wells, Jr.
Secretary-Treasurer	Mrs. Erwin W. Lee
Baptist Women Director	Mrs. Eugene Hardin
Ass't. BW Director	Mrs. Raymond Blanchard, Jr.
Baptist Young Women Director	Mrs. Larry Price
Ass't, BYW Director	Mrs. Larry Bell
Acteens Director	Mrs. Ted Lockerman
Ass't. Acteens Director	Mrs. Byron Bass
GA Director	Mrs. Hugh Matthews
Ass't. GA Director	Mrs. DeWitt King
Mission Friends Director	Mrs. Andy Wood
Ass't. Mission Friends Director	Mrs. Elliott Tew
Mission Action Director	Mrs. Johnny Carlton
Ass't. Mission Action Director	Mrs. Albert Kaleel
Centennial Chairman	Mrs. Edwin Peterson
Area Director(Clinton)	Mrs. Robert E. Strickland
Area Director(Garland-Star)	Mrs. Janie Strickland
Area Director(Mount Olive)	Mrs. Virginia Hines
Area Director(Faison-Warsaw)	Mrs. Katie Kirby
Area Director(Wallace-Rose Hill)	Mrs. Linda Hawes

The officers were installed with prayer of dedication by Mrs. Coleman Carter.

Special music "Thou Art Worthy" was presented by Grove Park Baptist Church Choir.

Mrs. Eugene Hardin invited the 77th Annual Session (April, 1986) to meet with Sharon Baptist Church, Shiloh Church assisting.

Mrs. Erwin Lee, Place Committee chairman, announced meeting schedule for next five years:

1986	77th Annual Session	Sharon Baptist Church, Shiloh assisting
1987	78th Annual Session	Mount Olive Baptist Church
1988	79th Annual Session	Mount Gilead Baptist Church
1989	80th Annual Session	Johnson Baptist Church, Magnolia assist.
1990	81st Annual Session	Corinth Baptist Church

The speaker for the evening session was Dr. I. Ruth Martin, Associate Professor of Religion, Pembroke State University. She was introduced by Rev. Mack Musselwhite. Dr. Martin spent six weeks during the summer of 1984 in Liberia as a volunteer missionary. She brought an inspiring and challenging missions message. Information regarding Bibles for Liberia was given. Dr. Martin gave the benediction.

Respectfully submitted,
Mrs. H.J. Register, Director
Mrs. Erwin W. Lee, Secretary

195 Registered
27 Churches represented

FINANCIAL REPORT:

1984-85 Budget	$1,215.00
Balance 04-25-85	$1,184.57

HISTORY OF ROWAN BAPTIST CHURCH

Twenty-seven years before the signing of the Declaration of Independence, Edward Brown had enough members to form a church in the community now known as Rowan. Great Cohara Baptist Church was formed in 1749, a General Baptist Church lax in doctrine but placing great emphasis on the necessity of the new birth. The minutes later began calling the church Rowan without explanation as to the time of or reason for the name change. The first building was a log structure located about a mile and a half from the present location and was used for the first struggling ten years. Harsh restrictions were placed on churches during the Colonial period and Rowan suffered especially from Governor Tryon's strictly enforced laws including the one that forbade any minister other than one of the Church of England to perform marriage ceremonies. Edward Brown had been trained in the Church of England but was later converted, baptized and ordained a Baptist preacher. He served until his death in 1783.

On October 15, 1759, the church reorganized as a Particular Baptist Church and rebuilt the log building, which was used until 1808 when the first structure was erected, called Rowan Meeting House and used until 1903, nearly all of the 19th century. The building was reflective of the life of the time. On the side, up next to the pulpit was the front door where all women and girls sat on the preacher's left. In the end of the building opposite the pulpit was a door entered by men and boys who sat on the other side. Across the end of the building behind the pulpit was a room which could be used by slaves to hear the sermon through a shutter-type window.

The fourth building program involved erecting another frame structure in 1902-03. On October 9, 1910 a special meeting was called for the purpose of appointing a committee to study enlarging the building. A note of the cost is entered in the March, 1912 minutes: $573.87. Membership during the four-year period of J.M. Page's pastorate (1906-10) increased from 50 to 150 and the minutes indicate the spiritual condition was "the best in the history of the church".

At a meeting December 5, 1937, the trustees were authorized to sell the church building and to put the money from such sale into a new building. The construction of the first brick building was under the direction of Monroe Marshburn, a member of the church, and with the pastoral guidance of H.G. Bryant.

The educational plant was replaced in 1953 with L.C. Boney as contractor and M.M. Johnson as pastor. Redecoration and carpeting in the sanctuary; central heat and air conditioning; and paving of parking areas were undertaken and completed during 1962-64. The massive oaks and whispering pines that were for 200 years shade for fellowship among the members after Sunday worship, remain in the memory of some members. The church bell had been missed since the erection of the brick building, so in 1971, the people voted to rebuild the front porch and to add a steeple with an electrically-controlled bell.

In 1982 the building was expanded to include the addition of office, library, fellowship hall and classrooms.

The first mention of a member of the church being ordained to preach was in April 1785, when "Fleet Cooper was ordained and given the pastoral care of the church." He is mentioned again as pastor for a brief time in 1801. Other ministers from Rowan include Joshua Sikes in 1790, H.H. Duncan in 1875, Ellis Pope in 1947, Milton Boone in 1950 and Tommy Denton in 1973.

Roberts "for the purpose of organizing a church at Clinton."

The first mention of Sunday School is on the second Sunday in March, 1877, when J.J. Stringfield was elected superintendent. For a number of years the Sunday School met at 2:30 on Sunday afternoons. Preaching was on Saturday night and Sunday morning.

October 1, 1911, the church met in conference and appointed "three committeemen to act during the association and to see that not any picture taking should be allowed on the church ground and also to keep off any salesmen of any kind."

Minutes indicated that over the years a strict watch was kept over the morals of the members. Members were visited and called before the congregation for walking disorderly. In 1859 a resolution was adopted to exclude members for intoxication. It was not unusual for one to confess to the church and ask forgiveness for misbehavior. No attendance was sure to call for a visit by a committee from the church.

At a meeting on March 8, 1913, Pastor DeLoatch told the people they needed to increase personal services by looking after members temporally as well as spiritually. Committees were appointed for visitation and "to look after the sick" and to report at later meetings.

The Woman's Missionary Union was organized in 1888 in the Southern Baptist Convention and the local group held its first meeting in 1906 under the leadership of Mrs. Berta Peterson, under an oak tree in the backyard at the home of Mrs. Kate Evans.

The church has had an active training program since the Baptist Young People's Union was organized in the early 1930's.

The Brotherhood was organized at Rowan in 1946.

At a business meeting on February 3, 1924 it was decided that a pastor's home be built on land donated for that purpose by Mr. and Mrs. John Peterson. A two-story house was built on the donated site located at Highway #421, about a mile west of the church. On November 14, 1929, the house burned; it was replaced with a new one, much of the physical labor being performed by the pastor and his wife. This house was sold when the church built the present pastorium in 1959.

On October 30, 1949, Rowan's bicentennial was celebrated with an all-day program that drew a crowd of several hundred people. The morning sermon was delivered by former Pastor Edward A. Walker. Other former pastors in attendance were J.M. Page, N.E. Gresham, and H.C Bryant. Dr. R. R. McCullouch was pastor at the time of the celebration.

Currently Michael Shook is pastor. Living pastors are M.M. Johnson, E.S. Morgan and E.C. Chamblee.

SUNDAY SCHOOL REPORT

"And seeing the multitudes, he [Christ] went up into a mountain: and when he was set, his disciples came unto Him:

2. And He opened His mouth, and He taught them..." Matthew 5:1 - 2. As we hear the scripture we must believe in a growing Sunday School. Those multitudes are still with us today and we have the privilege of bringing them into our Sunday School to be taught God's Word.

The past five years, 1980-1985 have been growth years in our Sunday Schools. "8.5 by '85" has paid off in our churches by having more people in Bible study than ever before. In the past couple of years our own Association has seen a slowing up of a loss trend and last year was up about 28. "8.5 by '85" is now behind us with victories in some areas and some losses in others. We must now look to the future.

"Victory Now/Challenge Tomorrow" was the theme of this year's state Sunday School Fall Conferences. It expresses a great truth. We have had victories but now we have challenges to face. A recent survey has shown that only one out of eight Americans are enrolled in Bible study. "Challenge 10/90" has been conceived to reach these people for Bible study and Christ. "Challenge 10/90" is a challenge to have 10 million people enrolled in our Sunday Schools by 1990.

Your local ASSISTeam has been expanded this year to help our churches to enroll people and improve Bible study in our Sunday Schools. Last year the team led several associational conferences. Several team members were invited into at least 12 of our churches to lead studies or for personal consultation. We commend the team for their diligent work among our churches. We look forward to even greater work this coming year.

Respectfully submitted,
James Hartsell, Chairman

EVANGELISM REPORT

Evangelism is not an option in our churches. Our Lord's clearest

At the writing of this report 1984-85 baptism
available. However, during simultaneous campaig
baptisms always increases, oftimes greatly so. Let
New America"   will see many won to the Lord.
A goal is that all persons in North Carolina wi
Christ by the end of 1986. Let us strive that all in
will hear.

Respectfully submitted
Dennis Knight, Chairma

WOMANS' MISSIONARY UNION REPORT
"By Love Compelled" was the WMU emphas
objective was to involve each church member in a
ministry and witness, with mission action as the major
North Carolina WMU has launched a grow
Grow With Us" which is North Carolina's part of
"Vision 88". The challenge is to double our member
is the centennial year for WMU-SBC. WMU in Easter
reported 1726 members as of October 1, 1984.   Our g
Associational leaders were trained at Ca
Goldsboro. A leader conference for church WMU v
October 4, 1984 at the Warsaw Church.
Mission Action activities included gifts to
Correctional Center for Women in Raleigh, Health I
Migrant Ministries, monies given to help the
self-involvement for many of the ladies in the differ
Association.
The Annual Session was held at Grove I
with 195 in attendance and 27 churches represented.
The ladies were involved in Mission Action
Ministries of our Association, and helping with Ch
Women at NC Correctional Center.
The Annual Session was hosted by G
Twenty-seven out of forty-one churches were repres
one-hundred and ninety-five in attendance. Gr
delicious meal. In the evening session the choir of
mood for worship and Dr. I. Ruth Martin challenge
should not be just words and talk; it must be tru
itself in action." (I John 3:18 TEV).

Respectfully submi
Helen Register, Di

VACATION BIBLE SCHOOL REPORT
This has been a good year for Vacation Bible
26, 1985, 100 VBS workers from 22 churches attend
VBS Clinic. The conferences were led by members
Later in the spring, on May 9, David Moore led
Mission VBS and Backyard Bible Clubs. Seven wer
this clinic.

-32-

Church	Enroll-ment	Avg. Att.	No Days	Hours Daily	Prof. Faith	Achieve ment Level
Beulah	73	67	5	3	0	*
Brown	68	58	5	2	0	Merit
Calvary	89	85	6	2½	1	Distinguished
Clinton	92	70	5	2½	*	*
Concord	70	64	6	2½	0	Advanced
Corinth	80	72	5	2½	0	Merit
Evergreen	65	61	5	2½	*	*
Faison	90	73	6	*	*	Merit
Garner's Chapel	26	25	5	2½	0	*
Grove Park	119	89	6	2½	0	Merit
Immanuel	100	82	5	2	0	Merit
Ingold	65	57	5	2½	0	Merit
Island Creek	75	47	5	2	0	*
Kenansville	65	62	5	3	0	*
Magnolia	99	75	5	2	0	Merit
Mount Olive	169	146	5	3	0	Merit
Mount Vernon	85	71	5	2½	2	Merit
New Hope	30	28	5	2½	0	Merit
Piney Grove	101	80	5	2½	4	*
Poplar Grove	28	27	5	2½	0	Merit
Poston	90	75	5	3	7	Advanced
Rose Hill	55	53	5	3	*	*
Rowan	103	90	5	3	4	Distinguished
Sharon	60	56	5	2	0	Merit
Siloam	67	56	5	3	0	*
Teachey	24	19	5	2½	0	*
Turkey	75	61	5	2½	*	Advanced
Warsaw	61	59	5	1½	2	*

* Not Indicated

CHURCH MUSIC REPORT

In Colossians 3:16 we read "Let the word of Christ dwell in you richly in all wisdom; teaching and admonishing one another in psalms and hymns and spiritual songs, singing with grace in your hearts to the Lord." The churches in Eastern Baptist Association take great joy in spreading the "word of Christ" through song. As they join their voices in praise to Him each Sunday in their churches, they "teach" young Christians the very foundation of our faith, and they remind older Christians of great Biblical truths to sustain them in their daily walk with the Master. Therefore, their task becomes one of missions - - to develop and strengthen believers through music. What a responsibility and what a challenge! May we all be willing to accept this task and move forward for Jesus as ministers through song.

Respectfully submitted,
Jean Hatch, Chairman

ORDINATION COMMITTEE REPORT

The Ordination Committee interviewed and ordained two new pastors during 1985. Scott Bass of the Mount Gilead Church , and Arledge Castles of the Poston Church.

Respectfully submitted,
Donald Coley, Chairman

NOMINATING COMMITTEE REPORT

The Nominating Committee places in nomination the names of   the following persons to serve in positions as indicated for the A s sociational Year, 1985-1986:

GENERAL OFFICERS

Moderator	Lucille Yancey
Vice-Moderator	Dennis Knight
Clerk	David Moore
Associate Clerk	Farrell Miller
Treasurer	Bill Boyette
Associate Treasurer	Jo Neal Robinson

BROTHERHOOD

Director	Woody Brinson

CHURCH MUSIC

Director	Raymond Futch

SUNDAY SCHOOL

Director	James Hartsell
Teaching Improvement & Training	David Moore
Outreach Leader	Lynn Hilton
Vacation Bible School	Dennis Knight

Adult

Younger	Michael Shook
Median Adult	Mack Musselwhite
Senior Adult	Debbie Futch
Homebound	Charlotte Hartsell

Youth

Senior Hi	L.E. Williamson
Junior Hi	Ric Durham

Children

Younger	Cathy Hopkins
Middle	Naomi Moore
Older	Andy Wood

Pre-School
    Middle   Jenny Strickland
    Older   Tempie Wood

Special
   Mentally Handicapped   Margaret Musselwhite

CHURCH TRAINING

Director   Hal Bilbo
Adult   Randy Outland
Youth   Rose Pleasant
Children   Janie Brown & Denise Smith

WOMANS MISSIONARY UNION

Director   Helen Register
Assistant Director   Mary Evelyn Wells
Enlistment/Enlargement   Mary Evelyn Wells
Secretary/Treasurer   Edith Lee
Baptist Women Director   Donis Hardin
Assistant Baptist Women Director Shelby Blanchard
Baptist Young Women Director   Cynthia Price
Assistant BYW Director   Carrie Bell
Acteens Director   Gloria Lockerman
Assistant Acteens Director   Donna Bass
GA Director   Phyllis Matthews
Assistant GA Director   Ruth King
Mission Friends Director   Tempie Wood
Assistant Mission Friends Director Frances Tew
Mission Action Director   Connie Carlton
Mission Action Assistant Director Jane Kaleel
Centennial Chairman   Inez Peterson
Area Directors:
   Clinton Area   Louise Strickland
   Garland & Star Area   Janie Strickland
   Mount Olive Area   Virginia Hines
   Faison & Warsaw Area   Katie Kirby
   Wallace-Rose Hill Area   Linda Hawes

SCHEDULE OF MEETING PLACES FOR WMU ANNUAL SESSION
1986   77th Annual Session   Sharon Baptist Church
1987   78th Annual Session   Mount Olive Baptist Church
1988   79th Annual Session   Mount Gilead Baptist Church
1989   80th Annual Session   Johnson Baptist Church

ASSOCIATIONAL MISSIONS DEVELOPMENT PROGRAM

MISSIONS COUNCIL
   Davis Benton, Director   Margaret Musselwhite
   Kenneth Goodson   Doris Carroll
   James Pardue   Mary Lee Jones
   Florence Hoover   Andy Wood

COMPONENTS

DEAF MINISTRIES

Mary Lee Jones, Chairman
Sylvia Knight
Phyllis Durham

MIGRANT MINISTRIES

Andy Wood, Chairman
Gail Naylor
Wilson Spencer
Lynn Hilton
Jane Kaleel

LITERACY MINISTRIES

Florence Hoover, Chairman
Faye Gaddy
Thelma Davis

MENTALLY HANDICAPPED MINISTRIES

Margaret Musselwhite, Chairman
Judith Pardue
Hanna Farmer

SENIOR ADULT MINISTRIES

Doris Carroll, Chairman
Joyce Warren
Lori Jackson
Lois Colwell

TRUSTEES

DeWitt King		1988
Charles L. Matthis	(Unexpired term)	1987
Larry Harper, Chairman		1986

DENOMINATIONAL REPRESENTATIVES

American Bible Society	H.J. Register
Childrens' Homes	John A. Johnson
Baptist Retirement Homes	Millard M. Johnson
Christian Education	
Cooperative Program	Albert Pope
Annuity Board	Waldo Early
Baptist Foundation	Ken Durham
Baptist Hospital	Gerald Quinn
Christian Literature/Biblical Recorder	T. N. Cooper

Presented by: Farrell Miller, Chairman
George McGill
H.J. Register
Charles Lee Pope
Jane Kaleel
Lois Colwell

LITERACY COMMITTEE REPORT

During February (16th and 23rd) a Literacy Workshop was held at Clinton First to train teachers (persons) to teach reading and writing using the Laubach method. Lib Loftis, a teacher certified by the Home Mission Board, taught this workshop on Saturdays. Nineteen participated in this workshop and sixteen received certificates of completion.

Thelma Davis and Florence Hoover are tutoring thirteen Hispanic men at Turkey Baptist Church on Wednesday nights weekly, for two hours.

An ESOL (English for speakers of other languages) Workshop is scheduled for November 14, 15 and 16 on Thursday and Friday nights from 7:00 - 10:00 P.M. and on Saturday from 8:30 A.M. to 3:30 P.M.

We need much work in many areas of our association. We need volunteers - women or men. If you speak and write English, you qualify to participate. Now is the time to get trained. Please help! We need you.

Respectfully submitted,
Florence Hoover, Chairman

SENIOR ADULT MINISTRIES COMMITTEE REPORT

The Senior Adult Ministry Committee of Eastern Baptist Association has endeavored to increase the fellowship of Senior Adults throughout the Association by sponsoring rallies, conferences and trips, and through development of Senior Adult groups in the local church.

The first edition of the Senior Adult Newsletter was mailed in September to pastors and Senior Adult representatives in the local churches. The newsletter's purpose is to promote Eastern Baptist Association Senior Adult activities and events of interest to Senior Adults. Senior Adults are also encouraged to use their time and talents in volunteer service and ministry in Eastern Baptist Association.

Respectfully submitted,
Senior Adult Committee

MENTALLY HANDICAPPED MINISTRY COMMITTEE REPORT

The Mentally Handicapped Ministry Committee sponsored the Annual Christmas Banquet for the Mentally Handicapped at Rowan Church. Churches across the Association provided food and gifts for the approximately fifty people in attendance. Special music was presented by Rev. and Mrs. Hal Bilbo and the devotional thought was given by Rev. Michael Shook.

Margaret Musselwhite, a committee member and an ASSISTeam member specializing in the mentally handicapped Sunday School ministry, has led in several Sunday School leadership conferences and is available for training in the local church upon request.

Respectfully submitted,
Mentally Handicapped Committee

REPORT OF SPANISH MINISTRY

The Spanish ministry of First Baptist Church has grown out of the ministry to migrants sponsored by our Association. After our team went to a migrant camp last summer, we began to be aware that some of these people had become residents of our area.

The State Convention sent three Spanish speaking people into our area to conduct a census. This census revealed, that indeed, there were Spanish speaking residents, and recommended that a Bible Class begin.

Rev. Mauricio Vargas conducted worship services on Sunday afternoons to begin the ministry. Then Rev. Augerro from Fayetteville was called as interim pastor. Then on June 1, 1985 Rev. William Ortego was called as minister.

Since June 1, services have been held each Sunday afternoon with Bible study before the worship hour. Attendance has reached a high of 50 with the average around 35. Seven people have been baptized and others attending are considering making this decision.

William has now enrolled in Campbell University for three days a week. He plans to marry in December and his wife also plans to attend Campbell.

This beginning ministry is now taking some form and we look forward to a more stable and growing ministry next year.

Respectfully submitted,
Rev. James Pardue, Clinton FBC

POSTON DEAF MINISTRY REPORT

Poston Baptist Church has for several years been praying that God would open up a way for a deaf ministry to be started in the church. The need was manifested by a deaf person being a member and no interpreter available to interpret God's Word. Her Sunday School class sponsored a banquet several years, around Thanksgiving, for the deaf in the area. Attendance at the banquet increased to such a degree that the church voted to undergird expenses for the banquet.

In 1983 a deaf committee was formed in the Association and in 1984 a service for the deaf was held in April at Corinth Church; a picnic was given by First Baptist Church, Warsaw, in August and the Annual Banquet was held at Poston in November.

Early in 1985 the Eastern Association voted to sponsor monthly services for the deaf with one-half of the the salary coming from the convention - a salary of $100.00 per week was designated. Poston accepted the challenge of sponsoring the ministry by offering facilities and on February 6 the church voted to call Arledge Castles, deaf student at Southeastern Seminary, Wake Forest, North Carolina, on a monthly basis with no expense to the church in regards to salary.

Work was begun in February but very soon the deaf began to ask why they could not have services every Sunday, and on May 19, 1985 in a special called business meeting the church voted to allocate $1500.00 to the deaf ministry and called Arledge Castles as pastor to the deaf. Arledge moved his travel trailer behind the church and is using facilities at the church; he travels from Wake Forest each week end and spends the night in the trailer and does out-reach work among the deaf in the area.

Sixteen deaf people have been enrolled and 5 have made professions of faith and been baptized into the fellowship.

On September 29 Arledge Castles was ordained in the First Baptist Church, Columbia, South Carolina, his home church. First Baptist had given him much support in the past and requested they be allowed this privilege and on the 75th anniversary of deaf work in the church, they ordained him. This is the first deaf person to be ordained into the gospel ministry in the State of South Carolina. Poston participated in the service with the presentation of a Bible from the church. Mary Boney, Chairman of the deaf ministry of the church made the presentation.

Respectfully submitted
Poston Baptist Church - Mary Boney, Chairman

MIGRANT MINISTRY COMMITTEE REPORT

Eastern Baptist Association has experienced the best year ever in Migrant Ministry because of the support of our churches and committed volunteers. A plus in the ministry has been the addition of Rev. William Ortega as pastor of the Mission of First Baptist Church, Clinton. He has been an asset to the Association as he has preached, witnessed and led Hispanics to Christ. We are appreciative to First Baptist Church, Clinton for working closely with us in Migrant Ministry.

The following facts give an overview of the year's ministry:

- Over 90 Hispanics made professions of faith
- 3 summer student missionaries were employed by the Association:
    1)Brenda Nowell, Campbell University graduate completed her third year with us
    2)Belinda Davis, Pembroke State University sophomore
    3) Jerry Miller, Ouachita Baptist University graduate
    (A Home Mission Board summer missionary)
- 5 Christian Service Corps Volunteers served in Eastern Association
    Clara Segars, Gainesville, Georgia
    Sue Williams, Raleigh, North Carolina
    Mary Grizzard, Emporia, Virginia
    Bernice Smith, Seaboard, North Carolina
    Vicki Puckett, Okeechobee, Florida
- Transportation was provided by Rowan Church, First Baptist, Clinton and Calvary Church
- Four Youth Mission Groups led in Backyard Bible Clubs: Piney Grove Church, First Baptist Church, Fayetteville, Georgia, First Baptist of Wallace, N.C, and Warsaw Baptist Church.
- 4 Migrant Evangelism Teams - Calvary Church, First Baptist, Clinton, Piney Grove and Island Creek
- Kings Worship Leadership, June 4 - August 6(Summer) (Tuesday Night Hispanic Services) Immanuel Church, Calypso Church, Rowan, Calvary, Poplar Grove, Magnolia and First Baptist of Mount Olive.
- Approximately 500 health kits distributed; food and clothing distributed to approximately 300 people. Over 250 Bibles dispersed
- Migrant summer school ministry at North Duplin Elementary led by First Baptist Church of Mount Olive - approximately 80-100 children involved

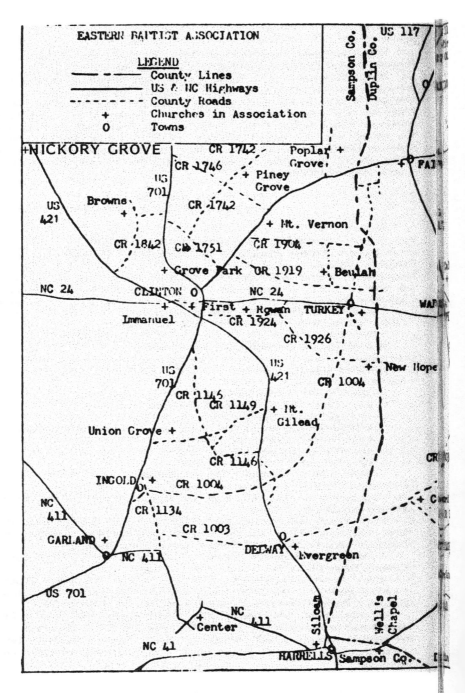

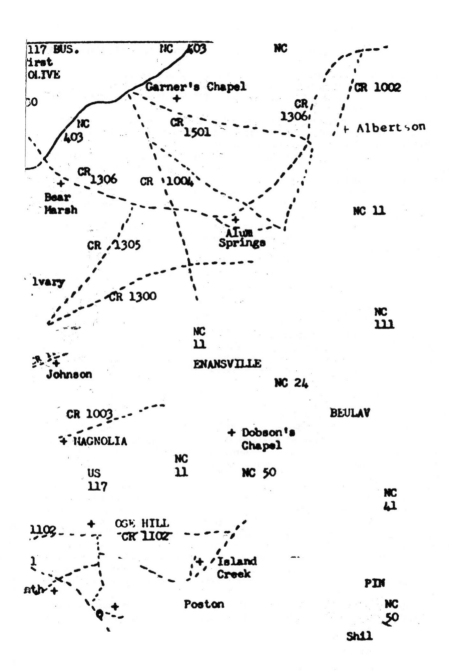

- Summer Migrant Ministry orientation workshop held May 23, Calvary Church
- Recreation equipment received from Brotherhood of Warsaw and Calypso Churches
- Clothes Closet coordinator - Jane Kaleel (1½ years service)
- Annual Summer Migrant Ministry Appreciation Pig Pickin' August 13 at First Baptist Church, Clinton shelter; 125 in attendance representing over 300 volunteers from our churches
- Video tapes received from Baptist State Convention Language Missions Dept. for ministry with Haitians. The tapes are French Creole worship services led by Rev. Wilfred Lubin
- Various items as health kits, clothing, etc. and financial gifts received from churches, mission groups and individuals from across Eastern Baptist Association
- A dedicated Migrant Ministry committee led by Andy Wood with committed members, Gail Naylor , Lynn Hilton, Jane Kaleel, Wilson Spencer and Charles Adams
- The Committee thanks each church for making available its resources to keep this vital ministry going and growing. Pray as we continue to expand our ministries

Respectfully submitted,
Andy Wood, Chairman

MISSIONS DEVELOPMENT PROGRAM REPORT

1984-85 was a challenging and exciting year in Missions Development across Eastern Baptist Association. Our ministries continued to grow and reach people for Christ. The support shown by every church is appreciated and is demonstrated through the following events, plans and actions of the Missions Council and the Executive Board.

- Annual Meeting Actions - October 30, 1985 1) "Missions Committee" changed to "Missions Council" 2) Christian Social Ministries Director title changed to Mission Ministries Director 3) Establishment of the Missions Development Program; All changes were recommended by the Constitution Committee of Eastern Baptist Association after changes in terminology and suggested organizational patterns in A Baptist Association, 1984, a Home Mission Board publication and the Associational WMU Manual, 1984.
- The Missions Council endorsed and the Executive Board approved(2-11-85): 1) the establishment of a Spanish Language Mission at First Baptist Church Clinton and 2) that a $2,000. contribution be made from the Association Reserve Fund to assist in securing a Spanish pastor for the Language Mission. In June, 1985 Rev. William Ortega began a full time ministry to Hispanics as pastor of the mission 3) the establishment of a Deaf Mission at Poston Church, Wallace with Rev. Arledge Castles leading the Sunday School and worship services one Sunday a month. In March Mr. Castles began leading in the services every week.
- Endorsement of Beginner and Advanced Sign Language Classes at Wallace - Rose Hill High School through James Sprunt Technical College.

Promoted Associational Emphasis Week, "The Association: Missions With A Personal Touch", May 20-26, 1985; 04-29-85 the Executive Board approved the appeal for a special offering for the Mission Development Program Ministries.

    - 16 people were certified as Laubach tutors. Plans are made for a November 1985 English As A Second Language Workshop.

    - 1985-86 Budget and calendars were developed by all committees

    - Four Missions Council members attended Key Leadership Conference at Ridgecrest in May. Those attending were Florence Hoover, Rev. Andy Wood, Rev. James Pardue and Cathy Hopkins.

    - 7-29-85 the Executive Board approved the Cooperative Agreement requests being sent to the Baptist State Convention for budget consideration

    - A Senior Adult Newsletter began circulation in September 1985

    - An experimental ministry in cooperation with the Baptist State Convention of North Carolina for the development of a balanced ministry in a nursing care facility and discovering a volunteer chaplain for the facility. Target facility Guardian Care in Kenansville with Rev. Ernest (Ed) Johnson as volunteer chaplain.

We are proud of all of our ministry committees for their diligent work during the past year. We expect new ministries to develop in the coming months and years as we work together in Eastern Baptist Association missions development.

> Respectfully submitted,
> Davis Benton,
> Missions Development Program Director

CLOTHING CLOSET REPORT

This has been an interesting year for the clothing closet. In February and March about 40 people worked to sort clothing and assist with a clothing sale. On March 22-23 we sold items at .10¢-.25¢. Donald Starling donated the use of his warehouse.

From May - August, 62 people filled requests for clothing and household items for 175 people. If you could see the faces of people as they receive bags of clothing, and see the children as they "show off" their new clothing, you would realize this is truly a ministry.

Due to unfortunate circumstances, we had to dispose of many of the items left in the main room of the clothing closet; however, we did have boxes of items that had not been sorted, including boxes of winter items. Since mid-September two ladies have gone each week to sort and hang items on hand.

The clothing closet is to serve the clothing needs of our Association. If you know of needs, please contact the Association office or Jane Kaleel(592-2043). If you have clothing or household items to donate, please be sure they are clean and mended. It would help if they are sized.

A word of thanks is in order to Grove Park Church for allowing us the use of two rooms. A prayer request: we need more space. We also need people to volunteer their time to help. Are you available?

> Respectfully submitted,
> Jane Kaleel, Co-ordinator

-43-

BUDGET

EASTERN BAPTIST ASSOCIATION
1985 - 86

ADMINISTRATIVE SUPPORT MINISTRIES

Director of Missions

1110	Salary	12,750.00	
1120	Housing	7,338.00	
1130	Travel	4,000.00	
1140	Annuity	1,200.00	
1150	Insurance	2,712.00	
1160	Convention & Conferences	1,000.00	
1170	Social Security Offset	2,300.00	
	Total		31,300.00

Secretary

1210	Salary	5,616.00	
1220	Social Security(Assoc. part)	413.00	
	Total		6,029.00

Office Expense

1310	Repairs	500.00	
1320	Copier Service	750.00	
1330	Supplies	1,500.00	
1340	Printing	600.00	
1350	Postage	1,400.00	
1360	Telephone	1,000.00	
	Total		5,750.00

Equipment Expense

1410	Purchase of Equipmen	250.00	
	Total		250.00

Associational Minutes

1510	Expense of Minutes	1,200.00	
	Total		1,200.00

Lending Library

1610	Materials	200.00	
	Total		200.00

Associational Officers Training

1710	Expenses	200.00	
	Total		200.00

TOTAL ADMINISTRATIVE SUPPORT MINISTRIES $ 44,929.00

MISSION DEVELOPMENT MINISTRIES

Mission Ministries Director

2110	Salary	14,550.00	
2130	Travel	3,600.00	
2140	Annuity	1,200.00	
2150	Conferences	200.00	
2170	Social Security(Assoc. part)	1,070.00	
	Total		20,620.00

Office Expense

2210	Supplies	400.00	
2220	Postage	400.00	
2230	Telephone(Long Distance)	500.00	
	Total		1,300.00

Mission Advance

2240	Hunger Fund	6,760.00	
2241	Emergency Fund	540.00	
2243	Church-type Missions	2,000.00	
2244	Mount Olive College BSU	200.00	
	Total		9,500.00

Migrant Ministry

2311	Salary	1,800.00	
2312	Social Security	-0-	
2313	Travel	2,770.00	
2314	Meals	-0-	
2315	Housing	1,200.00	
2316	Speaker Expense	300.00	
2317	Supplies	300.00	
2318	Film Rental	270.00	
2320	Unforeseen Expenses	200.00	
	Total		6,840.00

Deaf Ministries

2410	Activities	350.00	
	Total		350.00

Literacy Ministry

2510	Activities	100.00	
	Total		100.00

Senior Adult Ministry

2610	Activities	300.00	
	Total		300.00

Mentally Handicapped Ministry

2710	Activities	500.00	
	Total		500.00

Associational Leader Training

2810	Expenses	575.00	
	Total		575.00

TOTAL MISSION DEVELOPMENT MINISTRIES $ 40,085.00

CHURCH DEVELOPMENT MINISTRIES

Sunday School

3011	Activities	325.00	
3013	Assoc. Leader Training	330.00	
	Total		655.00

Church Training

3021	Activities	220.00	
3023	Assoc. Leader Training	345.00	
	Total		565.00

	Womans Missionary Union			
3031	Activities	400.00		
3033	Assoc. Leader Training	690.00		
	Total		1,090.00	
	Brotherhood			
3041	Activities	100.00		
3043	Assoc. Leader Training	50.00		
	Total		150.00	
	Music			
3051	Activities	100.00		
3053	Assoc. Leader Training	50.00		
	Total		150.00	
	Evangelism			
3061	Activities	125.00		
3063	Assoc. Leader Training	100.00		
	Total		225.00	
	Media Library			
3071	Activities	100.00		
3073	Assoc. Leader Training	100.00		
	Total		200.00	
	Pastor Support			
3091	Activities	60.00		
3093	Assoc. Leader Training	50.00		
	Total		110.00	
	Stewardship			
3101	Activities	60.00		
3103	Assoc. Leader Training	50.00		
	Total		110.00	
	TOTAL CHURCH DEVELOPMENT MINISTRIES			$ 3,255.00

FELLOWSHIP MINISTRIES

	Ministers Conference			
5110	Speaker Expense	100.00		
5130	Assoc. Leader Training	50.00		
	Total		150.00	
	Annual Meeting			
5210	Expenses	300.00		
	Total		300.00	
	TOTAL FELLOWSHIP MINISTRIES			450.00

MISCELLANEOUS

6100	Unforeseen Expenses	300.00		
6300	N.C. Sales Tax Paid	400.00		
	Total		700.00	
	TOTAL MISCELLANEOUS			700.00

7110	Reserved for Special Account	
7120	Reserved for Special Account	
7130	Reserved for Special Account	
GRAND TOTAL BUDGET		89,419.00

ANTICIPATED INCOME

900	Churches - Regular Contributions	57,089.00
902	Churches - Associational Minutes	1,200.00
904	Baptist State Convention	19,480.00
908	Copier Fees	150.00
910	Interest - IMMA Housing	1,800.00
912	Interest - N-O-W Account Checking	500.00
914	Special Gifts from Churches(Ledger Record Total)	500.00
915	Special Gifts from Individuals (Ledger Record Total)	1,000.00
916	North Carolina Sales Tax Refund	400.00
917	Transfer from Reserve Fund(Hunger & Emergency Funds	7,300.00
918	Other Receipts (Itemized by Donors)	-0-
	TOTAL ANTICIPATED RECEIPTS	$89,419.00

CHURCH CONTRIBUTIONS TO ASSOCIATIONAL MISSIONS

CHURCH	1983	1985	1985
Albertson	150.00	150.00	150.00
Alum Springs	340.00	360.00	400.00
Bear Marsh	300.00	300.00	300.00
Beulah	611.38	705.01	807.38
Brown	85.00	100.00	40.00
Calvary	809.02	1,116.22	849.07
*Calypso	300.00	300.00	648.00
Center	462.75	433.38	186.53
Clinton	2,675.00	3,975.00	5,410.76
Concord	596.79	499.79	390.07
Corinth	1,440.00	1,470.98	1,610.89
Dobson Chapel	635.25	648.75	1,034.13
Evergreen	180.00	300.00	240.00
Faison	496.95	399.45	423.48
Garland	883.26	861.53	986.81
Garner's Chapel	150.00	150.00	150.00
Grove Park	1,635.96	2,124.96	2,334.54
*Hickory Grove(Came to EBA Jan. 24, 1983)		520.00	640.00
Immanuel	1,622.00	3,434.00	4,061.50
Ingold	400.00	500.00	500.00
Island Creek	792.00	792.00	900.00
Johnson	1,136.42	1,130.61	911.81
Kenansville	300.00	300.00	1,100.00
Magnolia	707.93	682.00	727.31
Mount Gilead	1,376.99	900.00	1,369.00
Mount Olive	3,375.00	3,875.00	4,375.00
Mount Vernon	530.00	530.00	530.00
New Hope	650.00	350.00	350.00
Piney Grove	375.00	225.00	339.80
Poplar Grove	-0-	500.00	400.00
Poston	1,600.00	1,980.00	2,640.00
Rose Hill	1,276.00	1,100.00	1,200.00
Rowan	1,571.00	1,785.00	2,100.00
Sharon	900.00	1,200.00	1,200.00
Shiloh	1,124.19	1,299.51	1,541.58
Siloam	400.00	400.00	400.00

Teachey	580.00	600.00	825.00
Turkey	896.64	975.80	1,111.78
Union Grove	187.16	141.27	192.17
Warsaw	1,755.00	1,462.52	2,047.50
Wells Chapel	778.20	816.30	941.70
TOTAL	$36,334.89	$39,394.06	$46,365.81

*Calypso joined Neuse Association July, 1985
**Hickory Grove came into Eastern Association January 24, 1983

TREASURER'S REPORT
GENERAL FUND

RECEIPTS

Brought Forward October 1, 1984		$ 5,548.47
Church Regular Contributions	$46,365.81	
Associational Minutes	964.00	
Baptist State Convention	27,210.00	
Copier Fees	77.06	
Interest IMMA (Housing)	1,854.56	
Interest NOW Account	445.00	
Disaster Relief	2,500.00	
Emergency Fund	200.00	
Other Receipts	7,004.28	
Transfer from Reserve:		
Spanish Mission	2,000.00	
Rhoda & Commodore Davis Memorial Fund	3,300.00	
Unrestricted for General Fund	735.86	
TOTAL RECEIPTS		92,856.57
TOTAL AVAILABLE FUNDS		98,405.04

EXPENDITURES

ADMINISTRATIVE SUPPORT MINISTRIES

Director of Mission		
Salary	11,500.00	
Housing	7,250.00	
Travel	4,000.00	
Annuity	760.76	
Insurance	2,581.23	
Conventions & Conferences	600.00	
Social Security Offset	2,300.00	
Total		28,991.99
Secretary (Part Time)		
Salary	5,400.00	
Social Security	494.35	
Total		5,894.35
Office Expense		
Repairs	752.70	
Copier Service	530.50	
Supplies	1,092.37	
Printing	933.60	

Postage	1,233.43	
Telephone	1,010.74	
Total		5,553.34
Equipment Purchase		788.50
Associational Minutes		725.00
Lending Library		155.52
Associational Officers Training		164.19
TOTAL ADMINISTRATIVE MINISTRIES			42,272.89

MISSIONS DEVELOPMENT MINISTRIES

Mission Ministries Director

Salary	14,050.00	
Travel	3,600.00	
Annuity	1,200.00	
Conferences	82.09	
Social Security	988.73	
Total		19,920.82

Office Expense

Promotion	86.18	
Postage	461.24	
Telephone	461.01	
Total		1,008.43
Hunger Fund		1,518.11

Migrant Ministry

Student Salaries	2,750.99	
Social Security	241.82	
Travel	1,844.66	
Meals	623.43	
Housing	703.06	
Speaker Expenses	325.00	
Supplies	511.82	
Film Rental	215.18	
Leader Training	41.04	
Unforeseen Expenses	253.65	
Total		7,509.66

Deaf Ministries

Activity	532.00	
Leader Training	40.00	
Total		572.00

Literacy Ministry

Activities	124.54	
Leader Training	-0-	
Total		124.54

Senior Adult Ministry

Activities	-0-	
Leader Training	-0-	
Total		-0-

Mentally Handicapped Ministry

Activities	37.55	
Leader Training	-0-	
Total		37.55

CHURCH DEVELOPMENT MINISTRIES

Sunday School
Activities	389.07	
Promotion	48.41	
Leader Training	137.69	
Total		584.17

Church Training
Activities	175.00	
Promotion	56.49	
Leader Training	41.04	
Total		272.53

Womans Missionary Union
Activities	239.00	
Promotion	11.60	
Leader Training	584.74	
Total		835.34

Brotherhood
Activities	8.00	
Promotion	2.00	
Leader Training	50.75	
Total		60.75

Church Music
Activities	-0-	
Promotion	14.75	
Leadership Training	41.04	
Total		55.79

Evangelism Committee
Activities	-0-	
Promotion	160.40	
Leader Training	-0-	
Total		160.40

Media Library Committee
Activities	-0-	
Promotion	-0-	
Leader Training	105.96	
Total		105.96

Mission Council
Activities	233.17	
Promotion	13.26	
Leader Training	25.94	
Total		274.37

Pastor Support Committee
Activities	-0-	
Promotion	-0-	
Leader Training	-0-	
Total		-0-

Stewardship Committee
Activities	-0-	
Promotion	-0-	
Leader Training	-0-	
		-0-

TOTAL CHURCH DEVELOPMENT MINISTRIES 2,349.31

MISSION ADVANCE MINISTRIES
   Mount Olive College BSU   200.00
TOTAL MISSION ADVANCE MINISTRIES 200.00

FELLOWSHIP MINISTRIES:
Ministers Conference
    Speakers Expense   10.78
    Promotion   83.86
    Leader Training   41.04
    Total   135.68

Annual Meeting   178.00
Associational Fellowship Meals   950.26
TOTAL FELLOWSHIP MINISTRIES 1,863.94

MISCELLANEOUS
Unforeseen Expenses   370.75
N.C. Sales Tax   125.82
TOTAL MISCELLANEOUS 496.57

SPECIAL ACCOUNTS
    Disaster Relief Fund   2,545.89
    Emergency Fund   995.60
    Spanish Mission Fund   2,000.00
    Re-payment(transfer) to Reserve Fund 12,461.11
TOTAL SPECIAL ACCOUNTS 18,002.60

TOTAL EXPENDITURES 95,276.42
BALANCE 3,128.62
PLUS PAYROLL TAX PAYABLE 402.54
BALANCE SEPTEMBER 30, 1985 $3,531.16

STATEMENT OF CASH ASSETS

GENERAL FUND
    Balance 09/30/85   3,128.62
    Plus Payroll Tax Payable   402.54
    Balance 09/30/85   3,531.16

FUNDS FROM SALE OF MISSIONARY HOME
    Beginning Principal Balance   22,394.00
    Interest Revenue   1,990.85
    Interest Revenue transferred to
      General Fund   09/30/85   (1,854.56)
      Ending Balance 9-30-85 Interest   136.29
      Principal   22,394.00

RESERVE FUND
    Beginning Balance 10-1-84   2,267.96
    Deposits   12.461.11
    Interest Earned   118.48
    Transferred to General Fund   (6,235.86)
Ending Balance 09-30-85   8,681.69

BAPTIST CENTER FUND
    Beginning Balance 10/1/84   5,934.11
    Interest Earned   505.19
    Ending Balance 09-30-85 $6,439.30

TOTAL CASH ASSETS $41,182.4

SCHEDULE OF MEETING PLACES OF EASTERN ASSOCIATION

. . .

1986
1st Day *Warsaw
          Calvary

2nd Day *Bear Marsh
          Alum Springs

1987
1st Day *Kenansville
          Albertson

2nd Day *Corinth
          Teachey

1988
1st Day Rose Hill
2nd Day *Immanuel
          Hickory Grove

1989
1st Day *Faison
          Poplar Grove

2nd Day *Garland
          Ingold
          Center

1990
1st Day *Island Creek
          Dobson's Chapel

2nd Day *Grove Park
          Brown

1991
1st Day Clinton, First

2nd Day *Magnolia
          Concord
          Johnson

1992
1st Day Mount Olive

2nd Day *Mount Gilead
          Union Grove

1993
1st Day *Siloam
          Evergreen
2nd Day *Turkey
          Beulah
          New Hope

1994
1st Day *Piney Grove
          Mount Vernon

2nd Day *Sharon
          Shiloh

1995
1st Day   Rowan

2nd Day *Poston
          Wells Chapel

*Meeting Place
Other listed churches assisting with meal on respective days

RULES OF ORDER

1. At the meeting of the Association the moderator elected at the preceding session shall preside. In case of his absence, the Vice Moderator shall preside.

2. Each session of the Association shall be opened with religious exercises.

3. At each daily session and previous to proceeding to business the associational clerk shall be requested to announce the number of churches represented and the total number of messengers representing these churches. When it is determined that a majority of the churches are represented the moderator shall declare the Association duly constituted. It shall be necessary for a majority of the churches to be represented for the Association to transact business other than adjournment. The proceedings of the first day of the Annual Session shall be read the morning of the second day and the proceedings of the second day shall be read at the first Council of the Association to meet following the Annual Meeting.

4. The members shall observe toward the officers and each other that courtesy which belongs to Christians.

5. Any member wishing to speak shall arise and address the presiding officers and shall confine himself strictly to the question under consideration and avoid personalities.

6. No member shall speak more than twice on the same question without permission.

7. All motions seconded shall be definitely stated by the presiding officer before discussion.

8. No motion shall be withdrawn after discussion.

9. When a question is under discussion, no motion nor proposition shall be received except to adjourn, to lay on the table, to amend, to commit, or to postpone to a definite time, which several motions shall have preference in the order in which they are stated.

10. After a motion has been decided, any member having voted in the majority may move a re-consideration.

11. All questions except such as relate to the Constitution shall be decided by a majority vote.

12. The Association shall have the right to decide what subjects shall be admitted to consideration.

13. The rules of order may be altered or amended at any session of the Association by a majority vote.

CONSTITUTION

PREAMBLE

We, the Missionary Baptist Churches of Jesus Christ, composing the EASTERN BAPTIST ASSOCIATION, convinced of the necessity of an association of churches in order to promote fellowship, missions, education, Christian service, the preaching of the gospel, and to cooperate with the Baptist State Convention of North Carolina and the Southern Baptist Convention in their work, do hereby agree and subscribe to the following articles.

ARTICLE 1. NAMES

This association shall be known and denominated as the North Carolina EASTERN BAPTIST ASSOCIATION.

ARTICLE II. PURPOSE

The purpose of this association shall be the promotion of Christ's kingdom among men, and the means of accomplishing this shall be in strict conformity to the New Testament.

ARTICLE III. AUTHORITY

This association claims to be independent and sovereign in its own sphere, but shall never attempt to exercise any authority over the internal affairs of the churches.

ARTICLE IV. COMPOSITION

This association shall be composed of all ordained ministers who are members or pastors of member churches, the general officers of the association, the director of missions, and three messengers from each church with an additional messenger for every one-hundred members over the first one-hundred, no church being allowed more than ten messengers.

ARTICLE V. MEETINGS

The Annual Session of the Association shall commence on Monday after the fourth Lord's Day in October. The church year for the churches of the Association shall commence on October 1, and end on September 30.

ARTICLE VI. OFFICERS

The officers of the Association shall be a moderator, a vice moderator, a clerk, an associate clerk, the chairman of the Historical Committee, a treasurer and an associate treasurer. All officers shall be elected annually except the chairman of the Historical Committee who is the senior member of the Historical Committee. The moderator shall not be elected to serve more than two full years at one period and shall assume office at the close of the Annual Session at which time he is elected.

ARTICLE VII. TRUSTEES

The Association shall have three (3) trustees who shall serve three-year terms in rotation, the replacement to be elected by the Association annually.

ARTICLE VIII. EXECUTIVE BOARD

The Association shall have an Executive Board consisting of the general officers of the Association; the director of missions, the Mission Ministries Director; the directors of associational Brotherhood, Church Music, Church Training, Sunday School, and Womans Missionary Union; retired pastors in the Association; and two lay persons (men or women) from each church to be elected by the church and whose names shall be included in the church letter to the Association.

ARTICLE IX. ASSOCIATIONAL COUNCIL

The Association shall have an Associational Council consisting of the officers of the Executive Board; the directors of associational Brotherhood, Church Music, Church Training, Mission Ministries Development Program, Sunday School, and Womans Missionary Union; the chairpersons of Evangelism, Media Library, Pastoral Support, and Stewardship; the director of missions and the Missions Ministries director.

ARTICLE X. MISSIONS DEVELOPMENT PROGRAM

The Association shall have a Missions Development Program organization consisting of three (3) at-large members, of which one shall be the Mission Development director; the component programs representing all mission ministries conducted by the Association; the Mission Ministries director; a representative of Brotherhood, and a representative of Womans Missionary Union.

ARTICLE XI. COMMITTEES

The Association shall have such committees as may be deemed necessary for orderly and efficient achievement of the Association's purpose. Members on standing committees shall be on the rotating basis with one-third of the members rotating off each year. Members completing a three year term shall not be eligible for re-election until one year has passed. A member elected to fill an unexpired term shall be eligible for election to a full term following the completion of the unexpired term.

ARTICLE XII. CHURCH PROGRAMS

The Association shall organize groups of officers for the five (5) church programs: Sunday School, Church Training, Women's Missionary Union, Music and Brotherhood.

ARTICLE XIII. VISITORS

The Association may invite visiting and corresponding brethren to seats and extend to them the privilege of the body, except that of voting.

ARTICLE XIV. MISCELLANEOUS

The Association shall not maintain a fellowship with any church which neglects to observe gospel order.

ARTICLE XV. CONSTITUTIONAL CHANGES

This constitution may be amended on the second day of any Annual Session by a vote of two-thirds of the messengers present provided the proposed changes have been presented on the first day of the Annual Session.

BY-LAWS
ARTICLE I. DUTIES OF OFFICERS

A. MODERATOR - The moderator on the first day of each Annual Session of the Association shall appoint the following committees to function during the session: Place and Preacher; Resolutions; and Memorials. At the last regular meeting of the Executive Board before the Annual Session of the Association, the moderator shall appoint a Constitutional Committee to serve during the Annual Session, and a Committee-on-Committees.

It shall be the duty of the moderator to enforce an observance of the constitution, preserve order, decide all questions of order, vote in case of a tie, and act as chairman of the Executive Board.

B. VICE MODERATOR - It shall be the duty of the vice moderator to preside in the absence of or at the request of the moderator, to give other appropriate assistance to the moderator, and to succeed to the office of moderator, if and when, during his tenure of office the office of moderator becomes vacant.

C. CLERK - It shall be the duty of the clerk to record the proceedings of each Annual Session, superintend their printing and distribution, and serve as secretary of the Executive Board and Associational Council.

It shall be the clerks duty to report the actions of the Executive Board to the Annual Sessions of the Association. He shall report the actions of the Associational Council to the next meeting of the Board or to the Annual Session of the Association, which ever comes first.

D. ASSOCIATE CLERK - It shall be the duty of the associate clerk to register the messengers, to report upon request the number of these churches, and to perform such other duties as are usually performed by an associate clerk.

E. TREASURER - It shall be the duty of the treasurer to receive all funds contributed by the churches or collected during the Annual Session of this body, to distribute all funds received as ordered by the Association, and to make to the Association an annual report of the condition of the treasury.

F. ASSOCIATE TREASURER - It shall be the duties of the associate treasurer to assist the treasurer in the performance of the treasurers' duties as directed by the treasurer.

ARTICLE II. DUTIES OF TRUSTEES

The Trustees shall be the representative of the Association in legal matters, and shall perform such duties as the Association or the Executive Board may prescribe.

ARTICLE III. EXECUTIVE BOARD

A. OFFICERS - The officers of the Executive Board shall be: moderator, vice moderator, clerk, associate clerk, treasurer, and associate treasurer. The corresponding officers of the association elected during the last Annual Session of the Association shall serve in these positions on the Executive Board.

B. DUTIES - The Executive Board shall cooperate with the Baptist State Convention of North Carolina in its program for the furtherance of the work fostered by the body within the bounds of the Association; It shall act for the Association on any matters requiring attention between Annual Sessions of the Association; and it shall have the power to fill any vacancies on the Board during the year. The clerk shall make a report of the work of the Executive Board at the Annual Session of the Association. The director of missions or other workers employed by the Association shall make a quarterly report to the Executive Board in order that the said Board shall be prepared to make a full report to this body.

C. MEETINGS - The Executive Board shall meet once each quarter, other than in the quarter of the Annual Session, at a time and place designated by the Board. The moderator shall serve as chairman of the Board. With proper notice of the meeting being given to all members, and when it is determined that a majority of the churches are represented the chairman shall declare the Board duly constituted.

ARTICLE IV. COMMITTEES

A. STANDING COMMITTEES - A majority shall constitute a quorum for each committee.
1. ELECTION OF COMMITTEES: All committee members shall be persons who have demonstrated talent for performing the work of the committee, or who have stated a willingness to receive training to equip them for the work of the committee.
Standing committees shall be formed from a slate of persons selected, notified, secured to serve, and nominated by the Committee on Committees. The nominees, then, must be elected by the Association in its annual session. Special committees shall be recommended when deemed appropriate to perform the business and ministry of the Association, and are subject to the approval of the Executive Board. These committee posts shall be filled by the Committee on Committees from a slate of persons selected, notified, secured to serve , nominated and presented to and elected by the Executive Board. These committtees shall have definitely prescribed duties and a definite term of service before they are established.

2. STEWARDSHIP COMMITTEE: The Stewardship Committee shall be composed of nine (9) members. This committee shall be responsible for recommending a budget to the Association in its Annual Session, for the distribution of all Associational funds and for devising plans for raising such funds as are necessary for carrying on the associational programs. The Stewardship Committee shall lead a program of biblical stewardship education and promotion among the churches and on the associational level. The associational treasurer shall be a member of this committee. The Stewardship Committee shall have the financial records of the association audited annually.

3. EVANGELISM COMMITTEE: The Evangelism Committee shall be composed of three (3) members. It shall be the duty of this committee to promote evangelism both in the local church and on an associational level. It shall serve to link the Association with state and south-wide departments of evangelism and shall use every available means for fostering the cause of winning the lost to Christ.

4. MEDIA LIBRARY COMMITTEE: The Media Library Committee shall be composed of three (3) members duly elected by the association and resource personnel as appointed by the moderator whose duty it shall be to encourage the establishing and promotion of libraries in churches.

5. PASTORAL SUPPORT COMMITTEE: The Pastoral Support Committee shall be composed of three (3) members whose duties shall be to provide an on-going continuing program of help to pastors and church staff members in areas of need. The program shall include guidance for career assessment; spiritual, emotional, and physical needs of pastors and church staff.

6. PROGRAM COMMITTEE: The Program Committee shall be composed of three (3) members. It shall be their duty to arrange the program of the Annual Session of the Association and for all other sessions which may be called.

7. ORDINATION COMMITTTEE: The Ordination Committee shall be composed of six (6) members (pastors and deacons). This committee shall offer to any church, upon request, advice and assistance in the examination and ordination of deacons and ministers.

8. HISTORICAL COMMITTEE: The Historical Committee shall consist of three (3) members. The commmittee shall obtain and edit the histories of two churches each year to be included in the minutes, and shall maintain an up-to-date history of the Association. The senior member of the committee shall be the chairman.

9. NOMINATING COMMITTEE: The Nominating Committee shall be composed of six (6) members. It shall be the duty of this committee to submit nominations to the Association in session for the Associational general officers (with the floor open for nominations) as well as for representatives to denominational agencies and interests for the following year and to fill any vacancies which may occur during the year. This committee shall also be responsible for forwarding to the Executive Board at their second meeting for approval and to the association for election, the directors of Brotherhood, Sunday School,

Womans' Missionary Union, Church Training, Church Music and Missions Development Program. The Church Development Program directors shall then become members of the Nominating Committee. The Nominating Committee shall present to the Executive Board at their third meeting, a complete slate of officers for the five Church Program Organizations and the Missions Development Program

10. PROPERTIES COMMITTEE: The Properties Committee shall be composed of three (3) members. It shall be the duties of this committee to maintain an up-to-date inventory of all properties and equipment owned by the Association and make recommendations concerning purchase or disposition of properties and equipment.

B. APPOINTED COMMITTEES:

1. CONSTITUTION AND BY-LAWS COMMITTEE: This committee shall be composed of three (3) members, whose duty it shall be to study and recommend changes in the Constitution and By-Laws and bring reports as necessary to the Association.

2. PLACE AND PREACHER COMMITTEE: This committee shall be composed of three(3) members, whose duty it shall be to make the Association aware of the rotating system of meeting places, and to recommend to the Association in the Annual Session a place or places for meeting, along with a preacher and alternate for the sermon for the following year.

3. RESOLUTIONS COMMITTEE: This committee shall be composed of three (3) members whose duty it shall be to study all resolutions referred to it by the Association or the Executive Board and report suitable resolutions at the Annual Session.

4. MEMORIALS COMMITTEE: This committee shall be composed of three (3) members whose duty it shall be to prepare and present at the Annual Session an appropriate program of memorial for those of our number who have died during the preceeding year. These names may be secured from the letters to the Association from the member churches.

5. COMMITTEE ON COMMITTEES: This committee shall be composed of six (6) members whose duty it shall be to select and nominate persons for the standing committees and shall appoint successors when vacancies occur during the year.

ARTICLE V. DUTIES OF CHURCH PROGRAM DIRECTORS

A. THE ASSOCIATIONAL SUNDAY SCHOOL DIRECTOR shall promote and supervise the Sunday School program of the Association, and shall be responsible for the direction of Vacation Bible School work of the Association in cooperation with the director of missions.

B. THE ASSOCIATIONAL CHURCH TRAINING DIRECTOR shall promote and supervise the Church Training Program of the Association in cooperation with the director of missions.

C. THE ASSOCIATIONAL WOMAN'S MISSIONARY UNION DIRECTOR shall promote and supervise the Woman's Missionary Union Program of the Association, cooperating with the director of missions, and in keeping with the Constitution and By-Laws of the Woman's Missionary Union of the EASTERN BAPTIST ASSOCIATION.

D. THE ASSOCIATIONAL BROTHERHOOD DIRECTOR shall promote and supervise the Brotherhood Program of the Association in cooperation with the director of mission.

E. THE ASSOCIATIONAL MUSIC DIRECTOR shall promote and supervise the Church Music Program of the Association in cooperation with the director of missions.

ARTICLE VI. MISSIONS DEVELOPMENT PROGRAM

A. PURPOSE - The purpose of the Missions Development Program shall be to lead the Association to address the priority of mission needs in the area.

B. ORGANIZATION

    1. MISSIONS COUNCIL. The Missions Council shall be composed of the three at-large members of the Missions Development Program; the Missions Ministries director; the chairpersons of all component programs; the Brotherhood director and the Womans Missionary Union missions action director. The Mission Developmen Program director shall serve as chairperson. The Missions Council shall work with the Mission Ministries director in discovering, analyzing and presenting to the Association or the Executive Board new opportunities for mission ministries; and in coordination of the mission ministries of the Missions Development Program. Upon determining a new mission ministry is needed, the Missions Council shall prepare a written description of the component program containing its composition and functions. Each new component program shall be presented to the Association or the Executive Board for approval.

    2. COMPONENT PROGRAMS

    a. DEAF MINISTRIES - The Deaf Ministries Program shall be composed of three (3) members whose duties shall be to plan, promote, and evaluate mission ministries to hearing-impaired persons. The Deaf Ministries Program shall provide assistance to churches through their missionary education organizations in the development of ministries to hearing-impaired persons in local communities and in the churches' participation in deaf ministries conducted by the association through enlistment, training, and guidance of volunteers in these ministries.

    b. LITERACY MINISTRIES - The Literacy Ministries Program shall be composed of three (3) members whose duties shall be to plan, promote, and evaluate missions ministries designed to assist non-English-speaking persons in developing or improving reading skills. The Literacy Ministries Program shall provide assistance to the churches through their missionary education organization in development through enlistment, training, and guidance of volunteers in these ministries.

c. MENTALLY HANDICAPPED MINISTRIES - The Mentally Handicapped Ministries Program shall be composed of three (3) members whose duties shall be to plan, promote, and evaluate ministries to mentally handicapped persons. The Mentally Handicapped Ministries Program shall provide assistance to churches through their missionary education organizations in development of ministries to mentally handicapped persons in the local communities and in the churches participation in mentally handicapped ministries conducted in the association through enlistment, training, and guidance of volunteers in these ministries.

d. MIGRANT MINISTRIES - The Migrant Ministries Program shall be composed of six (6) persons whose duties shall be to plan, promote, and evaluate the Associations ministries to Migrant farm laborers. The Migrant Ministries Program shall provide assistance to churches through their missionary education organizations in providing ministries to migrant farm laborers in local communities and in the churches' participation in migrant ministries conducted by the Association through enlistment, training, and guidance of volunteers in these ministries.

e. SENIOR ADULT MINISTRIES - The Senior Adult Ministries Program shall be composed of three (3) members whose duties shall be to plan, promote, and evaluate ministries to senior adults. The Senior Adult Ministries Program shall provide assistance to churches through their missionary education organizations in development of ministries to senior adults in local communities and in the churches' participation in senior adult ministries conducted by the assocation through enlistment, training, and guidance of volunteers in these ministries.

ARTICLE VII. ASSOCIATIONAL COUNCIL

A. PURPOSE - The purpose of the Associational Council shall be to provide a consultative, advisory, and coordinative service to the Association and its various programs and committees.

B. DUTIES - The duties of the Associational Council shall be: provide for communication between associational officers, organizations, and committees; study church needs in the association and needs of the people in the area of the association; propose long-range and short-range goals for the association; prepare and recommend plans for involving organizations and committees appropriately in attaining goals; review and coordinate plans made by the organizations and committees and relate these to the attainment of goals; evaluate the use of resources; and report through appropriate channels progress made toward attainment of associational goals. The Council shall exercise general supervision of the work of the director of missions. In the event the position of director of missions becomes vacant, the Council shall recommend to the Association or the Executive Board for approval, a search committee whose duties shall be to seek prayerfully a person to fill the positions.

C. Officers - The officers of the Associational Council shall be the chairman and the secretary. The moderator shall serve as chairman.

The Associational clerk shall be the secretary. In the absence of the secretary, the chairman shall appoint a temporary secretary.

ARTICLE VIII. BY-LAWS CHANGES

These by-laws may be amended on the second day of any Annual Session by a vote of the majority of the messengers present and voting, providing the proposed changes have been presented on the first day of the Annual Session.